MAPPING INDIGENOUS PRESENCE

Critical Issues in Indigenous Studies

Jeffrey P. Shepherd and Myla Vicenti Carpio
Series Editors

Mapping Indigenous Presence

*North Scandinavian
and North American
Perspectives*

Edited by
KATHRYN W. SHANLEY
AND BJØRG EVJEN

Foreword by
S. JAMES ANAYA

THE UNIVERSITY OF
ARIZONA PRESS

TUCSON

The University of Arizona Press
www.uapress.arizona.edu

Printed in the United States of America
20   19   18   17   16   15   6   5   4   3   2   1

ISBN-13: 978-0-8165-3152-3 (paper)

Jacket designed by Leigh McDonald
Jacket image: *Waiting for the Ice* by Corky Clairemont

Publication of this book is made possible in part by funding from the University of Tromsø.

Library of Congress Cataloging-in-Publication Data
Mapping indigenous presence : north Scandinavian and North American perspectives /
edited by Kathryn W. Shanley and Bjørg Evjen ; foreword by S. James Anaya.
   pages cm — (Critical issues in indigenous studies)
   Includes bibliographical references and index.
   ISBN 978-0-8165-3152-3 (pbk. : alk. paper)
   1. Sami (European people)—Norway—Cross-cultural studies.   2. Indians of
North America—Montana—Cross-cultural studies.   I. Shanley, Kathryn W.
(Kathryn Winona), 1947– editor.   II. Evjen, Bjørg, editor.   III. Series: Critical
issues in indigenous studies.
   DL442.L3M34 2015
   305.894'570481—dc23
                          2014040111

Contents

Foreword

Looking to the Future for Indigenous Peoples' Rights

S. James Anaya

Every place we turn today, we hear talk of globalization. The word found its way irreversibly into our everyday vocabulary back in the 1980s, and in 2000 the International Monetary Fund solidified its use through the declaration that globalization involves trade, capital, migration of peoples, and dissemination of knowledge.[1] An information explosion occurred with the availability of news through new forms of media, especially social networks. For the past several decades our world seems closer as we all become exposed to knowledge of changes happening all over the world. We see how people live in every imaginable geography: vast deserts, highest mountains, seemingly endless plains, rolling hills, lush green islands surrounded by water, tall-grass prairies, and fields of formidable ice and snow. Images of wars and natural disasters bombard us daily along with reports about the monetary happenings in the global market and the acceleration of climate change. As citizens of the world, we must sort through the information as media pundits postulate what democracy means, and we must decide for ourselves what matters most in globalization for the health of all human beings and the environment.

Given our increasing understanding of the interconnectedness of all peoples, regions, and ecological systems, media can be a powerful force in making the world aware that Indigenous peoples inhabit large areas of the planet from the Arctic to the islands of the South Pacific. The Idle No More movement in Canada is a prime example of increased awareness through media, with its flash mob gatherings and crucial dissemination of facts in grassroots movements. Indigenous peoples comprise, or are the descendants of, the people who originally inhabited lands before settlers arrived. Indigenous peoples typically function as stewards of the environments in the places they continue to live and call home. Others displaced through settler colonialism also seek recognition and emancipation.

With the spread of colonialism for the past many centuries, occupation and settlement of regions previously inhabited primarily by Indigenous peoples has resulted in the loss of Indigenous land ownership and control; mining and other toxic industries in Indigenous regions have become increasingly and alarmingly part of a pattern of dispossession. Nonetheless, Indigenous people's cultures continue and remain distinct within their ancestral territories and within countries that often hardly recognize their existence. Many Indigenous peoples struggle to be recognized and have their ways of life respected; Sámi people of the European far north and the Native American nations of Montana are among them.

The inclusion of Indigenous peoples in the global consciousness undeniably came to the fore with the passage of the United Nations Declaration on the Rights of Indigenous Peoples on September 13, 2007. Although the document represented the collective Indigenous efforts over the past half-century to be heard in the United Nations, the issues addressed have been with us for a long time. As we now call upon the governments of the world to honor their commitment to social justice for Indigenous peoples, a complementary academic movement seeks to deepen and broaden understanding of the shared realities, histories, and economies that shape the future of the planet through global interconnectedness. *Mapping Indigenous Presence* brings together scholars from two distinct regions—the University of Tromsø in northern Norway and the University of Montana in southwestern Montana—to reflect on topics essential to understanding Indigenous life in those regions and in the larger societies in which they abide.

I am happy to see this comparative volume come together. In 2011, in my capacity as United Nations Special Rapporteur on the Rights of Indigenous Peoples, I developed a report on the situation of the Sámi people in the Sápmi Region of Norway, Sweden, and Finland.[2] (Sámi people also live in Russia; however, their specific conditions were not addressed in the report.) Although I noted that in those three countries a relatively high level of attention was being paid to Indigenous issues, I also hoped that the Nordic countries would provide an example to the world by how they treat the Sámi, the Indigenous peoples of those northerly regions that span four countries. By building solidarity among Sámi people, the Sámi Parliament has played an important role in drawing attention to Sámi struggles by providing political vision. Genuine self-determination, effective enjoyment of rights to their lands, territories, and resources, as well as language preservation efforts are keys to the Sámi's vitality and future continuance as Indigenous peoples. Cultural activities and scholarship are also central to their revitalization and political voice. Education provides not only the Sámi people with culturally appropriate instruction but also allows for transmission of knowledge about their histories and culture to the wider public.

Two recommendations in my report on Sápmiland are that the Nordic governments "develop and implement measures to increase awareness about the Sámi people within the media and the public at large," with Sámi people involved in that process, and that "awareness about the Sámi people should be promoted . . . through primary, secondary, and university school curricula." This important collection of essays works in harmony with those goals in that its comparative approach and individual perspectives provide vital scholarly work that can be used in classrooms to further the study of Indigenous peoples' cultures, histories, political struggles, and arts. Global awareness of shared histories and interests among Indigenous peoples, such as the Sámi people of Norway and the Indigenous nations of Montana, adds to knowledge about what land-based cultures face in modernity and will continue to face until the governments of the nations within which they abide recognize their full right to exist and to continue their cultural and political practices. I applaud the authors included in this text for their steadfast effort to increase awareness of Indigenous knowledge, histories, cultures, and issues from the past, as well as of contemporary realities and challenges.

Similarly, I reported in 2012 on the situation of Indigenous peoples in the United States, following consultations with a number of Indigenous nations, organizations, and individuals, as well as with U.S. government officials in Washington, DC, Arizona, Alaska, Oregon, and Washington.[3] Based on information gathered about Indigenous peoples throughout the country, the report concluded that American Indians, Alaska Natives, and Native Hawaiians function within vibrant communities; nonetheless, they have suffered and continue to suffer from a range of misguided governmental policies, dishonored treaties, and other oppressions within the United States as a whole. Widespread historical wrongs manifest themselves in various social and political indicators of disadvantage and impediments toward their full realization of the goals of the Declaration on the Rights of Indigenous Peoples. Although steps have been taken to address the disadvantaged conditions of Indigenous peoples in the United States and the historical deprivation of their rights, much more needs to be done within a genuine spirit of reconciliation.

Mapping Indigenous Presence takes as its fundamental principle the idea that Indigenous studies scholarship should involve rigor. Such work seeks to set the historical record straight by writing against the grain of stereotypes of Indigenous peoples as savages who need to be governed, whose languages and cultures do not measure up to the cultures and languages of Europe, who need to be Christianized, and whose lands should be "developed" in a manner fitting with the settler-colonialist project. The contemporary perspectives gathered here attest to the importance of the roles Indigenous people have played as overseers of their own lands and resources, as creators of their own cultural richness, and as political entities capable of governing themselves.

Notes

1. According to the *Globalisation and Global Economic News* website (http://www.globalisation.eu/), globalization has led to the abuse of "hundreds of thousands of people in developing countries all around the world. It has caused great disruption to lives and produced very few noticeable benefits in return." Proponents, on the other hand, argue that globalization has helped to reduce poverty. Both are no doubt true, but the focus on market and economic issues eclipses the high stakes Indigenous peoples have in globalization and the long history of their exploitation by so-called developed countries.

2. The Situation of the Sámi People of the Sápmi Region of Norway, Sweden, and Finland, UN Doc. A/HRC/18/35/Add.2 (2011). For a copy of my reports, go to: http://www.ohchr.org/EN/Issues/IPeoples/SRIndigenousPeoples/Pages/ SRIPeoplesIndex.aspx

3. The Situation of Indigenous Peoples in the United States of America, UN Doc. A/HRC/21/54 (2012).

Acknowledgments

We would like to thank the Norwegian Research Council for funding our Partnerships in Higher Education grant proposal and the University of Montana Office of the Provost and International Programs for supplementing the grant. In addition, we are indebted to the faculty and staff of the Centre for Sámi Studies at the University of Tromsø and the Native American Studies Department at the University of Montana for their support, without which this project would not have been possible. Faculty from Norway and Montana who devoted considerable time to our efforts, but who were not part of this anthology deserve our special thanks: Angelica Lawson (University of Minnesota) and Else Grete Broderstad (University of Tromsø). Special thanks to Phyllis Duran, Jerryll Moreno, Allyson Carter, and the staff at the University of Arizona Press for their assistance along the way in preparing the manuscript.

We would also like to thank the Confederated Salish Kootenai tribal council, Salish culture committee, faculty, and staff at Salish Kootenai and Stone Child Colleges, and the late Robert Swan of RJS and Associates on the Rocky Boy's Reservation for welcoming our delegation and offering their words of wisdom and support. Special thanks to Hayden Ausland, University of Montana, for his relentless and dedicated efforts to create scholarly links between the universities in Tromsø and Montana. We are exceedingly grateful for the loving support and inspiration offered to us by David L. Moore and Einar Niemi.

MAPPING INDIGENOUS PRESENCE

Montana

●
Helena

The lower forty-eight U.S. states with Montana highlighted. Map by Matthew Nordhagen.

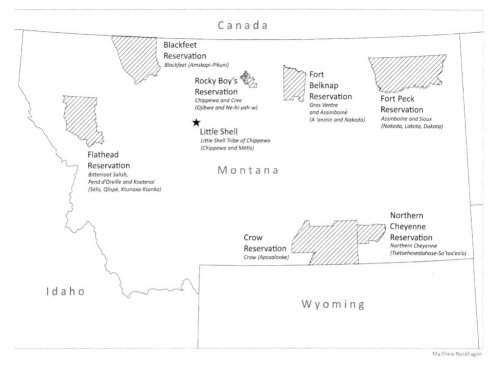

Canada

Blackfeet
Reservation
Blackfeet (Amskapi-Pikuni)

Rocky Boy's
Reservation
*Chippewa and Cree
(Ojibwe and Ne-hi-yah-w)*

★
Little Shell
*Little Shell Tribe of Chippewa
(Chippewa and Métis)*

Fort
Belknap
Reservation
*Gros Ventre
and Assiniboinè
(A 'aninin and Nakoda)*

Fort Peck
Reservation
*Assinboine and Sioux
(Nakoda, Lakota, Dakota)*

Flathead
Reservation
*Bitterroot Salish,
Pend d'Oreille and Kootenai
(Sélis, Qlispé, Ktunaxa-Ksanka)*

Montana

Northern
Cheyenne
Reservation
*Northern Cheyenne
(Tsetsehesestahase-So'taa'eo'o)*

Crow
Reservation
Crow (Apsaalooke)

Idaho

Wyoming

Matthew Nordhagen

Indian reservations and tribes in the state of Montana. Map by Matthew Nordhagen.

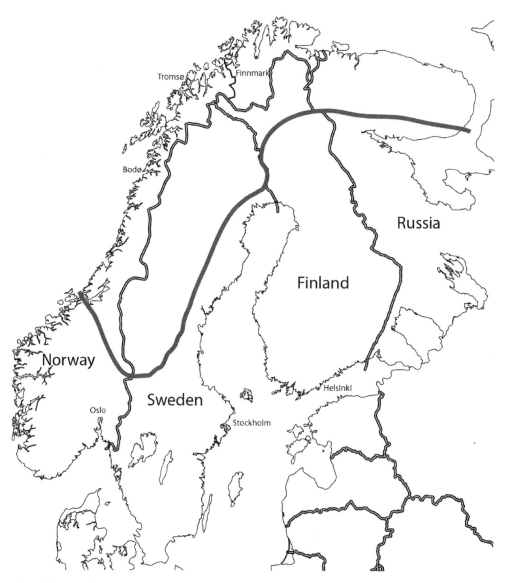

Map of Sápmi, the Sámi homeland spanning Norway, Finland, Sweden, and Russia. Map by Bjorn Hatteng, Centre for Sámi Studies.

"Mapping" Indigenous Presence

The Declaration on the Rights of Indigenous Peoples at Rhetorical Turns and Tipping Points

Kathryn W. Shanley

And then for just a little while I thought I saw beneath [the flowering tree] in the shade the circled village of people and every living thing with roots or legs or wings, and all were happy. "[The Flowering Tree] shall stand in the center of the nation's circle," said the Grandfather, "a cane to walk with and a people's heart; and by your powers you shall make it bloom."
—NICHOLAS BLACK ELK, "THE GREAT VISION," *BLACK ELK SPEAKS*

For one Sámi myth has it that when the Great Spirit created the people who were to become the ancestral mothers and fathers of the Sámi, he knew the difficulties that awaited them. In order to give them something in which to believe . . . he placed the living, beating heart of a two-year-old female reindeer at the center of the earth, so that each time the Sámi felt their existence threatened, they could simply put their ears to the ground and listen for the heartbeat beneath. If the heart was still beating, their future was secure, and their problems would be solved.
—HARALD GASKI, "SONG, POETRY, AND IMAGE IN WRITING"

To be human is to think spatially. Communities from ancient to contemporary times have created conceptual and literal places within spaces for themselves—homelands to inhabit as part of who they/we are—and we often map ways of declaring sacred "centers" within such places. In our everyday speech we frequently employ the metaphor of "mapping" to frame our ways of thinking about everything from how we plan to spend the day to how we imagine our future lives.[1] The metaphor of the map represents the way time and thoughts configure our "home ground." In that sense, we are what we imagine, and home is an organizing principle for who we imagine we are. In discussing "experiential grounding," George Lakoff and Mark Johnson, cognitive linguists renowned for their work on metaphors, state that "our most fundamental concepts are organized in terms of one or more spatialization metaphors" (Lakoff and Johnson 1980, 17). Actual "locations or places are constitutional elements of space," as Helander-Renvall notes, and "places within an existential space can also be understood as centers of meaning and purpose" (Helander-Renvall 2009, 46). For Indigenous peoples—people vitally connected to geographical locations—place means both an imagined home and a vibrantly interactive space inhabited by many sentient beings, what Western thinkers might call a "metaphysical" space. Place means kinship in its broadest terms. Epistemological differences between Western and Indigenous thinkers begin with—for lack of a better word—a different stance toward inhabiting spaces that is characterized by degree and type of engagement. "Indigenous people are people of place, and the nature of place is embedded in their language," states Tewa scientist Gregory Cajete. "The physical, cognitive, and emotional orientation of a people is a kind of 'map' they carry in their heads and transfer from generation to generation" (Cajete 2004, 46). Throughout the world, the *real* business of mapping—the dividing up of space and assigning ownership or character—is captured in the dichotomous rhetorical constructions of "Indigenous and postmodern," "developing," and—what?—"developed?" "first and third worlds," "North and South," and so forth. As Shari Huhndorf remarks, in *Mapping the Americas: The Transnational Politics of Contemporary Native Culture*, the governmental maps constitute documents of colonial possession and the names on maps carry the weight of histories of dispossession, disappearance, and displacement (Huhndorf 2009a).[2]

When used in the context of Indigenous peoples' rights, mapping represents the acknowledgment of their full peoplehood (human rights) and the boundaries of literal homelands, the political control of which frequently remains contested.[3] Lourdes Alberto, in speaking about our current academic discourses, says that "the field of transnationalism remains a necessary site in which to interrogate the possible colonial legacies that often obscure the Indigenous presence" (Alberto 2012, 39). Although contemporary Indigenous peoples complicatedly occupy many locations and are subject to variable political and cultural circumstances, we recognize in this text, first, the place-based identities that serve as their legacy, and we use it as a theoretical framework. When it comes to "maps," as well as "fields" of study, the metaphors layer themselves deeply into our languages of identity and location in time, space, and our promise of continuance and continuity. Indigenous peoples constitute themselves around literal geographic places, and their self-determination efforts occur within those places literally or, as is the case with people in diaspora, symbolically. Often peoples conceive of themselves across or despite borders that others envision—even legally maintained borders. Indigeneity sits in places. Indigenous rights begin with the places they have inhabited and/or continue to inhabit. While that fact may be obvious to those of us who work in the field of Indigenous studies— people doing legal, historical, cultural, literary, political, and artistic work— the fact is by no means obvious to people from dominant cultures.

Mapping Indigenous Presence: North Scandinavian and North American Perspectives is a collection of essays adding to a growing body of work in Indigenous studies that addresses the rights, issues, and concerns Indigenous people face as peoples within settler nation-states. This volume does so by providing scholarship that illuminates the histories, cultures, politics, education, laws, health, and literatures of Indigenous peoples. Our focus on Native people in Norway and Montana, although linked because our institutions are located in northerly climates, involves a tremendous diversity of cultural, political, and social history. Recognizing that we cannot hope to capture all that can be said about the Sámis of Norway and the Native Americans of Montana, we offer a smattering of what we know by addressing the following: research methodologies in humanities (Bjørg Evjen and David R. M. Beck) and social sciences (Annjeanette E. Belcourt, Gyda Swaney, and Allyson Kelley); education (Phyllis Ngai, Unn-Doris Karlsen Bæk, and Gry Paulgaard); cultural pluralism and Native American literature (David L. Moore); natural resource management (Robin Saha and Jennifer Hill-Hart); lawmaking regarding Indigenous land rights (Øyvind Ravna); film studies (Bob Boyer); performance art and postcolonial studies (Laura Castor); and literature and linguistics (Harald Gaski). Similarities and differences are the point of the collaboration, within individual essays and among all of them. These essays represent a conversation in which we scholars of Sámi and Native American studies participated, in discussions about the Indigenous presence in our respective places. We were keenly interested in our shared visions for global reckoning, as well as full recognition of rights for Indigenous peoples.

The anthology developed through a series of faculty exchanges and workshops between the University of Tromsø's Centre for Sámi Studies and the University of Montana's Native American Studies that took place over four years between 2008 and 2012 (see Bjørg Evjen's Afterword). Since our first faculty workshop took place in October 2008 in Tromsø at the same time as a United Nations (UN) committee on Indigenous people and development, we have taken the Declaration on the Rights of Indigenous Peoples (UNDRIP) as core to our vision for increasing the knowledge of Indigenous peoples in our respective geographies and for bringing their continued presence to the new global map through our scholarship. Our scholarship provides comparative cross-cultural perspectives vital in the field of Indigenous Studies, and, at its heart, the collaborative effort seeks most to expand knowledge for educational purposes, in particular for graduate study in Indigenous Studies. Montana in the Pacific Northwest of the United States and Finnmark in northern Norway are regions of the world inhabited by Indigenous people for millennia; they provide historical, political, and cultural information that lend themselves to useful comparison and contrast, since they share in the global history of colonization, and yet differ in their legal and cultural particulars. For example, the tribal nations in Montana were all impacted in one way or another by the Hellgate Treaty of 1855, just as the Sámi people of Fennoscandia have been affected by agreements between the Sámi parliament and the Norwegian government. Else Grete Broderstad, Sámi political scientist, aptly points out how the self-determination of Native peoples involves a dynamic between Indigenous and non-Indigenous. She writes, "a perspective on indigenous self-determination, as well as a need to include these perspectives in nonindigenous actions and ideas concerning governing and citizenship, imply a focus on shared destiny and reciprocal dependency. The political voyage happens in the same waters and reciprocal dependency appears particularly evident in relation to land rights and the need for resource access" (Broderstad 2011, 898–99).

Our hope in putting together this anthology is to shed light on the shared destiny and reciprocal dependency Native Americans and Sámis each have with the people and the government in their respective countries and on how Native American and Sámi peoples bear a mutual interest in self-determination as Indigenous peoples. Seeking recognition within our political and cultural spheres entails a complex—even convoluted—process of decolonization that involves many things, not the least of which are community activism, research, arts, literature, economics, education, resource management, politics, legal pursuit of social justice, and religious revitalization. The collection of essays here presents many perspectives on the means toward achieving self-determination.[4]

Recognition of the Global Presence of Indigenous People

With the United Nations' vote of 143 in favor, 11 abstentions, and 4 against ratifying UNDRIP on September 13, 2007, Indigenous peoples around the world made their way onto the map of global recognition. After a decades-long struggle, Indigenous peoples were finally seen as fully human in the human rights discourse. Their presence in international legal discourse has been conspicuously obscured, even though the UN passed the Universal Declaration of Human Rights (Declaration) in 1948 after World War II to prevent future genocides. A UN press release after the passage of UNDRIP stated that it (UNDRIP) "represent(s) the dynamic development of international legal norms, and it reflects the commitment of the UN's member states to move in certain directions."[5] "Certain directions" thus becomes another metaphorical mapping of "roads" to be taken, at the end of which one may or may not see laws passed that create new legal norms. Originally lacking endorsement by the United States, Canada, New Zealand, and Australia,[6] passage of UNDRIP nonetheless represents something of a symbolic milestone in which "nationhood" takes on new meanings, and to borrow Nicholas Black Elk's words, "the circled village" includes "every living thing with roots or legs or wings" (Neihardt 2000, 23). Global acknowledgment of Indigenous peoples' rights entails a shift in Western philosophy inasmuch as such recognition affirms group rights—the right to exist as distinct peoples and to reproduce—are equal to individual human rights. Henry Minde notes that, "the American view dominated when the new system of human rights was established in the UN after the World War II. This view concentrates on discrimination of persons belonging to different minorities, that is, a concentration on the principles of individual and universal rights" (Minde 2001, 110). The quasi-legal or unbinding nature of UNDRIP nonetheless empowers a rhetoric that carries with it the pressure of environmental tipping points and signifies new meanings for the word "Indigenous" as people who often function as stewards of place, in a fullness of human dignity. Not coincidentally, Indigenous peoples inhabit some of the richest areas in the world. And, though frequently seen as impoverished or not seen at all, those peoples and their philosophies dictate ways of life reliant upon maintenance of biodiversity. UNDRIP, in a sense, brings together a legal recognition by uniting a human rights rhetoric with a newly acknowledged view of global change brought about by the increasing awareness of and alarm regarding environmental tipping points. As stated in *Transitions and Tipping Points in Complex Environmental Systems*, "just as the first view of the planet Earth from space helped crystallize a global perspective and an environmental awareness, the advent of a global, interconnected, and interdisciplinary data networks will be important in fostering international, collective action to address environmental problems" (AC-ERE 2009, 8; Field et al. 2014).

While counting Indigenous people may not be easy (population estimates run between 300 and 350 million, 5 to 6 percent of the world's population), ascertaining the size of their land bases seems nearly impossible, especially given their status as peoples, which continues to identify inseparability with the environment. Acknowledging the significant presence of Indigenous people as inhabitants of the planet flies in the face of theorists who resist concepts of cultural identity primarily or inextricably based on situated knowledge; and, it challenges the idea that unique knowledge and ways of knowing are situated in place, rather than "universal" as in the Western European epistemological paradigm. Part of the destructive legacy of colonialism stems from the idea that knowledge must be transportable—like goods—as a universal in order for it to be valuable. Yet, moving from metaphor to actual peoples in actual places and/or people displaced from their original spaces and places remains crucial for grasping their rights in a rights-based discourse. As awareness of the importance of valuing eco- and ethnodiversity has increased, so has the appreciation for place-based rights and responsibilities. The law has not caught up with that growing awareness.

Asserting place-based rights—rights based on long-standing tenure in a particular geographical place—goes against over a half-millennium of Western European legal frameworks for colonizing Indigenous lands, dominating the peoples, and capturing the resources. As Robert J. Miller so aptly states in the introduction to *Discovering Indigenous Lands: The Doctrine of Discovery in the English Colonies*, which he coauthored,

> when English explorers and other Europeans planted their national flags and religious symbols in "newly discovered" lands, as many paintings depict, they were not just thanking God for a safe voyage. Instead they were undertaking a well-recognized legal procedure and ritual mandated by international law and designed to create their country's legal claim over the "newly discovered" lands and peoples. (Miller et al. 2010, 2)

The inhabitants of those places had vastly different ideas, and came to object to the assumptions on the part of European nations. Although often referred to as a legal fiction, the internationally known Doctrine of

Discovery "was nothing more than an attempt to put a patina of legality on the armed confiscation of the assets of Indigenous peoples," argues Miller and others (Miller et al. 2010, 6). Centuries later, the U.S. Supreme Court, according to Miller and colleagues, defined the Doctrine of Discovery implicitly through ten tenets identified in the *Johnson v. McIntosh* case of 1823: 1) the "first European country to discover lands unknown to other Europeans gained property and sovereignty rights over the lands"; 2) "physical possessions had to occur within a reasonable length of time after the first discovery to create a complete title to the land for the discovering country"; 3) the European countries claiming discovery "acquired a property right of preemption, that is, the sole power and authority to buy the land from the Indigenous peoples and governments"; 4) "Indigenous nations and peoples were considered . . . to have lost the full property and ownership over their lands"; 5) "the inhabitants of those lands were also considered to have lost some of their inherent sovereign powers and their rights to free trade and diplomatic relations on an international scale"; 6) the "discovery element provided that Europeans had a claim to a reasonable and significant amount of land contiguous to and surrounding their actual settlements and discovered lands"; 7) Indigenous lands were considered "to be empty, wasted, and available to be claimed," an idea known as *terra nullius*; 8) peoples who were not professed Christians "did not possess the same human and natural law rights to land, sovereignty, and self-determination as Christian peoples"; 9) the European concept of "civilization" definitively had not been bestowed upon Indigenous peoples by God, "and, therefore, Christians had a responsibility to bring 'civilization' to them, to exercise paternity and guardianship powers over them"; and 10) "just wars" were within European purview and "allegedly justified the invasion, conquest, and acquisition of Indigenous lands in certain circumstances" (Miller et al. 2010, 6–8). All the tenets set forth in the Marshall decisions of the early nineteenth century resonate with the social justice sought by Indigenous peoples today.

Coming to terms with UNDRIP thus means defining key words and "mapping" our intellectual terrain. Over the last several decades, but especially since the 2007 signing of the UNDRIP, the term *Indigenous* has grown in usage; it is nonetheless difficult to define. The United Nations uses the following working definition.[7]

Indigenous communities, peoples, and nations are those which, having a historical continuity with preinvasion and precolonial societies that developed on their territories, consider themselves distinct from other sectors of the societies now prevailing on those territories, or parts of them. They form at present nondominant sectors of society and are determined to preserve, develop, and transmit to future generations their ancestral territories, and their ethnic identity, as the basis of their continued existence as peoples, in accordance with their own cultural patterns, social institutions, and legal system.

Long-standing, place-based cultural identity from tenure in particular geographical locations provides the crux of difference between Indigenous people and other societies that have come to dominate in those places. The fact sheet of the Permanent Forum on Indigenous Issues (Forum) further elaborates the above definition to include those people who self-identify as indigenous peoples "at the individual level and [are] accepted by the community as their member" and who have "resolve[d] to maintain and reproduce their ancestral environments and systems as distinctive peoples and communities." Indigenous people are more easily identified, according to the Forum, than defined, and they reside in at least seventy countries. Local naming remains the most accurate designations for them, particularly in the language of the peoples themselves.

Any way of designating Indigenous, however, emphasizes *peoples* as more than what is loosely designated as a population group. *Indigenism*, a term intended to identify the human rights movement associated with protecting Indigeneity, represents a "revolt" of sorts, a resistance to "the forces of cultural uniformity and against the appropriation of Indigenous peoples' sovereignty by states," according to Ronald Niezen, author of *The Origins of Indigenism*. The movement results from resistance to colonialism. He writes that the

> main premise is that by removing [Indigenous] people from their land, educating their children in state schools, eliminating their languages, and usurping their own systems of justice and conflict resolution, states are imposing a gray uniformity on all humanity, stifling and suppressing the creative cultural energies of those who are *most knowledgeable and prescient about the forces of nature*. (Niezen 2003, 2 [emphasis added])

The growth of global environmentalism since the 1960s has led to gradually increased recognition of the presence of Indigenous peoples and of those peoples' unique stewardship roles in their homelands. Moreover, the systematic control over Indigenous peoples' lives and ways of living and the outright efforts to destroy the people culturally and/or physically is finally being seen—at least in some political sectors—as a result of global imperialist ideology that was first manifest in the Doctrine of Discovery (see Coates 2004, 120–43). The multidimensional nature of that ideology has been carefully addressed in UNDRIP.

Indigenous Peoples and Ecological Systems Thinking

Though often seen as a cliché related to Native people, closeness to nature here becomes the ethical hinge-pin in media for the argument to preserve racial and ethnic minority peoples' rights in light of current global climate change—what Derrick Bell, Jr., terms *"interest convergence"* when describing the civil rights movement. That is, dominant powers see a self-interest that coexists with the needs of the oppressed. Traditional ecological knowledge (TEK) is the new vocabulary for an old set of Indigenous epistemological practices, and the need to acknowledge Indigenous land tenure comes with the heightened awareness of the global diminution of biodiversity. Further, TEK, as situated in Indigenous societies, "incorporates understanding of ecological relationships about biota, ecosystems, and places" into cultural practices related to interspecies relations, as well as belief systems (Reo and Whyte 2012, 15). Moving beyond interest convergence toward historical reckoning with and accountability for past actions will necessitate deepening understandings of the power of place in shaping human consciousness (Bell 1995, 20). The kinds of commitments to cultural identity that arise from place-centered philosophy lead to deferring levels and types of ethical engagement. UNDRIP links tribal people across the globe both through their shared history of colonial domination and their fundamentally place- and kinship-based worldviews.

The Indigenous peoples of Norway and the United States share the challenges of coming to terms with settler colonialism in their respective places, and they share the experience of being peoples who also have a presence within their respective geographies at the same time as they inhabit multicultural worlds and move in and out of other locations within their respective dominant nation-states. To one degree or another, Indigenous presence problematizes those nations' hegemonic definition of themselves as Norwegians or as Americans. In the United States extant treaties made between sovereigns create boundaries and territories where rights constantly play out in convoluted and contested ways. In Montana, although the "Medicine Line" (international boundary between the United States and Canada) creates a semipermeable barrier for tribal people, such as the Blackfeet Nation, identity for many is tribal before it is American or Canadian.

Given the history of the making and breaking of treaties and other agreements over the centuries, it remains to be seen how the UN's 2007 recognition of Indigenous peoples' rights will be allowed to play out in regard to control over natural resources, as well as Indigenous land ownership and self-determination. After all, the idea of "sustainable development" has only relatively recently entered global discourses as a way of integrating "local communities into larger social and economic frameworks," as noted by Paul Jull in his essay in *Indigenous Peoples: Resource Management and Global Rights* (Jull 2003, 21). Regardless, the merging of the metaphorical and the literal in the UNDRIP signals a crucial movement away from an aspect of Western thinking that has trapped Indigenous people in Western ideas of "the natural" or "the wilderness" for many centuries. The concept is that as "wild" people they have no "place" in a future and that they must and will evolve away from the being "undeveloped." In other words, Indigenous people who inhabit areas designated as "wilderness," as "undeveloped," or "under-developed" are not capable of managing those places in modern ways (see Lummis 1996). In the United States such thinking over the past century and a half has resulted in the growth of a system of governmental paternalism through the U.S. Department of the Interior (USDI), and within it the Bureau of Indian Affairs. The USDI abrogated rights of Indigenous peoples by declaring Native people wards of the state and their lands and resources best held in "trust." Moreover, legitimizing the concept of "Indigenous" allows for a wide range of peoples to be seen as allied through histories of imperial domination, as well as vested interests in sustainability of resources and ways of life within their homelands. Writing before the passage of UNDRIP, Jull discusses resource development in relation to the differences between "wealthy educated countries like Norway, Sweden, and Finland," on the one hand, and other countries in places such as South America, on the other, where extraordinary corporate and governmental oppression exists. Indigenous peoples in those South American countries must even at times be careful not to be identified when they meet with other Indigenous peoples regarding land and resources. Yet, Indigenous people often need protection and support from allies outside their regions as they struggle against corporate forces seeking to destroy their homelands. Jull writes that "the era of Indigenous internationalism began in 1973 at the Arctic Peoples Conference with Greenlandic, Sámi, and Northern Canadian Indigenous hinterland peoples sharing their experiences of 'frontier' resource development pressure and other aspects of marginalization by government and industry" (Jull 2003, 25). When Indigenous peoples from around the world become part of a global "imagined community," the voices and needs of the least politically powerful have a better chance to be heard (Anderson 1983).

More than a political shift, UNDRIP envisions epistemological shifts, especially in regard to environmental tipping points. The same social value system that has evolved over the past five centuries, stemming from the Doctrine of Discovery, has led to a split between what is called "human" and what is called "nature." Indigenous studies illuminates that fissure between Western and Indigenous scientific thinking. In their introduction to *Postcolonial Ecologies*, Elizabeth DeLoughrey and George B. Handley write that "place encodes time, suggesting that histories embedded in the land and sea have always provided vital and dynamic methodologies for understanding the transformative impact of empire and the anticolonial epistemologies it tries to suppress" (DeLoughrey and Handley 2011, 4). In other words they argue "Western discourses of nature and the environment have been shaped by the history of empire" (DeLoughrey and Handley 2011, 4). Mary Louise Pratt observes that the "Linnaeus system alone launched a European knowledge-building enterprise of unprecedented scale and appeal" (Pratt 1992, 25).

This represented a "radically new mapping of global space through one common language (Latin)," Pratt asserts, an action that brought about "a new European 'planetary consciousness'" (DeLoughrey and Handley 2011, 10). Domination and exploitation through taxonomies of nature and maps of Indigenous peoples and their lands go hand-in-hand with discourses of identifying Indigenous people as "savages," evolutionarily backward, and therefore, by way of either their corruption or their innocence, unable to govern themselves or to provide oversight to their homelands and resources, and eventually their very own children. In settler-colonialist ideology "progress" centrally involves a movement of Indigenous people into a mainstream society and a designation of "nature" into special areas void of human inhabitants. Use of "wilderness" areas then becomes governed by the state and limited to recreational or capitalist exploitation (for example, in harvesting trees), as seen fit by the state.

Further, UNDRIP attempts to recover (or uncover, depending on the legal state of ownership) rights of communal ownership and control and, more importantly, a right to be a people—distinct and fruitful. Made up of nineteen introductory paragraphs and forty-five articles, UNDRIP "cover[s] a wide range of human rights and fundamental freedoms related to Indigenous peoples, including the right to preserve and develop their cultural characteristics and distinct identities, ownership and use of traditional lands and natural resources, and protection against genocide" (Asian Indigenous and Tribal Peoples Network [AITPN] July 26, 2006, 1). It also "covers rights related to religion, language, and education, and the right to participate in the political, economic, and social life of the society in which indigenous peoples live" (AITPN 2006, 1). The most controversial aspect of UNDRIP, and perhaps the reason four nations would not initially sign it, rests with the fact that it "recognizes the right to self-determination, to self-government in matters related to Indigenous affairs, and the honoring of treaties and agreements concluded with indigenous peoples" (AITPN 2006, 1).

Why is UNDRIP so important, even though four prominent nations were slow to recognize its validity? In symbolic terms, Indigenous peoples and the ways in which they are treated should no longer be hidden behind or within the discourses of colonialism and neocolonialism in its many oppressive forms: scientific, political, educational, or popular/cultural media. With UNDRIP, the first step in truth and reconciliation has been made: an acknowledgment of the need for social justice for Indigenous Peoples and for empowerment. (Since Nuremberg and beginning with South Africa after apartheid, at least thirty "truth and reconciliation" commissions have been set up around the world. Most notable are those commissions seeking redress for the atrocities of forced boarding school education.) As the AITPN details, "from denial of entry to the League of Nations to the adoption of the Draft Declaration [UNDRIP] to exclusion from the 'WE THE PEOPLES OF THE UNITED NATIONS' of the Charter of the United Nations, Indigenous peoples had to consistently overcome exclusion. International human rights instruments failed to include Indigenous peoples. Critical Indigenous rights are not found in normative legal frameworks" (AITPN 2006, 2). They were not on the world "map" in the minds of UN ambassadors, and they had no recourse in regard to international human rights remedies.

S. James Anaya, author of *Indigenous Peoples in International Law*, was appointed in 2008 to serve as UN Special Rapporteur on the Situation of Human Rights and Fundamental Freedom of Indigenous Peoples. With Anaya's appointment, Indigenous people have a place in that world political body legally and symbolically.[8] The importance of oversight or watchdog positions, such as that of the Special Rapporteur, should never be underestimated. In his book Anaya details the evolution of Western thought relative to Indigenous peoples in North America since the European invasion of the continent. Bartolomé de las Casas and Francisco de Vitoria of the late fifteenth and early sixteenth centuries regarded Native people to be human, no small matter at the time. Anaya writes that "within [the] historical jurisprudential frame, the threshold question for determining the rights and status of the American Indians was whether they were rational human beings" (Anaya 2004, 17). Over the next two centuries, Western thinking evolved a differentiation between "the natural rights of individuals and the natural rights of states" that allowed for the domination of people by the state for "the common good" (Anaya 2004, 20). Despite Indigenous peoples being seen as human, they were regarded as un-Christian and evolutionarily backward, and therefore subject to domination. Vitoria opened the door early on by writing about American Indians and seeing them as "unfit to found or administer a lawful state" (quoted in Anaya 2004, 18). Therein lies the seed of the federal paternalism originating in the Doctrine of Discovery that continues to this day, as well as the implicit definition of the Western European nation-state. An insidious discourse of dominance hides in the idea that the nation-state's rights trump the rights of the Indigenous nations residing within. Military, political, economic, educational, and religious domination has followed.

In the early decades of the nineteenth century in the United States, three Supreme Court decisions chiseled into law the idea of there being no tribal institutional equivalent to that of the nation-state. Chief Justice Marshall wrote majority legal opinions amidst the controversy of removal of Cherokee and other southeastern Indian nations to Oklahoma. He deemed Cherokees as "quasi-sovereign, domestic dependent nations," which removed them from international law since "tribal societies [were seen] as not qualifying as nations or states and hence as without full rights to group autonomy or ancestral lands" (Anaya 2004, 23). They were, ironically, "civilized" enough to have developed a written language, produced a written literature and a newspaper through their printing press, formed their own Supreme Court, maintained successful farming and animal husbandry homesteads, and developed other modes of economic development. Their removal, which Cherokees termed the "Trail of Tears," represented a historical moment of extreme social injustice in U.S. history. Although the Supreme Court opposed removal, the premises in Chief Justice Marshall's argument "meant that Indian tribes and other Indigenous peoples, not qualifying as states, could not participate in the shaping of international law, nor could they look to it to affirm the rights that had once been deemed to inhere in them by natural or divine law" (Anaya 2004, 27). The act of signing treaties itself should serve as an indication of Indigenous peoples' inherent rights despite the legal fiction decreeing that European nation-states have the right to claim previously undiscovered territories. Indigenous peoples within nation-states carry forward with unique world-views and histories that define land ownership and usage—recourse to rights—yet, such determinations by and large continue to rest within the dominant culture's legal system. Norway has only begun to codify Sámi land rights over the past twenty-five to thirty years, for example.

Exclusion of Indigenous peoples from previous international law, such as the Declaration in 1948, resulted from complicated nation-states' fears of potential loss of sovereignty in forming alliances. Paul Lauren, author of *The Evolution of International Human Rights: Visions Seen*, points out the difficulty in such agreements at that time. He writes, "any international guarantees of human rights by their very nature would impinge on the claimed prerogatives of national sovereignty and domestic jurisdiction." He further explains, "most of those imperial powers were military allies neces-sary for defeating common enemies and not at all inclined to surrender their possessions or their prerogatives of national sovereignty" (Lauren 2011, 158). The pattern of Indigenous peoples' exclusion continued for decades. The unwillingness of world powers to give up control over Indigenous peoples and their lands has also continued, as is evident by the countries who would not initially sign UNDRIP.

D'Arcy McNickle is a noted Métis scholar, creative writer, enrolled tribal member from the Flathead Reservation, and an advocate for American Indian rights. In his 1973 text, *Native American Tribalism: Indian Survivals and Renewals*, he writes,

> The United States Court of Claims, in reviewing an Indian case at the end of the last century . . . found the legal situation anomalous, a situa-tion "unknown to the common law or the civil law or to any system of municipal law. [American Indians] were neither citizens nor aliens; they were neither persons nor slaves; they were wards of the nation, and yet . . . were little else than prisoners of war while war did not exist." (McNickle 1973, 87)

The sad truth of such a statement is reflected through a well-documented history of American Indian disenfranchisement due to policies of forced assimilation into European American worldview, policies that included re-ligious oppression and mandatory boarding school attendance. Tribal people were alienated from their lands through legal and illegal means, including the usurpation and flooding of tribal homelands by "right of Eminent Domain." As Beth Piatote amply details in her book *Domestic Subjects:*

Gender, Citizenship, and the Law in Native American Literature, such assimilative policies held as their core the goal to disintegrate the tribal family and thereby to destroy the communal connection of the people to each other and to the land (Piatote 2012). "Homeland" takes on new meaning when seen in light of land appropriation through marriage law in settlercolonial situations.

Sámi people faced similar assimilation policy efforts, particularly during the nineteenth century, as a program of Norwegianization forbade the Sámi use of their own language, forced attendance of Sámi youth in boarding schools, and characterized Sámi cultural traditions, lifeways, and history as backward. According to Harald Gaski and Henry Minde, renowned scholars of Sámi history, the policies that were put in place that forced Sámi children into boarding schools altered their livelihoods and culture dramatically and almost eliminated their language (Bremmer 2012). Gradually, Sámi people in the four countries where they reside (Norway, Finland, Sweden, and Russia) have come into visibility through international Indigenous alliances and activism. Through the formation of the Sámi Parliament, they have gained a considerable political voice in Norway, Sweden, and Finland.

Forty years after the UN human rights awareness, American Indigenous peoples face new forms of theft of lands and resources, in addition to the environmental racism in policies and practices that cause devastating health problems and early death. The Declaration provides a means of international redress that globalizes Indigenous identities and Indigenous resistances to assimilative and appropriative policies by nation-states. The ways and means of the resistances vary widely according to place, state structure, and cultural particularities. Nonetheless, the commonalities of Indigenous experience shared among people lend strength to each struggle—no matter whether it is in Venezuela in its efforts to return control of capital to the Indigenous people or in the United States where the struggle continues among Western Shoshone people to reclaim what has been unlawfully taken from them by encroachment.

Reimagining Indigenous Self-Determination Through Education

Many struggles for social justice for Indigenous peoples now crucially take place in courts of law and in assemblies where the social infrastructure is built and funded. Educational reformation and transformation, however, also offer the grounds for rebuilding Native nations and thereby become a high priority in claiming the full rights to self-determination. As two Native North American scholars, Marie Battiste (Mi'kmaq) and James (Sa'ke'j) Youngblood Henderson (Chickasaw), remind us, "the military, political, and economic subjugation of Indigenous peoples has been well documented, as have social, cultural, and linguistic pressures and the ensuing damage to Indigenous communities, but no force has been more effective in oppressing Indigenous knowledge and heritage than the educational system" (Battiste and Henderson 2000, 86). Transforming our thinking around Indigenous issues carries a complex imperative to assure the survival not only of Indigenous ideas, but also of the communities from which traditional knowledge has been generated, is maintained, and critically, has sometimes been lost. For the Sámi of Norway, those knowledge systems involve reindeer herding traditions, seafaring, and fishing traditions. For American Indians in Montana, those knowledge systems involve mountain and high plains cultural survival knowledge—ranging from fire regulation to bison management. From communities to classrooms, Indigenous knowledge spans generations today in new terms and with new methods.

The intergenerational historical trauma from displacement, dispossession, oppression, and deracination requires dynamic educational systems and educators committed to making a difference in terms of positive outcomes in tribal peoples' lives. Indigenous pedagogy also needs to be properly valued. In the words of Gregory Cajete, Tewa scientist and educator, "as a whole, traditional tribal education revolved around experiential learning (learning by doing or seeing), storytelling (learning by listening and imagining), ritual/ceremony (learning through initiation), dreaming (learning through unconscious imagery), tutoring (learning through apprenticeship), and artistic creation (learning through creative synthesis)" (Cajete 1994, 34). Sápmi and Indian Country in Montana support tribally based educational institutions that hold the preservation of cultural perspectives and the enrichment of Indigenous knowledge as important educational priorities.

Within the public schools in Montana, Indigenous peoples have faced obstacles in making their presence felt. Developing educational curricula that teach American Indian history has been met with obstacles at the levels of classroom teaching and administration—pipeline issues exist for students and knowledge. In regard to curricular reform fostering a bigger-picture history, Montana is uniquely positioned to provide an educational model for others in its recognition of Indigenous peoples' rights to respectful representation. The state's constitution (amended in 1972) mandates the dissemination of American Indian history. Article X, Section 1(2) of the Montana Constitution reads: "the state recognizes the distinct and unique cultural heritage of American Indians and is committed in its educational goals to the preservation of their cultural integrity."[9] The 1972 Montana Constitution is the only state constitution in the United States that recognizes the unique cultural heritage of the Native peoples of Montana and mandates that the history of Native people be taught throughout its educational system and that schools involve local tribal communities and Native parents in assuring that the spirit of the law is upheld. As with all laws governing the recognition of and respect for Indigenous knowledge, the threat that legal scaffolding will be taken away looms large, particularly in political winds sweeping for corporate domination of natural resources.

Putting teeth into the constitutional mandate has taken many years, however. The Montana legislature passed the Native American Studies Act to realize the vision put forth in the constitution, but after a couple of years, the state teachers brought it down by changing one word, making Native American studies desired but not required. Some speculate that originally the efforts to fulfill the constitutional mandate failed to provide a much-needed grandfather clause that would have addressed the issues around continuing education raised by the more senior teachers who offered the greatest resistance to the statute. After floundering for over two decades, legislation in 1999, House Bill 528, attempted once again to remedy the American Indian/Alaska Native achievement gap. That bill passed and became statute; since then the governor has given each tribal college and the landless, state-recognized Little Shell Chippewa people monies to develop histories of their reservations and tribes. The governor also gave $17 million to the Office of Public Instruction to turn the histories into curricula. With the resources provided by the state, "seven essential understandings" were developed. They called first for understanding that a great diversity exists among the twelve tribal nations of Montana, in terms of their histories, governments, languages, and cultures. Second, individual American Indians develop uniquely—"there is no generic American Indian." Third, in modern Native life, traditional beliefs and spirituality continue; in other words, "tribal cultures, traditions, and languages are still practiced" today. Fourth, the reservations of today are places "reserved by tribes for their own use through treaties, statutes, and executive orders . . . not 'given' to them." Although in a few instances, reservations were created by executive orders of the U.S. president for a variety of reasons. Fifth, federal policies conceived and enacted throughout mainstream American history continue to shape who American Indian people are today. Sixth, "history is a story most often related through the subjective experience of the teller." Because "histories are being rediscovered and revised," what has been thought about American Indian history has changed and will change with the addition of Indigenous scholarship and perspectives." Finally, "under the American legal system, Indian tribes have sovereign powers, separate and independent from the federal and state governments."[10]

Those seven essential understandings, though specifically created for Montana's Indian Education for All, can be adapted as essential Indigenous studies understandings, since they involve basic ideas about identity formation of groups and individuals, continuity of cultures, what Indigenous homelands are and how they are governed, how contemporary Native communities reflect centuries of colonial intrusion and domination, how history (at its best) involves dynamic revisions and transformations, and most importantly, that Indigenous people have inherently sovereign rights. In some respects, as intellectual understandings, the detailing itself of their essential nature makes obvious a new mapping of ideas that renders Native people visible. The UNDRIP details each of those ideas while maintaining the general rubric of Indigenous peoples' rights. This collection reflects scholars' efforts to add a voice and a vision that illuminates "the disjuncture in the ideologies that have underpinned the development of [imperial] world order" (Stewart-Harawira 2005, 56).

Among Sámi peoples, educational transformation and development also play an important role in the realization of their full human rights. In his 2010 report on Sámi people's self-determination struggles, S. James Anaya presented a report to the Human Rights Council on a study he conducted on Sápmi "land, water, and natural resource rights, and the situation of youth, with particular focus on education and language" in Norway, Finland, and Sweden. He made recommendations, and he added that "despite the expressed commitment of the Governments of Norway, Sweden, and Finland to protect the rights of the Sámi people, the challenges ahead in Sápmi are significant," and that "overcoming the harm inflicted by the discrimination and extensive assimilation policies carried out throughout history in the Nordic countries will require serious commitment, political will, and hard work" (Anaya 2010, 2). As with Montana's constitutional mandate to respect American Indian histories and cultures throughout the state's educational system, the commitment to do so must be shown by political will to keep the laws in place that assure such social justice initiatives, to fund them, and to put in the hard work to make certain they continue. Education, historically used by colonial powers to assimilate and deracinate Native peoples, can and has become a tool of liberation from the legacy of colonialism.

Preserving Place-Based Visions

I began this introduction with the words of Nicholas Black Elk as a way of providing the frame of an Indigenous visionary. Black Elk was a man whose deepest desire was to see his people's hopes and dreams blossom in generations to come and for them to continue their existence as distinct yet powerfully dynamic people. In an important sense he anticipated that UNDRIP would be signed, even as he worked within the Catholic Church as a catechist to keep spiritual hope alive. The power of his vision carried him through many hard times in his life. In Black Elk's vision the holy person gave him "a cane to walk with and a people's heart"—images that suggest, first, something to help the aged and infirm visionary through life and by extension, all of us (help in carrying on). Second, "a people's heart" would also lighten his load, since it signals a noble responsibility, as well as a guide. Being communally and holistically grounded through a deep sense of the responsibility toward others reminds him of his relations in the world.[11] As the foundational Sámi myth would have it, placing the reindeer's heart in its homeland, so that putting an ear to the ground to catch the beating of the reindeer heart could renew hope and give courage and strength to the people to carry on their ways as Indigenous peoples. On a model of living for the seventh generation from now, nothing could be more pressing than attending to traditional ecological knowledge— what Indigenous peoples, such as the peoples of Sápmi and of Montana, see as a web of interconnectedness.

Notes

1. Mapping as a metaphor for conceptualizing done by colonizing forces and by Native people has a notable early usage in Hugh Brody's *Maps and Dreams*. More recently, René Oyono, Peter Mbile, Marina France, and Solange Bandiaky, in "Mapping Communities, Mapping Rights: Participatory Community Mapping as Rights Contestation in Cameroon" (2010), discuss jurisdictional issues in regard to the "dualism between legitimacy and legality," the former being the concept held by the Indigenous people themselves.

2. See Lummis's (1996) *Radical Democracy* for a discussion of the problematic use of the term "development."

3. Boundaries may actually be part of the problem of domination of territories where, for example, a people have traditionally hunted or seasonally inhabited.

4. Our conversations within this text reflect the areas of expertise and specialization of the people involved in the project, rather than what might be the case with another type of anthology where an editor seeks out authors with particular expertise and specialization to contribute to a text. Our collaboration, therefore, led to some

people working on jointly authored chapters and others contributing from their individual research and voice. It is our hope that our conversation serves the needs of scholars and students to learn about our peoples.

5. http://indigenouspeoples.nl/indigenous-peoples/rights-of-indigenous-peoples/international-law.

6. Since then, the United States, New Zealand, Australia, and Canada have endorsed UNDRIP, with qualifications.

7. "Indigenous Peoples." *United Nations Permanent Forum on Indigenous Issues.* http://www.un.org/esa/sodev/unpfii.

8. Over the past thirty-plus years, many committees have been created within the UN to address a wide range of needs of Indigenous people globally and in specific locations. Shari Huhndorf (2009b, 361) states that, "Indigenous peoples have adapted maps, despite their historical uses, to secure 'restorative justice' and, in particular, to establish claims to territory. Whereas European maps have defined and controlled space by erasing indigenous peoples and transforming American geographies into geometrical configurations (the 'wilderness' or 'virgin land' of colonial discourse)."

9. "Indian Education." Montana Office of Public Instruction. http://opi.mt.gov/programs/indianed/. Accessed November 12, 2012.

10. "Indian Education for All." *Montana Office of Public Instruction.* http://opi.mt.gov/programs/indianed/. Accessed November 12, 2012.

11. While I recognize that Neihardt made changes to shape the manuscript of Black Elk's story, as Black Elk related it, this part truthfully reflects Black Elk's philosophy.

References

AC-ERE (Advisory Committee for Environmental Research and Education). 2009. Transitions and Tipping Points in Complex Environmental Systems. NSF Report No. 7. Washington, DC: National Science Foundation.

AITPN (Asian Indigenous and Tribal Peoples Network). 2006. "A UN Declaration on the Rights of Indigenous Peoples: Right and Wrong Sides of History." *Indigenous Issues (The Occasional Briefing Papers of the AITPN).* Janakpuri, New Delhi-110058, India, July 26.

Alberto, Lourdes. 2012. "Topographies of Indigenism: Mexico, Decolonial Indigenism, and the Chicana Transnational Subject in Ana Castillo's Mixquiahuala Letters." In *Comparative Indigeneities of the Americas: Toward a Hemispheric Approach,* edited by M. Bianet Castellanos, Lourdes Gutiérrez Nájera, and Arturo J. Aldama, 39–66. Tucson, AZ: University of Arizona Press.

Anaya, S. James. 2004. *Indigenous Peoples in International Law.* 2nd ed. New York: Oxford University Press.

———. 2010. *Report of the Special Rapporteur on the Situation of Human Rights and Fundamental Freedoms of Indigenous People, Preliminary Note on the Situation of Sámi People in the Sápmi Region Spanning Norway, Sweden and Finland.* Human Rights Council, Fifteenth Session, Agenda Item 3, Promotion and Protection of all Human Rights, Civil, Political, Economic, Social and Cultural Rights, Including the Right to Development. July 7, 1–3.

Anderson, Benedict. 1983. *Imagined Communities*. New York and London: New Left Books.

Battiste, Marie, and James Youngblood Henderson. 2000. *Protecting Indigenous Knowledge and Heritage: A Global Challenge*. Saskatoon, SK: Purich Publishing.

Bell, Derek A., Jr. 1995. "*Brown v. Board of Education* and the Interest Convergence Dilemma." In *Critical Race Theory: The Key Writings That Formed the Movement*, edited by Kimberle Crenshaw, Neil Cotanda, Gary Peller, and Kendall Thomas, 20–29. New York: The New Press.

Bremmer, Michael Terry. 2012. "Assessing the Role of Shame and Honor During the Alta Conflict." MA thesis. University of Montana, Missoula.

Broderstad, Else Grete. 2011. "The Promises and Challenges of Indigenous Self-Determination: the Sámi Case." *International Journal* 66(4):893–907.

Brody, Hugh. 1981. *Maps and Dreams: Indians and the Colombian River Frontier*. London: Jill Norman & Hobhouse.

Cajete, Gregory. 1994. *Look to the Mountain: An Ecology of Indigenous Education*. Skyland, NC: Kivaki Press.

———. 2004. "Philosophy of Native Science." In *Native American Thought*, edited by Anne Water, 45–47. Malden, MA: Blackwell Publishing.

Coates, Ken S. 2004. *A Global History of Indigenous Peoples: Struggle and Survival*. New York: Palgrave MacMillan.

DeLoughrey, Elizabeth, and George B. Handley, eds. 2011. *Postcolonial Ecologies: Literatures of the Environment*. New York: Oxford University Press.

Field, Christopher B., Vicente R. Barros, Michael D. Mastrandrea, Katharine J. Mach, Mohamed A.-K. Abdrabo, W. Neil Adger, Yury A. Anokhin, et al. 2014. *Climate Change 2014: Impacts, Adaptations, and Vulnerability*. WGII AR5 Phase I Report Launch. March 31, 2014. https://ipcc-wg2.gov/AR5/images/uploads/IPCC_WG2AR5_SPM_Approved.pdf. (downloaded May 25, 2014).

Gaski, Harald. 2011. "Song, Poetry, and Image in Writing: Sámi Literature." *Nordlit* 27:33–54.

Helander-Renvall, Elina. 2009. "Animism, Personhood and the Nature of Reality: Sámi Perspectives." *Polard Record* 46(236):44–56. Cambridge, MA: Cambridge University Press.

Huhndorf, Shari. 2009a. *Mapping the Americas: The Transnational Politics of Contemporary Native Culture*. Ithaca: Cornell University Press.

———. 2009b. "Picture Revolution: Transnationalism, American Studies, and the Politics of Contemporary Native Culture." *American Quarterly* 61(2):359–81.

Jakobsen, Jonas. 2011. "Education, Recognition and the Sámi People of Norway." In *Writing Postcolonial Histories of Intercultural Education*, edited by H. Niedrig and C. Ydesen, 1–9. New York: Peter Lang Publishing.

Josephsen, Eva. 2007. "Gáldu Cála." *Journal of Indigenous Peoples' Rights*. No 1. Kautokeino, Norway: Gáldu Cála Resource Center.

Jull, Peter. 2003. "The Politics of Sustainable Development: Reconciliation in Indigenous Hinterlands." In *Indigenous Peoples: Resource Management and Global Rights*, edited by Svein Jentoft, Henry Minde, and Ragnar Nilsen, 21–44. The Netherlands: Eubron.

Lakoff, George, and Mark Johnson. 1980. *Metaphors We Live By*. Chicago: University of Chicago Press.

Lauren, Paul. 2011. *The Evolution of International Human Rights: Visions Seen.* Pennsylvania Studies in Human Rights, 3rd ed. Philadelphia, PA: University of Pennsylvania Press.

Lummis, C. Douglas. 1996. *Radical Democracy.* Ithaca and London: Cornell University Press.

McNickle, D'Arcy. 1973. *Native American Tribalism: Indian Survivals and Renewals.* London: Oxford University Press.

Miller, Robert J., Jacinta Ruru, Larissa Behrendt, and Tracey Lindberg. 2010. *Discovering Indigenous Lands: The Doctrine of Discovery in the English Colonies.* New York: Oxford University Press.

Minde, Henry. 2003. "The Challenge of Indigenism: The Struggle for Sámi Land Rights and Self-Government in Norway 1960–1990." In *Indigenous Peoples: Resource Management and Global Studies,* edited by Svein Jentoft, Henry Minde, and Ragnar Nilsen, 75–106. The Netherlands: Eburon Delft.

———. 2001. "Sámi Land Rights in Norway: A Test Case for Indigenous Peoples." *International Journal on Minority and Group Rights* 8:107–25. Kluwer Law International.

Neihardt, John G. 2000. *Black Elk Speaks.* Lincoln: University of Nebraska Press.

Niezen, Ronald. 2003. *The Origins of Indigenism: Human Rights and the Politics of Identity.* Berkeley: University of California Press.

Oyono, René, Peter Mbile, Marina France, and Solange Bandiaky. 2010. "Mapping Communities, Mapping Rights: Participatory Community Mapping as Rights Contestation in Cameroon." *Policy Matters* 17:156–60.

Piatote, Beth. 2012. *Domestic Subjects: Gender, Citizenship, and Law in Native American Literature.* New Haven, CT: Yale University Press.

Pratt, Mary Louise. *Imperial Eyes: Travel Writing and Transculturation.* New York: Routledge, 1992.

Reo, Nicholas James, and Kyle Powys Whyte. 2012. "Hunting and Morality as Elements of Traditional Ecological Knowledge." *Human Ecology* 40:15–27.

Stewart-Harawira, Makere. 2005. *The New Imperial Order: Indigenous Responses to Globalization.* London and New York: Zed Books.

United Nations Department of Economic and Social Affairs, Division for Social Policy and Development, Secretariat of the Permanent Forum on Indigenous Issues. "The Concept of Indigenous Peoples." www.un.org/en/development/desa/index.html.

United Nations Declaration on the Rights of Indigenous Peoples, adopted September 13, 2007. United Nations Permanent Forum on Indigenous Issues. Fact Sheet. http://www.un.org/esa/socdev/unpfii/documents/5session_factsheet1.pdf. Accessed February 5, 2012.

CHAPTER ONE

Growing Indigenous Influence on Research, Extended Perspectives, and a New Methodology

A Historical Approach

Bjørg Evjen and David R. M. Beck

How are we to understand the historical context leading up to today's "Indigenous methodology" in the social sciences and humanities? Study of the growing Indigenous influence on research over the last 150 years in Norway and the United States shows how the dynamics in the encounters between researchers and the researched have become increasingly complicated. Originally put in a passive role as the objects of research, old ethnic peoples and Sámis in Norway and Native Americans in the United States today have become active participants and researchers. Researchers and their research must be placed and understood within the contemporary ideological contexts in which they live or have lived, since the situation of the researcher undoubtedly reflects the social and political conditions of the time. Analysis of research demonstrates how the researcher's perspective on Indigenous peoples and cultures consequently has changed over time and how the Indigenous role as researchers has increased. To what extent do these changes include an extended and new perspective, and to what extent is the change the consequence of a new methodology and a reflection of the international Indigenous revitalization movements? How do patterns of change in research agendas and methods compare between Norway and the United States?

 In recent decades a new focus on research and research methodology has arisen. Various methodological concepts including Western research,

27

Indigenous methodology, and decolonizing methodology are now considered to play key roles in the analysis of research. One hundred years ago it would have been unthinkable for a Sámi, and somewhat rare for a Native American, to stand up to be an active participant in research. There was no concept of an Indigenous methodology. What happened to research on topics of relevance for Indigenous peoples?

Many contemporary scholars are fully aware of the changing research milieu that includes a change in power of the academic, cultural, and political sort (e.g., Niemi 1983; Stordal 2008; Trouillot 1995). Research serves as a tool of power and defines the history of the past or present. It includes those doing research and those being researched. This chapter focuses on the historical development of these changes. On the Norwegian end, our focus is on research in Sápmi in general, with examples from research conducted in a smaller part of Sápmi, namely in the Lule Sámi area. No Kvens were living in this area. In the 1900s the Sámi part of the population of Tysfjord was sought out for several large international research projects. The U.S. picture is more complex. Scholars and collectors visited hundreds of communities for large and small research projects resulting in publications, archival holdings, and museum collections. Only a very few of these relationships will be highlighted here with the intention of elucidating broad themes.

Indigenous peoples have become the focus of increasingly nuanced studies. Museums and universities began large-scale ethnographic (not to mention artifact and human remains) collecting projects in the late nineteenth century with varying degrees of cooperation from and exploitation of Native American community members and scholars. To what extent did the same patterns appear in Norway and the United States regarding the focus of research and the encounter between the researcher and the researched? What were the key differences? How can this be explained? The main lines of relevant historical development serve as backdrops and will be sketched briefly step-by-step.

Time of Enlightenment, the First Step

The years preceding the mid-nineteenth century when research on minorities was broadly characterized by exoticism throughout the Western world will be considered first. Non-Norwegians were to be integrated "naturally" into Norwegian society. In Norway, as in the rest of Scandinavia, senior officials, often vicars, mostly coming from the southern part of the country, wrote in their journals or in books of travel about the people they met, not the least on the strange and exotic Sámi population. Although Norway was christened around 1000 AD, it wasn't until 1700 that missionaries were sent north to christen the people living there. Reports and letters from the missionaries tell about a pre-Christian worldview. Through stories and drawings they mediate an understanding of Sámi as a people living in and close to nature (Nordnorske samlinger 1938–1947). In North America most of the early observations of Indigenous people were recorded by missionaries, travelers/explorers, or government officials, and Indians were represented as objects of proselytization (Thwaites, 1896–1901). As time went on, Native people were viewed as "savage," either in romanticized terms as the "noble savage" living in harmony with nature, or fearful terms, such as the "savage savage" threatening the safety of the European invading settler societies (Berkhofer 1978; Pearce 1967). Documenting Native peoples became a key component of America's expansion to the west by the early nineteenth century.

The pastor Olav Holm of the parish in Tysfjord (1878–1884) carried a residue of this attitude and a transition representing what was to come. He arrived in local societies where different ethnic groups lived close together, which was new to him. He took a great interest in the Sámi. Holm studied the cultural diversity of the area and wrote books and several articles for newspapers and periodicals (cf. Evjen 1998). In many contexts Pastor Holm is especially mentioned as an example of the condescending attitude of majority society toward the Sámi. In his work *Fra en nordlandsk Prestegaard (From a Nordland Parsonage)*, he describes meeting with the Sámi of Tysfjord. Not surprisingly, his account is colored by the distance between the state officials and his subjects, and it gives an exotic picture of the Sámi while highlighting positive and negative qualities. Thus, he is struck with wonder when Sámi children demonstrate especially strong powers of reasoning in arriving at answers to his questions and states, "it is remarkable how quick these youngsters can be with answers to questions when—it must be noted—they have had a good teacher. Truths pop into their minds from nowhere, as it were" (Holm 1923, 129). Many times he remarks on how beautiful some Sámi can be, as if this were something unexpected that had to be emphasized for his readers.

Holm's writings reflect the changing attitude in the culture of the time from exoticism to nationalism; his were clearly influenced by the attitudes of social Darwinism. He wrote that "the White man's" culture was superior to that of the Sámi. While central in the work mentioned above, the Sámi are not mentioned in his 1889 *Det norske Folks Historie*

(*The History of the Norwegian People*). The influence of nationalism meant that any historical account had to stress the homogeneity of Norwegian culture. Given this point of view, the Sámi were too different and a minority to boot. However, Pastor Holm collected enough stories, myths, names, and so on for an entire book about them. For unknown reasons it was not published, but the manuscript for *Lapperne* (The Lapps) can be found in the manuscript collection of the library at the University of Oslo. Holm viewed the Sámi as if they were one homogenous group rooted in an Eastern culture. He described them in a 1907 publication in the following manner, a well-known attitude in the contemporary context of his time.

> I believe the Lapp is all but immune to what, to us, is higher culture, which is the level of our culture at this time. As far as I can see, he lacks the preconditions to create a social order that requires diligence, respect for rules, and a basic discipline in all aspects of higher form of social existence . . . for which the Asiatic nomad is not well suited, no matter how long he has been permanently settled. (Holm 1907, 16)

In North America and the United States the fascination with American Indians was strong, even if the attitudes toward them were similar to those toward the Sámi in Norway. The Jesuit missionaries in the north and the Spanish invaders in the south wrote copiously about their perceptions of Indian people from the first encounters onward. Missionaries sent news back to their European bases in the form of letters in order to raise funds; they emphasized the backwardness of Indian communities and glorified their successes in bringing them to Christ (Thwaites 1896–1901). Spanish America in the sixteenth through eighteenth centuries developed the legal system that would come to characterize a significant foundation of the modern United States' Indian policy, defining American Indians as culturally inferior to Europeans (Anaya 2004). This definition gave Euro-Americans a special obligation, in their view, to bring about massive cultural change to the people in Native American communities.

By the early nineteenth century the United States had begun its expansion across the continent in earnest, which culminated in the dispossession of nearly all tribal land and resources by the end of the century. The "cant of conquest," to borrow a term from Frances Jennings (1976), informed the reservation and assimilation policies that accompanied and followed it. American Indians were viewed as childlike, without religion, and lacking real social and governing institutions. They were also treated as curiosities and alternatively as peoples to be feared (the savage savage) or emulated (the noble savage). Ironically, even as Indian lands were being taken from them, as Indian people were being killed in warfare and massacres, and as Indian cultures were coming under heavy assault, non-Indian people idolized their own perceptions of Native American culture (Deloria 1999).

Government-sponsored explorations to the west in the early nineteenth century generally included orders to report on conditions in Indian Country so that governing officials back east could be better informed in their efforts to expand American influence across the continent. This would become a pattern for the next century and a half or more. Lewis and Clark and Zebulon Pike, in their famous expeditions, recorded data regarding the American Indian people they encountered as did Jedidiah Morse in his commissioned report of the conditions of American Indian tribes. Although this information lacked the perspective of the Native Americans themselves, it came to guide federal relations with tribes (Coues 1895; Morse 1822; Ronda 1984; Salish-Pend d'Oreille Culture Committee and Elders Cultural Advisory Council 2005).

Occasionally during this era observers recorded ethnographic material about Indians because they were curious. These were largely descriptive and judgmental. At times these could provide valuable details of everything from social relations to tribal customs, as in the case of Edwin James and the Menominee in 1815. James was stationed at the military fort at Green Bay and recorded a lengthy journal providing ethnographic description of Menominee customs and practices. More often, however, these recorded observations described violent encounters, such as those of Jedidiah Smith with Indians in Oregon, or cultural misunderstanding, such as that between Alexander McLeod and Coos tribal people. The latter expressed frustration in his journal in 1826 at being unable to ascertain the location of trapping grounds from tribal leaders, who after all were simply protecting access to their resources. All of these types of narratives are marred by ethnocentric assumptions of Western cultural superiority (Beck 2002, 2009; Davies 1961; Kasprycki 1990).

Historian Robert E. Bieder, in his seminal work on early American ethnologists, observes that in the nineteenth century, ethnologists' work purportedly influenced policy makers, though he questions the extent to which this actually occurred. Some, such as Henry Rowe Schoolcraft, actually worked for the government in the field of Indian relations and directly applied their observations to their actions in the field. Ethnologists in these years were still concerned with defining how and where American Indians fit into the development of human societies, whether they were a separately developed race, and the extent to which environment shaped people and vice versa. Their various works often reflected the scientific theories they propounded more than the peoples they studied (Bieder 1986).

Nationalism, the Second Step

In the second step, from approximately 1850 to 1940, nationalism held sway. Indigenous peoples were viewed as "outsiders" who should be brought into the life of the dominant culture. A nation was meant to consist of one culturally homogenous population. In Norway a lot of effort was put into defining everybody as one and the same in the policy of Norwegianization, including sending children to Norwegian schools. In Sweden the policy of Swedenization was a bit different but was nevertheless founded in the same kind of national policy. While in Norway this policy can be labeled as "assimilation," in Sweden to a certain extent it was "segregation." Reindeer-herding Sámi were organized in *Samebyer*, that is, local areas where reindeer husbandry was allowed and where children went to Sámi speaking schools. In the United States nationalism followed the era of "separation," as even the meager lands set aside for Indian tribes were increasingly coveted by Americans. In this U.S. era, reservations were established in small remnants of tribal homelands, and then Americans laid siege to them to dispossess tribes from their resources and individuals from their cultural affiliation. The federal policy of forced assimilation was enacted in an effort at Americanization.

In the decades prior to World War I, Norwegian researchers held German universities and researchers in the highest regard, including the German's focus on finding national human physical features and races. This was the heyday of social Darwinism with its agenda of the racial superiority of "the white man." The attitude at the time strongly favored the assimilation of "the outsiders" into society. In addition, there was a negative attitude in the dominant society regarding the position of reindeer-herding Sámi and the sea Sámi. The latter were often portrayed as if they stood on the lowest rung of the social status ladder (Eriksen and Niemi 1981; Helland 1908). To what degree this also was considered to be true internally amongst the Sámi has so far not been the subject of research.

German dominance changed with the outbreak of the war in 1914. After that a meeting place for Nordic researchers was formed with the establishment of the Institute for Comparative Cultures with its own publication series. The study of the Arctic peoples became one of the main tasks with a primary focus on the Sámi. Norway was obliged to do research on them before they "yield for the modern culture's homogenizing influence" (Stang 1925, 62). The Sámi was a small population with "an exotic and strange language and culture." Thus, the results from the future research were expected to be rich and meaningful (Stang 1925, 62).

During these years, cultures of Arctic peoples with particular emphasis on the Sámi culture became a main area of interest for the Norwegian Scientific Society and the Ethnographic Museum, which also produced their own publications. In this context we can especially point out the North Norwegian collections in which the Sámi culture was strongly represented.

Linguist Just Qvigstad held a great interest in the Sámi people and saw it as a task of major importance to collect Sámi materials while there still was time (Hansen 1991). Qvigstad had contacted none other than Holm to become better informed about the conditions in Tysfjord. He took a special interest in the sea Sámi. Among other things, he took on the task of examining the sea Sámi dialect called *Finnagiella* or the old Tysfjord dialect. This dialect was significantly different from the one spoken by the mountain Sámi in the same area (Qvigstad 1925, 18). According to Qvigstad, the dialect was close to extinction to some extent because of the influence from the mountain Sámi and Norwegianism. The Lule Sámi dialect of the mountain Sámi still held its own against Norwegian influence (Qvigstad 1888, 1925).

Qvigstad managed to collect samples of Finnagiella, but he was not able to learn the language. According to oral tradition, he paid a sea Sámi to come and visit him in his hometown Tromsø and share his knowledge. Another story relates how Qvigstad, when visiting Tysfjord, even had to follow an informant in a rowboat across the fjord to get information. The sea Sámi disliked Qvigstad comparing and claiming a common origin for mountain and sea Sámi; the relationship between the researcher and the researched was somewhat strained. He succeeded only to some extent and did not manage to define the language grammatically. He only gave an overview list of the words he managed to find. Today we do not know much more about Finnagiella aside from that found by Qvigstad.

Of a more ethnocultural documentation was his collection of oral tales, published between 1927 and 1929 (Amundsen 1972, 61f). Qvigstad also wanted to document the extent of the Sámi population in the Lule Sámi area. In 1929 he published *Sjøfinnene i Nordland* (*Sea Sami in Nordland*), where he quantifies and documents a sea Sámi settlement on the basis of several source categories. Tysfjord's work shows the highest number of sea

Sámi in Nordland County (Qvigstad 1929). Decades were to pass before researchers picked up this thread.

Qvigstad maintained contact with Nordic and European linguists to stay informed and develop new research projects. There was, among others, K. B. Wiklund with whom he documented cross-border reindeer herding. This Swedish researcher also documented the cross-border activity in his own publication. Two publications dealing with the same subject must be seen in the context of the breakup of the union with Sweden in 1905 when Norway became completely independent. The Swedish researcher Wiklund wanted to reveal all the Swedish Sámi that seasonally were moving from the Swedish side of the border to the Norwegian side, while the Norwegian researcher Qvigstad wanted to focus the Norwegian Sámi using the same areas (Wiklund 1908; Wiklund and Qvigstad 1909). Nationalism still held a strong position.

Language and stories were popular objects of collection and recording in the United States at this time as well. Ethnologists working for the Smithsonian National Museum of Natural History, regional museum anthropologists and ethnologists, and some university scholars all undertook projects. The ethnologists fanned out across Indian Country. Some specialized in languages and cultures of specific tribal communities; others collected more generally. In order to collect effectively, these scholars collaborated with tribal members in their communities, and the relationships that resulted were complex and varied.

Walter James Hoffman, a Smithsonian ethnologist, voiced the justifications for collecting stories and languages that would be used for generations to come. He studied the religious ceremonies first of the Ojibwe and then the Menominee tribes in the late nineteenth century. When Menominee leaders, including Neopit, became aware of this, they met with Hoffman in Washington, DC, and asked him to conduct a similar study for them "in order that their version of the traditions and dramatized forms of initiation could be studied and preserved 'for the information of future generations of the Menomini'" (Hoffman 1896, 11). For generations to come, ethnologists and tribal elders reasoned that the old ways were dying out and they needed to be recorded to preserve them (Densmore 1932; Dusenberry 1998; Slotkin 1952, 1957). In fact, in popular culture among reformers, political and bureaucratic officials, and scholars, American Indians were viewed as a "dying race." This meant that Americans expected Indians to disappear as distinct peoples, communities, and cultures (Beck 2001). Such was also the attitude in Scandinavia toward the Sámi (Evjen and Hansen 2008).

Ethnologists, linguists, and folklorists all collected stories in tribal languages and in English. Sometimes they would be published in both languages, sometimes in English. Often the published stories were distillations of much more comprehensive sets of field notes. Many times the notes were collected by local tribal members for the ethnologists (Bloomfield 1928; Saokio Heritage 2009; Skinner and Satterlee 1913).

In a few cases American Indians themselves conducted the ethnological work. Most well-known among these individuals was William A. Jones, a Fox tribal member who earned a doctorate in anthropology from Columbia University and studied under Franz Boas. In 1904 Jones became the first American Indian to earn a PhD in anthropology. A skilled linguist, he worked within the museum world until he met an untimely death in the Philippines in 1908 (LaPier and Beck 2012).

The idea in these cases was that tribal languages were dying, and in order to preserve them, either for the future of tribal members or of science, they needed to be recorded. Probably the most prolific recorder of tribal languages in the first half of the twentieth century was John Peabody Harrington, who gathered stories for tribes throughout California and the Pacific Coast (Kraus International Publications Microfilm, 1981).

Physical Measurements of the "Other"

Around the turn of the century, research became intensely focused on "races" and the "Other" to determine, among other things, the differences between ethnic groups of people. One method was the so-called skull measurements, physical measurements that included not just the head, but also other parts of the body of the living and dead. Military physicians all over Norway gathered data in conjunction with drafts for military service, data that also was categorized according to ethnicity.

International research projects were undertaken in order to make physical measurements of ethnic groups (Schreiner 1935, 1939). In Norway this was done with Sámi, Kven, and Norwegians. Tysfjord was one of a number of Norwegian areas included in the study. Extensive materials were also collected in Sweden. The leading researchers in Norway were the physician Kristian E. Schreiner and his wife Alette. Initially they wanted to examine the sea Sámi part of the population because they had been told that they were the original inhabitants. They changed their approach to focus on a particular fjord—the Hellemo Fjord—when they learned that the sea Sámi were scattered across the area. In this fjord lived descendants of sea and mountain Sámi. Schreiner's measurements in Tysfjord in 1914 and 1921 were taken of 210 Sámi, with as many as 28 measurements per person. It turned out it was not possible to assign exact measurements to any distinctive features of Sámi people; they were as different amongst themselves as the people of London, according to Schreiner (1935). The results of the international research also did not provide any basis for clear patterns. It was problematic, if not impossible, to determine original physical features of the members of an ethnic group.

In the generations to follow, the descriptions from these encounters between Sámi and researchers have become veritable migratory tales. There are still people who remember these events. Different versions have been told in which the Sámi had to be physically restrained while the measurements were taken. Many refused to undress, not surprisingly, making it impossible to take measurements of their bodies. Others present at these measurement sessions supposedly found the whole scene interesting. They probably were not familiar with the theories that could only be tested with their participation. This situation was an extreme case of using the Sámi as passive research objects. The results of the investigations conducted in 1914 and 1921 were published in German and English and printed in the publications of the Scientific Society, *Vitenskapsselskapets skrifter*. This made them all but inaccessible for the local population (Evjen 1998; Schreiner 1932, 1935, 1939).

Since this was part of broadly conceived international research projects, similar testing was conducted in the United States at this time. The new science of physical anthropology was increasingly used to shape or reinforce policy. This was done on living people and the dead, on fresh corpses and older remains. Some of this research was sponsored by the Smithsonian Institution, the national museum of the United States. The research on the living was used to determine the extent to which American Indian individuals were "full blood" versus "mixed blood." By the late nineteenth century Indian competency and tribal membership were considered by federal officials to be based on the degree to which Indians ancestors were Indian or white. The more white blood that Indians had, the more competent they were deemed to be. This led to a blood quantum–based identification system that still exists in many tribal communities in the United States.

As American entrepreneurs in the late nineteenth and early twentieth centuries schemed ways to disenfranchise Indian communities and individuals from their lands and resources, anthropological testing, with a scientific imprimatur, became a valuable tool for federal officials who sided more often with resource extractors than with tribes. In Minnesota, for example, when logging interests hoped to gain access to valuable timber resources, they brought in nationally renowned scientists, such as Albert Jenks and Aleš Hrdlička, to determine who was full-blood and who was mixed-blood tribal members. As tribal lands were allotted, the federal government had more authority to sell resources belonging to full-bloods, and the private market played a larger role in relation to mixed-bloods. Testing, such as judging whether individuals resembled facial casts of full-bloods, how curly their hair was, the size of their feet, and how quickly their natural color returned to their skin when it was scratched upon, formed the basis of the judgment. Unfortunately, this "science" was used in massive resource dispossession of some of the richest forestland in the United States (Beaulieu 1984).

Hrdlička's knowledge was based in part on his skull and human remains collection work with the Smithsonian. In fact, before the 1906 Antiquities Act protected human remains and burials for scientific research, Hrdlička published a how-to manual for collecting human remains through the United States Government Printing Office. He emphasized the value of robbing fresh graves in which skin was still in relatively good shape on the corpses and the value of collecting the remains of children. He urged amateurs to send these collections to the national museum for study. He also included color markers similar to modern paint chips so that the collector could judge skin color (Hrdlička 1904). Even one of the key figures in American anthropology, Franz Boas, participated in the collection of these remains for study and display. But he complained in his diary that "it is most unpleasant work to steal bones from graves, but what is the use, someone has to do it. . . . Yesterday I wrote to the Museum in Washington asking whether they would consider buying skulls this winter for $600; if they will, I shall collect assiduously. Without having such a connection I would not do it" (Boas in Kosslak 1999, 134).

The U.S. Army and museum officials made such collections and used them as part of studies that reinforced social Darwinistic theories. Skulls collected by army officials that later went to the Smithsonian, for example, were classified to rank the intelligence of racial groups. When the skulls did not match preconceived hierarchical assumptions, the data were manipulated in various ways to prove that Caucasians were the most intelligent race, while other racial groups lacked the cranial capacity to meet those same standards. These encounters with collectors and the loss of ancestors were remembered with sorrow and anger in tribal communities throughout the country. In 1990 after tribal member Curly Bear Wagner conducted research at the Smithsonian, the Blackfeet Tribe of Montana recovered some remains, which had been collected by an army doctor. They then held a ceremony for the repatriation and reburial of these ancestors. Oral histories among the Menominee also have revealed the horrific memories of tribal elders who in the early twentieth century in their childhood saw graves rifled (Beck 2010; Bieder 1986; Gould 1981; Hinsley 1981).

In Neiden, Norway, protests arose when outsiders came to open graves and remove the skeletons. Sámi and Kven also put spells on the diggers to stop them but without success. A researcher at the University of Oslo processed and stored the material. After a long process of negotiation, in September 2011, the remains of ninety-five persons were brought back and reburied in Neiden.

Increasing Focus on the Sea Sámi

In the 1920s it was claimed that only the reindeer-herding Sámi had an exotic culture different from the Norwegians. The sea Sámi had been living close to the Norwegians using their language and clothing, and thus were of a lesser interest as research objects (Stang 1925, 74). However, shortly after World War II, there was a renewed focus on the sea Sámi portion of the population. It began in Finnmark with teacher Anders Larsen's book *About the Sea Sámi* written in the Sámi language in 1947 and translated into Norwegian in 1950. Larsen was himself a sea Sámi, but he was not a researcher. His account presented the sea Sámi culture through the activities of everyday life. He published his knowledge and familiarity of the sea Sámi after the strong urging of Qvigstad. Larsen's publications broke new ground— an attempt to reveal the distinctiveness of sea Sámi culture and way of life seen from the vantage point of "the Other." However, it fell to the ethnologist Knut Kolsrud to make the sea Sámi culture of the Lule Sámi area the focus of scholarly attention.

Kolsrud's 1947 doctoral dissertation dealt with the Sámi people of the area north of Tysfjord, Ofoten, and *Finnefolket i Ofoten*. This was a seminal work for later research on Sámi and especially sea Sámi culture, settlement, and way of life. Kolsrud demonstrated how the sea Sámi originally made up a clear majority in Ofoten but later over the centuries were pushed aside by Norwegian migration into the area. He was also the first to document and analyze how the special jurisdictional institution known as *Finneodelen* (special allodium rights) functioned in relation to the traditional sea Sámi sites and settlements in Ofoten.

During Kolsrud's doctoral defense, a discussion ensued among the non-Sámi academics about the background for the seasonal movements—between the winter settlements and summer pastures from outer to inner parts of the fjords. This could be documented among some of the sea Sámi population of Nordland. On the basis of this publication, Kolsrud published the study *Sommersete* (*Summer Pasture*) in 1961. In this work he documented that the population of Tysfjord around 1600 was almost totally Sámi and that the varied economic adaption of the sea Sámi was quite similar to that of Ofoten. The only exception was that the majority regularly moved seasonally to summer pastures because of the need to add feeding resources for raising cattle. Together with Qvigstad's earlier investigations, Kolsrud's works on Ofoten and Tysfjord were to become an important foundation for later research on sea Sámi history in the Lule Sámi area (Evjen and Hansen 2008).

This encounter between the researcher and the sea Sámi occurred on the basis of the researcher's archival studies and interviews. Kolsrud also sought to become informed about conditions by questioning his contemporary sea Sámi relatives.

Post–World War II, the Third Step

A new attitude emerged and gradually left Norwegian nationalism behind. The new trend arose from the welfare state; the egalitarianism subsequently provided a space for pluralism—that is a greater appreciation for diversity in society (Niemi 1983). On an international level the number of researchers increased as did the number of international research networks in the days of globalization.

The Sámi and the Kven were the two ethnic groups in Norway considered to be "the exotic" and "the outsiders," although they had lived in the country from time immemorial. Increasingly after World War II these groups contributed to the consciousness of cultural pluralism of North Norwegian society. In addition, a growing sense of ethnic consciousness took place on the part of the people being studied—in this context the Lule Sámi on the Norwegian side of the border. This development is clearly reflected in the growth and building of ethnopolitical organizations. Among the Sámi, the first wave of ethnopolitical mobilization came at the beginning of the 1900s. It was dominated by southern Sámi initiators but did not attract a large following and almost disappeared in the period between the world wars. After 1950 the buildup continued with the establishment of

Nordic and national Sámi institutions, but it was not until the politicized 1960s and 1970s that ethnopolitics had a wider impact (cf. Minde 1997, 134). The National Association of Norwegian Sámi, (NSR [Norske Samers Riksforbund]) was formed in 1968 and 1969 when only Sámi were accorded full membership. The "NSR was probably a sign that the Sámi themselves were increasingly in charge" (Drivenes 1994, 265).

Several aspects of social changes after World War II had a bearing on Sámi research. The egalitarian principle was one of the underpinnings on which Norwegian society was built after the war. This forms the basis for the following characterization of Sámi culture in *Nordnorsk kulturhistorie* (North Norwegian Cultural History). "It would seem that Norwegian social democracy found it difficult to support the Sámi cultural awakening. The rhetoric of social democracy about social solidarity and national unity meant that social differences within the nation had to be reduced and— given such an ideological perspective, it was difficult to attach much value to developing minority cultures" (Drivenes 1994, 265).

Another aspect of the social change was the opening of a space in the field for a Sámi scholar to conduct Sámi studies. There was mainly cross-border reindeer herding in the Lule Sámi area with summer residence on the Norwegian side of the border and in winter on the Swedish side. On the Swedish side of the border, the geographer Israel Ruong, subsequently professor in Sámi language, published in the 1940s and later several works on reindeer herding, as well as works on the permanently settled Sámi. Ruong found the area south of Tysfjord, Pite Lappmark, especially interesting because their linguistic, ethnological, and cultural borders crossed between the forest and mountain Sámi areas. He himself was Pite Sámi from the southernmost part of the Lule Sámi area. This time it was an account by the Other; researcher and the objects of research were Sámi. The topics were, however, not different from earlier research.

In the 1960s an American-financed project on employment and out-migration from North Norway, known as the *Isolationsprosjektet* (Isolation Project) was started. Aspiring professor Per Mathiesen, who also took part in the project, gave an analytic discourse on the position of the researcher taking part in this project pertaining to the living conditions of the Other. The research results were intended to be given to the minorities to provide them with information regarding how the majority society made decisions of importance for the minority. The aim was to provide the Sámi with the tools necessary to formulate, present, and implement their political causes, in this case concerning housing conditions (Mathiesen 1970, 64).

Inner Finnmark was one of the places researched. Ringvassøy in Troms was another place, and Tysfjord was a third one. Tysfjord's neighboring municipalities of Hamarøy and Sørfold were included to a lesser degree. From their publications it can be read that professor of sociology Vilhelm Aubert and his assistant Lina Homme got to know Sámi society from the inside in their attempt to find answers to their sociological questions. Their research reports reveal that there were close, more personal connections between researcher and research subjects under the impetus of Aubert's initiative and Homme's enthusiasm. The economy, poverty, and place of religion, youth, and sexual morality were some of the themes analyzed in their work. The research demonstrated that the Sámi part of the population struggled with problems of poverty, as well as issues related to culture and powerlessness. But Aubert and Homme also showed how Sámi society was imbued with solidarity, tolerance, and openness (Aubert and Homme 1965, 1970; Homme 1969). This was the time of another big international trend on how states wanted to help Indigenous groups in the north to improve living conditions with housing projects.

The postwar years in the United States saw a shift in Indian policy as congress decided to downsize the federal government. One part of this effort led to the "termination" policy intended to put an end to the political-legal relationship between tribes and the United States—one of the most destructive policies foisted on tribes in U.S. history. During the 1950s and 1960s the U.S. Congress passed laws terminating the relationships between more than 100 tribes and the United States, which threw tribal communities into massive upheaval and further impoverished already socioeconomically challenged communities (Beck 2009; Burt 1982; Fixico 1986; Metcalf 2007; Ulrich 2010).

Congressional leaders and federal administrators believed that in order for termination to be complete and lasting, Indian claims against the federal government needed to be settled once and for all. These claims derived from illegally taken resources and lands during the treaty-making era, the allotment era, and other times. Up until the 1940s tribes made these claims through the United States Court of Claims, but there were so many tribal claims that in 1946 the U.S. Congress decided to establish a separate Indian Claims Commission (ICC). This was intended to operate for five years; instead, it conducted work for more than three decades. It only made final adjudication in a handful of the hundreds of cases filed, so in the end it was not successful in its established aims (Rosenthal 1985).

The ICC process involved lengthy hearings into individual cases, and the need for evidence led to the establishment of the field of ethnohistory. Scholars combined anthropological fieldwork and archival documentary research to build evidence of tribal occupation and use of lands in order to prove their cases. The process ensconced the scholars as experts in Indian history and culture in the legal realm and within academia (McMillen 2007). It would not be until the 1960s and 1970s that American Indians would begin the process of actively inserting themselves into the academic world on a relatively larger scale in order to take some control over the interpretation of their histories and communities to the outside world.

Demand for Active Participation

The next big international project involving Tysfjord Sámi again elicited negative reactions. In the 1980s professor of pedagogy Karl Jan Solstad led the Norwegian branch of an international research project titled The Developmental Conditions of Growing Up in Sámi Communities. The project was financed by the van Leer Foundation, an international fund that usually supported projects for at-risk groups in nonindustrialized countries. The board changed the guidelines of the fund to allow for Sámi participation. The project was assigned to Nordlandsforskning (Nordland Research) in Bodø and became the largest project ever in terms of its financial framework.

The goal of the project was to enhance the environment in which Sámi children were brought up and to reduce any possible discrimination. There was also a desire to stimulate the use of Sámi language and culture in the school environment. Evenes, Hattfjelldal, and Tysfjord were the chosen areas to promote this development. It turned out that the conversations with the parents, meant to be one of the starting points for the project, could not take place as a matter of course. The Sámi part of the population was reluctant to come forward.

A similar project was undertaken at the same time in Tornedal on the Swedish side of the Lule Sámi area. In the Norwegian final report, an interesting difference between the two projects was highlighted. On the Swedish side, the project director was Sámi in spite of the fact that the project was not explicitly directed toward the Sámi community. The project was considered a success. On the Norwegian side, the project was led by non-Sámi and was specifically directed toward the Sámi community. As indicated above, the Norwegian project was marred by problems in its implementation.

Representatives of the local Sámi association, established in 1979, had strong objections to the implementation of the van Leer project. They claimed that the project represented the attitudes of the past that the Norwegian majority knew best and made decisions without the Sámi having a seat at the table (Høgmo 1992, 68). The Sámi population would no longer participate as passive research objects for the representatives of majority society. They insisted on real influence in the project.

The time had come for this change. Thanks to the efforts and active voice of local Sámi, the van Leer project was now to have a Sámi participant from the local community. A tangible and positive result of the project was the production of Sámi teaching aids for use in school (cf. Beaulieu 1984; Eriksen and Skjelnes undated; Grenersen 1995; Høgmo 1992; Isaksen undated and restricted; Jensen 1991; Solstad 1981).

The United States saw a major shift begin to occur in the late 1960s during the heyday of the civil rights movement. Vine Deloria, Jr., famously penned a caustic article on the role of anthropologists in tribal communities for *Playboy* magazine, which was a chapter in his iconic book *Custer Died for Your Sins.* This awoke in Indian Country and in popular American culture a recognition that scholars working with tribal groups generally did so for their own gain, often without considering the value of their work to the tribal communities and individuals they were studying. While there had previously been some recognition of this within anthropological circles, such as Sol Tax's development of the subfield of action anthropology, Deloria's work shifted the general scholarly view significantly (Deloria 1968, 1969; Stanley 1996; Tax 1988).

Popular historians and academic scholars alike took note and began to seek correctives. For example, David Armour's work *Massacre at Mackinaw—1763*, an edited version of Alexander Henry's journal, was retitled *Attack at Michilimackinac, 1763*, reflecting a different view of the circumstances of war (1966, 1971). George and Louise Spindler also changed the title of a study they published on the Menominee tribe in the wake of the Menominee's successful battle to overturn the federal policy of termination that had stripped them of the legal political relationship with the federal government. Originally in 1971 their work was titled *Dreamers without Power*, in reference to Menominee religious tradition. They renamed the book *Dreamers with Power* when it was reissued in 1984.

Even at this time very few American Indian individuals were entering the academy. Deloria and Beatrice Medicine (anthropology), Elizabeth Cook-Lynn (Native American Studies), and David Edmunds and Don Fixico (history) were among the handful of Indian scholars doing research and writing on tribal communities during the 1970s and early 1980s. Young tribal leaders were participating in scholarly led workshops with the result that many became activists (Cobb 2008). The newly established American Indian Graduate Program in Albuquerque was beginning to fund American Indian students' graduate education, which led to a significant increase of Indian lawyers.

In the 1970s American Indian leaders from a variety of walks of life were working to change federal policy away from the destructive termination era to the modern era of self-determination. Many tribal leaders earning college and advanced degrees were putting their education to work within or on behalf of their communities, either in the local or national context. Some were establishing tribal colleges in their communities, which was a movement that would in many cases lead to instruction and study conducted from within the context of community knowledge and methodologies. Some three dozen tribal colleges in the United States are now members of the American Indian Higher Education Consortium.

Ethnopolitical Revitalization, the Fourth Step

Ethnopolitical revitalization came with the watershed moment in the relationship between the Sámi and the Norwegian state after the opposition to a planned damming of the Alta-Kautokeino River system. What followed was the establishment of the Sámi Parliament in 1989, which was a part of and led to further political and cultural revival and mobilization on ethnic grounds. These events also reflect an international trend where political and cultural revitalization arose in many parts of the Indigenous world.

Sámi Research on Sámi Topics

Increased Sámi consciousness has also led to the establishment of institutions to strengthen Sámi education and research. Several Sámi institutions were established, such as The Nordic Sámi Institute in 1973 and the Nordic Council of Ministers. In 1982, a commission for higher Sámi education was appointed (Norwegian Official Utredninger [NOU] 1985, 24). The Sámi Education Council and the Sámi University College were established in 1976 and 1989, respectively (Stordal 2008). In 1996 the education council set up a branch office at Árran, a Lule Sámi center in Tysfjord, with the Lule Sámi language as a field of study. The center was opened in 1994. Thus, the area has a high profile Sámi institution at the local level. The University in Nordland has an office at Árran. The same university established two chairs in 1998 for the study of Lule Sámi language and culture.

Sámi students in the 1970s and 1980s were mainly drawn to Sámi topics of general interest. For example, many papers were written on Sámi and non-Sámi settlement patterns, organizing in the old siida system, ethnopolitics, and Læstadianism, a religious revelation. It is interesting to learn that many of them chose to write about Indigenous people in America rather than from their own areas. In the 1990s, the challenges of bilingual education were revisited. Topics dealing specifically with the Lule Sámi area gradually became more common, as for example, the struggle to retain the Hellefjord settlement, the Lule Sámi dialect, Lule Sámi handicrafts, Lule Sámi yoik, and religious issues in the area (cf. Evjen 1999 for a more comprehensive treatment).

Student work reflects changes in contemporary social and political conditions in the same manner as the research mentioned above. Here we find an ethnopolitical consciousness and an appreciation for a pluralistic society.

Dissemination of Research to and by the Other

As we have seen, earlier research has, for the most part, been done, and the results disseminated, by researchers coming from the outside. Ascertaining the results of the research was, however, not without some difficulty for those Lule Sámi who might be interested in such insight. In large measure, this was because many of the publications had restricted access, that is they were not open to general inspection. Furthermore, Alette Schreiner wrote her report from Tysfjord in German, while Kristian E. Schreiner, to all intents and purposes, published his results in German and English. Aubert and Lina Homme published their major sociological reports in English with restricted access to both. Homme's reports from Tysfjord, Hamarøy, and Sørfold were also restricted. The final report from the van Leer project was written in English (Høgmo 1992). Publishing in another language other than Norwegian/Sámi is not uncommon in projects involving international cooperation and must be understood as an act of communicating with an international research community. Final reports are usually restricted for reasons of privacy. However, paternalistic attitudes might also be at work. In other words, there might be a wish to protect the population from insights that—in the view of the researcher—are too complex or painful, or they might be subject to misunderstanding.

It is not only researchers and research institutions from the outside who keep information and material out of the public domain. Many Sámi students have chosen to allow only limited access to their papers. As in the case of researchers, the reasons may be many and complex. First, it might be a matter of privacy. The Lule Sámi constitutes a small group where individuals can be easily recognized. Second, it could be about a desire to protect the Sámi community. New knowledge is withheld to avoid misunderstandings and inappropriate use, something which is probably the case in regard to papers with religious themes. Third, the reason might be to avoid internal criticism and to shield against anticipated disagreement and internal conflict. The restriction also prevents students and researchers from the outside from gaining access and finding fault with the conclusions. Most student papers are, however, open and available. Irrespective of any cases of individuals being held back, Sámi participation in research is now a fact of life.

Inadequate communication of results to those participating in the investigations has given rise to myths of various kinds. One such myth is that researchers made so many strange discoveries and came to such unbelievable conclusions that publication would be imprudent. Or, the researcher had crossed the line and publication would show that the people had been exploited. This is part of a wider discussion of research ethics, which is not pursued any further here.

As changes occurred in the political arena in Indian Country and within the walls of the academy, the landscape in the United States also began to shift. Increasingly, tribal knowledge became valued in the outside world as it had always been to a greater or lesser extent within Indian Country. On the governmental level, regulations for development more frequently required tribal input about cultural resource studies of lands where building or construction was going to occur. Today such work cannot be done without tribal input utilizing community-based knowledge. For example, the 1990 Native American Graves Protection and Repatriation Act (NAGPRA) requires consultation with tribal authorities whose remains and cemeteries are uncovered in construction projects. And after the 1992 amendments, Section 106 of the National Historic Preservation Act requires consultation with Tribal Historic Preservation Offices for cultural impact studies related to development (Advisory Council on Historic Preservation).

As tribal colleges and ethnic studies programs in mainstream colleges and universities developed, tribally based knowledge became increasingly important in scholarly studies. Whereas in the past it had been preserved because of fears that cultures were going extinct, it was now valued for what could be learned about modern Indigenous America and what lessons it could provide in terms of the relationship of tribal groups to modern society. The preeminent Native American studies scholar Elizabeth Cook-Lynn (2007) has defined the unique status of Indian Country and the field of Native American studies as reliant on two foundations: Indigeneity and sovereignty. Both of these themes have increasingly become platforms of study in and of Indian Country by Indian and non-Indian scholars. Despite all of this, Indigenous perspectives are often still marginalized within the academy, as there is a tendency for academics to be more comfortable with people like themselves. This means that tribal members who grew up immersed in tribal communities are less likely to be considered as colleagues than those who grew up in more cosmopolitan settings that mainstream Americans can identify with (Medicine 2001).

Increased Focus on Cultural Pluralism, a Fifth Step Possible

Qvigstad and Kolsrud's groundbreaking research on the sea Sámi part of the population was not quickly followed by increased research on this theme in the Lule Sámi area. However, in 1982 an issue of *Ottar* from the Tromsø Museum was published with the title *Kystsamisk bosetting* (Coastal Sámi Settlement). An issue of *Ottar* from the previous year dealt with the Alta controversy and had raised questions about the rights of the sea Sámi (Bjørklund 1981, 31). As is well-known, the Alta controversy primarily involved the rights of reindeer-herding Sámi. In the 1982 introduction, the point is made that the name "coastal Sámi" is used instead of sea Sámi, in order to include all Sámi permanently settled by the sea. No mention is made of the argument also possibly being a wish to avoid using the term sea Sámi. Going back 100 years, the social hierarchy among groups of Sámi had, as earlier mentioned, placed the sea Sámi at the bottom. Among the authors there was also Lule Sámi who received the concept positively. At that time it was better to be coastal Sámi than sea Sámi. Today a strong revitalization has lifted the sea Sámi status.

Over the next quarter-century the research landscape in Norway continued to shift. The Norwegian Research Council (NFR) is a central institution that has strongly influenced contemporary research. Through its grants, NFR determines more directly what it sees as the most promising inquiries for future research. In the first Sámi research program, which began in the fall of 2007, there is increased investment in Sámi research topics in general, but in addition, there is also a strong influence on focusing on the Sámi as a heterogeneous group and on developing a Sámi scientific language. In other words, the national government has become strongly involved in this endeavor.

Recent research represents the pluralistic view. In Evjen and Hansen's 2008 anthology, *Nordlands kulturelle mangfold, etniske relasjoner i historisk perspektiv* (*The Cultural Diversity of Nordland, Ethnic Conditions in Historical Perspective*), the authors focus especially on the sea Sámi in history by identifying them in the sources, their part of the population, and their participation in various livelihoods. In this anthology, the emergence of reindeer herding in the area also is pushed farther back in time than it previously had been. Sámi and non-Sámi were represented, and the text has summaries in the Lule Sámi language. Some ten years prior this would have been a sensation.

The Other in a New Position

In the same project the demand was made that the Sámi institution Árran should play an active part in administrating the project. An attitude emerged among the Sámi and gave the impression that the researchers were representatives of the Other. Obviously, one could no longer take for granted that the Other was representing the minority. This can be seen in a broader context, providing the most recent step of developing the encounter between the researcher and the researched Sámi.

Over the last decade Indigenous researchers have come up with what is called a "decolonizing methodology." It maintains that Indigenous research should be designed by those understanding the culture to ensure that Indigenous peoples' knowledge is the foundation (Smith 1999, 15). Research should be conducted by "those who understand the culture." It further reads that research should be disseminated back to people in a language they can understand "in order to support them in their desire to be subjects rather than objects of research" (Porsanger 2004, 117; Smith 1999, 15). In between the lines it is recognized that "those who understand" come from the minority group. The Other would then be a part of the majority group.

Other features in this methodology are more challenging. The term *research* is understood as the way in which science has been and still is implicated in the excesses of imperialism. It is argued that a deep understanding of Indigenous cultures can only be achieved by a member of that culture. Consequently, an outsider's understanding is biased. Such a line of argument has been connected to international ethnopolitical revitalization since the 1970s and the power of defining the research focus. This is a part of an international discourse involving "those who understand the culture." An important issue follows and raises the question of who has the power or the monopoly to create such a definition. Much of the debate over the criteria for participation is a variation of the "question of ethnic monopoly" (Thuen 1995).

A bias of dominant-culture researchers is not the only problem when discussing decolonizing history. Those coming from outside Indigenous culture approach Indigenous peoples' cultures and histories from within the experience of the colonial state. This results in different research questions, methods, and interpretations that too often presume Indigenous deficiency, even when researchers mean well. They produce an Indigenous studies rather than decolonizing methodology or history. In line with this, the present chapter portrays how research on Indigenous peoples has changed with historically changing societal attitudes and suggests possibilities for new understandings when Indigenous scholars define research questions.

Programs of preferential treatment should not be seen to replace one type of monopoly (by Western academic structures) with another (Indigenous), but as an important step in establishing a context of genuinely equal opportunity (Saugestad 1998, 9). In research, academic competence rather than ethnic identity must be given priority. The arguments pro and contra the "decolonizing methodology" are taken up in national and international academic fora. The international trend is moving on and taking its point of departure from the fact that the educational level is increasing, especially among the Sámi. In fact, the Sámi in Norway are among the highest educated Indigenous people (Stordal 2008, 255). In a recent international anthology, one-third of the presentations are on the politics of knowledge, and they discuss how higher education and research can build a vision for the future when conducted by the Other in either understanding of the word (Minde 2008). The Other had shifted from one group to the other, from the minority to the majority.

Indigenous researchers are also increasingly becoming trained within conventional research areas and contribute to the advancement of knowledge within those long-standing fields. In some cases they are working within conventional academic theory in those fields, and in some cases they are reshaping that theory. This is adding to the multiplicity of voices across the academy and creating an enriched research environment that cuts across the board. This is increasingly significant as cross- and multi-disciplinary work is becoming the norm.

Taking the topic in this article as a point of departure, the new methodologies can be seen as the final step in a line of change from the nineteenth century and up until today and as such is part of an interesting process. On the other hand, these methodologies can also be viewed as being the first step in creating knowledge about Indigenous communities from a multiplicity of perspectives. It can be concluded that any form of domination is detrimental to the ideals of intellectual freedom, and more importantly, to understanding our world. The Other, as an insider or an outsider, may present different knowledge, a difference that together provides a broader picture of an Indigenous culture than by either one of them alone.

Conclusion

The role of Indigenous peoples in relation to research has changed significantly over time in the United States and Norway. During the five stages presented here, most encounters that took place in the two areas were remarkably similar, showing that what happened was more than a result of national politics and mentality. Research in the larger and ethnically more complex United States and the smaller and less diverse Norway were to a large extent reflective of international trends.

A bird's-eye view of the development of the encounter between researcher and the Other over time shows that from the first step when missionaries and state officials saw the minority groups as noble savages, through to step two with a focus on race and homogenization in the period of nationalism, the Indigenous minority groups were passive objects of research. After World War II, in step three, society opened up for pluralism, and Indigenous researchers increasingly demanded to actively participate. After an ethnopolitical and cultural revitalization, the encounter between researchers and the researched in step four had the character of Indigenous people fulfilling both positions. In step five more Indigenous researchers design research by themselves, and scholarship now has increasingly included work from those who see their own culture from the inside.

Political connections also reflected the international trends. Instruments used on national political levels are surprisingly similar. The role of missionaries in Christianizing the minorities and educating them in reading Christian texts, the effort to immerse the children in the values of the majority culture through the use of boarding schools, and the gathering of human remains and items of cultural patrimony by research museums all occurred at similar times in both countries. So did the shift in the research roles of Indigenous peoples.

We also find major differences. For example, while the United States vacillated between segregating American Indians on reservations and forcing or encouraging them to leave reservation communities to assimilate into American society (although on an unequal basis), in Norway the policy of assimilation focused entirely on forcing everybody to be Norwegians living in the Norwegian society. Demonstrative of this, land-use issues, on-reservation and off-reservation, dominated much of the relationship between Indian tribes and the United States. This was not a main case in Norway mostly because colonization happened in another way and in another time.

In both places, however, researchers served as representatives of colonial powers during the first three steps described above. In the United States they often turned the focus of their research efforts to policy justification and policy manipulation that served in large degrees to diminish the strength of Indigenous communities. The national governments often used the results of the research to enforce power over those communities and, by the late nineteenth and early twentieth centuries, results were increasingly used to define those communities as vanishing or diminishing. In Norway this was found in the Lule Sámi community but only to a smaller extent in the society elsewhere. Ironically, it was at this time that Native people became involved in the research. The initial involvement was primarily as informants, but many served more in the role of collaborators. Even when the Indigenous role was more proactive, it was subordinated or hidden by the researcher. This was the case throughout the first half of the twentieth century. It was not until after World War II that Indigenous community members were able to begin to use this research for the benefit of their societies and communities.

The next step though was for the Other to begin to conduct the research themselves and beyond that to drive the focus of the research. This began in the latter half of the twentieth century, particularly after the 1960s and 1970s when worldwide movements to expand the rights of minority peoples coalesced with Indigenous efforts at increased self-governance. It has been a long, slowly developing process of change that more recently has brought about a call for not only an Indigenous direction of research, but for research in Indigenous communities to be defined by Indigenous values and methods. Research questions should be raised from within Indigenous communities themselves. Indigenous theory should drive such research so that it is meaningful and beneficial to Indigenous communities. The development of such theory is in its early stages and is contested within Indigenous communities and the academy. It is incumbent upon those of us working with Indigenous communities and in the fields focusing on Indigenous community research to understand the changes and participate in the academic dialogue (re)defining those changes.

References

Advisory Council on Historic Preservation. n.d. http://www.achp.gov/.

Amundsen, L. 1972. *Instituttet for sammenlignende kulturforskning, 1922–1972*. Universitetsforlaget: Oslo-Bergen-Tromsø.

Anaya, S. James. 2004. *Indigenous Peoples in International Law*. 2nd ed. New York: Oxford University Press.

Armour, D. A., ed. 1966. *Massacre at Mackinac: Alexander Henry's Travels and Adventures in Canada and the Indian Territories Between the Years 1760 and 1764*. Mackinac Island, MI: Mackinac State Park Commission.

———. 1971. *Attack at Michilimackinac: Alexander Henry's Travels and Adventures in Canada and the Indian Territories Between the Years 1760 and 1764*. Mackinac Island, MI: Mackinac Island State Park Commission.

Aubert, V., and L. Homme. 1965. *Hellemofjorden*. Report, Institute for Social Research, Department of Sociology, Oslo.

———. 1970. *Orjo Vuodna*. Institute for Social Research, Department of Sociology, Oslo.

Beaulieu, D. L. 1984. "Curly Hair and Big Feet: Physical Anthropology and the Implementation of Land Allotment on the White Earth Chippewa Reservation." *American Indian Quarterly* 8(4):281–314.

Beck, D. R. M. 2001. "The Myth of the Vanishing Race," *Edward S. Curtis's The North American Indian*. Northwestern University Library and Library of Congress. http://memory.loc.gov/ammem/award98/ienhtml/essay2.html.

———. 2002. *Siege and Survival: History of the Menominee Indians, 1634–1856*. Lincoln: University of Nebraska Press.

———. 2009. *Seeking Recognition: The Termination and Restoration of the Coos, Lower Umpqua, and Siuslaw Indians, 1855–1984*. Lincoln: University of Nebraska Press.

———. 2010. "'Collecting Among the Menomini': Cultural Assault in Twentieth Century Wisconsin." *American Indian Quarterly* 34(2):157–93.

Berkhofer, R. F. 1978. *The White Man's Indian: Images of the American Indian from Columbus to the Present*. New York: Alfred A. Knopf.

Bieder, R. E. 1986. *Science Encounters the Indian, 1820–1880: The Early Years of American Ethnology*. Norman: University of Oklahoma Press.

Bjørklund, I. 1981. "Hva med sjøsamene?" *Ottar* 129:31–34. University of Tromsø.

Bloomfield, L. 1928. *Menomini Texts*. New York: G. L. Strechert & Co.

Burt, L. W. 1982. *Tribalism in Crisis, Federal Indian Policy, 1953–1961*. Albuquerque: University of New Mexico Press.

Cobb, D. M. 2008. *Native Activism in Cold War America: The Struggle for Sovereignty*. Lawrence: University Press of Kansas.

Cook-Lynn, E. 2007. *New Indians, Old Wars*. Champaign: University of Illinois Press.

Coues, E., ed. 1895. *The Expeditions of Zebulon Montgomery Pike*. New York: Francis P. Harper.

Davies, K. G., ed. 1961. *Peter Skene Ogden's Snake Country Journal, 1826–1827*. Publications of Hudson Bay's Record Society 23. London: The Hudson's Bay Record Society.

Deloria, P. 1999. *Playing Indian*. New Haven, CT: Yale University Press.

Deloria, V., Jr. 1968. *Custer Died for Your Sins: An Indian Manifesto*. Norman: University of Oklahoma Press.

———. 1969. "Custer Died for Your Sins." *Playboy* 16(8):131–32, 172–75.

Densmore, F. 1932. *Menominee Music*. Washington, DC: Government Printing Office.

Drivenes, E. A. 1994. *Nordnorsk kulturhistorie* (North Norwegian Cultural History), 1:265. Oslo: Gyldendal.

Dusenberry, V. (1962) 1998. *The Montana Cree: A Study in Religious Persistence*. Norman: University of Oklahoma Press.

Eriksen, K. E., and Niemi, E., eds. 1981. *Den finske fare: sikkerhetsproblemer og minoritetspolitikk i nord, 1860–1940*. Oslo: Universitetsforlaget.

Evjen, B. 1998. *Et sammensatt fellesskap, Tysfjord kommune, 1869–1950*. Tysfjord Municipality.

———. 1999. "Fra eksotiske forskningsobjekt til aktive forskere." In *Bårjås*, Árran, luleSámisk museum. Tysfjord, 12–23.

Evjen, B., and L. I. Hansen. eds. 2008. *Nordlands kulturelle mangfold, etniske relasjoner i historisk perspektiv. (The Cultural Diversity of Nordland, Ethnic Conditions in Historical Perspective)*. Oslo: Pax.

Fixico, D. L. 1986. *Termination and Relocation: Federal Indian Policy, 1945–1960*. Albuquerque: University of New Mexico Press.

Gould, S. J. 1981. *The Mismeasure of Man*. New York: W. W. Norton & Co.

Grenersen, G. 1995. "Kulturell gjenreisning i et markeSámisk kjerneområde." PhD diss., University of Tromsø.

Hansen, L. I. 1991. "Kulturforsker Just Qvigstad." Doctoral lecture given at the University of Tromsø.

Helland, A. 1908. *Norges land og folk. Topografisk-statistisk beskrevet XVIII Nordland amt. Annen del*. Kristiania.

Hinsley, C. 1981. *Savages and Scientists: The Smithsonian Institution and the Development of American Anthropology, 1846–1910*. Washington, DC: Smithsonian Press.

Hoffman, W. J. 1896. *The Menomini Indians*. Report attached to the Fourteenth Annual Report of the U.S. Bureau of Ethnology to the Secretary of the Smithsonian Institution, 1892–93. Washington, DC: Government Printing Office.

Holm, O. 1889. *Det norske folks historie*. Christiania: Cammermeyer.

———. 1907. "Lidt om Tysfjord—Lapper," unpublished manuscript.

———. 1923. *Fra en nordlandsk prestegaard*. Oslo: Aschehoug.

Homme, L. 1969. *Nordisk nykolonialisme: Sámiske problem i dag*. Oslo: Samlaget.

Høgmo, A. 1992. Developing Minority Education in the North: A Comparative Study of Two Bicultural Educational Programmes in Respectively Northern Norway and Northern Sweden Initiated and Financed by the Van Leer Foundation in Netherland, NF—rapport 31, Nordland Research Institute, Bodø.

Hrdlička, A. 1904. "Directions for Collecting Information and Specimens for Physical Anthropology." Washington, DC: Government Printing Office.

Jennings, F. 1976. *The Invasion of America: Indians, Colonialism, and the Cant of Conquest*. New York: W. W. Norton & Co.

Jensen, Eivand Bråstad. 1991. *Fra fornorskningspolitikk mot kulturelt mangfold*. Stonglandseidet: Nordkalottforlaget.

Kasprycki, S. S. 1990. "'A Lover of All Knowledge,' Edwin James and Menominee Ethnography." *European Review of Native American Studies* 4(1):1–9.

Kolsrud, K. 1947. "Finnefolket i Ofoten. En studie i Ofotens demografi og sjøfinnenes etnografi i eldre tid," *Nordnorske samlinger* VIII, Oslo.

———. 1961. Sommersete, in Nesheim, A: Bind 5, *Sámiske samlinger*, Oslo.

Kosslak, R. M. 1999. "The Native American Graves Protection and Repatriation Act: The Death Knell for Scientific Study?" *American Indian Law Review* 24(1):129–51.

Kraus International Publications Microfilm. 1981. *The Papers of John Peabody Harrington in the Smithsonian Institution, 1907–1955*. Millwood, NY: Kraus International Publications Microfilm.

LaPier, R. R., and D. R. M. Beck. 2012. "Crossroads for a Culture." *Chicago History* Spring, 22–43.

Larsen, A. 1947/1950. Om sjøsamene, *Tromsø museums årsskrifter*, Universitetet i Tromsø.

Mathiesen, P. 1970. Boligreising og nasjonal tilpasning hos den Sámiske minoritetsgruppe, INAS report no. 70–1. Oslo: Institute of Applied Social Research.

McMillen, C. W. 2007. *Making Indian Law: The Hualapai Land Case and the Birth of Ethnohistory*. New Haven, CT: Yale University Press.

Medicine, B. 2001. *Learning to Be an Anthropologist and Remaining Native*. Champaign: University of Illinois Press.

Metcalf, R. W. 2007. *Termination's Legacy: The Discarded Indians of Utah*. Lincoln: University of Nebraska Press.

Minde, H. 1997. "Historien om Stuoranjárga," unpublished manuscript.

———, ed. 2008. *Indigenous Peoples: Self-Determination, Knowledge, Indigeneity*. Delft: Eburon.

Morse, J. 1822. *A Report to the Secretary of War of the United States on Indian Affairs*. New Haven, CT: S. Converse.

Niemi, E. 1983. "History of Minorities: The Sámi and the Kvens." In *Making a Historical Culture: Historiography in Norway*, edited by W. H. Hubbard, J. E. Myhre, T. Nordby, and S. Sogner, 325–43. Oslo-Copenhagen-Stockholm-Boston: Scandinavian University Press.

NOU (Norwegian Official Utredninger) 1985:24, *Samisk kultur og utdanning. Videregående opplæring for samer*, Samekulturutvalget, Kulturdepartementet.

Nordnorske samlinger. 1938–1947. Vols 1–8, Etnografiske museum, Oslo.

Ottar. 1982. KystSámisk bosetting (Coastal Sámi Settlement) Populærvitenskaplig tidsskrift fra Tromsø Museum 4, Universitetet i Tromsø.

Pearce, R. H. 1967. *Savagism and Civilization: A Study of the Indian and the American Mind*. Baltimore: Johns Hopkins Press.

Porsanger, J. 2004. "An Essay About Indigenous Methods." Norlit15/2004 Universitetet i Tromsø.

Qvigstad, J. 1888. "Lappische Sprachproben." *Journal de la Societe Finno—Ougrienne*, Finland.

————. 1925. *Die Lappischen Dialecte in Norwegen.* Oslo: Etnografiske Museums Skrifter.

————. 1929. *Sjøfinnene i Nordland, Tromsø museums skrifter.* Universitetet i Tromsø.

Ronda, J. P. 1984. *Lewis and Clark Among the Indians.* Lincoln: University of Nebraska Press.

Rosenthal, H. D. 1985. "Indian Claims and the American Conscience: A Brief History of the Indian Claims Commission." In *Irredeemable America: The Indians' Estate and Land Claims,* edited by Imre Sutton, 35–70. Albuquerque: University of New Mexico Press.

Ruong, I. 1937. "Fjällapparna i Jukkasjärvvi socken." *Geographica.* Skrifter från Universitetets geografiske Institution, Uppsala.

Salish-Pend d'Oreille Culture Committee and Elders Cultural Advisory Council. 2005. *The Salish People and the Lewis and Clark Expedition.* Lincoln: University of Nebraska Press.

Saokio Heritage. 2009. http://www.saokioheritage.com.

Saugestad, S. 1998. "Research On, With and By Indigenous Peoples, Reflections on the Insider and Outsider Perspectives in Anthropology, with Examples from the University of Tromsø and the University of Botswana." Paper presented to CHAGS 8, Osaka October.

Schreiner, A. 1932. *Antropologische Lokaluntersuchungen in Norge, Hellemo.* Oslo: Det norske vitenskapsakademi.

Schreiner, K. E. 1935. *Zur Oestologie der Lappen.* Oslo: Institutt for Sammenligende Kulturforskning.

————. 1939. *Crania Norvegica.* Oslo: Institutt for Sammenligende Kulturforskning.

Skinner A., and J. V. Satterlee. 1913. *Folklore of the Menominee Indians.* Vol. 13, Part 3 of *Anthropological Papers of the American Museum of Natural History.* New York: Published by Order of the Trustees.

Slotkin, J. S. 1952. "Menomini Peyotism: A Study of Individual Variation in a Primary Group with a Homogenous Culture." *Transactions of the American Philosophical Society* 42(4):535–700.

————. 1957. *The Menomini Pow Wow: A Study in Cultural Decay.* Milwaukee: Milwaukee Public Museum Publications in Anthropology No. 4.

Smith, L. T. 1999. *Decolonizing Methodologies.* London: Zed Books.

Solstad, K. 1981. "Locally Relevant Curricula in Rural Norway: The Lofoten Islands Example/Karl Jan Solstad." In *Rural Education in Urbanized Nations: Issues and Innovations,* edited by Jonathan P. Sher. Boulder, CO: Westview Press.

Spindler, G. and L. Spindler. 1971. *Dreamers without Power: The Menomini Indians.* New York: Holt, Rinehart, and Winston.

————. 1984. *Dreamers with Power: The Menominee.* Long Grove, IL: Waveland Press.

Stang, F., ed. 1925. *Fire innledningsforelesninger, holdt 4–8. September 1924.* Oslo: H. Aschehoug & Co.

Stanley, S. 1996. "Community, Action, and Continuity: A Narrative Vita of Sol Tax." *Current Anthropology* 37:1 Supplement, S131–S137.

Stordal, V. 2008. "Nation Building Through Knowledge Building: The Discourse of Sámi Higher Education and Research in Norway." In *Indigenous Peoples: Self-Determination, Knowledge, Indigeneity,* edited by H. Minde, S. Jentoft, and G. Midré. Delft: Eburon.

Tax, S. 1988. "Pride and Puzzlement: A Retro-introspective Record of 60 Years in Anthropology." *Annual Review of Anthropology* 17:1–21.

Thuen, T. 1995. *Quest for Equity: Norway and the Sámi Challenge.* Newfoundland: Institute of Social and Economic Research.

Thwaites, R. G., ed. 1896–1901. *The Jesuit Relations and Allied Documents.* Cleveland: The Burrows Brothers Company.

Trouillot, M.-R. 1995. *Silencing the Past: Power and the Production of History.* Boston: Beacon Press.

Ulrich, R. 2010. *American Indian Nations from Termination to Restoration, 1953–2006.* Lincoln: University of Nebraska Press.

Wiklund, K. 1908. *De Svenska nomadlapparnas flyttningar till Norge i äldre och nyare tid.* Uppsala: Almqvist & Wiksell.

Wiklund, K., and J. Qvigstad. 1909. Reinbeitekommissionen af 1907. Dokumenter angaaende flytlapperne m.m. II. Samlede efter reinbeitekommissionens opdrag af rektor J. Qvigstad and professor K.B. Wiklund, Kristiania.

CHAPTER TWO

Indigenous Methodologies in Research

Social Justice and Sovereignty as the Foundations of Community-Based Research

Annjeanette E. Belcourt, Gyda Swaney, and Allyson Kelley

Throughout time Indigenous communities have used their own cultural expertise to assess, validate, and apply experiential knowledge to improve the health of their communities and members. These inferential methods were based on generations of lived experiences gained within the context of a myriad of American Indian and Alaska Native (AIAN) communities surviving, and even thriving, within challenging and diverse geographic conditions. These Indigenous methodologies mirrored aspects of Western science by sharing principles of hypothesis testing to assess reliability, generalizability, and a variety of differential forms of validity or accuracy. They were based on the premise that health and survival require a balance of physical, spiritual, emotional, social, and economic factors, and to achieve and maintain this balance, Indigenous methodologies were needed to test, validate, and experiment. However, these methods were unique to each individual tribal community and thus varied based upon the relevant primary socioeconomic resources that were shaped by geography, tribal history, lifeways, and sociological factors influencing daily life for Indigenous nations. Recently, Western science has begun to recognize the significance of the Indigenous methodologies and how implementing these principles improves research approaches and the impact of research aimed at improving the health inequalities and disparities that many Indigenous communities experience (Botha 2011; Kovach 2009; Smith 2005; Wilson 2008).

Specifically, it is important to recognize the severe and pronounced inequalities that impact Indigenous communities in the United States and throughout the global community. For example, in 2013, 27 percent of Indigenous groups in the United States lived in poverty compared to 14.3 percent of the general population (Macartney, Bishaw, and Fontenot 2013). The reality is that the rates of poverty and associated severe health disparities among families and individuals living on reservations are much higher. On average, Indigenous groups in the United States experience fewer educational opportunities and lower educational attainment, and 75 percent earned a high school diploma in 2006 compared with 91 percent of White students (DeVoe and Darling-Churchill 2008).

American Indians and Alaska Natives have the lowest life expectancy of any racial/ethnic group in the United States, and they have the highest age-adjusted mortality rates in the nation; they are often double that of the combined rates for the U.S. population (1,480 per 100,000 people [Christensen and Kightlinger 2013]). On average AIANs have a life expectancy that is 4.6 years less than other Americans, and the most common causes of mortality include complications due to diabetes, accidental death, homicide, suicide, and tuberculosis. The infant mortality rate, a sensitive indicator of general health of a population, has decreased recently but remains 24 percent greater for Native Americans than other groups. As a population, AIANs have lower educational attainment, higher unemployment, earn substantially less for full-time work, and are more likely to live in poverty than the total U.S. population. The reality is that the rates of poverty and associated severe health disparities among families and individuals living on reservations are much higher.

Poverty contributes to harsh living conditions that are far worse among AIANs than any ethnic group in the United States. Indigenous communities experience housing challenges related to physical problems (overcrowding and lack of plumbing or kitchens), affordability, homeownership, and homelessness. Rates of homelessness are more than three times higher among Indigenous U.S. groups compared with the general U.S. population ([23 percent] Kingsley, Mikelsons, and Herbig 2013). Combined, lower education, poverty, and harsh living conditions create injustices in which Indigenous people die at an earlier age and more frequently than other populations.

A multidimensional, culturally based Indigenous approach is needed to mitigate social unfairness effectively. To this end, Indigenous research must incorporate primary prevention aimed at reducing extreme poverty, improving access to economic and educational opportunities, improving access to adequate housing, and addressing structural racism. In this chapter we provide contextual information regarding Indigenous methodologies and how these methods can be used to address social wrongs while honoring the values and knowledge of Indigenous people. We provide an example of how AIANs have used an intertribal Institutional Review Board (IRB) to promote social justice via increased tribal participation in the regulation of research.

Native Americans, Social Justice, and Tribal Sovereignty

American Indians and Alaska Natives comprise many distinct and heterogeneous ethnocultural tribal/Indigenous groups in the United States. The 2010 U.S. Census reported that 2.9 million people identified their ethnicity as American Indian or Alaska Native along with another racial category, a 39 percent increase from 2000 (Norris, Vines, and Hoeffel 2012). An additional 2.3 million people identified their sole racial classification as American Indian or Alaska Native in the United States. The Bureau of Indian Affairs (BIA) recognizes 562 different tribal groups, each characterized by significant within-group variation and diversity, including distinct languages, ceremonial practices, cultural norms and customs, political structures, economies, and historical backgrounds. The diversity of AIAN populations is notable and is inclusive of groups that were historically subsistence hunter-gatherers, agriculturalists, and skilled tradesmen. Traditionally, AIAN groups lived by adapting to a wide variety of ecological conditions, ranging from arctic and subarctic, grassland plains, woodlands, ocean coastal areas, and desert regions. Ceremonies, languages, and social structures varied by tribal nation and locale, which has resulted in a remarkable history of intertribal cultural diversity. However, migration from ancestral homelands often leads to urbanized Indigenous populations, where traditional activities and diets are more difficult to maintain and practice due to the influence of the dominant Western culture.

Preferred identifiers for Indigenous peoples of North America vary by geographical and tribal group. Canadian Indigenous people have used the terms *First Nations*, as well as *Inuit* and *Metís*, while groups in the United States have used the terms *American Indian*, *Native American*, or *Alaska Native*. However, as a general rule most individuals' and tribal communities' preferred identifier is the name of their tribal nation in their Native language, such as Pikuni, Oglala Lakota, Anishinaabe, or Diné. The National Congress of the American Indian has supported the use of American Indian and Alaska Native as the recognized reference terms for the Indigenous peoples of the United States.

American Indians and Alaska Natives have the shared experience of significant population collapse, colonization, systematic oppression, and severe discriminatory practices that included forced relocation, direct warfare, the introduction of new and often fatal diseases into communities, forced removal of children to boarding or residential schools, language and cultural devastation policies, and severe systematic poverty and geographic isolation. This brief history sets the contextual stage for describing social justice and tribal sovereignty in community-based research.

Social justice is based on context, sociocultural aspects of history, and culture. We have chosen to use the term *social justice* to refer to individual or community egalitarianism, fairness, or equity as it pertains to Indigenous groups of the United States. When any of these factors are absent, an individual may experience disparities in health, education, or living conditions that are unfair, inequitable, and ultimately avoidable. Often Western scientists refer to the social determinants of health as oppression, health inequities, health disparities, undesirable social gradients, structural racism, social exclusion, and lack of social capacity. These determinants are intertwined with the past, present, and future context of AIAN communities and their health. In this chapter we use the term social justice in the milieu of community-based research, the social determinants of health and tribal sovereignty.

American Indian and Alaska Natives have established unique relationships with the U.S. federal government through the historical use of federal treaties and laws. American Indian and Alaska Native nations have established government-to-government relationships with the United States due to their unique status as sovereign Indigenous nations within this country. The treaties and laws from which these federal trust relationships and obligations emanate originated in the period of contact/seizure/colonization. During this time, AIAN nations forcibly gave up millions of acres of land in exchange for the provision of healthcare, education, and other rights as long as Indigenous nations exist within this nation or *As Long as the Grass Grows and the Rivers Flow* (Trafzer 2000). For example, the Indian Self-Determination and Education Assistance Act of 1975 gave tribal nations the authority to take over any Indian Health Service (IHS) or BIA functions. Other notable laws related to social justice and sovereignty include: the Snyder Act of 1921, the 1954 Transfer Act, the Indian Sanitations and Facilities Acts of 1959, the Indian Health Care Improvement Act of 1976, the Indian Child Welfare Act of 1978, and the Omnibus Drug Act of 1986. While beyond the scope of this chapter, it is vital to acknowledge these historic acts in AIAN history because they continue to mandate tribal sovereignty and the many unique treaty obligations of the U.S. government to Indigenous nations. Moreover, these acts demonstrate U.S. efforts to address historic injustices that unfortunately continue to persist and contextualize the continued disparities in health observed among Indigenous populations today.

Community-Based Participatory Research and Indigenous Methodologies

Reality is not an objective truth or facts to be discovered but includes the ways in which people involved with facts perceive them. The concrete reality is the connection between the subjectivity and objectivity, never objectivity isolated from subjectivity.
— PAULO FREIRE, *PEDAGOGY OF THE OPPRESSED*

Research is not just a highly moral and civilized search for knowledge; it is a set of very human activities that reproduce particular social relations of power.
— LINDA TUHIWAI SMITH, *DECOLONIZING METHODOLOGIES: RESEARCH AND INDIGENOUS PEOPLES*

Community-based participatory research (CBPR) is a collaborative form of inquiry well suited for Native communities. In the 1940s Kurt Lewin prompted researchers to think about ethics, courage, and power relations. His research focused on solving social problems through action research that would help practitioners. In his article, "Action Research and Minority Populations," he called for social scientists to have courage, "It needs the best of what the best among us can give, and the help of everybody" (Lewin 1946, 46). This call was repeated over the years through participatory action research in the fields of sociology, anthropology, community planning, and feminist theory (Minkler 2004; Wallerstien and Duran 2008). By 1970, there was an abundance of publications, history, and evidence to show that survey research had done little to address social injustice, power, and disparities. Budd Hall's (1975) seminal paper, "Participatory Research: An Approach for Change," describes the paradigm shift among Western researchers and the realization that knowledge is a form of power. His work, and that of others (Freire 1972; Wallerstein and Duran 2008) was instrumental in establishing the basis for participatory action research and CBPR as we know it today in which communities identify research priorities and implement them with little assistance from Western researchers or academic institutions. As Maori Scholar Smith (2005, 29) notes,

> the Western academy which claims theory as thoroughly Western . . . has constructed all the rules by which the Indigenous world has been theorized. . . . [As a result] Indigenous voices have been overwhelmingly silenced. The act, let alone the art and science of theorizing our own existence and realities, is not something which many Indigenous people assume is possible.

This history and paradigm shift is evident today in CBPR approaches that aim to address social injustice. Social equity and justice are the essential aspects of CBPR methods. The principles of CBPR highlight the fundamental recognition of appropriately engaging communities and individuals who participate in research. American Indian and Alaska Native communities have acknowledged that appropriately conducted research can be a powerful tool to redress the pervasive health disparities documented in health literature. Achieving such social justice and health equity, however, requires responsible scientific inquiry aimed at collaboratively identifying the underlying etiology of health disparities in AIAN populations. For example, the inclusion of Indigenous methodologies and a basic understanding of the ways in which cultural contexts and practices, such as ceremonies and rituals, facilitate social justice and Indigenous knowledge are required. As Vine Deloria, Jr. (1999a, 134) noted,

> modern science tends to use two kinds of questions to examine the world: (1) how does it work and (2) what use is it? These questions are natural for a people who think the world is constructed to serve their purposes. The old people might have used these two questions in their effort to understand the world, but it is certain that they always asked an additional question: what does it mean?

Building such Indigenous and scientific knowledge must include the perspective of the actual life experience of research participants and prioritize the service needs of Indigenous communities. This form of knowledge building has the best opportunity to inform health policy and practice innovations. In a systematic review of 70 CBPR papers published in the last decade, Salimi and colleagues (2012) found that CBPR has the potential to improve health and well-being in communities while decreasing the significant health disparities found to exist within AIAN communities (Beals et al. 2003; Denzin and Lincoln 2005; IHS 2002–2003).

It is now clear that, like CBPR, Indigenous methodologies are approaches that position and situate Indigenous people in the research arena. Indigenous methodologies implicitly honor the values and principles of CBPR but go beyond power dynamics, structural racism, and injustice. Indigenous methodologies are deeply rooted in a tribal community history, language, and way of being in the world as opposed to the CBPR history that is based largely on colonial imperialism. The Indigenous perspective is being revitalized, energized, and scientifically recognized by communities, researchers, universities, policy-making organizations, and funding agencies. The ethical and philosophical principles informing Indigenous methodologies call for research conducted with Indigenous populations to adopt community-situated, tribally informed, and Native scientist-led programs of inquiry (Burhansstipanov, Christopher, and Schumacher 2005; Fisher and Ball 2005; Mohatt et al. 2004). Porsanger (2004), however, cautions against privileging Indigenous scholars because there are so many "insider" views. Indigenous methodologies are "guided by tribal epistemologies, and tribal knowledge is not Western knowledge." Indigenous methodologies require an "outsider" to make a paradigm shift and to consider a more diverse and tribally accurate way to think about how research is done and what research means for Indigenous people.

Unlike CBPR and Western knowledge, Indigenous methodologies are difficult to define because Native people have their own knowledge systems. As Deloria (1999b, 35) writes, "the Indian perspective of the natural world . . . already has a fundamental principle of interpretation/observation that pervades everything that Indians think or experience. Thus verification of existing knowledge and the addition of new knowledge is simply a matter of adding to the already considerable body of information that Indians possess." Guiding principles and commonalities of CBPR, Western knowledge, and Indigenous methodologies are informed by understanding the shared meaning of different knowledge systems. This perspective and the commonalities of Indigenous values, ethics, and morals in the literature are reinforced by our collective experiences.

Indigenous methodologies are based on a relational worldview—the belief that all things are connected and interdependent—and rely on a holistic view of the universe. Indigenous methodologists have described the research framework as a "nest" that serves as a container for process and content. The process is necessarily one that values and honors good (or healthy) relationships: namely those based on respect, reciprocity, and responsibility. These values are present within many cultures and communities. However, these distinct, diverse, and tribally identified worldviews and principles guide Indigenous methodologies and emphasize community health and collective principles that promote humility, active listening, equitable relationships with human and nonhuman entities, group cohesion, and the spirit of generosity. These Indigenous values, shared by many other cultures, serve to promote communal wellness while simultaneously acknowledging the importance of culturally based or traditional methods of healing, knowledge acquisition, education, prevention, and intervention to mental health or physical forms of distress. Indigenous methodologies are rooted in spiritual epistemologies and guided by individual and community experience that is metaphysical in nature. The content and characteristics of Indigenous methodology may include researcher preparation, decolonizing ethics, gathering knowledge, making meaning, and giving back.

Is it possible for us to find a common ground—a place where we can begin to understand each other? We believe that the shared space of Indigenous and qualitative methodologies is common ground where "insiders" and "outsiders" and Western and Indigenous researchers can speak truth to each other. This space would benefit both and build a global perspective that could ultimately create a more effective and inclusive scientific perspective. Global health and public health requires that we strive to identify the places of commonality, as well as distinction.

Equally important, considering how the discriminatory and oppressive colonial practices have extended into the scientific history of this nation, is a history characterized by examples of unethical and even harmful research conducted on (not with) Indigenous populations. This legacy has established a frequently identified and historically rooted distrust of research for many Native people and communities. However, there is evidence that the decolonization of Western research is well underway. Most would agree that Western research has moved beyond positivist and postpositivist approaches into more flexible interpretations of the subjective reality in which Indigenous methodologies are situated. However, to move forward with Indigenous methodologies as a pathway for social justice, we must caution researchers that the past cannot be repeated. The history of Western research in the United States was, and sometimes is, a form of colonization, categorization, and structural racism.

The fundamental belief in the essential nature of objectification in research within Western science has led, over the centuries, to the abuse of

Native American research subjects. In the seventeenth and eighteenth centuries American Indian body parts, particularly skulls, were collected from war sites and studied by military doctors to "reveal character and mental capacity" (Hodge 2012, 434). In the 1950s the United States Air Force (USAF) used Native elders to recruit 120 non-English speaking Alaska Natives for a study involving radioactive iodine. The Alaska Native participants were required to ingest radioactive iodine over 200 times resulting in their suffering from unsafe exposure to radiation. The USAF wanted to know if Natives survived the cold by having higher metabolisms. Results of this research found the obvious: Natives did not have higher metabolisms, but they knew how to dress and eat for the cold weather. The research involved breastfeeding women, women of childbearing age, and their children. Furthermore, the USAF did not obtain consent from individuals or collect demographic information to allow for follow-up that would address undesirable health outcomes related to overexposure to radiation. Most troubling is what Shore writes about the research abuse, that Natives were "trading their participation for much needed medical treatment in rural villages" (Hodge 2012, 434).

Another study conducted in the 1950s by the U.S. Public Health Service (PHS) involved Navajo uranium miners. The aim of the study was to examine how radon in mines impacted health outcomes. The PHS had never gained consent of the miners and did not inform them of the known risks of lung cancer from exposure to radon (Samet et al. 1984). Other populations throughout the global community have been exploited as research subjects—so much so that in 1948 after World War II, the United Nations created the Universal Declaration of Human Rights ([Declaration] United Nations 1948). This Declaration was based on equality and dignity for all human beings and the idea that fundamental rights and freedoms were not luxuries but necessities for all people.

Even with the exploitative aspects of the research history, what we have learned through the Declaration is that well-intentioned researchers can enact a series of events that have ultimately resulted in unintended or unanticipated negative impacts upon Indigenous communities. In 1972 researchers from the northeastern United States entered an Alaska Native community to examine attitudes and values about alcohol use and collect psychological histories and data on the people's drinking habits. Researchers reported that alcohol use and social problems related to cultural changes were due to increasing wealth associated with oil development. Researchers went beyond describing the results and made recommendations for how the community should deal with alcohol use, including establishing alcohol education programs, slowing the cash flow to communities, and investing in projects elsewhere. This research culminated in a *New York Times* headline January 22, 1980: "Alcohol Plagues Eskimos, Sudden Wealth Sparks Epidemic of Alcoholism." An investigation into the research findings called into question the results of the study, identifying them as erroneous and promoting sensational statistics. Publications and reports from this research were deemed ethnocentric and parochial, demeaning, and denigrating to the Inupiat people (Foulks 1989, 12). This well-known study represents what one faculty member from the Inupiat University of the Arctic in Barrow, Alaska, called a faulty methodological orientation of research and a superficial understanding by researchers (Foulks 1989, 12). While it may be subjective to determine whether these conclusions are accurate, it is certainly the case that research that does not prioritize Indigenous voices and methodologies places Indigenous communities and science at risk. Researchers may not realize how their conclusions play into longtime patterns of oppressive power over communities by governments and churches.

More recently, researchers from Arizona State University collected DNA from members of the Havasupai Tribe. This small tribe has one of the highest rates of diabetes in the nation, and researchers promised tribal members that their DNA might provide insight to this health issue. However, the researchers used the DNA for other purposes: to examine mental illness, traditions, and theories about where the tribe originated that were in direct opposition to the tribal creation stories and spiritual beliefs. The research was only discovered when a Havasupai undergraduate student happened to attend a public lecture on the research findings. In 2010 the university's board of regents agreed to pay forty-one tribal members $700,000 and to provide other forms of assistance to the tribe including the return of blood samples from the tribal community (Harmon 2010).

Faulty methodological research orientations have unfortunately persisted in Indigenous communities. Community-based participatory research provides a paradigm of orientation to research that, based on Indigenous research standards, holds the potential to promote tribal sovereignty and equitable community engagement. Western scientific inquiry is guided by principles of beneficence and the idea that the benefits of research be wisely balanced with the potential risks to human participants. These elements of social justice frame future approaches that hold promise to promote knowledge, health, and benefits for Indigenous communities.

Community-Based Participatory Research and Social Justice

The emergence of CBPR holds significant promise to Native communities and to the more global pursuit of social justice because it has and will promote social change. Community-based participatory research includes principles that are complementary to the intersection of Indigenous knowledge and Western science because Native people have the knowledge of cultural and contextual factors that contribute to understanding disparate conditions. Western-trained scientists are proficient in the language and methodologies required to communicate the results of research within the dominant Western biomedical worldview. However, translating these findings in effective and applied ways within Indigenous cultures requires that Indigenous viewpoints, knowledge systems, and healing methods be understood, acknowledged, and when appropriate, integrated.

The key principles of CBPR foster respectful relationships, utilize a strengths-based perspective to build capacity, and facilitate co-learning and collaborative, equitable partnerships in all components of the research project. The cyclical and iterative process assures that the dissemination of findings and knowledge are shared appropriately and in a manner that will redress the social inequities experienced by AIAN communities. Within the literature there are numerous reports of successful CBPR approaches rooted in Indigenous epistemologies that lead to social justice. The People Awakening Project, but one example, used participatory action research, a form of CBPR, to examine community needs relating to alcohol abuse, prevention, and treatment (Mohatt et al. 2004). The research relied on Indigenous values and ways of knowing combined with culturally adapted quantitative methodologies to generate an in-depth understanding of sobriety. The results of the research empowered communities and led to awareness about positive factors that could help more effectively to support sobriety for Native people within this community.

Quantitative methodologies rooted in Western science frequently clash with Indigenous methodologies because they require research to be generalizable, valid, repeatable, and measurable, and they are driven by hypotheses testing and a biomedical model. Quantitative methodologies articulate differences using numbers but fail to account for the complex contextual and cultural differences in Indigenous populations. Another criticism of quantitative methodologies is that they fail to address the reasons for which numeric differences exist. For example, in a 1990 study about poverty, suicide, and homicide among Native Americans, data from twelve

IHS areas were examined to ascertain if there was a relationship between poverty and suicide or homicide. Statistical analyses reported significant correlations between these variables in eleven of the twelve IHS areas. However, the quantitative methodology failed to explain why the service area with the highest rate of poverty had the lowest rate of suicide and homicide (Young 1990). Curiously, one year later, the same author published another study with similar results but relied on anomie and social learning theory as explanations for the differences rather than examining culturally protective factors that were likely related to the resilience of the community (Young 1991). This research relied solely on quantitative methodologies and called for more research to examine differences. This research is an example of how Western-trained researchers often try to quantify what Indigenous people already know—in this case, poverty, suicide, and homicide rates are elevated in some Indigenous communities. Such research is unethical by many standards; more specifically, it perpetuates stereotypes about AIANs and fails to provide any tangible benefit to AIAN communities. Research driven by Western scientific principles has failed to address social injustice, and rather describes, relates, quantifies, and generalizes differences in research outcomes found within Native communities, as described above. Research based on these aims often results in more funding for Western-trained scientists to conduct additional inquiry with or on Native communities, but this form of research fails to address the reasons for which injustices exist. Little of the research funding reaches the community in ways that ameliorate social issues or injustices. Further, the Western scientific research agenda often fails to promote Native researchers, and Indigenous people continue to be objectified. Thus, explanations found within qualitative research methodologies via in-depth interviews, oral histories, and lived experiences are needed to address injustices experienced by and in Indigenous communities.

Determining the cross-cultural equivalence of measures is complex and often requires a step-wise validation of multiple dimensions. A rigorous approach would ensure equivalence of five major dimensions: content, conceptual, semantic, technical, and criterion equivalence. For the purposes of this chapter, two of these concepts will be briefly discussed here. Content equivalence refers to the process in which each item is examined to ensure it is relevant to the worldview of the culture being studied. Conceptual equivalence refers to the idea that a measure is assessing the same theoretical concept in each culture. For example, does an Indigenous group have a theoretical concept such as "depression," and if so, how does it compare or contrast to the Western theoretical concept? In addition, do the

Western quantitative measures developed to categorize levels of depression fit with the Indigenous group's worldview? Careful examination of theoretical concepts and measurement of the concepts are required. A critical analysis ensures researchers and the researched that what is being studied is relevant and respectful (Shore et al. 1987).

Cultural validity strategies take into account and understand that cultures will have different worldviews, beliefs, practices, and relational styles. Researchers are susceptible to bias that could detrimentally affect instrument selections and their applications. Cultural validity strategies ensure tribal communities and researchers that the work conducted will not be offensive and that it will be respectful. Focus groups have been used to validate a measure culturally. This methodology has enabled researchers to learn from the people being studied, generate data that can enrich and inform the concepts being examined, and inform item development on measures. This step is of critical importance and reduces the likelihood researchers will impose their own ethnocentric bias and arrive at erroneous conclusions about an Indigenous population. A side benefit of focus groups is that they also provide space for in-depth, generative discussions that strengthen and deepen researcher-researched relationships, produce greater understanding of differing worldviews, and facilitate co-learning.

Indigenous and non-Indigenous scholars have identified the importance of qualitative research. There is significant potential benefit from examining the ethnographic etiological understandings, healing methodologies, and ways of assessing research questions and interventions. Weiss, one of the first researchers to use a qualitative method of inquiry, reported that as a graduate student in the 1930s he conducted "depth interviews" for American manufacturers to ascertain why people purchased or failed to purchase various products (Weiss 1994). Weiss found qualitative interviewing useful, continued to use it, and eventually came to believe it was preferable when endeavoring to understand the complex experiences of people. Weiss maintains that "an open and trusting alliance" between the interviewer and the participant is a requirement for an effective interview. From these humble beginnings a quiet revolution was launched. Qualitative research investigates in an in-depth and holistic fashion, typically through the collection of rich narrative data using a flexible research design in an effort to understand a phenomenon. The history of qualitative, as well as mixed-methodological, science tells the story of a movement inclusive of reformation and transformation. Many Native, as well as non-Native scholars, would agree that all inquiry is moral and political (Beals et al. 2003; Denzin and Lincoln 2005; Norton and Manson 1996).

Qualitative research methodologies have routinely been used by researchers who study oppression, domination, suppression, alienation, and hegemony. As a consequence of this important research, participants previously ignored were given voice: women, feminists, people with disabilities, sexual minorities, and Indigenous people. The agenda for the third edition of Denzin and Lincoln's (2005) book, *The Sage Handbook of Qualitative Research*, was to provide a platform from which scholars could "create and imagine a free democratic society" and "change the world in positive ways."

Qualitative researchers maintain that our underlying beliefs guide the selection of research questions and methodology just as surely as they shape our actions. When we inquire about the nature of reality, by virtue of asking the question we are acknowledging the notion that there are many realities (ontology). Likewise, when we inquire about the relationship between the researcher and the researched, we must also make decisions about how to engage in the research process. As we explore the role of values, we acknowledge that research is value laden and biased. And finally, when we ask what the process of research is, we are using inductive logic, studying the topic within its context, and using an emerging methodological design. Knowledge and understanding emerge through the inductive approach.

Applying a Western theoretical model to an Indigenous population can, at its best, impose a poorly fitting model and, at its worst, promote ethnocentric assumptions that may actually harm the community of the research focus. Minimizing this risk requires that researchers develop theory and methods appropriate to Indigenous people by including them in all aspects of the research. Grounded theory is the methodology that enables this to occur; grounded theory allows for the inductive construction or generation of a theory from the data. By grounding theory in data, grounded theory researchers address some of the common criticisms of qualitative research methods, namely that they are theoretical. Also, grounded theory allows researchers to test previous theories and modify them so they are more appropriate for the population. For example, in a study by Hernandez, Antone, and Cornelius (1999), grounded theory was used to test the theory of integration among First Nations clients with diabetes and to assess how clients perceive their diabetes, how they live with diabetes, and the most appropriate education strategies for the population. Autoethnography is a qualitative research method based on firsthand experiences that allow researchers to explore personal interaction through social, cultural, or political contexts (Atkinson et al. 2002). Ethnography tends to focus on an entire cultural group, and a "good ethnography" requires a prolonged stay at the research site where the researcher endeavors to stay engaged with the methodological process in the context and to reduce the "distance" and the "objective separateness" between her/himself and those being researched (Guba and Lincoln 1988; Wolcott 1999). Denzin and Lincoln (2005) are optimistic regarding ethnographers' abilities to move the discourse forward, and they are hopeful that their research will also contribute to a more socially just world. As ethnographers have inquired about the experience of marginalized people, they have often included participants in the design, data collection, analysis, and write up. As a consequence, the participants' "voices" are heard throughout the research process. Included in this methodology are advocacy roles and an action agenda for change. Nevertheless, quantitative and qualitative research is subject to regulations imposed by the U.S. federal government, and research with sovereign Indigenous communities requires additional protections. Indigenous communities within the United States have begun systematically to claim and assert their sovereign rights to regulate human subject protections for research.

Federal Guidelines and Institutional Review Boards

Current federal guidelines for research involving human subjects do not address multiple challenges and possibilities existent within Indigenous research contexts. The definition of research found in 45 C.F.R § 46 is a systematic investigation, including research development, testing, and evaluation designed to develop or contribute to generalizable knowledge. However, the prioritized relational worldview found within Indigenous communities requires specific adaptations to the definition and regulation of research (Cross 1997). This integration begins with tribes, as sovereign independent nations, defines what research is, and then creates policies that address gaps in the current federal research protection guidelines. The unique cultural and social implications of research among Indigenous communities require oversights of human research protections established by the Belmont Report, as well as protections for the community (Alderte 1996; Freeman and Romero 2002; U.S. Department of Health and Human Services 1979).

There is a growing awareness within Indigenous communities of what constitutes research based on a Western worldview. As an example, in 2009 tribal health directors and elected tribal leaders from Montana and Wyoming met in Billings, Montana, at the Montana Wyoming Tribal Leaders

Council to discuss the development of an intertribal IRB and the current context in which research occurs and is regulated within AIAN communities. Attendees were most concerned with the need for Indigenous methodologies to address known health disparities through interventions that work. Attendees felt research that would not result in a tangible community benefit was unethical. Many attendees also voiced the need for research that gives back to the community in the way of teaching, tribal scholarships, infrastructure building, and sustainability. Emerging constructs, such as community-level needs for confidentiality, differential definitions of human subjects research inclusive of blood tissue samples, and the need for AIAN scientific and community reviewers emerged as distinctive themes of this consensus-building effort.

The discussion led to the development of an intertribal IRB and prompted a fundamental shift in the way that research is written, funded, monitored, and implemented within Native communities served by the intertribal consortium. A call for social justice again underscores the need for inclusive forms of scientific practice within Indigenous communities.

Many tribes have developed IRBs and have stressed the need for research that would translate into increased knowledge in the communities based on tribal research priorities and strategic health, environment, and education plans (Montana-Wyoming Tribal Leaders Council 2010). Tribal leaders also have voiced the need for clear documentation of the tribe's rights to the data and all publication rights.

Multitribal or tribal IRBs include tribal research and epidemiology centers, urban and rural Indian health boards, tribal colleges, and tribal governments (Office for Human Research Protections 2005). In order to serve both community interests and federal human subject protection regulations held in 45 C.F.R § 46, most tribal IRBs have been established using the federal requirements for research regulation, and additional protections have been added to address areas not covered by the federal regulations (Sahota n.d.). For example, 45 C.F.R § 46 does not address publication of private communal knowledge; protection of communities; respect for elders and knowledge of a community; respect for AIAN communities, their strengths, and survival; promotion of resiliency and active community involvement; or respect for and promotion of tribal sovereignty. In response to this, many tribal IRBs have additional protections including community-level protections, review by cultural committees or elders, Indigenous values, publication and dissemination agreements, issues related to monetary benefits versus exploitation, and consideration of the meaning of research questions within the context of the cultural relationships upon which research questions are premised (Kelley et al. 2013).

In the tragic history of research in the United States on Native people, tribal or community IRBs are not mentioned. In 1974 the National Commission for the Protections of Human Subjects of Biomedical and Behavioral Research was established in response to concerns about human subjects' protections in biomedical research. From this, the U.S. Congress passed the National Research Act requiring IRB approval for all federally funded research involving human subjects. In 1979 the Belmont Report was published outlining ethical principles and guidelines for the protection of human subjects in research. Then, in 1997 President Clinton apologized to African American survivors of the Tuskegee syphilis experiment, yet none of these acts or apologies addressed the research injustices on Native people or lands. There remains a lack of awareness about the history of research on Native people in the United States. This lack of awareness leads to flawed research approaches, harms communities, and perpetuates a Western-dominated research agenda where the oversight of human protections is given to the Western institutions.

When Western institutions regulate their own research, they often cannot be objective. Nor, seemingly, can Western institutions and their IRBs begin to understand the social injustices experienced by Native communities as a direct result of the Eurocentric dominant research paradigms embraced by many Western-trained researchers.

Researchers must be aware of the differences in culture and context within AIAN communities when conducting research in cultures different from the ones from which they come. A brief review of research on Native people suggests that when researchers are not aware of the cultural and community context, the outcomes have questionable meaning to tribes. Research must acknowledge tribal sovereignty and its implications. Research that fails to acknowledge differences is viewed as exploitation by many tribes and advocates for social justice. We feel it is possible to reverse social injustice and promote social contexts that determine desirable health outcomes in Native communities.

Conclusion

Inclusion of a multidimensional, culturally centered, Indigenous approach to research is required to pursue social justice more effectively and reduce health disparities for AIAN populations in the United States. Indigenous research approaches must also seek to incorporate primary prevention aimed at reducing extreme poverty, improving access to economic and educational opportunities, improving access to adequate housing, and addressing structural forms of racism. In this chapter we have described the context in which Indigenous methodologies can be used to promote social justice and honor the values and knowledge of Indigenous people. We have provided a summary of the use of intertribal IRBs as a means to promote social justice via increased tribal participation in the regulation of research regulation with AIAN populations. Indigenous methodologies span thousands of years; however, only recently has Western science become interested in how such methodologies may improve the accuracy and depth of research outcomes. Within this effort to promote a more just, inclusive, equitable, and ultimately accurate portrayal of science, there is promise for Native people who experience injustice to hope for a future of improved Indigenous health. Developing more effective and just scientific knowledge and methods for Indigenous populations can improve more global efforts to promote health and reduce disparities in morbidity and mortality for diverse populations.

References

Alderte, E. 1996. "The Formulation of a Health Research Agenda by and for Indigenous Peoples: Contesting the Western Scientific Paradigm." *The Journal of Alternative and Complementary Medicine* 2(3):377–85.

Atkinson, P., A. Coffey, S. Delamont, J. Lofland, and L. Lofland, eds. 2002. *Handbook of Ethnography*. London: Sage.

Beals, J., S. M. Manson, C. M. Mitchell, P. Spicer, and AI-SUPERPFP Team. 2003. "Cultural Specificity and Comparison in Psychiatric Epidemiology: Walking the Tightrope in American Indian Research." *Culture, Medicine and Psychiatry* 27:259–89.

Botha, L. 2011. "Mixing Methods as a Process Towards Indigenous Methodologies." *International Journal of Social Research Methodology* 14(4):313–25.

Burhansstipanov, L., S. Christopher, and A. Schumacher. 2005. "Lessons Learned from Community-Based Participatory Research in Indian Country." *Cancer Control* 12(2):70–76.

Christensen, M., and L. Kightlinger. 2013. "Premature Mortality Patterns Among American Indians in South Dakota, 2000–2010." *American Journal of Preventive Medicine* 44(5):465–71.

Cross, T. 1997. "National Indian Child Welfare Association: Understanding the Relational Worldview in Indian Families." *Pathways Practice Digest* 12(4):n.p.

Deloria, Vine, Jr. 1999a. "Traditional Technology." In *Spirit and Reason: The Vine Deloria, Jr., Reader*, edited by B. Deloria, K. Foehner, and S. Scinta, 129–36. Golden, CO: Fulcrum Publishing.

———. 1999b. "Relativity, Relatedness, and Reality." In *Spirit and Reason: The Vine Deloria, Jr., Reader*, edited by B. Deloria, K. Foehner, and S. Scinta, 32–39. Golden, CO: Fulcrum Publishing.

Denzin, Norman K., and Yvonna S. Lincoln, eds. 2005. *The Sage Handbook of Qualitative Research*. Thousand Oaks, CA: Sage.

DeVoe, J., and K. Darling-Churchill. 2008. *Status and Trends in the Education of American Indians and Alaska Natives (NCES 2008–084)*. National Center for Education Statistics, Institute of Education Sciences. Washington, DC: U.S. Department of Education.

Duran, Eduardo. 2006. *Healing the Soul Wound: Counseling with American Indians and Other Native Peoples*. New York: U.S. Teachers College Press.

Fisher, P. A., and T. J. Ball. 2005. "Balancing Empiricism and Local Cultural Knowledge in the Design of Prevention Research." *Journal of Urban Health* 82(2):44–55.

Foulks, E. F. 1989. "Misalliances in the Barrow Alcohol Study." *American Indian and Alaska Native Mental Health Research* 2(3):7–17.

Freeman, W. L., and F. C. Romero. 2002. "Community Consultation to Evaluate Group Risk." *Institutional Review Board: Management and Function*, edited by R. Amdur and E. Bankert, 160–64. Sudbury, MA: Jones and Bartlett.

Freire, P. 1972. *Pedagogy of the Oppressed*. London: Penguin.

Guba, E., and Y. S. Lincoln. 1988. "Do Inquiry Paradigms Imply Inquiry Methodologies?" In *Qualitative Approaches to Evaluation in Education*, edited by D. M. Fetterman, 89–115. New York: Praeger.

Hall, B. L. 1975. "Participatory Research: An Approach for Change." *Convergence* 8(2):24–31.

Harmon, A. 2010. "Indian Tribe Wins Fight to Limit Research of Its DNA." *New York Times*, April 21.

Hernandez, C. A., I. Antone, and I. Cornelius. 1999. "A Grounded Theory Study of the Experience of Type 2 Diabetes Mellitus in First Nations Adults in Canada." *Journal of Transcultural Nursing* 10(3):220–28.

Hodge, F. S. 2012. "No Meaningful Apology for American Indian Unethical Research Abuses." *Ethics and Behavior* 22(6):431–44.

IHS (Indian Health Service). 2002–2003. *Trends in Indian Health*, Rockville, MD: U.S. Department of Health and Human Services.

Johnson, E. A., and E. R. Rhoades. 2000. "The History and Organization of Indian Health Services and Systems." In *American Indian Health: Innovations in Healthcare, Promotion, and Policy*, edited by E. R. Rhoades, 82. Baltimore: Johns Hopkins University Press.

Kelley, A., A. Belcourt-Dittloff, C. Belcourt, and G. Belcourt. 2013. "Research Ethics and Indigenous Communities." *American Journal of Public Health* 103:2146–52.

Kingsley, G. T., M. Mikelsons, and C. Herbig. 2013. *Housing Problems and Needs of American Indians and Alaska Natives*. BiblioGov.

Kovach, M. 2009. *Indigenous Methodologies: Characteristics, Conversations, and Contexts*. Toronto: University of Toronto Press.

Lewin, K. 1946. "Action Research and Minority Populations." *Journal of Social Issues* 2(4):34–46.

Macartney, S., A. Bishaw, and K. Fontenot. 2013. "Poverty Rates for Selected Detailed Race and Hispanic Groups by State and Place: 2007–2011." In *American Community Survey Briefs*. Washington, DC: U.S. Census Bureau.

Minkler, M. 2004. "Ethical Challenges for the 'Outside' Researcher in Community-Based Participatory Research." *Health, Education and Behavior* 31(6):684–97.

Mohatt, G. V., K. L. Hazel, J. Allen, M. Stachelrodt, C. Hensel, and R. Fath. 2004. "Unheard Alaska: Culturally Anchored Participatory Action Research on Sobriety with Alaska Natives." *American Journal of Community Psychology* 33(3):263–73.

Montana-Wyoming Tribal Leaders Council. 2010. "Grant Awards and Research in Montana Wyoming Indian Country." Paper presented at the Executive Board Meeting, Billings, Montana.

Norris, T., P. Vines, and E. Hoeffel. 2012. "The American Indian and Alaska Native Population: 2010." In *2010 Census Briefs.* Washington, DC: U.S. Census Bureau.

Norton, I. M., and S. M. Manson. 1996. "Research in American Indian and Alaska Native Communities: Navigating the Cultural Universe of Values and Process." *Journal of Consulting and Clinical Psychology* 64(5):856–60.

Office for Human Research Protections. 2005. "Code of Federal Regulations 45 Cfr 46 Definitions." Washington, DC: United States Department of Health and Human Services.

Porsanger, J. 2004. "An Essay About Indigenous Methodology." *Nordlit* 15:105–20.

Sahota, P. C. n.d. "Research Regulation in American Indian/Alaska Native Communities: Policy and Practice Considerations." NCAI Policy Research Center. Available at www.ncaiprc.org/research-publications-papers. Accessed September 2009.

Salimi, Y., K. Shahandeh, H. Malekafzali, N. Loori, A. Kheiltash, E. Jamshidi, A.S. Frouzan, and R. Majdzadeh. 2012. "Is Community-Based Participatory Research (CBPR) Useful? A Systematic Review on Papers in a Decade." *International Journal of Preventive Medicine* 3(6):386–93.

Samet, J. M., D. M. Kutvirt, R. J. Waxweiler, and C. R. Key. 1984. "Uranium Mining and Lung Cancer in Navajo Men." *New England Journal of Medicine* 310(23):1481–84.

Shore, J. H., S. M. Manson, J. D. Bloom, G. Keepers, and G. Neligh. 1987. "A Pilot Study of Depression among American Indian Patients with Research Diagnostic Criteria." *American Indian and Alaska Native Mental Health Research* 1(2):4–15.

Smith, L. T. 2005. *Decolonizing Methodologies: Research and Indigenous Peoples.* Dunedin: Zed Books.

Thomas, D. H. 2000. *Skull Wars: Kennewick Man, Archaeology, and the Battle for Native American Identity.* New York: Basic Books.

Trafzer, Clifford E. 2000. *As Long as the Grass Shall Grow and Rivers Flow: A History of Native Americans.* Independence, KY: Cengage Learning.

United Nations. 1948. *The Universal Declaration of Human Rights.* http://www.un.org /en/documents/udhr/.

U.S. Department of Health and Human Services. 1979. *The Belmont Report: Ethical Principles and Guidelines for the Protection of Human Subjects of Research.* The National Commission for the Protection of Human Subjects of Biomedical and Behavioral Research, Office of the Secretary. Washington, DC.

Wallerstein, N., and B. Duran. 2008. "The Theoretical, Historical, and Practice Roots of CBPR." In *Community-Based Participatory Research for Health: From Process to Outcomes,* edited by M. Minkler and N. Wallerstein, 25–46. San Francisco, CA: Jossey-Bass.

Weber-Pillwax, C. 2001. "What Is Indigenous Research?" *Canadian Journal of Native Education* 25(2):166–74.

Weiss, R. S. 1994. *Learning from Strangers: The Art and Method of Qualitative Interview Studies*. New York: The Free Press.

Wilson, Angela Cavender, and Michael Yellow Bird. 2005. *For Indigenous Eyes Only: A Decolonization Handbook*. School of American Research Native America Series. Santa Fe, NM: School of American Research.

Wilson, S. 2008. *Research Is Ceremony: Indigenous Research Methods*. Halifax, NS: Fernwood Publishing.

Wolcott, H. F. 1999. *Ethnography: A Way of Seeing*. Walnut Creek, CA: AltaMira.

Young, Thomas J. 1990. "Poverty, suicide, and homicide among Native Americans." *Psychological Reports* 67(3f):1153–54.

———. 1991. "Suicide and Homicide Among Native Americans: Anomie or Social Learning?" *Psychological Reports* 68(3c):1137–38.

CHAPTER THREE

Indigenous Education in the Norwegian and U.S. Contexts

Phyllis Ngai, Unn-Doris Karlsen Bæk,
and Gry Paulgaard

The United Nations (UN) Declaration on the Rights of Indigenous Peoples (UNDRIP) affirms that "Indigenous peoples have the right to the dignity and diversity of their cultures, traditions, histories, and aspirations, which shall be appropriately reflected in education and public information" (UN 2007). This international agreement represents a long-overdue governmental affirmation of Indigenous peoples' rights, including rights to culturally responsive education and rights to be free from any forms of racism transmitted through education and public information. Norway, along with 144 other UN member nations, endorsed the declaration in 2007. The United States initially refused to endorse it, but reversed its decision in 2010. The declaration stipulates that "states shall take effective measures, in consultation and cooperation with the Indigenous peoples concerned, to combat prejudice and eliminate discrimination and to promote tolerance, understanding and good relations among Indigenous peoples and all other segments of society." This declaration helps define Indigenous education in the twenty-first century by calling attention to two strands: first, educating Indigenous youths in and through their cultures; and second, educating all citizens about Indigenous people and their heritages. Indigenous education includes teaching Indigenous youths to learn in their language and to be nurtured in their ancestral culture. Indigenous education also involves shifting the focus of non-Native educational institutions from assimilating Indigenous peoples to educating the whole society about Indigenous perspectives, cultures, histories, and people.

Our chapter explores the issues and implications of the two strands of Indigenous education in the national contexts of the United States and Norway. At the local/global intersection issues hindering fulfillment of UNDRIP emerge as common across national borders. Against the historical backdrop, the first part of the chapter attempts to map out educational policy shifts over time and to understand the impacts of different forms of Indigenous education on American Indian and Sámi students. The overall discussion builds upon a comparative perspective that facilitates transnational sharing of inspiration and ideas for removing barriers to the spirit of UNDRIP.

The U.S. Context

In the United States, people who identify themselves as American Indians or Alaska Natives constitute about 1.7 percent of the U.S. population, or 5.2 million U.S. residents (Norris, Vines, and Hoeffel 2012). They represent different cultures, languages, and homelands (NCNASL 2008).[1] Between 2000 and 2010, the American Indian and Alaskan Native population increased almost twice as fast as the total U.S. population (Norris, Vines, and Hoeffel 2012). This is a young population; its approximate median age is 25 years compared to 35 years for all races in the United States (IHS 2012). Based on the 2003–2005 data, the life expectancy of Native Americans (72.6 years) is 5.2 years less than all other races in the United States (IHS 2012). Although the educational experiences vary across Indigenous groups, most Native people on the continent share similar tribulations and triumphs, resistance, and resiliency in reaction to the U.S. government's Indian policy. Formal education is a nontraditional concept to Native American people. Formal schools are a relatively new way to educate youths in Indigenous communities. Historically, school is a white man's tool to eliminate the distinctive cultural and linguistic traditions of Indigenous people. David Beaulieu (2000, 37), a White Earth Chippewa tribal member, explains that "schools have traditionally served the needs of the larger society and have not focused on the needs of small isolated and primarily rural American Indian communities that have their own specific ideas about the goals of development and the role of education in meeting community needs." As Native people regain self-determination, tribally controlled schools have begun to refocus the social, cultural, and economic context of their communities for purposes and goals of Indigenous education.

While some Native students attend tribally controlled schools on reservations, more than 90 percent of all Native American students nationwide attend regular public schools or so-called mainstream schools side-by-side with non-Natives (Oakes and Maday 2009, 2). Recently, the numbers of Natives attending urban schools with a majority of non-Native student population are growing (NCNASL 2008). When Native students attend public schools, their education is outside the control of their tribes, although parental involvement is encouraged in schools receiving federal funding designated for supporting Native students.[2]

The governing body of public schools that serve students of all backgrounds, including Native students, is the state legislature. State legislators, only about 1 percent of whom are Natives nationwide (NCSL 2009), are the ones responsible for appropriations and policy that impact education for more than 90 percent of Native students in the United States (NCNASL 2008). To date, out of the fifty states, only eleven have passed legislation mandating instruction in tribal culture, history, and/or government to all students in K–12 public schools. Implied in the laws concerning Indigenous education in public schools are the goals of creating an inclusive learning environment for Native students and educating non-Native students about the Indigenous people of the country. In *Power and Place: Indian Education in America*, Vine Deloria, Jr., succinctly captures the evolving meanings of American Indian education.

> Formal Indian education in America stretches all the way from reservation preschools in rural Native communities to prestigious urban universities far away from Indian cultural centers. The educational journey of modern Indian people is one spanning two distinct value systems and worldviews. It is an adventure in which the Native American sacred view must inevitably encounter the material and pragmatic focus of the larger American society. In that meeting ground lays an opportunity for the two cultures to both teach and learn from each other. (Deloria and Wildcat 2001, v)

The Norwegian Context

In Norway, the Sámi population is the only group with official status as Indigenous people.[3] The status as Indigenous people brings with it specific rights regarding education, to which we will return later. Even though the Sámi have been accepted as *one* Indigenous people in Norway, we are at the same time talking about different subgroups related to geographic location, occupational structure, language, and degree of assimilation into the *fornorskningspolitikken* (Norwegian majority culture) (Solstad 2009). The Sámi population is located all over Norway (and Sweden, Finland, and Russia); the core areas for the population are in the northern parts of Norway (Nordland, Troms, and Finnmark counties). In this chapter we will mainly focus on the education in the core areas of Finnmark.

It is not possible to state the size of the Sámi population in Norway specifically and accurately. From approximately 1850 to 1950 the official state policy of assimilation required that Sámi people give up their culture and identity and become part of the fornorskningspolitikken. As a result of this assimilation policy, giving up or hiding one's original Sámi identity were strategies that many chose. There have been and still are different opinions as to who can be considered a Sámi (Pettersen 2004), and opinions differ at the individual, institutional, and national levels. Also, up until this date, no systematic national census has been carried out to register Sámi background. There are, however, different estimates available. According to the Nordic Sámi Institute, the total number of the Sámi population is between 50,000 and 80,000 people; two-thirds reside in Norway. Since two-thirds of the entire Sámi population live in Norway, it has a special responsibility to sustain and develop Sámi culture and language.

In many ways, the Sámi people in Norway have experienced a challenging relationship with the Norwegian educational system, given that for 100 years, the official government policy regarding the Sámi population was to assimilate them into the Norwegian society. The educational system was a crucial measure through which "the Sámi were to be systematically Norwegianized" (Hirvonen 2008, 17). The national educational policy specified that the Sámi people were to attend Norwegian schools and use the Norwegian language in school. Educators made few efforts to adjust teaching to accommodate children who did not master the Norwegian language but instead spoke Sámi as their first and only language (Solstad 2009). During the second half of the nineteenth century, important international conventions affirmed the rights of Indigenous people, and those international agreements helped formalize Norway's obligations toward the Sámi people; hence, the assimilation policy became history. In 1989 the Norwegian government established two important Sámi institutions: the *Samediggi* (Sámi Parliament) and the Sámi College. In 1997 the government implemented the first special Sámi curriculum for compulsory primary and lower secondary schooling. Since the latest Norwegian educational reform in 2006, the Knowledge Promotion Reform, the special Sámi curriculum (the Sámi National Curriculum for Knowledge Promotion) has included compulsory and secondary education. According to Solstad (2009), no other nation-state has implemented a specific formal national curriculum for an Indigenous people.

Sámi education in Norway is first and foremost defined as education for Sámi children, and the most important tool in this regard is the Sámi National Curriculum implemented in schools located within Sámi municipalities. However, the regular National Curriculum also includes elements aimed at educating all Norwegian children in the Sámi culture. The present Sámi National Curriculum enables municipalities and individual schools to determine the degree to which students learn Sámi language and culture, ranging from receiving the full compulsory schooling in Sámi to studying Sámi language and culture as an optional subject. In recent years about twenty schools in the Sámi Administrative Area and about ten schools outside this area used the Sámi curriculum. Nationally, nearly 200 schools, including Sámi schools, teach Sámi as a subject (Hirvonen 2008, 21–22).

Comparison

How do the trajectories of Indigenous education in Norway and the United States connect across oceans and mountains? In Norway and the United States, the meanings and implications of Indigenous education have changed over time. In the recent decades national initiatives for Indigenous education that build upon the ideal of self-determination and equity are gaining momentum in both countries. With rights to self-determination, Indigenous communities in both national contexts are striving to ensure high-quality, culturally relevant education for Indigenous students (Aikio-Puoskari 2009; Beaulieu 2000, 43; Henriksen 2009, 26). However, Indigenous education is not just a local issue. As Nyseth and Pedersen (2005, 76) point out, "the enlargement of awareness, which sees Sámi as an Indigenous people, implies a change from local and specific ethnic group identification to the general concept of Indigenousness, where the Sámi become part of the international movement of Indigenous peoples." A similar expansion of perspective also has emerged in the United States as illustrated by the Americans for Indian Opportunity Ambassador program that aims to provide budding Native leaders in North America to connect nationally and internationally.

Further, Indigenous education is not an issue for Indigenous people only. The question of how Indigenous education can be integrated into mainstream education systems in ways that benefit all students (Native and non-Native) in culturally plural societies needs to be addressed. In the following section we situate our transnational exploration for new pedagogical insights in the separate but parallel historical experiences of the two countries. We recognize that lifting Indigenous education out of the margin (geographically and pedagogically) and centralizing it in mainstream education is not and cannot be the *only* effort contributing to the thriving of Indigenous peoples. But we posit that the educational outcomes, that is a deep understanding of and a profound appreciation for Indigeneity, resulting from such a shift are likely to lead to social change beneficial to Native students and their non-Native classmates in an interconnected world.

Historical Trends: National Policy Concerning Indigenous in the United States and Norway

The United States and American Indian Experience

Indigenous education is a complex policy issue in the United States. A historical review reveals "the inherent paradox in a system that requires the government to provide education for Native Americans while at the same time promoting self-determination among Indigenous people" (Barnhardt 2001, 25). In its recent report on the education of Native children, the National Caucus of Native American State Legislators reminds us that "the responsibility of the federal government to provide for the health, education, and well-being of tribal citizens in perpetuity came with the millions of acres of land ceded by Native American tribes through treaties to the federal government—which allowed creation of this country" (NCNASL 2008, 8). Against such a historical backdrop, discussions about Indigenous education at the national level often focus on education of American Indian children, teenagers, adults, and communities by mainstream educational institutions, even though Indigenous education rightfully includes education of American Indian children by their parents, extended families, and communities. The reason, according to Tippeconnic (2000, 34), is that the public education arena is perceived by American Indian scholars and educators as a domain of resistance and reclamation of Indigenous rights. Not until genuine, effective Indian education that aims to nurture Native children through culturally appropriate approaches and serves to inform non-Native students of the value of Indigenous perspectives is included in public education will Indigenous peoples' rights to the dignity and diversity of their cultures, traditions, histories, and aspirations be fully honored by local and national governments. Decolonizing knowledges and centralizing Indigenous perspectives in the mainstream educational domain is part of the struggle for reclaiming voice (Freire 1970; Smith 1999).

The history of Indian education can be divided into two broad periods: the missionary period (1568–1870) and the federal period (1870–1968). In the late nineteenth century the federal American Indian boarding school system reflected the Native peoples' loss of political power and economic status (Juneau 2001, 21; Trafzer et al. 2006). For decades, national government boarding schools constituted the predominant form of assimilative Indigenous education around the country. Many tribal members were "rounded up" (a descriptive term used by some Natives) by U.S. government officials and sent to boarding schools to receive "Whiteman" education in other states (Juneau 2001). Although some Indian parents willingly let their children enroll in boarding schools to learn some skills for earning money (Ellis 2006), many youngsters were forced to leave their families and communities behind with no protection from any tribal or non-tribal authority (Trafzer et al. 2006).

Most U.S. legislation involving Indigenous students in the United States can be traced to the federal period, 1870–1968 (Swisher and Tippeconnic 1999, 66). A turning point in the U.S. history of Indigenous education is marked by the 1928 *Meriam Report*, an extensive commissioned survey of Indian social and economic conditions, which called for new attitudes and approaches toward education of Native children. At that time, about 40 percent of all Native children attended schools controlled by the Bureau of Indian Affairs, a federal agency. The report recommended "a major reformation of American Indian education with Indian involvement at all levels of the educational process" and contained specific recommendations that education be tied to communities and that Native language and culture be included in the development of the curriculum (Barnhardt 2001, 12; Huff 1997; Tippeconnic 2000). This attitudinal shift marked the beginning of the nationwide advocacy of culturally responsive education for Native students in the United States.

In the 1930s and 1940s, national educational policies concerning American Indians appeared to be more sympathetic toward Native identity maintenance and intergenerational transmission of Native languages and cultures than in previous decades. Boundaries around a safety zone of tolerable cultural difference started to loosen up (Lomawaima and McCarty 2006). However, language and cultural learning among Native youths continued to be limited to isolated places. During that period, "Indians had a right to 'remain an Indian,' as long as they remained on their reservation or allotment land and did not compete for jobs" (Lomawaima and McCarty 2006, 73). The door had opened for language and cultural revitalization, but only for scattered local efforts.

In many ways, Indigenous education in the United States is a movement of rejecting assimilation and striving for self-determination, as the critical consciousness of governmental obligation to safeguard Indigenous rights is emerging locally and globally. This movement toward Indian control of Indian education "started in the 1960s, secured legislation in the 1970s, survived the 1980s, picked up momentum in the 1990s, and promises to gain even greater significance beyond 2000" (Tippeconnic 1999, 33). The journey has been a slow and rocky one. Although some regression has occurred from time to time in the U.S. political scene, Native peoples' perseverance has been fruitful. For instance, during the 1950s and 1960s, federal policy swung back to cultural intolerance. In reaction, local, tribal, and national Indian leaders and young people started to speak up about the value of heritage languages and cultures. Throughout the mid-twentieth century, American Indian leadership built up strength "formally to reject the idea of 'termination' that aimed to strip Natives of their 'Indianness' through assimilationist policies" (Bill 1990, 21). It took nearly two decades for the American public to become receptive to their messages (Lomawaima and McCarty 2006, 116).

The year 1970, when President Nixon called for a new national policy of "self-determination" for the American Indian people, represents another turning point. Nixon delivered a message to the U.S. Congress on Indian policy promising "self-determination without termination" and declaring that "every Indian community wishing to do so should be able to control its own Indian schools" (American Indian Policy Review Commission 1976, 111). Subsequently, the Indian Education Act of 1972 mandated that schools develop programs to meet the culturally related academic needs of American Indian students. The call for involving Indian parents in the education of Indian children emerged to reinforce the political rhetoric of acknowledging self-determination of Indigenous people; however, it was not until 1975 that the Indian Self-Determination and Indian Assistance Act authorized tribes to contract with the national government to administer schools for Indian students (Swisher and Tippeconnic 1999). This gradual shift of ideology at the national level allowed an increasing number of American Indian communities to develop their own language and culture educational programs for the first time in history (Juneau 2001, 39). Moreover, hope that Native-controlled schools would provide vitality to learning through Indigenous languages and cultures started to surface

(Lomawaima and McCarty 2006). At that time, some non-Native lawmakers began to recognize the governmental obligation to include Indigenous perspectives in public education.

A stark reversal of the past assimilative educational policies appeared in the 1990 Native American Languages Act. This was the first U.S. government policy statement that committed the nation to preserve, protect, and promote the rights and freedom of Native Americans to use, practice, and develop Native languages as a vehicle for formal and informal education (Swisher and Tippeconnic 1999, 74). Throughout the 1990s, American Indian education became synonymous with integrating tribal languages and cultures into the education of Native children, which is commonly known as the culturally responsive approach.

Toward the second half of the 1990s, educators' motivations for adopting culturally responsive approaches to education of American Indians shifted from self-determination to bridging the achievement gap of Native students. The change in emphasis became apparent in the 1994 Title IX of the Improving America's Schools Act, which provided supplemental funds to local educational agencies to reform school programs serving Indian children by developing demonstration projects to improve the achievement of Indian children (Swisher and Tippeconnic 1999, 74). In 1998 President Clinton issued Executive Order No. 13096 on American Indian and Alaska Native education that clearly conveyed a pledge aimed toward "improving the academic performance and reducing the dropout rate" of Indigenous students (Brayboy and Castagno 2009, 34).

The national commitment to use culturally responsive education to bridge the achievement gap among Native students did not continue through the turn of the century. Under the Bush administration, the 2004 Executive Order 13336 focused U.S. educators' attention on helping Indigenous students meet the goals established in the No Child Left Behind Act of 2001, a standardized test-driven mandate for improving academic achievements of all students. Since then, schools have been under pressure to prepare students for standardized testing, which often contradicts the culturally responsive approaches that many educators believe contribute to the academic success of Native youths (Brayboy and Castagno 2009, 34).

During the past thirty years, educators and others have been struggling with the question of how best to educate Indigenous students in public schools. Recent demographic trends indicate that most Native students attend school side-by-side with non-Native students. According to 2010 Census data, the majority of the American Indian and Alaska Native population (78 percent) lives outside of American Indian and Alaska Native areas.

In addition, out of the total 4.6 million people residing in American Indian areas, 77 percent do not identify as American Indian and Alaska Natives (Norris, Vines, and Hoeffel 2012). As the demographics change, it may be necessary to shift the research focus of Indigenous education in the United States from educating Indian students in isolation on reservations or rural tribal schools to addressing their needs in public schools with mixed populations.

The Norwegian and Sámi Experience

The educational system in Norway has been instrumental in carrying out the Norwegian government's assimilation policies. As in U.S. Indigenous education, the period around the seventeenth to mid-eighteenth century can be characterized as the missionary period. The Christian mission started schooling for Sámi and Kven, another ethnic minority in Northern Norway descended from Finnish immigrants in 1714, which was a period when the government did not distinguish between Sámi and Kven (Evjen 2004). The aim was primarily to transform all of "the heathens" into "good Christians" (Solstad 2009). One important goal of the missionary effort was to teach literacy to the Sámi people so that they could read the Bible. In order to achieve this as effectively as possible, the language of instruction was the Sámi language (Jensen 2005). In 1717 a school was established by the missionaries to produce teachers and missionaries among the Sámi population and for the translation of textbooks and the Bible to Sámi (Jensen 2005). The belief at the time was that if Sámi people received education in Sámi, they would want to learn Norwegian in order to be able to attain a higher level of acculturation.

In the mid-eighteenth century, the prevailing view on the Sámi changed. Opposition against the use of Sámi language in school increased. In the mid-nineteenth century "a harsh and overtly assimilationist official policy" came into effect (Aikio-Puoskari 2009, 243). For decades, the use of Sámi language and yoiking, singing in the traditional Sámi way, were prohibited in the school. During this period, Norwegian authorities implemented a number of measures aimed at total assimilation of Sámi people into fornorskningspolitikken. One such measure was *Finnefondet*, established in 1851 by the Norwegian Parliament. The aim of Finnefondet was to promote teaching of Norwegian language and culture in Sámi districts. The percentage of the national government budget allocated for assimilation initiatives of the Sámi populations in Finnmark and the northern part of Troms County from Finnefondet at the beginning of the nineteenth century was larger than the total allowance for Sámi purposes in Norway at the beginning of the twentieth century (Minde 2005, 18). For instance, non-Sámi teachers working in Sámi areas received higher wages than teachers working in other areas through Finnefondet. They could also apply for extra salaries if they could document that their work in teaching Norwegian to Sámi students had been a success. The fund also financed an extensive governmental building of boarding schools for Sámi children where the children spent most of the year away from parents and families. One of the reasons for the extensive governmental effort in establishing boarding schools was to disperse Sámi settlement in the northern part of the country. These institutions operated in the service of assimilation (Meløy 1980).

The boarding schools were institutions where the Sámi children lived in Norwegian milieus with Norwegian language and culture. As part of the assimilative educational approach, all school personnel, including school principals and teachers, were Norwegians (Jensen 2005). There were reports of traumatic experiences from pupils coming to the governmental boarding schools without understanding the Norwegian language. Some Sámi students reported punishment when they used their Sámi language (Stølen 2007). The strict regulations of language use and behavior at the boarding schools were not formally removed until 1959 when a new education act came into effect.

The shift in the view on the Sámi from the mid-nineteenth century can be understood in light of two ideological trends that had a strong holding in Norway—and in the rest of Europe—at the time: nationalism and social Darwinism (Jensen 2005). When it comes to nationalism, the emphasis was on the promotion and construction of an independent Norwegian nation-state based on sovereignty and homogeneity. This must, of course, be understood against the backdrop of Norway's long history of subjugation under foreign rule—first by Denmark and then by Sweden. Norway finally achieved its sovereignty as a nation-state in 1905 with its liberation from Sweden. A period of high national consciousness and a drive to build a nation-state followed. Ethnic diversity, especially in the northern areas, represented a threat to the national unity of a nation-state characterized by a mostly homogeneous population that shared the same language, culture, and customs (Eriksen and Niemi 1981, 371; Jensen 2005, 46). The Norwegian government considered assimilation of the Sámi population a prerequisite for identification with the Norwegian nation-state.

Scholars describe how social Darwinism influenced the assimilation policy (Jensen 2005; Lorentz 1991). According to social Darwinism the survival of selective ethnic and social groups is based on an evolutionary paradigm, which explicates a differentiation between civilized and "savage" or "primitive" groups. The political consequences of such a perspective is that ethnic minorities are considered to be at a lower stage of development, less civilized than the majority and, thus, have to be assimilated to the culture, language, and standards of the majority (Jensen 2005). The understanding of Sámi people as primitive and the majority Norwegian population as civilized served to legitimize the assimilation policy.

A third motive was security policy; that is, protecting Norway's borders in the north against the threat from Finland (Eriksen and Niemi 1981). This was legitimized by security policy on strengthening the national control of the northern part of Norway where the population consisted of different ethnic groups. As there was fear that Russian troops, and later Finnish troops would invade and occupy the northern areas of Norway, politicians generated different initiatives to protect the northern borders. The government considered assimilation of the Sámi population one important security procedure to secure loyalty to the Norwegian nation.

These three main political and cultural trends—nationalism, social Darwinism, and security policy—together had an important impact on Indigenous education in Norway. The educational system became the most important institution for the assimilation policy. The school arena has even been described as the battlefield of assimilation (Niemi 1997). Niemi claims that the teachers were the combatants involved in the implementation of a long-lasting and continual assimilation process purposely intended and initiated by the governmental authorities.

Even though some of the ideological patrimony that laid the foundation for the assimilation policy was heavily compromised as a result of Nazi influence prior to and during World War II, the assimilation policy continued to receive general political support until the mid-nineteenth century. In some geographical locations, especially along the coastal areas of Finnmark County and the northern part of Troms County, the Sámi population was dramatically reduced not by demographic factors, such as out-migration, but as a result of the assimilation policy (Bjørklund 1985; Nielsen 1986). Among the few Sámi people who received, for example, teacher education, the opposition against the assimilation policy was, however, strong, and they received support among Norwegian groupings. The opposition claimed the rights for Sámi students to use, learn, and be taught in the Sámi language. It did, however, take several decades before this was formally realized. All the way up until 1959, it was official educational policy that teachers were only to use Sámi language in their teaching if it was strictly necessary (Höem 2007; Jensen 2005).

After 1959, a clear break from the aggressive assimilationist policy carried out by the Norwegian government (Solstad 2009) began. New perspectives on Sámi educational issues became more and more visible in official documents. According to Solstad, this departure from the active assimilation policy not only had to do with internal Norwegian circumstances, it also reflected international trends regarding new perspectives on human value and human rights. The most influential document in this regard was the United Nations' Declaration of Human Rights of 1948. Since then, a number of school reforms gradually strengthened the rights of Sámi children to education in and through their heritage language and culture. Since the late 1960s schools have officially been able to use Sámi at the primary level. The education law of 1975, which was reinforced by 1985 legislation, required teaching in the Sámi language upon Sámi parents' requests.

Norway's formal acceptance of Sámi as an Indigenous people and their rights within the nation-state and the state's obligations toward the Sámi led to the addition of a new paragraph to Norwegian law in 1988, Section 110A. This is the "Sámi Paragraph," which states that the authorities are to guarantee that the Sámi people can secure and develop their language, culture, and societal life. This paragraph is of crucial importance to Sámi policy on Sámi education. Sámi education is an extremely important tool to ensure the existence and maintenance of Sámi culture and language for future generations. The passing of Sámi Act (SáL 1987) and the Sámi Language Act (SáLGn 1992) expanded opportunities for teaching and learning through Sámi (Hirvonen 2008, 18).

Despite the harsh assimilation policy carried out by the Norwegian government toward the Sámi people, other trends within Norwegian educational history and educational policy allowed for the implementation of a specific Sámi curriculum. The idea of equitable education for all has constituted an important foundation for *enhetsskolen* (Norwegian educational policy). The goal of the Norwegian schools has been "to provide for all children—independent of abilities, economy and social status, religious or cultural background, and geography—equitable and adapted education within a common frame, with common laws and curricula" (Norwegian Ministry of Education 1998, 28). Official educational policy documents state that the principle of equitable education is secured through the premise that education shall be adapted to individuals' abilities, developmental levels, and needs and to local diversity (ibid.). In this way the foundation for the development of perspectives attending to the culturally specific needs of Sámi children and adolescents was already present.

Official Norwegian policy regarding the Sámi people largely relates to the outline for the Nordic Sámi Convention of 2006 (for Norway, Sweden, and Finland) concerning language and education rights (Åhrén 2007; Solstad 2009). According to the convention, the Sámi have the right to use, develop, and revitalize their language and traditions (article 23). The states have a duty to actively promote these rights (article 24). Article 26 of the declaration states that Sámi education shall adapt to Sámi students' cultural backgrounds. The convention distinguishes between the rights to language and education of the Sámi population living within the traditional Sámi areas and the Sámi population residing outside of those areas. The Sámi population residing within the traditional Sámi areas shall have access to education in and through the medium of the Sámi language. Sámi children and adolescents living outside the Sámi areas shall have access to education in the Sámi language and through the medium of the Sámi language to the extent it can be deemed reasonable in the specific area.

As already mentioned, the first national curriculum developed especially for Sámi education (L97S) was introduced at the compulsory primary education level in 1997. In 2006 the government implemented a second Sámi national curriculum in primary and secondary education (LK06S). This separate curriculum is implemented in Sámi municipalities subject to the Sámi Language Act.[4] In the Sámi National Curriculum the subject curricula are partly separate curricula, such as for the Sámi language and for *duodjii* (traditional Sámi handcrafts), and partly adapted parallel curricula, such as for natural science, music, and so on.

Several governmental levels and institutions are important when it comes to ensuring Sámi education. First, the Sámi Parliament has the responsibility for developing the Sámi National Curriculum in order to guarantee the curriculum is adapted to the cultural backgrounds and particular needs of Sámi children and adolescents. According to the Norwegian Education Act of 1998, § 6–4, the Sámi Parliament is responsible for developing curriculum for Sámi students in compulsory education and for teaching Sámi language and specific Sámi subjects in secondary education, for example the Sámi craft, doudjii. The Sámi Parliament is also responsible for providing regulations about Sámi-related contents within the different subjects in the general school. The Sámi Parliament also distributes economic support grants every year for motivating students in upper secondary school to learn the Sámi language, for increasing the competence among teachers who teach in and on the Sámi language, and for developing teaching aids for Sámi education.

Second, the *fylkesmannen* (chief state-level representative at the county level) in Nordland, Troms, and Finnmark is also important and has the advisory and control functions toward the municipalities and counties that manage and run the schools. The fylkesmann's role is to make sure that Sámi people's right to education in their language is kept. The fylkesmann also administers the economic support systems for teaching in the Sámi language in the municipalities of their counties.

Third, municipalities and counties own the school, and as such they are responsible to see to it that the education is in accordance with laws and regulations, including the Sámi National Curriculum. The school owners also are responsible for developing local curriculum, where appropriate, as a frame for individual schools' educational plans (Nygaard and Kramvig 2009). The schools themselves must then evaluate which kind of organization and which teaching methods are the best fit for realizing the teaching plans for individual Sámi students (ibid.).

Transnational Connections: Shared Experience and Shared Challenges

From Assimilation to Self-Determination

The histories of Indigenous education in the United States and Norway are different in many respects but comparable in other ways. Obviously, the definition of Indigenous education has changed over time in both countries, as local and global political influences intersect gradually to pressure for national and international agreements on promoting and protecting Indigenous rights. The shared trajectory started with assimilation, which defined Indigenous education in the two nations until the twentieth century. The first schools set up for American Indian and Sámi children were intended by missionaries primarily to "civilize" and assimilate the target Indigenous populations (Spring 2007, 24–25). Boarding schools in both countries operated to deculturalize Native children and disintegrate Indigenous communities. Historically, as told by Native American authors, European American educators attempted to eliminate Native Americans' "Indianness," so as to assimilate the Native population into the newly established dominant White culture and the value system of a Christian, European American society (Reynolds 2005, 48). The goals of public education for American Indians were "to transform Indian people and societies and to eradicate Indian self-government, self-determination, and self-education" (Lomawaima 1999, 5; Tippeconnic 1999, 43). In Norway Sámi people experienced similar forms of assimilative public education. In a special issue of the *Journal of Indigenous Peoples Rights* on Sámi self-determination,

Henriksen (2009, 22) reports that "there was broad agreement that the national school system [in Norway] has by and large contributed to colonizing the Sámi's way of thinking."

One of the stated main goals of assimilative education for Indigenous populations was national unity in the United States and Norway.[5] Indigenous languages and cultures, along with other minority heritages, were considered a threat to solidarity in both countries throughout history. In Norway politicians maintained that cultural and linguistic homogeneity were required to resist external political threat. In the United States politicians argued that cultural and linguistic homogeneity was a basic ingredient of nationalism. A reversal of such mentality has recently started to emerge in both national contexts. Seeing homogeneity as the ideal has gradually begun to be replaced by recognition of the value of cultural diversity, while multicultural policies are slowly gaining support in wider spectrums of both societies. The national trends in both national contexts are at least steering away from a blatant deficit-assimilation approach of destroying languages and cultures toward a more amiable position of tolerance and acceptance (Tippeconnic 2000).

In both countries, national affirmation of the Indigenous right to self-determination played a key role in changing the nature of Indigenous education. In the United States over the past few decades, a number of national policies supported American Indian tribes' autonomy in administering schools for Indian students and educating the young in their heritage languages and cultures (Swisher and Tippeconnic 1999, 70). In Norway the establishment of the Sámi Parliament positively influenced the progress of the Sámi School as defined by a national Sámi curriculum (Hirvonen 2008, 18, 21). In the 1990s the U.S. and Norwegian governments passed legislation to support the use of Indigenous language as the vehicle for educating Indigenous students. At present, Aikio-Puoskari (2009, 241) posits, "the most important issues are the right to self-determination in education and the potential of reviving the language and culture with the help of the school." The resulting Sámi National Curriculum parallels the culturally responsible education model promoted for education of American Indian youths. Over the past decade or so advocates of Indigenous education in both countries have focused not only on language preservation, but also on the content of instruction and on "the position of Native culture in education" (Aikio-Puoskari 2009, 241; Starnes 2006). Despite the shared experience, scholars and educators in the United States and Norway can find inspiration through this transnational connection. The transformation of Indigenous education in Norway has been propelled by an advocacy for equal rights, while in the United States the foundation of progress has built upon a respect for tribal sovereignty.

Marginalization of Indigenous Education

While education of Sámi and American Indian and Alaska Native youths is becoming less driven by assimilation policies, schools serving mixed populations are becoming increasingly inclusive of Indigenous languages and cultures. Yet Indigenous education remains in the margin first in the field of education nationally and, second, in mainstream schools serving mixed student populations, including Indigenous students in both countries. In the United States, for example, Indigenous education is a rare subject of discussion at national educational conferences except at meetings with specific focus on American Indian education. A search through the Education Resources Information Center database, the most extensive database of educational-related literature in the United States with over one million records, produced only about forty articles published in peer-reviewed journals (except for journals with a specific focus on American Indian education) between 1990 and 2011, that directly address issues related to Indigenous education. It appears that the education of Indigenous youth and the education of all students about Indigenous history, culture, and perspectives are not priorities for mainstream policy makers and educators.

Tippeconnic observes that over the years the U.S. government has paid adequate lip service to the importance of Indigenous education, but in reality Indigenous education has not received much attention at the national, state, and local levels. What is left out of the discussion and established parameters of citizenship education is the issue of tribal nationhood and the dual citizenship that Native Americans carry. Writer (2010, 71) points out, "if schools' citizenship education does not address the historical and contemporary context of Native American citizenship, then this is evidence of ongoing colonization and the practice of cultural imperialism." In other words, the destructive effects of colonizing educational policies and practices require conscientious attention to the special status of Native American tribes as sovereign nations and Indigenous peoples' rights to culturally relevant education.

Indigenous education is commonly treated by U.S. educational leaders as a remedy for previously ethnocentric curricula and culturally insensitive delivery to Indigenous populations, rather than as high-quality education that incorporates Indigenous perspectives, values, and methodologies. A majority of the research studies and publications about Indigenous education primarily concern practices in reservation schools and tribally operated schools (Freng, Frend, and Moore 2007, 53), even though nowadays more than 90 percent of all American Indian students nationwide attend mainstream schools side-by-side with non-Indian students (Oakes and Maday 2009, 2). Advocacy for improved Indigenous education in schools seldom expands beyond "saving the failing Indian child." Furthermore, in the U.S. educational system, minimal curricular attention is paid to Indigenous peoples' histories and contributions. To date, Native American history is mostly restricted to college courses (Writer 2010). Only recently have Native American issues appeared in some states' K–12 curriculum (McCoy 2005). When references related to Native Americans are included in commercial textbooks and history classes used in mainstream schools, they are often presented from the Eurocentric perspective (Huff 1997; Loewen 1995; Skinner 1999). The history taught in schools and transmitted in public forums still serves to deny the experiences and silence the perspectives of Native Americans (Writer 2010, 75). For instance, social studies, as a core subject in U.S. schools, often blatantly "excludes the history of a race existing an estimated forty thousand years on this continent. Excluded also are the accomplishments of Indians that built cities, codified laws, produced 48 percent of the world's crops, built seaworthy boats, mapped out roads and trade routes, practiced medicine, and invented tools still used today" (Huff 1997, xx). Many public schools around the country continue to omit educating students about the meanings of tribal sovereignty and the legitimacy of Native Americans' special status in relations to state and national governments. Thus, Native Americans continue to suffer prejudice springing from lack of understanding, for example, about certain compensations promised by intergovernmental treaty agreements.[6]

One of the differences between the U.S. and the Norwegian context is that Indigenous tribes in the United States are sovereign nations, while Sámi people do not have the same status in Norway. In a special issue of the *Journal of Indigenous Peoples Rights* on Sámi self-determination, John Henriksen (2009, 7) reports that "for a long time . . . key Sámi politicians have sought to nuance the debate on Sámi self-determination, not least by emphasising that the need for recognition of the Sámi people's right to self-determination is not related to a desire to secede from existing nation states."

In the Norwegian context, according to Henriksen (2008, 34), "neither state authorities nor the Sámi parliaments have given priority to the question of greater Sámi self-determination in the education and schools sector." Limited information and teaching materials on Sámi children's rights are available. There is a lack of knowledge among teachers and school administrators on Sámi children's rights (Henriksen 2009). Moreover, Sámi education "must always be adapted to and adjusted in respect of national educational plans and framework conditions. . . . Weak financial parameters place limits on the development of a separate Sámi school system" (Henriksen 2009, 25). Regardless of the backgrounds of student populations, the local educational norm is always based on national teaching plans. Education provided for children in Sámi communities or education of Sámi students in schools with mixed populations must always adapt to the National Curriculum plans (Henriksen 2008, 34). This standardized approach undercuts the spirit of Indigenous education aiming to educate students in and through their heritage languages and cultures. Access to education adjusted to one's Sámi background is only possible in certain geographical areas, particularly in the core Sámi areas of Finnmark and the northern part of Troms County. According to Solstad (2009), access to Sámi education becomes weaker the further away one lives from the traditional Sámi core areas.

A large percentage of the Sámi population in Norway lives outside the core Sámi areas in the northern part, as well as other parts of the country, such as in the capital city, Oslo. Much of the teaching in Sámi language outside of the Sámi municipalities is done through distance teaching in primary and secondary education. Despite the existence of the Sámi National Curriculum, Sámi-speaking students are not receiving the same level of support in their local communities to learn the Sámi language as Norwegian-speaking students receive in relation to their culture and language (Helander 2004; Magga 2004). Helander (2004) also points out that there is a lack of effort among educators to help students understand why it is useful to employ the Sámi language in one's day-to-day life.

The U.S. and Norwegian Native population demographic patterns in relation to the extent of Indigenous education implementation are parallel in significant ways (see also statistics reported above in the section The United States and American Indian Experience). While most Native people live outside of Indian reservations or Sámi core areas, Indigenous education in the form of culturally relevant curricula is more accessible on reservations or in core areas. For instance, in state of Montana (where Ngai resides) more Native people live on reservations than in other parts of the United States. Here, Indian students can access, for example, Indigenous language courses in public schools on reservations but not beyond.[7] Tribally and privately funded Native language immersion programs exist only on reservations but not outside (Ngai 2012). Although there are more opportunities for learning Native languages and cultures on reservations, the public school curricula in these locations remain determined by state and national educational plans and standards. As in Norway, the standardized approach mandated by the U.S. government (see the No Child Left Behind Act, 10) has left little room for culturally relevant instruction for Indian students even on reservations.

In the United States and Norway, Indigenous education is marginalized in mainstream schools; in other words, even culturally responsive approaches and the Sámi National Curriculum implemented with good intentions continue to be subsumed under the larger national cultural framework. Educators continue to rely on and advocate for the one-size-fits-all model (Brayboy and Castagno 2009, 31) in both countries. Another key reason for marginalization is the lack of an appealing pedagogical framework for guiding teachers to integrate Indigenous education meaningfully for all students (Native and non-Native). Given the small percentage of Native students in most mainstream schools and the demands of standardized testing, Indigenous cultures, histories, languages, and contemporary issues easily fall by the wayside. Indigenous education needs to operate as an essential component of mainstream curricula in order to receive moral and practical support in the school system. If educators perceive Indigenous education as complementary to core subject curricula and as valuable education for all students (Native and non-Native) they would be willing to invest time, energy, and resources to integrate Indigenous education into classroom learning within and outside of Indian reservations and Sámi Administrative Areas. Only when all citizens are educated about Native histories, perspectives, and issues will stereotypes and maltreatments by dominant powers that continue to traumatize Native people be replaced by healing, equity, and mutual respect.

Perpetuation of Stereotypes About Indigenous People

Marginalization of Indigenous education left unchecked the wide spread of stereotypes about Indigenous people in both societies. Historically, Norway's social Darwinism justified educational efforts that built upon the stereotypes of Indigenous people as "uncivilized." A similar misperception was normalized and popularized through symbols, print materials, and media images for generations in U.S. society (Huff 1997). In *To Live Heroically: Institutional Racism and American Indian Education*, Delores Huff (Cherokee) points out that before the "enlightenment" (pre-1980s) textbooks referred to Native Americans "as savages, beasts to be exterminated, pagans, and uncivilized" (Huff 1997, xx). Today's fictional films, advertising, newspapers, music, and product images continue "to dehumanize and silence American Indians . . . [which] gives voice to the dominant culture" (Miller and Ross 2004, 255). When the mainstream media perpetuate stereotypes of Native people, it serves to maintain the power imbalance that privileges the dominate group, uphold the superiority claim of the oppressor, and deepen internalized colonization experienced by the oppressed. The image of the buckskins, beads, and feathers identified with Indians of the early nineteenth century remains in the media (Sanchez 2003). Indigenous peoples on the American continent are "depicted as historic artifacts, or are represented in children's stories as if the modern Indian does not exist" (Huff 1997). The pervasive stereotypes of American Indians vary "over time and place from the 'artificially idealistic' (noble savage) to present-day images of 'mystical environmentalists' or uneducated, alcoholic bingo-players confined to reservations" (Mihesuah 1996, 9). Students are still taught that "Columbus 'discovered' America and Indian peoples, that the Sioux were primitive nomads who could not assimilate even with the assistance of the United States government, and that conditions of poverty are not a social cumulative inequality, but are an indication that Indians cannot take care of themselves" (Fenelon and LeBeau 2006, 26). Generations of Native children have gone through school "confused and fragmented." Beneath these insulting images are "hidden and mixed messages" that "tear away at the fiber of their self-esteem" (Huff 1997, xx). The prevailing stereotypes also impact how non-Indians relate to Indian people and how Indian people relate to one another.

Similarly, Sámi people have been represented as the "Other" in relation to Norwegians for centuries. The stereotypical images may have included positive and negative connotations, but the coding of the Sámi people as different from Norwegians has been more or less constant over the years. Images of Sámi people as naïve and underdeveloped, with their closeness to nature interpreted and characterized as primitive, have been widespread in literature and visual representations. The negative stereotypes about Sámi people existed in what was the most authoritative and official texts describing the Norwegian reality in the eighteenth and nineteenth centuries (Mathisen 2001, 88). In many respects, texts and educators portrayed the Sámi people as opponents to civilization, health, and Christianity, since the modern "civilized" life has been defined by those who had and have the power to produce the official narratives (Mathisen 2001). One of the officially declared aims of the assimilation policy was to "bring them

[Sámi people] forward to maturity (mands modenhet)—if it is possible. This is a lasting goal of education" (Lund 2003, 17).

Today, stereotypes about Sámi people, as is true also of stereotypes about other Indigenous peoples, are pursued in a great variety of narratives through myths, historical documents, visual and verbal representations, and written texts. Common to all such representations is the existence of a cognitive division between the modern, rational world and the less rational, wilder, and sometimes even degenerated world of otherness. This can be termed as a temporization of culture and ethnicity, including primitivism and evolutionism, where the difference lies in the positive versus the negative evaluation (Friedman 1996; Paulgaard 2009). Even though representations of Sámi life and culture are perceived as "positive" connections, as in the representation of "the noble savage" within tourism, the core contrast between the primitive and the civilized prevails.

When repeated often enough, stereotypes begin to represent a "reality of images" (Eder 2006), playing an influential role in the narrative construction of reality. To help reverse the trend, educators need to integrate accurate, constructive, and inspiring materials about Indigenous people into mainstream education.

Indigenous Education as Multicultural Education for All in U.S. and Norwegian Classrooms

According to UNDRIP, an Indigenous education in the twenty-first century needs to be culturally relevant education for Indigenous youths alongside a multicultural education that informs the non-Native students about Indigenous history, culture, people, and their perspectives on contemporary issues. To end marginalization, one possible approach is to integrate Indigenous education into mainstream education. Above and beyond mere rhetoric, we envision genuine integration that includes Indigenous perspectives along with the perspectives of the majority and minority groups in a culturally plural society. The multicultural education model proposed by James A. Banks (2002), a widely respected U.S. scholar in the field of education, offers inspiration. Under this model, educators first need to discard the idea that Indigenous education is an "add-on" and reject the "cultural additive" approach. Through this approach, teachers would merely add contents about diverse cultural groups to the curriculum without changing its basic structure and would emphasize the mastery of low-level facts about Native peoples. Instead, we advocate the transformative multicultural approach through which students study historical, social, artistic, and literary events and concepts from multiple, local and international ethnic and cultural perspectives (Banks 2002). Mainstream perspectives and Indigenous perspectives are among those to be investigated on the basis that they are equally valid and valuable for educational purposes. This approach "differs fundamentally from the additive approach. It changes the canon, paradigms, and basic assumptions of the curriculum" (Banks 2002, 31). Major goals of this approach are as follows:

1. To help students to understand knowledge as a social construction;
2. To listen to the voices of the dominant groups and of the oppressed;
3. To analyze one's perspective in contrast to another on events and situations;
4. To think critically; and ultimately
5. To take personal, social, and civic actions related to the concepts, problems, and issues studied (Banks 2002).

To bring about change in attitudes toward Indigenous people in society, we envision that Indigenous education operates as a form of transformative multicultural education for all students (regardless of ethnic background). Its implementation would be based on the principles of critical pedagogy that aims to bring about sustainable development of genuinely democratic societies. Henry Giroux's explanation of critical pedagogy helps us visualize how integration of Indigenous education into mainstream education can transpire.

> Critical pedagogy must address the challenge of providing students with the competencies they need to cultivate the capacity for critical judgment, to thoughtfully connect politics to social responsibility and expand their own sense of agency in order to curb the excesses of dominant power, to revitalize a sense of public commitment, and to expand democratic relations. Animated by a spirit of critique and possibility, critical pedagogy at its best attempts to provoke students to deliberate, resist, and cultivate a range of capacities that enable them to move beyond the world they already know without insisting on a fixed set of meanings. (2001, 20)

In other words, Indigenous education should encourage all learners to "contest the dominant views of democracy" (Griroux 2001, 21) and to articulate a genuine democracy that is free from the shackle of "Western, linear political framework" (Grande 2004, 34). It should motivate teachers, students, schools, and communities to contribute to "increased social justice, equality, and improvement in the quality of life for all constituencies with the larger society" (Grande 2004, 34). Sandy Grande, author of *Red Pedagogy*, distinguishes Indigenization from democratization. The former is about enfranchisement and the latter is about sovereignty (Grande 2004). In our view both are viable concepts for comparative analysis in Indigenous education when implemented as transformative multicultural education for all.

In recent years discussions about Indigenous education have expanded to include the significance of educating all citizens about Indigenous issues, cultures, and histories. For instance, in *Next Steps Research and Practice to Advance Indian Education*, the first text for college classrooms about American Indian education written entirely by Native people, Linda Skinner (Choctaw) maintains that "Indian education should come to mean not just the education of Indians, but also education about Indians" (Skinner 1999, 120). Eleven out of the fifty states in the union have passed legislation mandating instruction in tribal culture, history, and/or government to all students in K–12 public schools. The state of Montana is at the forefront of integrating Indigenous education into mainstream education. In 1999 the Montana Legislature passed state law MCA 20–1–501, known as Indian Education For All (IEFA). The law requires that public schools implement programs to fulfill the inclusive Indian education intent found in Mont. Const. of 1972 art. X, § 1(2), which stipulates that the state "recognizes the distinct and unique cultural heritage of the American Indians and is committed in its educational goals to the preservation of their cultural heritage." Likewise, in the Norwegian context, one of the main goals of the Sámi National Curriculum is "that every student [regardless of ethnic background] in the Sámi area should learn about Sámi culture" (Hirvonen 2008, 29). The current generation of policy makers and educators in both countries understand that the general public's ignorance of the lives of Indigenous people directly and indirectly hurts current generations of Indigenous youths.

In the U.S. context, the Education Committee of the National Caucus of Native American State Legislators recommends (1) teaching Native customs, history, and legal obligations to all students (Native and non-Native) and (2) providing professional development to instill cultural sensitivity for teachers and administrators (NCNASL 2008). Without rejecting the role mainstream schools can play in Indigenous education, Grande (2004, 19) reminds us that Indigenous education would be constructive only if it is

accompanied by social change. She cautions that "unless educational reform happens concurrently with analyses of the forces of colonialism, it can
only serve as a deeply insufficient (if not negligent) Band-Aid over the in-
cessant wounds of imperialism." For instance, in the 1960s Mexican
American students throughout the Southwest United States were able to
convince public schools to provide culturally relevant pedagogical and curriculum support through Mexican American studies courses. Unexpectedly,
in January 2011, the state of Arizona outlawed Tucson's Mexican-
American studies program based on the false belief that ethnic studies
programs are anti-white and hence serve to divide the nation. A year later,
state government officials confiscated books used in those programs, including several key texts used in Native American Studies, such as *Pedagogy of
the Oppressed* by Paulo Freire and *Rethinking Columbus: The Next 500 Years*
by Bill Bigelow, under the perverted assumption that books challenging
dominant viewpoints promote "ethnic resentment" (Rothberg 2012). This
case illustrates that, without equal status based on citizens' and policy
makers' full acceptance of diversity, education of and about minority perspectives can be short lived and is subject to local political changes, such as
state legislation. With such realization, we maintain that social transformation will most likely occur through education of future generations. We
place our hopes in the young. Indigenous education can be a constructive
vehicle for social change; however, it will not survive and thrive without
legal backing. What is absent in the U.S. context but present in the Norwegian context is the legal protection that Indigenous education enjoys at
the national level.

The Norwegian state has been founded on the geographic territory of
diverse ethnic groups, and this fact has consequences for education in Norway. All students shall, through their compulsory education, gain insight
into and knowledge about the Norwegian and the Sámi. Knowledge about
the Sámi culture, therefore, is implemented as a part of the general National Curriculum that serves as a guideline for all schools in Norway. The
general part of the National Curriculum states that "Sámi language and
culture is a part of the common heritage which Norway has a special responsibility for protecting." Section 6.4 in Norway's Education Act instructs
schools to "teach about the Sámi population and their language, culture,
and societal life in relation to the different subject areas in schools. Within
frames decided by the Ministry of Education, the Sámi Parliament provides
regulations when it comes to the contents of such teaching. For example,
the Sámi Parliament seeks to ensure that Sámi issues are emphasized in
the National Curriculum and its competence goals. The Sámi Parliament

also has had a leading role in developing the contents of the Sámi National Curriculum. Through compulsory education, all students in Norway are to receive knowledge about and insight into Sámi history, culture, and societal life.

In order for integration of Indigenous education to take root locally and nationally, new pedagogical approaches that guide teacher preparation, curriculum development, and classroom implementation are urgently needed (Aikio-Puoskari 2009, 255; Juneau and Broaddus 2006). In this part of the chapter, we explore several pedagogical ideas that help conceptualize Indigenous education as an integral part of mainstream education for all students regardless of ethnic background. From our perspective, Indigenous education can be an enhancing component of high-quality basic education for all in the United States and Norway, because it advances transnational citizenship education, transformative social justice education, education for critical democracy, and place-based education for sustainable development.

Indigenous Education as Citizenship Education

Citizenship and citizenship education are notions that merit renewed scrutiny at a time when support for assimilation declines and respect for self-determination rises in both local and global contexts. Norwegian and U.S. educators are called, either by a critical consciousness or the changing social and political atmosphere, to reconsider the goals of citizenship education, as the melting-pot ideology is yielding to an appreciation for synergy in recent years. As citizenship education involves inclusion and understanding of the historical and political contexts of all citizens, its teachers are responsible for helping students understand the complexity of both nations' "politically situated past and present relationships with and obligations to" Indigenous people (Dewey 1938; Writer 2010, 70) and for including interethnic relationship building into the educational process. Such "inclusive, transformative citizenship education" can be realized through collaboration among teachers, school administrators, policy makers, and Indigenous community leaders who are committed to incorporating Indigenous histories and perspectives in school teaching and learning (Writer 2010, 77). If educators and policy makers are to live up to the spirit of UNDRIP, Indigenous education must become part of the mainstream citizenship education. Specifically, it must nurture in the young a deep sense of respect and appreciation for diverse perspectives and fluid identities that allows one to feel grounded in multiple sociocultural contexts. The current generations live in the midst of frequent intercultural and transnational exchanges and interflows. The line between whites and Indians, for instance, is blurred by multicultural learning, living, and working conditions that are becoming increasingly commonplace. Today's students need to develop the abilities to move back and forth and to function effectively within and across different identities and associations (de Courtivron 2000).

The current literature about citizenship education has begun to include issues related to globalization in connection with local and national affiliations. For instance, Banks has refined his vision of citizenship education over the years to include a global perspective. Recently, he called for educational support for students "to attain clarified and reflective cultural, national, regional, and global identifications and understand how these identities are interrelated and constructed" (Banks 2008, 135). This educational objective reflects the reality of an increasingly interconnected, interdependent world, in which the local or the Indigenous is not only locally or nationally defined but also involved in global ethnopolitical matters and discourses. Thus, Indigenous education fits naturally into citizenship education that aims to nurture in students a critical consciousness of the locally/ globally intertwined human conditions and a sense of responsibility for collaborating across historical, sociocultural, and national boundaries on solving problems of local/global significance. Such issues include, but are not limited to, global warming and climate change, diminishing biocultural diversity, threatened food and water security, lack of health equity, environmental injustice, and perpetual racism (Ngai and Koehn 2011). Indigenous peoples, along with other victims of colonization, have been suffering physically and psychologically from most (if not all) of these consequences of ill-perceived superiority for too long.

Indigenous Education as Social Justice Education

Pedagogical approaches that aim to lay the foundation for critical democracy are closely related to Indigenous education. Critical democracy involves more than respect for "a benignly neutral diversity that 'celebrates' cultural differences" (Lomawaima and McCarty 2006, 281). It requires minds that are able first to discern and manage complexity (Noguera and Cohen 2006, 574–75); second, to perceive connections among inequities across place and time; third, to grow from the strengths uncovered in the unique components of the diversity in one's midst; fourth, to imagine different ways of being (Quin 2009, 118); fifth, to entertain seriously perspectives that differ from " 'the powers that be' " (Merryfield 2001, 254); and last, to become conscious and accepting of individual and social responsibility for actions that can bring about justice in our communities and the larger society (Freire 1970). Indigenous education aimed at educating all students about the histories, experiences, and perspectives of Indigenous peoples embodies all of these educational objectives (Ngai and Koehn 2010a).

To take the vision of transformative Indigenous education one step farther is to connect it to social justice education, which promotes social action based on an understanding of critical democracy (Carlisle, Jackson, and George 2006; Grande 2004, 28). The principles of social justice education apply logically and effectively to Indigenous education. Social justice education guides students to work toward enhancing equity across multiple social identity groups, including Indigenous groups. Consistent with Indigenous education, social justice education sets to accomplish the following steps:

1. To encourage all students to participate in knowledge construction;
2. To acknowledge, value, and build upon students' existing knowledge, interests, cultural, and linguistic resources;
3. To work in reciprocal partnership with students' families and communities;
4. To teach explicitly about activism, power, and inequity in schools and society (Dover 2009, 509); and
5. To recognize and validate the cultural identities of students (Banks 2008, 135).

In the United States and Norway, Indigenous people survived hundreds of years of coercive assimilation and are striving to retain their own cultures and historical identities in the face of cultural domination in the education system and globalization. Through education for social justice, educators can address these issues to produce a truthful curriculum about the makeup of the culturally plural societies and the disparity experienced by different peoples in both countries. Teachers can integrate Indigenous education into the social justice-education curriculum through Indigenous history, cultural understanding, Indigenous worldview, actual analysis of contemporary social structures, and awareness of social justice struggles. When analytic and emotional competencies translate into reflective social action, Indigenous education has lived up to the spirit of critical democracy (Pittman 2009).

Indigenous Education for Sustainable Development

Indigenous education also can be an effective form of education for sustainable development (or vice versa) when implemented as place-based or place-conscious education. Education for sustainable development integrates the social, environmental, economic, and cultural dimensions of development and generates awareness of our interdependence. Indigenous perspectives can enrich discussions concerning sustainable development issues, such as environmental protection and biodiversity, as Indigenous values and knowledges "contribute to the necessary requisite variety needed for diversity" (Bhawuk 2008, 306).

Further, education for sustainable development promotes Indigenous values, such as peace and respect for others and for the wider natural and social environment (UNESCO 2014) through contextualized and experiential learning in and about the place where students reside and claim stewardship. A place-based pedagogical approach prompts students to reach beyond the classroom to experience the place and connect face-to-face with people who possess different backgrounds. By interacting with local Indigenous communities and learning about the places taken care of by Natives for thousands of years, students experience a new, inspiring worldview with the potential to transform their attitudes and empower their conscious and unconscious actions toward harmonious living (Quin 2009, 117). For instance, when students study selected local tribal perspective(s) in the United States or the Sámi perspective in Norway, along with additional cultural perspective(s), they learn to appreciate the wisdom in different worldviews, alternative solutions to shared problems, the power of synergy, and unity within diversity (Ngai and Koehn 2010b). Such learning transformations lay the foundation for further education that equips students to make ethical decisions on important global and local issues.

Conclusion

Throughout history, the meanings and implications of Indigenous education have been carried by the ebbs and flows of national and international politics. While backward movements emerged from time to time locally and globally, UNDRIP, endorsed by all UN members within the first decade, promises to propel Indigenous education forward through the rest of this century. The international agreement reiterates the importance of culturally relevant education for Indigenous youths; it also calls for promoting intercultural understanding for facilitating development of positive Native/non-Native relationships. In this chapter we have shown that the definition of Indigenous education has changed over time in the United States and Norway. Indigenous education has evolved from being a limited tool of assimilation to a potentially transformative, educational, nurturing ground where respect for diversity and social justice can flourish. Toward the end of this chapter, we suggested some pedagogical approaches that might contribute to further progress through moving Indigenous education out of its long-time marginalization to the central stage of mainstream education.

Today most Indigenous students learn side-by-side with their non-Native classmates. While a majority of American Indians attend public schools outside of a homogenous Indian reservation setting, an increasing number of Sámi live outside of the Sámi Administrative Areas (Huss 2008). This demographical trend calls for more expansive pedagogical approaches to Indigenous education. We propose implementing Indigenous education as part of mainstream citizenship education, social justice education, and education for sustainable development. The suggested integrated pedagogy promises to expand Indigenous education to benefit all students regardless of heritage background (Natives and non-Natives) in the contemporary interconnected reality.

The extent to which mainstreaming Indigenous education will succeed in bringing about positive attitudes toward Indigenous peoples and their rightful place in society depends on the effectiveness of implementation. For instance, Ngai's research on a pilot IEFA program that aimed to integrate Indigenous perspectives into mainstream classroom learning in an elementary school in Montana indicates that certain instructional strategies are effective in facilitating the development of positive attitudes toward interacting with American Indians. This outcome carries the potential to improve future interracial relationships among Indians and non-Indians, but some teaching approaches fail to improve students' attitudes (Ngai and Koehn, 2010a).[8] Therefore, careful design of lessons and thoughtful implementation of learning activities are imperative for fulfilling the potential benefits of the proposed pedagogical shift concerning Indigenous education.

For Native students, integrating Indigenous education into mainstream education is a powerful way of celebrating Indigenous identity and heritage. Such curricular integration can serve the purposes of culturally responsive education and enhance students' efficacy beyond their immediate ethnic communities and cultures. There is growing research providing evidence of the effectiveness of the culturally responsive model in improving academic success among American Indian and Sámi children (Evjen 2004; Freng, Frend, and Moore 2007, 53; Gay 2000; Jensen 2005; Ladson-Billings 1995; Pewewardy 1994). Using culturally responsive approaches in mainstream classrooms affirms rather than denies the cultures students bring to school. Such pedagogy taps students' cultural strength instead of focusing on deficits. It serves to foster a climate in which students are capable of "maximizing their cultural identity in order to gain confidence to learn and succeed in the mainstream educational setting" (Hirvonen 2008, 22; Brayboy and Castagno 2009). It promises to create in Native students a sense of belonging in school (Huffman 2010, 171). It can serve to replace malignant stereotypes about Indigenous people and the history of poisoned interracial relationships with positive interracial relations and respect for diversity in schools. In this way it can improve the mental health of Native youth (Pewewardy 1998; Pewewardy and Fitzpatrick 2009).

Traditionally, teaching and learning about heritage cultures and values occurred within extended families. Although the traditional intergenerational transmission of Indigenous knowledge can be simulated in respected elders' private living rooms or tribal and Sámi schools in Native-dominated regions, these secluded settings are luxuries for only a handful. To fulfill the goal of vitalizing Indigenous knowledges and identities, a place where most children are involved in learning is needed. Mainstream classrooms can be the place. Experienced Indigenous education pioneers, such as Joyce Silverthorne (1997) of the Salish Tribe, point out that collaboration among the whole community (including non-Native members) is needed to reverse the trend. The survival of Indigenous knowledges and the nurturing of Native youths should not and cannot be shouldered by mainstream school systems alone. Hualapai educator Lucille Watahomigie (1998, 7) maintains that "schools can build on the knowledge of the home and bring informal, family- and community-based language [and cultural] experiences to the process of formal learning." Teresa McCarty (2008, 175), long-time American Indian education advocate, points out that public schools "in tandem with other social institutions . . . can be a strategic resource for exerting Indigenous language and education rights."

Moreover, the integrated pedagogy proposed in this chapter aligns with the goals of "socioculturally responsive education" advocated by Lee and

Cerecer (2010, 200), as it recognizes "how Native youths' lives are not solely defined by their Native culture, but are also inclusive of social influences, such as the mainstream media, family income and occupations, tribal economic development, off-reservation residence, and peer influences." Genuine cultural inclusion necessary for the academic success of Indian students, for instance, involves not only drawing from Indigenous worldviews but, at the same time, providing an "enriched curriculum that promotes students' abilities to move freely between the tribal cultures and other American cultures and to contribute to the society in which they live" (Freng, Frend, and Moore 2007, 53). Along the same vein, the Sámi National Curriculum aims to "bring the cultural heritage to life, motivate students to make use of the local culture, and provide children and young people with the desire to become active and innovative in both Sámi and Norwegian societies" (KUF 1998, 816, quoted in Hirvonen 2008, 21). The proposed integrated pedagogy aims to support Native students to grow from being bicultural to becoming transcultural. Being transcultural, students need not forgo any parts of themselves. Integrating Indigenous education into mainstream education would be a step forward from the traditional culturally responsive approach. In the confluence of cultures in culturally plural societies of an interconnected world, education for Native youths means more than resisting assimilation and keeping traditional cultures and languages alive. It also is about helping Native youths to become comfortable and successful in their Indigenous communities and the mainstream society. Inupiaq scholar Leona Okakok reiterates that "educating a child means equipping him or her with the capability to succeed in the world he or she will live" (1989, 253 quoted in Brayboy and Castagno 2009, 34). Their world today spans beyond isolated Indian reservations or Sámi core areas. Their identities (individual and collective) stretch from the past to the present and from local to global. Thus, Indigenous education aiming to nurture Native youths needs to involve more than preservation and restoration. Education in the mainstream setting, as the theme statement of the 2008 World's Indigenous People's Conference on Education posits, "provides us [Indigenous people] with a broad set of options to shape our own futures and with tools to tell our own stories to the wider community; our challenge is to balance the learning from formal systems within our own traditions." Recognizing that centralizing Indigenous education in public school systems is not and cannot be the only movement contributing to the thriving of Indigenous peoples, we believe that such demarginalization is a step toward decolonization, promising to bring about social change through educating the young (Native and non-Native) about the value of Indigenous knowledges, the oppressive conditions faced by Indigenous peoples, and "Indigenous peoples' rights to dignity and diversity of their cultures, traditions, histories, and aspirations" (UN 2007).

For the non-Native students, integrating Indigenous education into mainstream education exerts an equally transforming impact. The U.S. historian J. W. Loewen, author of *Lies That Teachers Told Me: Everything Your American History Textbook Got Wrong*, asserts that "learning about marginalized perspectives of the minority in society and the first people of the country can change how non-Natives view history and how the majority project themselves into the future as citizens and conscientious individuals" (Loewen 1995, 301). Indigenous education incorporating teaching about national and transnational citizenship, social justice, critical democracy, and sustainable development would serve to nurture in all students *analytic, functional, communicative, emotional,* and *creative* competencies that are vital for peaceful, meaningful living locally and globally (Koehn and Rosenau 2010).[9] After all, effective, sustainable Indigenous education contributes to the well-being of all lives on earth because, according to Luisa Maffi (2007, 56), there is an "intimate link between cultural and linguistic identity, worldviews, and knowledge systems, on the one hand, and on the other, the lands and territories they occupy and from which they drive material and non-material sustenance." To illustrate, Oviedo and Maffi (2000) report that 4,635 (about 67 percent) of the world's ethnolinguistic groups overlap with 225 ecoregions, which are reservoirs of high biodiversity.[10] Thus, thriving Indigeneity means a thriving bio- and ethnosphere.

We agree that efforts to enhance Indigenous education in the twenty-first century should align "not only with educational change and the adoption of a curriculum, but also with much wider issues—the social and political changes that concern the meeting of different cultures" (Hirvonen 2008, 22). The proposed integrated pedagogy promises to break through the persistent marginalization and isolation and to broaden and deepen the impacts of Indigenous education. What does it take for such transformation to occur? While further research is needed to answer remaining questions, such as whose knowledge is actually chosen to be transmitted through Indigenous education (Huss 2008, 131) and what Indigenous knowledge is today, hope shines through the emerging academic and political discourse that explicates a desire to collaborate among Natives and non-Natives locally, nationally, and internationally.

Notes

1. In this chapter, we use the terms *American Indians, Indians, Native Americans,* or *Natives* interchangeably to refer to Indigenous people in the United States.

2. The complication of serving American Indian students in education involves answering the question of who an American Indian is. According to Jack Utter (1993, 11–12),

> for U.S. census purposes . . . an Indian is anyone who declares himself or herself to be one. Thus, the concept of Indian as used by Bureau of the Census does not denote scientific or biological definition but, rather, is an indication of the race with which a person identifies. Tribal groups, themselves, have differing criteria for who is an Indian of their tribe. . . . Many federal laws and regulations define 'Indian,' and these various definitions take on great significance when they control the distribution of funds and services or regulate the application of civil and criminal law.

Students who choose not to identify themselves as Indians or who cannot be identified as Indians would likely be treated by school administrators as non-Indians. However, the culturally responsive education model calls for pedagogies that include students' own cultures and languages in classroom teaching and learning. In other words, self-identification overrides any legal or tribal definitions in the context of culturally responsive education.

3. The term "Natives" is used interchangeably with the term "Indigenous people" in the U.S. and the Norwegian contexts. The term "non-Natives" is used to refer to citizens who are not of Indigenous descent in both the U.S. and Norwegian contexts.

4. Municipalities where the Sámi language has the same status as the Norwegian language as an official language.

5. The "melting pot" ideology, which idealized assimilating all ethnicities and cultures into one, had shaped public policies since the mid-nineteenth century through the twentieth century (see Sollars 1987). In a section entitled "Allotment and Assimilation" in *A Different Mirror*, Ronald Takaki reports that

> to advance and civilize the Indians, the white reformers argued, the tribal system had to be destroyed, for it was perpetuating "habits and nomadic barbarism" and "savagery." . . . The key to civilizing Indians was to convert them into individual landowners. . . . [The white reformers declared that] allotment was designed to make them [Indians] more independent and self-reliant. . . . "The aggressive and enterprising Anglo-Saxons" would set up their farms "side by side" with Indian farms, and "in a little while contact alone" would lead Indians to emulate the work ethic of their white neighbors. . . . There will be a school-house built, with Indian children and white children together. . . . They will readily learn the tongue of the white race. . . . They will readily learn the ways of civilization. . . . This conversion of Indians into individual landowners was ceremonialized at "last-arrow" pageants. (Takaki 1993, 235)

This ceremony is parallel to the one where people were dumped into water and came up "American" described in *Beyond Ethnicity* by Werner Sollars (1987) about Americanizing immigrants into the "melting pot."

6. In regard to the stereotype held by many non-Indians that American Indians "get a free ride from the government," Devon Mihesuah (1996, 88) explains that

> some Indians do receive various forms of aid from the U.S. government, but this aid is a result of treaty agreements in which the tribe in question ceded (often by force) most of its land in exchange for government protection of the remaining tribal land, and health and educational aid, among other things. . . . Since the government holds the land in trust for Indians, it is the government that collects the lease money, which in turn distributes the money to tribes.

7. The majority of American Indian students enrolled in public schools on Montana's reservations receive some exposure to the local Indigenous language. For example, Arlee District on the Flathead Reservation offers a K–12 Salish language program along with a K–12 Native American Studies program. The current language program allows for twenty minutes of Salish instruction once a week in kindergarten and first grade and twice a week in grades 2–6. In the middle school Salish is an elective class for one semester (an hour every day for nine weeks). In the high school the language is available as an elective class for four years. In the public schools on the Rocky Boy's Reservation a Cree teacher teaches Cree language and culture to K–6 children for approximately thirty minutes per week. Grades 7–8 students are required to take one semester of Cree language class. Cree language classes are available as an elective for grade 9–12 students (Voyd Pierre, personal communication, September 2008). In the Lame Deer Public School District, near the Northern Cheyenne Reservation, Cheyenne language classes are offered K–12. Grades K–6 students meet with their Northern Cheyenne culture teacher twice a week. The course available for grades 7–12 meets every day during the trimester or semester. Cultural activities, including language, are held twice a week after school. Some Cheyenne culture, but not the language, is integrated into the mainstream curriculum (Gary Hopkins, Title III program director, personal communication, November 2008). In Browning Public Schools, on the Blackfeet reservation, the Blackfeet language is taught at K–12. The Blackfeet teachers meet one hour per week with K–8 students. Blackfeet words are integrated into the mainstream reading and math curriculum. Grades 9–12 students can take an elective Blackfeet language course (Marilyn Bullshoe, Director of Blackfeet-Native American Studies Program in Browning Public Schools, personal communication, November 2008). In Montana there are three Native language immersion schools— Nkwusm (the Salish immersion school), the Piegan Institute (the Blackfeet immersion school), and the White Clay Immersion School that teaches in Gros Ventre.

8. Specifically, Ngai and Koehn's (2010a) study findings reveal urgent and challenging questions that call for clarification by Native communities and IEFA advocates: (1) Should IEFA focus on educating non-Indians about local American Indian cultures and histories or on improving current interracial relations? (2) Should IEFA stress the history of oppression and marginalization in academic subject learning or should it focus on guiding intercultural growth through learning about living cultures and resilient peoples as a vital part of an inclusive society (see also Grande, 2004)? (3) Should

IEFA focus on validating the value of Indigenous cultures and their status in the scheme of world knowledges and/or on helping learners develop empathy toward American Indian people in the name of social justice? (4) Should IEFA primarily be presented as an academic subject captured in texts or as an ethical obligation to learn about and experience the place in which we live and the perspectives of our neighbors? (5) Should an emphasis on teaching about local Indigenous histories and traditions take precedence over helping students relate to contemporary American Indian communities and their ever-evolving cultures? Although the goals of an Indian-education program can be manifold, these either-or questions push one to think deeply in order to prioritize and focus. The results reported in Ngai and Koehn's publication (2010a) indicate that each classroom approach, depending on the teacher's focus, tends to achieve only one or some of the desired outcomes.

9. Analytic competence involves the ability to link others' conditions to one's own circumstances and vice versa and to discern effective transactional strategies that help bridge differences. Creative/imaginative competence means the ability to tap into diverse cultural perspectives for inspiration to solve problems. Emotional competence allows one to open up to divergent cultural influences and to develop a sense of cross-cultural efficacy. The communicative dimension includes language and intercultural communication skills that facilitate conflict resolution, negotiation, and collaboration. Functional adroitness includes the ability to develop and maintain positive interpersonal and working relationships with different people (Koehn and Rosenau 2010).

10. Ken Hale (1992) contends that linguistic diversity shares the same level of importance with diversity in the zoological and botanical worlds. The threat to linguistic diversity not only coincides with, but has brought about, the threat to biodiversity. Ranka Bjelijac-Babic (2000, 3) explains that "there is an intrinsic and causal link between biological diversity and linguistic diversity" in the sense that a local language embodies a special stock of local knowledge about the natural environment. One of the reasons for the striking correlation between countries with areas of high biodiversity and countries with high numbers of Indigenous languages is that "over time, as human communities interact closely with the local environment, modifying it as they adapt to life in specific ecological niches, they acquire intimate and specialized knowledge of the environment and how to use and manage it for individual and group survival. This knowledge becomes encoded and transmitted through the local languages" (Oviedo and Maffi 2000, 13).

References

Åhrén, M. 2007. "The Saami Convention." *Journal of Indigenous Peoples Rights* 3:8–39.

Aikio-Puoskari, Ulla. 2009. "The Ethnic Revival, Language, and Education of the Sámi, an Indigenous People, in Three Nordic Countries (Finland, Norway, and Sweden)." In *Social Justice Through Multilingual Education*, edited by T. Skutnabb-Kangas, R. Phillipson, A. K. Mohanty, and M. Panda, 239–62. Buffalo, NY: Multilingual Matters.

American Indian Policy Review Commission. 1976. *Final Report*. Washington, DC: U.S. Government Printing Office.

Banks, James. 2002. *An Introduction to Multicultural Education*, 3rd ed. Boston: Allyn and Bacon.

——. 2008. "Diversity, Group Identity, and Citizenship Education in a Global Age." *Educational Researcher*, April, 129–37.

Barnhardt, C. 2001. "A History of Schooling for Alaska Native People." *Journal of American Indian Education* 40(1):1–30.

Beaulieu, D. 2000. "Comprehensive Reform and American Indian Education." *Journal of American Indian Education* 39(2):29–47.

Bhawuk, D. 2008. "Globalization and Indigenous Cultures: Homogenization or Differentiation." *International Journal Intercultural Relations* 32:305–17.

Bill, W. 1990. *From Boarding House to Self-Determining*. Helena: Montana Office of Public Instruction.

Bjelijac-Babic, Ranka. 2000. "6,000 Languages: An Embattled Heritage." *UNESCO Courier*. Available: http://www.unesco.org/courier/2000_04/uk/doss21.htm.

Bjørklund, Ivar. 1985. *Fjordfolket i Kvænangen* [The Fjord people in Kvænangen]. Oslo: Universitetsforlaget.

Bongo, M., L. Eriksen, and S. Germeten. 2009. "Læreplanverket for Kunnskapsløftet 2006 Sámisk (LK06S)—en analyse" [The National Curriculum for Knowledge Promotion 2006 Sámi (LK06S) in Norwegian]. In *Sámisk opplæring under LK06-Sámisk. Analyse av læreplan og tidlige tiltak for implementering* [Sámi education within LK06—Sámi. Analyses of National Curriculum and early interventions for implementation; in Norwegian], edited by K. J. Solstad, 94–141. Nordlandsforskning NF-rapport no. 3/2009. Bodø, Norway: Nordlandsforskning.

Brayboy, B. M. J., and A. E. Castagno. 2009. "Self-Determination Through Self-Education: Culturally Responsive Schooling for Indigenous Students in the USA." *Teaching Education* 20(1):31–53.

Carlisle, L. R., B. W. Jackson, and A. George. 2006. "Principles of Social Justice Education: The Social Justice Education in Schools Project." *Equity and Excellence in Education* 39(1):55–64.

de Courtivron, I. 2000. "Educating the Global Student, Whose Identity is Always a Matter of Choice." *Chronicle of Higher Education* 41(44):B4–5.

Deloria, V., Jr., and D. Wildcat. 2001. *Power and Place: Indian Education in America*. Golden, Colorado: American Indian Graduate Center and Fulcrum Resources.

Dewey, J. 1938. *Experience and Education*. New York: Collier Books.

Dover, A. G. 2009. "Teaching for Social Justice and K–12 Student Outcomes: A Conceptual Framework and Research Review." *Equity and Excellence in Education* 42(4):506–24.

Eder, Klaus. 2006. "Europe's Borders. The Narrative Construction of the Boundaries of Europe." *European Journal of Social Theory* 9(2):255–71.

Ellis, Clyde. 2006. "We Had a Lot of Fun, but of Course, that Wasn't the School Part." In *Boarding School Blues: Revisiting American Indian Educational Experiences*, edited by Clifford E. Trafzer, Jean A. Keller, and Lorene Sisquoc, 65–98. Lincoln: University of Nebraska Press.

Eriksen, Knut E., and Einar Niemi. 1981. *Den finske fare* [The Finish treath/danger]. Oslo: Universitetsforlaget.

Evjen, Bjørg. 2004. "Sámisk skolehistorie. Med eksempler fra Salten og Tysfjord" [Sámi School history. Examples from Salten and Tysfjord] *Årbok for norsk utdanningshistorie*, 81–94. utgivelsessted: Stiftelsen skolen.

Fenelon, J. V., and D. LeBeau. 2006. "Four Dimensions for Indian Education." In *Indigenous Education and Empowerment*, edited by I. Abu-Saad and D. Champagne, 21–56. New York: AltaMira Press.

Freng, S., A. Frend, and H. Moore. 2007. "Examining American Indians' Recall of Cultural Inclusion in School." *Journal of American Indian Education* 46(2):42–61.

Freire, P. 1970. *Pedagogy of the Oppressed*. New York: Continuum.

Friedman, Jonathan. 1996. *Cultural Identity and Global Process*. London: Sage Publications.

Gay, G. 2000. *Culturally Responsive Teaching: Theory, Research, and Practice*. New York: Teacher College Press.

Giroux, Henry. 2001. "Pedagogy of the Depressed: Beyond the New Politics of Cynicism." *College Literature* 28(3):1–32.

Grande, Sandy. 2004. *Red Pedagogy*. New York: Rowman and Littlefield Publishers.

Hale, K. 1992. "On Endangered Languages and the Safeguarding of Diversity." *Language* 68:1–3.

Helander, N. Ø. 2004. "Vurdering av begynneropplæring etter læreplan i Sámisk" (Evaluation of the beginner teaching after National Curriculum Sámi; in Norwegian). In *Sámisk skole i plan og praksis. Hvordan møte utfordringene i L97S? Evaluering av Reform 97* [Sámi school in plan and practice. How to meet the challenges in L97S? Evaluation of reform 97; in Norwegian], edited by V. Hirvonen, 82–100. Karasjok, Norway: Cálliid Lágádus-Forfatternes Forlag.

Henriksen, John B. 2008. "Sámi Self-Determination—Scope and Implementation." *Journal of Indigenous Peoples Rights* No. 2.

———. 2009. "Sámi Self-Determination. Autonomy and Self-Government: Education, Research and Culture." *Journal of Indigenous Peoples Rights* No. 2.

Hirvonen, Vuokko. 2008. "'Out on the Fells, I Feel Like a Sámi': Is There Linguistic and Cultural Equality in the Sámi School?" In *Can Schools Save Indigenous Languages? Policy and Practice on Four Continents*, edited by Nancy H. Hornberger, 15–41. New York: Palgrave Macmillan.

Höem, A. 2007. *Fra noaidiens verden til forskerens. Misjon, kunnskap og modernisering i sameland, 1715–2007* [From the world of the noaide to the world of the researcher. Mission, knowledge and modernization in Sámi Country 1715–2007]. Oslo, Norway: Novus Forlag.

Huff, D. J. 1997. *To Live Heroically: Institutional Racism and American Indian Education*. Albany: State University of New York Press.

Huffman, T. 2010. *Theoretical Perspectives on American Indian Education: Taking a New Look at Academic Success and the Achievement Gap*. New York: AltaMira Press.

Huss, Leena. 2008. "Revitalization Through Indigenous Education: A Forlorn Hope?" In *Can Schools Save Indigenous Languages? Policy and Practice on Four Continents*, edited by Nancy H. Hornberger, 125–35. New York: Palgrave Macmillan.

IHS (Indian Health Service, U.S. Department of Health and Human Services). 2012. *Indian Population*. Retrieved April 3, 2012, from http://www.ihs.gov/PublicAffairs/IHSBrochure/Population.asp.

Jensen, Eivind Bråstad. 2005. *Skoleverket og de tre stammers møte* [Education and the meeting of the three tribes]. Tromsø, Norway: Eureka Forlag.

Juneau, S. 2001. *A History and Foundation of American Indian Education Policy.* Helena: Montana Office of Public Instruction.

Juneau, D., and M. S. Broaddus. 2006. "And Still the Waters Flow: The Legacy of Indian Education in Montana." *Phi Delta, Kappan* 88(3):193–97.

Koehn, P. H., and J. N. Rosenau. 2010. *Transnational Competence: Empowering Professional Curriculums for Horizon-Rising Challenges.* Herndon, VA: Paradise.

Ladson-Billings, G. 1995. "Toward a Theory of Culturally Relevant Pedagogy." *American Education Research Journal* 35:465–91.

Lee, T. S., and P. D. Q. Cerecer. 2010. "(Re)claiming Native Youth Knowledge: Engaging in Socio-Culturally Responsive Teaching and Relationships." *Multicultural Perspectives* 12(4):199–205.

Loewen, J. W. 1995. *Lies My Teacher Told Me: Everything Your American History Textbook Got Wrong.* New York: Touchstone.

Lomawaima, K. T. 1999. "The Unnatural History of American Indian Education." In *Next Steps: Research and Practice to Advance Indian Education,* edited by K. G. Swisher and J. W. Tippeconnic III, 1–32. Charleston, WV: Clearinghouse on Rural Education and Small Schools.

Lomawaima, K. T., and T. L. McCarty. 2006. *To Remain an Indian: Lessons in Democracy from a Century of Native American Education.* Teachers College Columbia University.

Lorentz, Einhart. 1991. *Samefolket i historien* [The Sámi people in the history]. Oslo: Pax forlag.

Lund, Svein. 2003. *Sámisk skole eller Norsk Standard? Reformene i det norske skoleverket og Sámisk opplæring.* Karasjok: Davvi Girji.

Maffi, Luisa. 2007. "Bio-Cultural Diversity for Endogenous Development: Lessons from Research, Policy, and On-the-Ground Experiences." In *Endogenous Development and Bio-Cultural Diversity: The Interplay of Worldviews, Globalization, and Locality,* edited by B. Haverkort, 56–66. Leusden, The Netherlands: COMPAS.

Magga, O. H. 2004. "Sámisk som førstespråk i grunnskolen" [Sámi as first language in elementary education]. In *Sámisk skole i plan og praksis. Hvordan møte utfordringene i L97S? Evaluering av Reform 97* [Sámi school in plan and practice. How to meet the challenges in L97S? Evaluation of Reform 97], edited by V. Hirvonen, 50–81. Karasjok, Norway: Cálliid Lágádus-Forfatternes Forlag.

Mathisen, Stein R. 2001. "'Den naturlige samen': narrative konstruksjoner av 'de andre' i norsk tradisjon." In *Forestillinger om "Den Andre." Imagenes of Otherness,* edited by Line A. Ytrehus, 84–98. Kristiansand: Høyskoleforlaget.

McCarty, Teresa L. 2008. "Schools as Strategic Tools for Indigenous Language Revitalization: Lessons from Native America." In *Can Schools Save Indigenous Languages? Policy and Practice on Four Continents,* edited by Nancy H. Hornberger, 161–79. New York: Palgrave Macmillan.

McCoy, M. L. 2005. *Indian Education Legal Support Project: Compilation of State Indian Education Laws.* October. Retrieved January 2, 2009 from http://www.narf.org/pubs/edu/blue.pdf.

Meløy, L. Lind. 1980. *Internatliv i Finnmark* [Lives at the boarding schools in Finmark]. Oslo: Det norske samlaget.

Merryfield, M. M. 2001. "Pedagogy for Global Perspectives in Education: Studies of Teachers' Thinking and Practice." In *Changing Perspectives on International Education*, edited by P. O'Meara, H. D. Mehlinger, and R. M. Newman, 244–79. Bloomington: Indiana University Press.

Mihesuah, D. A. 1996. *American Indians: Stereotypes and Realities*. Atlanta: Clarity Press.

Miller, A., and S. D. Ross. 2004. "They Are Not Us: Framing of American Indians by the *Boston Globe*." *The Howard Journal of Communication* 15:245–59.

Minde, Henry. 2005. "Fornorskninga av samene—hvorfor, hvordan og hvilke følger" [Assimilation of the Sámi people—why, how and what kind of consequences]. *Sámisk skolehistorie 1*. Karasjok: Davvi Girji.

NCNASL (National Caucus of Native American State Legislators). 2008. "Striving to Achieve: Helping Native American Students Succeed." Retrieved August 4, 2011, from http://www.nativeamericanlegislators.org/default.aspx.

NCSL (National Conference of State Legislatures). 2009. "Numbers of Native Legislators." Retrieved Feb 21, 2010, from http://www.ncsl.org/Default.aspx?TabId=14762.

Ngai, P. B. 2012. *Crossing Mountains: Native American Language Education in Public Schools*. Lanham, MD: AltaMira Press.

Ngai, P. B., and P. H. Koehn. 2010a. "Implementing Montana's Indian-Education-For-All in a K–5 Public School: Implications for Classroom Teaching, Education Policy, and Native Communities." *Journal of American Indian Education* 49(1–2): 44–62.

———. 2010b. "Indigenous Studies and Intercultural Education: The Impact of a Place-Based Primary-School Program." *Intercultural Education* 21(6):597–606.

———. 2011. "Indigenous Education for Critical Democracy: Teacher Approaches and Learning Outcomes in a K–5 Indian-Education-For-All Program." *Equity and Excellence in Education* 44(2):249–69.

Nielsen, Reidar. 1986. *Folk uten fortid* [People without a past]. Oslo: Gyldendal.

Niemi, Einar. 1997. "Kulturmøte, etnisitet og statlig intervensjon på Nordkalotten." In *Den Nordiska mosaiken*, edited by Rut Bostrøm Andersen, Uppsala: Uppsala universitet.

Noguera, P., and R. Cohen. 2006. "Patriotism and Accountability: The Role of Educators in the War on Terrorism." *Phi Delta Kappan* 87(8):573–78.

Norris, T., P. Vines, and E. Hoeffel. 2012. "The American Indian and Alaska Native Population: 2010." Retrieved, April 11, 2012 http://www.census.gov/prod/cen2010/briefs/c2010br-10.pdf.

Norwegian Ministry of Education. 1998. Mot rikere mål [Towards richer goals; in Norwegian]. Report No. 28 (1998–1999) to the Storting. Oslo, Norway: Norwegian Ministry of Education.

Nygaard, V., and B. Kramvig. 2009. "Implementering av læreplan for Kunnskapsløftet 2006—Sámisk (LK06S) sett fra forvaltningsnivået" [Implementation of National Curriculum for Knowledge Promotion 2006—Sámi (LK06S) seen from the administrative level; in Norwegian]. In *Sámisk opplæring under LK06-Sámisk. Analyse av læreplan og tidlige tiltak for implementering* [Sámi education within LK06—Sámi. Analyses of National Curriculum and early interventions for implementation; in Norwegian], edited by K. J. Solstad, Side 52–40. Nordlandsforskning NF-rapport no. 3/2009. Bodø, Norway: Nordlandsforskning.

Nyseth, Torill, and Paul Pedersen. 2005. "Globalization from Below: The Revitalization of a Coastal Sámi Community in Northern Norway as Part of the Global Discourse in Indigenous Identity." In *Discourses and Silences: Indigenous Peoples, Risks, and Resistance*, edited by Garth Cant, Anake Goodall, and Justine Inns, 71–85. Canterbury, New Zealand: Department of Georgraphy, University of Canterbury.

Oakes, A., and T. Maday. 2009. "Engaging Native American Learners with Rigor and Cultural Relevance." *Issue Brief* (August) 30:1–10.

Oviedo, G., and L. Maffi. 2000. *Indigenous and Traditional Peoples of the World and Ecoregion Conservation*. Switzerland: WWF-World Wide Fund for Nature.

Paulgaard, Gry. 2009. "Cool and Crazy: Place Reinvention Through Filmmaking." *Place Reinvention: Northern Perspectives*, edited by Torill Nyseth and Arvid Viken, 145–63. Aldershot: Ashgate.

Pettersen, T. 2004. *The Right to Knowledge About Oneself: Preparing for Use of Numbers About Sámi as a Group—Some Normative Limitations and Possibilities*. Guovdageaidnu: Nordic Sámi Institute.

Pewewardy, C. 1994. "Culturally Responsive Pedagogy in Action: An American Indian Magnet School." In *Teaching Diverse Populations: Formulating a Knowledge Base*, edited by E. R. Hollins, J. E. King, and W. C. Hayman, 77–92. Albany: State University of New York Press.

———. 1998. "Fluff and Fathers: Treatment of American Indian in the Literature and the Classroom." *Equity and Excellence in Education* 31(1):69–76.

Pewewardy, C., and M. Fitzpatrick. 2009. "Working with American Indian Students and Families." *Intervention in School and Clinic* 45(91):91–98.

Pittman, C. T. 2009. "Multicultural Education and Social Justice Actions." *Intercultural Education* 20(2):173–86.

Quin, J. 2009. "Growing Social Justice Educators: A Pedagogical Framework for Social Justice Education." *Intercultural Education* 20(2):109–25.

Reynolds, R. J. 2005. "The Education of Indigenous Australian Students: Same Story, Different Hemisphere." *Multicultural Perspectives* 7(2):48–55.

Rothberg, Peter. 2012. "Challenging Arizona's Ban on Ethnic Studies." *The Nation*. February 1. Retrieved, April 5, 2012, http://www.thenation.com/blog/165989/chal lenging-arizonas-ban-ethnic-studies.

Sanchez, J. 2003. "How American Public Schools Using Down-Linked News Media Shape American Indian Identity." *The Howard Journal of Communication* 14: 39–48.

Silverthorne, J. A. 1997. "Language Preservation and Human Resources Development." In *Teaching Indigenous Languages*, edited by J. Reyhner, 105–15. Flagstaff: Northern Arizona University.

Skinner, Linda. 1999. "Teaching Through Traditions: Incorporating Languages and Culture into Curricula." In *Next Steps: Research and Practice to Advance Indian Education*, edited by K. G. Swisher and J. W. Tippeconnic III, 107–34. Charleston, WV: Clearinghouse on Rural Education and Small Schools.

Smith, Linda Tuhiwai. 1999. *Decolonizing Methodologies: Research and Indigenous Peoples*. New York: Zed Books Ltd.

Sollars, Werner. 1987. *Beyond Ethnicity: Consent and Descent in American Culture*. Cary, NC: Oxford University Press.

Solstad, K. J. 2009. "Bakgrunn—perspektiv—mål" [1. Background—perspectives—goals]. In *Sámisk opplæring under LK06-Sámisk. Analyse av læreplan og tidlige tiltak for implementering* [Sámi education within LK06—Sámi. Analyses of National Curriculum and early interventions for implementation; in Norwegian], edited by K. J. Solstad, 15–40. Nordlandsforskning NF-rapport no. 3/2009. Bodø, Norway: Nordlandsforskning.

Spring, Joel. 2007. *Deculturalization and the Struggle for Equality: A Brief History of the Education of Dominated Cultures in the United States*, 5th ed. Boston: McGraw Hill.

Starnes, B. A. 2006. "Montana's Indian Education for All: Toward an Education Worthy of American Ideals." *Phi Delta Kappan* 88(3):184–89.

Stølen, Gerd. 2007. *Den voksne ungdomsskoleeleven* [The adult pupil in secondary School] PhD avhandling, Universitetet i Tromsø.

Swisher, Karen, and John W. Tippeconnic, III, eds. 1999. *Next Steps: Research and Practice to Advance Indian Education*. Charleston, WV: Clearinghouse on Rural Education and Small Schools.

Takaki, Ronald. 1993. *A Different Mirror: A History of Multicultural America*. Boston: Little, Brown and Company.

Tippeconnic, John III. 1999. "Tribal Control of American Indian Education: Observations Since the 1960s with Implications for the Future." In *Next Steps: Research and Practice to Advance Indian Education*, edited by K. G. Swisher and J. W. Tippeconnic III, 33–52. Charleston, WV: Clearinghouse on Rural Education and Small Schools.

———. 2000. "Reflecting on the Past: Some Important Aspects of Indian Education to Consider as we Look Toward the Future." *Journal of American Indian Education* 39(2):39–48.

Trafzer, Clifford E., Jean A. Keller, and Lorene Sisquoc. 2006. *Boarding School Blues: Revisiting American Indian Educational Experiences*. Lincoln: University of Nebraska Press.

UNESCO. 2014. "Decade of Education for Sustainable Development." Retrieved from http://www.gdrc.org/sustdev/un-desd/key-action.html.

United Nations. 2007. "United Nations Declaration on the Rights of Indigenous Peoples." Retrieved, Feb 21, 2011 from http://www.un.org/esa/socdev/unpfii/en/drip.html.

Utter, Jack. 1993. *American Indians: Answers to Today's Questions*. Lake Ann, MI: National Woodlands.

Watahomigie, L. J. 1998. "The Native Language is a Gift: A Hualapai Language Autobiography." *International Journal of the Sociology of Languages* 132:5–7.

Writer, J. 2010. "Broadening the Meaning of Citizenship Education: Native Americans and Tribal Nationhood." *Action in Teacher Education* 32(2):70–81.

CHAPTER FOUR

"A Future for Indians as Indians"

D'Arcy McNickle's Pluralism and the Future of Indigenous Theory

David L. Moore

Codification of Inherent Rights

Indigenous movements worldwide, from Ecuador to Sámiland, from South Africa to India, from the UN Declaration on the Rights of Indigenous Peoples (UNDRIP) to the Zapatista Declarations, from circumpolar alliances to Native American reservations, to First Nations reserves, and to local rancherias are first of all about the land—and management of the land. The great tide of European colonialism that flowed for centuries has ebbed for decades and exposed islands, large and small, of resistance, resilience, and survivance in Indigenous communities on the land. Each of these communities has its unique political, historical, legal, and spiritual history. A volume such as this makes visible some of those islands and reveals that uniqueness, as well some of the connections across the various histories.

A thorough comparison of legal and political structures of tribal sovereignty between Native North America and Sámiland is beyond the scope of this chapter, but it is precisely the function of this present volume to stimulate such studies. Øyvind Ravna, in chapter 6 in his study of the Sámi, maps a historic shift in global political assumptions of Indigenous rights drawn from the United Nations' *International Labor Organization Convention No. 169*, as well as from the UNDRIP. Internationally, if not yet universally, he explains, we must assume that in states where there are minorities and in particular Indigenous peoples, the state has a responsibility to let these peoples participate in decision-making processes that concern them. The commitment to give Indigenous people substantial influence on decision-making, including participation in legislative processes, is binding. That commitment marks a trajectory that would warm the hearts of Indigenous ancestors who fought so hard for basic democratic rights on their land. I find it useful to identify that democratic right with pluralism, as I will explain.

In this context, I focus here on the ramifications for pluralistic political thought in the fiction of D'Arcy McNickle as they may relate to current Indigenous prospects in North America and beyond. The global Indigenous movement emerging at the turn of the twenty-first century offers international perspectives that shed light on McNickle's literary and political efforts for Indian rights across the prior century. And vice versa, McNickle's suggestions, explicit in his nonfiction and implicit in his fiction, shed light on pluralism in the emerging Indigenous movement worldwide.

One of the unique legal aspects of North American Indian reservations where McNickle worked and wrote, in contrast to other Indigenous histories, is the original and explicit "government-to-government" relationship (in late twentieth-century parlance) between Native nations and the U.S. government. This complex and changing set of legal relations was codified across American history in the U.S. Constitution (the "commerce clause"), in U.S. Supreme Court cases since "The Marshall Decisions" of the 1820s and 1830s, in the history of treaty making, and in legislative policy shifts toward incrementally increased recognition of "tribal sovereignty" in the twentieth century (most notably the Indian Reorganization Act of 1934 [IRA] and the Indian Self-Determination and Education Assistance Act of 1975). Colonial-era legal recognition of prior "aboriginal land rights" in the law also contributes to this unique government-to-government dynamic as it plays out in various ways across the United States and, eventually, Canada, Australia, New Zealand, Sámiland, and other colonized nations.

Numerous studies have mapped the history of that U.S. dynamic of tribal sovereignty.[1] I focus here on dramatic representations of that dynamic in a particular Native American writer whose homeland is the locus of a particular ongoing land dispute. Elsewhere in this volume, Robin Saha and Jennifer Hill-Hart chart the federal and international legal perspectives of a conflict over tribal management of the National Bison Range (NBR) on the Flathead Reservation of the Confederated Salish and Kootenai Tribes in Montana. (In a separate publication I have also offered a discourse analysis of the languages of land management issues on the NBR in contrast with Indigenous artistic expression on that same land.[2]) Rather than a history and policy analysis, such as Saha and Hill-Hart's, here I take a literary approach and aim through cross-cultural humanistic inquiry to suggest some principles of a tribal perspective eclipsed in that conflict. D'Arcy McNickle, a twentieth-century novelist, scholar, and activist from that reservation, fictionalized some of the early linked histories of the Flathead in dramatic ways that reflect on those recent political and legal negotiations for management of the land. What Saha and Hill-Hart refer to as contested "parity between the parties" in those negotiations becomes a discussion of the broader "government-to-government" relations between Native nations and the United States. McNickle dramatizes the lack of such parity, and by the tragic consequences of domination he underlines the practical principles of pluralism as the alternative that parity would permit.

Where the legal structures of "tribal sovereignty" in the United States offer a codification of aboriginal land rights, their historical weight puts political and ethical pressure on American society to adjust toward a more pluralistic regime. As Saha and Hill-Hart explain, the UNDRIP recognizes that hundreds of years of historical injustices have necessitated a shift in favor of greater power and influence for Indigenous people, and that such a shift requires constructive engagement and a complementary legal foundation. What McNickle recognized, even before the mid-century formation of the United Nations and its eventual declarations, is that the United States, because of its history of "tribal sovereignty," already has some aspects of such a "legal foundation." It is within this long-range perspective and context of lost and recovered sovereignty that many Native American writers and activists strive to reconfigure America's stories.

As context for Saha and Hill-Hart's detailed legal history of management issues surrounding the NBR, I compare the discursive strategies of McNickle, the Flathead Reservation's preeminent writer, in establishing a pluralist model of governance and management of the land. Where article 26 of UNDRIP states "Indigenous peoples have the right to the lands, territories, and resources which they have traditionally owned, occupied, or otherwise used or acquired," we may see a direction toward tribal sovereignty envisioned in the negative space of McNickle's tragic fiction, as such sovereignty is denied. Further, in the contentious prospect of "comanagement" of the NBR, we may also see the tribes'—and McNickle's—practical vision for pluralism in modern relations with settler colonialism. As Saha and Hill-Hart explain the pragmatic politics, because land repatriation appears to be politically impossible for now, comanagement of a unit, such as the NBR appears to afford an opportunity to advance Indigenous rights. Although they suggest how this historical and contemporary example may serve as an important step in the path to tribal management and toward the greater exercise of tribal sovereignty, I wonder if the pluralistic pragmatics of comanagement might not actually be an Indigenous end in itself. The tragic lessons that McNickle offers by the either-or politics of domination or resistance argue for an alternative politics of both-and that would redefine "sovereignty" in pluralistic terms. Let's look at McNickle's narratives for hints at such alternatives.

Democratic Difference as a Good in Itself

D'Arcy McNickle (1904–1977), of Métis and Flathead Salish Reservation background, was a Montana writer, activist, historian, and anthropologist with a national and international career. His attempts to incorporate Indigenous cultural values into academic discourse constitute a major artistic and political contribution throughout the twentieth century. In addition to his two major novels, *The Surrounded* (1936) and the posthumous *Wind from an Enemy Sky* (1978), his histories and commentaries, such as *They Came Here First: The Epic of the American Indian* (1949) and his summary book, *Native American Tribalism: Indian Survivals and Renewals* (1973), illuminate prospects for Indigenous cultural and political survival in the modern era.

Toward such survival as the ethical impulse of his writing, we may apply McNickle's representations of Native American community values to pluralism in postcolonial global society. Although it has its own discursive history, *pluralism* is a useful word for the leveling equilibrium of cultures that Indigenous voices have for centuries suggested reasonably to reverse colonialism and to elude slavery and conquest. Instead of the hierarchical conformities of "multicultural" assimilation, instead of the "melting pot," pluralism has always suggested a radically democratic social dynamic. Pluralism incorporates a social ethos of difference as the robust energy of community.[3] Yet even progressives in American politics tend to see in difference only a threat to solidarity, as "minority" activists know too well. The underlying concept, or presumption leading to precept, held by many on the right and the left, is that a utopian community must be homogenous. For context, this chapter explores potentialities and ramifications in McNickle's work that offer a concept of community that must be diverse, and I apply "pluralism" to that collection of potentials in his cross-cultural studies.

I suggest that the politics of pluralism underlie many Native writers' responses to colonial domination, with McNickle as an exemplary case.

Native voices have, in writing and oratory, offered modes of pluralistic interaction in various ways to Europeans and other settlers or invaders. In contrast to annihilation and assimilation, pluralism is a logical, one might even say natural, challenge to colonialism and then to exclusive and imperialistic nationalism. Native efforts at cross-cultural communication and equity required by pluralism began with the shoreline Taino greetings that Columbus saw only as naïve, and they have remained invisible to colonial eyes since The Admiral labeled *los indios* as potential slaves.[4]

Conversations about pluralism have clarified some of the ideas that colonized peoples have put forth over the last 500 years to offset the paradigm of a dominating center and of exploited or neglected margins. Under various names, such as feminism, Négritude, Black Power, Red Power, or tribal sovereignty, diverse social margins have invoked pluralism as a principle to resist being homogenized by the commodification processes of corporate capitalism. Pluralism would maintain differences of culture against such economic forces, and that steady insistence constitutes a joke on the American model of the melting pot.

McNickle is one of the clearest to enunciate this alternative, pluralistic approach to intercultural contact. His classic American Indian appeal to the humanity of the American oppressors does not suggest surrendering Native cultural difference. McNickle represents pluralism in his prose as a negative space, or a positive absence, as the background or substratum, in both the fiction and the nonfiction. Like the breath and silence between words, the frame of a painting, or the empty space in and around a sculpture, negative space is as much a part of expression as the foreground that seems to define while denying it. The positive absence of the ground as Indian land remains the illegal substratum of the American legal system designed to legitimize the modern economy—the American culture. Where that invisible presence of "the Indian" stands on the land, it remains in the American psyche and the American future.

Thus, in McNickle's fiction, the ideals of American pluralism are the absent presence behind the tragedies of American oppression. His strategic focus on tragedy maps the historical reality of the present, with pluralism as the ideal reality of past and future inside that present. Similarly, in nonfiction, McNickle's strategic focus on "the plight of the Indian" (McNickle 1973) under a century of failed federal policies echoes back from a pluralistic past and potential future into the unfolding present.

Part of what makes McNickle's prose so forceful is the rigor of his pluralism, his insistence on the one hand on maintaining the integrity of authentic difference, and his vision on the other of integrating sustained difference within American society. His tragic novels map the failure of integration due to the American, colonial assumption of superiority with the authority to assimilate and erase Native difference. His nonfiction, in contrast, maps the prospects, however dim, of integrating differences into a pluralist society. For example, in a preface to the 1975 edition of his ambitious study—*They Came Here First*—of the ancient to modern trajectory of Native cultures in North America, he directly affirms such pluralism from a Native point of view. Commenting on the long history of Indigenous adaptations before the colonial era, he wrote this more positive outlook during the same years he was completing *Wind from an Enemy Sky* as a fictional tragedy:

> The consequence of this development is that the venturing people who were the first to come into the New World and who adapted to its infinite variety may yet adapt to the conditions imposed by the competitive, acquisitive majority. But in adapting, by long experience, they will remain a separate and identifiable tradition, adding color to the fabric of American life. (quoted in Purdy 1990, 141)

It is telling that McNickle sets the creative agency for such a vision of American life within the ranks of "the venturing people who were the first to come" to this continent. Native people will remain separate, "adding color," while "the competitive, acquisitive majority" seems to continue imposing conditions on Native Americans. This is not a utopian vision, yet McNickle's view insists on a new story for this nation reinvented with its gradual recognition of its own Native American stories. McNickle himself is one of those storytellers, those reinventors.

By way of a working definition for "pluralism," I refer to Diana L. Eck, Harvard professor of comparative religion, for her four points about pluralism.

> First, pluralism is not diversity alone, but the energetic engagement with diversity. . . . Second, pluralism is not just tolerance, but the active seeking of understanding across lines of difference. . . . Third, pluralism is not relativism, but the encounter of commitments. The new paradigm of pluralism does not require us to leave our identities and our commitments behind, for pluralism is the encounter of commitments. It means holding our deepest differences, even our religious differences, not in isolation, but in relationship to one another. . . . Fourth, pluralism is based on dialogue. The language of pluralism is that of dialogue and

encounter, give and take, criticism and self-criticism. . . . Dialogue does not mean everyone at the "table" will agree with one another. Pluralism involves the commitment to being at the table—with one's commitments. (Eck 2012)

The active and open "encounter of commitments" in Eck's definition suggests the democratic energy of pluralism. Further, her unsentimental evocation of "dialogue" refocuses the dynamic of pluralism where, again, "difference is the robust energy of community."

Such an openness to dialogue and difference marked McNickle's activism, and even his leadership style, as we find in Dorothy Parker's biography. Evidently McNickle exercised a commitment to dialogics and pluralism quite different from standard adversarial modes of American culture. Parker explains his "passion for consensus," which, in my reading, reflects Eck's "commitment to being at the table."

As a leadership technique, struggling for consensus was more Indian than white; for McNickle, it had become almost axiomatic. . . . Some people perceived this search for a common ground among adversaries as a weakness. Vine Deloria, Jr., for instance, observed, "My impression of [McNickle] was that he would never take any controversial position on anything." For those who were accustomed to working within an adversarial framework of majority rule, McNickle's modus operandi could indeed be very frustrating, but it was also very Indian. (Parker 1992, 244)

Deloria's training and activism in law and legislation, as well as his Dakota Sioux cultural background, may have contributed to his comment on McNickle's avoidance of "any controversial position." McNickle's strategic stance may reflect his own training as a cultural anthropologist and his Flathead Salish cultural background—quite a different history from that of the Dakota Sioux, especially in terms of "any controversial position" in relations with the settler colonialists. Deloria certainly appreciated the "Indian" strategizing in McNickle's modus operandi. That a public intellectual and provocateur like Deloria would read McNickle's pluralism as passivity is not surprising in the context of their shared, lifelong fight against an adversarial American legal system that erases Indians.

As consensus is alien to American competitive and adversarial systems of thinking and behaving, McNickle's biographer touches on the context of this difference in more detail. "In a profile of Indian behavior, Nancy

Lurie describes this reach for consensus and notes, 'While often baffling to whites, the process is patterned, and Indian people of widely varying tribal backgrounds are able to conduct business together according to mutually understood rules'" (Parker 1992, 244–45). By such rules in many parts of Indian Country, McNickle was able to advocate within the heart of local communities because the strength of such a commitment to consensus underlies recognition and respect for difference. Add mainstream America's competitive drive to equate time with money, and the complex, time-consuming processes of consensus building remain as alien as its practical application in pluralism. Paradoxically, that common ground, which Parker describes in McNickle's logic of values, undergirds Eck's pluralist values and strategies of "engagement" beyond diversity. Common ground and consensus drive her pluralist theory of understanding beyond tolerance, her encounter of commitments beyond relativism, and her commitment to dialogue.

This contrary logic, which actually drives America's own *pluribus*,[5] has become clearer and more confused as American generations begin to recognize the historical fact of a multicultural, then pluralistic, nation against the ahistorical illogic of racial and ethnic exclusions. In Ishmael Reed's essay "What's American about America?" he cites the *New York Times* (June 23, 1983) a generation ago. "At the annual Lower East Side Jewish Festival yesterday, a Chinese woman ate a pizza slice in front of Ty Thuan Duc's Vietnamese grocery store. Beside her a Spanish-speaking family patronized a cart with two signs: 'Italian ices' and 'Kosher by Rabbi Alper.' And after the pastrami ran out, everybody ate knishes'" (Reed 1991, 4). It is hardly surprising anymore that global and local circumstances are forcing changes in historical categories and ways of thinking that never did fit events on the ground.

What remains less obvious, however, is how certain Native insights into the potentials of the American pluribus have driven writings by American Indians since the beginning of colonization and especially since the founding of the United States. Joseph Meeker's (1972, 167) "comic spirit" of social ecology, where, "morality is a matter of getting along with one's fellow creatures as well as possible" becomes the politics of pluralism in Native writers' responses to colonial domination. Throughout the western hemisphere, Native voices have, in writing and oratory, suggested pluralistic interaction in various ways with Europeans and other settlers or invaders.

Philosophically, pluralism as a term in European discourse has been set against monism, a multiplicity of causes against a single cause. Applying this juxtaposition to colonial binaries, Indigenous animism would be set against Euro-Christian theism. Indigenous racial difference would stand against colonial racial dominance; and Indigenous political and economic diversity would stand against centralized colonial and now corporate power.

In contemporary usage pluralism may be distinguished from multiculturalism by the tendency of the latter to homogenize difference. Multiculturalism, once an ethos of equality, has been co-opted as a term by corporate capital for entrée into diverse markets. Multiculturalism has become multicapitalism, the absorption of difference and resistance into mercantile hierarchies for the unidirectional revenue stream, that is, multiple markets. This is the tragic confusion of the financier, Adam Pell, in *Wind from an Enemy Sky* (McNickle 1978). Counterculture becomes multiculture becomes global capital culture, with the paradoxical effects of local monoculture. Examples range in colonial monocultures across the centuries from tobacco, to cotton, to pineapples, and to coffee. Yet a less cynical reading of multiculturalism recognizes that it still holds within it the seeds of what might more usefully be called pluralism.

In contrast to what might be called "market democracy," Anna Marie Smith extends the concept of radical democratic pluralism promoted by theorists Ernesto Laclau and Chantal Mouffe:

> The diversity among democratic differences must be affirmed as a good in itself; minority groups should never be asked to pay the price of cultural self-destruction through assimilation and disciplinary neutralization in exchange for inclusion, legitimacy, and recognition. Genuine "tolerance" must mean that minority groups are granted access to the material resources that they need to preserve their rights and to promote their distinct democratic differences. Genuine "multiculturalism" must mean not only the addition of minority democratic values, but also the opening up of the values held by the majority to the minorities' democratic critique, and the construction of a new set of shared community values through negotiation. (Smith 1998, 33)

There is a reason such theory is termed "radical." It goes to the root of modern, that is, American, social questions. If "minority groups should never be asked to pay the price of cultural self-destruction," then American history should never have happened. Diversity as a "good in itself" is the precise opposite of America's predominant imaginary where *unum* trumps pluribus. As I have written elsewhere, this dynamic, equating unity with sameness and difference with destruction, is itself the modern challenge of pluralism.[6] The ironies of Native American literature constitute a chorus of "democratic critiques" of "the values held by the majority." A pluralistic society would be seen as a horrifying hall of mirrors only by those who insist on seeing themselves in every other face. The hall of mirrors appears chaotic to those who would deny difference.

Although it frequently has blinded them to subtler dynamics of history, the hierarchical position of colonizing populations "naturally" has allowed them to desire and to assume that their power is a one-way street by which they can control the colonized—initially toward the mercantile center and gradually toward the dominant normative economy. Under ensuing oppression, the colonized populations have desired to see that exchange of power in reverse, as a two-way street, or even as a roundabout on a more reciprocal field of exchange. Moving beneath the advocacy of political and cultural pluralism versus monism lies the question of who has the power to change or control the other. In the dialectic of history, claiming such power to alter, assimilate, or even annihilate the subordinated population has backfired where the claim is based on the assumption that the dominating self will remain "the same," and that the thesis itself will not be synthesized with the antithesis.

This field of reversals is ripe for literary alternatives and pluralist politics. Reciprocity, rather than marginalization, isolation, or domination thus becomes a power strategy of pluralism as a form of irony, tragedy, and often comedy. The powerless, to survive, must recognize these dialectic implications for the powerful and then complicate the mutual transformations by drawing on a larger field, a set of other dialectical vectors. This is a logic of wise warriors, maddened and frustrated fighters, and even of jesters, tricksters, and clowns. These are the imaginative invocation of surprising factors by the seemingly foolish and powerless that undercuts and alters the powers that be. A power strategy of pluralism thus tends toward a wider field of reciprocity rather than marginalization, domination, or isolation. A more complex view of power relations on the part of the powerless means generally that Indigenous voices have recognized more clearly than their colonizers how the colonizers and their cultures may have been changed— acculturated—by Native contact.[7] Thus, the Lone Ranger and Tonto fistfight in heaven. What looked to the mainstream media like a clean hierarchy of white cowboy over Indian sidekick is shown by a Native author like Sherman Alexie to be a spiritual battle to reclaim history. The irony of this change in perspective, this invisible reversal, becomes the ground of a revised history, a revised story of survivance through pluralism.

Indian Survivals and Renewals: The Nonfiction

For more detailed discussion, let's turn first to gestures toward pluralism in examples of McNickle's nonfiction, as it will also contextualize the discussion of his fiction to follow. His exemplary nonfiction text is *Native American Tribalism: Indian Survivals and Renewals*, published in 1973 by Oxford University Press for London's Institute of Race Relations. A revised and expanded version of *The Indian Tribes of the United States*, which came out four years before McNickle's death, offers his summary perspective and reflects McNickle's professional and personal experiences across three-quarters of the twentieth century.

This vital publication emerged out of the tumultuous and promising '60s, as the early '70s produced not only this activist text but the most far-reaching federal legislation yet toward Native American autonomy, the American Indian Self-Determination and Education Assistance Act of 1975. The prospect of such a fundamental cultural and legal shift toward pluralism forms the thread woven through McNickle's history. It was under the administration of conservative president Richard Nixon, before his resignation in 1973, that the act was initially shaped by McNickle's colleagues, Native American activists, and legal scholars, such as Vine Deloria, Jr., and Suzan Shown Harjo. Even Nixon was able to articulate the emerging American values toward pluralism as in his address on July 8, 1970:

> The goal of any new national policy toward the Indian people [must be] to strengthen the Indian's sense of autonomy without threatening his sense of community. We must assure the Indian that he can assume control of his own life without being separated involuntarily from the tribal group. And we must make it clear that the Indians can become independent of federal control without being cut off from federal concern and federal support. (quoted in Parker 1992, 221)

Bypassing the generic language of "the Indian" in such a statement, we may say that this prescribed balance of "autonomy" and "community" would fit for a working definition of pluralism. As McNickle's biographer, Dorothy R. Parker, comments on this historic shift. "For the first time since the Bureau of Indian Affairs was established in 1824, it seemed that Indian communities might, as a matter of policy, be given time and space to learn the skills necessary to accommodate themselves to the modern world without violating their traditional values" (Parker 1992, 221). The closing decade of McNickle's life might thus have seemed somewhat of a vindication of his life work. While the 1975 Self-Determination Act was legislated two years after publication of *Native American Tribalism*, we can read in McNickle's accounts of earlier developments the values of pluralism echoing toward that future and beyond.

For example, Parker's phrase "to accommodate themselves" echoes McNickle's own characterizations of some features of the IRA, which was a major shift of policy, again toward pluralism, earlier in the century. However, in his insider's retrospective analysis of the emergence of the Indian New Deal, he observed that the idea that "there could be an alternative to assimilation" for Indians "was not pursued" directly after the *Meriam Report.* "It remained for the Indian people themselves, a full generation later, to plead the case for self-determination" (McNickle 1973, 92–93). He is referring here to the legislation for "self-determination" in the 1970s. Again, Indian communities and leadership were working for decades against deliberate "restriction of Indian freedom" (McNickle 1973, 88). Thus, it is all the more significant that McNickle makes visible a trend toward pluralism underneath policies that were willfully blind to pluralist values, as he writes, "until the third decade of the present century Indian policy was rooted in the assumption that the Indians would disappear. Authorities responsible for policy continued to refer to a diminishing population long after the growth had turned upward." McNickle's analysis clearly is aimed at reversing that root assumption.

Thus, quoting a 1938 *Report of the Commissioner of Indian Affairs* (in which office McNickle had worked during that period forty years before), McNickle valorizes a remarkable summary of the "new purpose" of the Indian New Deal:

> We, therefore, define our Indian policy somewhat as follows: so productively to use the monies appropriated by the Congress for Indians as to enable them, on good, adequate lands of their own, to earn decent livelihoods and lead self-respecting, organized lives in harmony with their own aims and ideals, as an integral part of American life. (quoted in McNickle 1973, 93)

As so often happens in these bureaucratic discussions of "freedom for Indians," we need to peel away the paternalism of federal discourse in order to get to the kernel of justice articulated here—even as we are analyzing, again, the gradual transformation of white supremacy into diverse plurality. That is, we have to pass through Robert Berkhofer's 1978 *White Man's Indian* in order to approach actual Indigenous realities. Thus, it is remarkable in terms of reshaping 1930s American mainstream identity to read here that Indian lives might become "an integral part of American life" if Indians themselves, by "their own aims and ideals," so choose.

Writing in retrospect, McNickle also affirmed the pluralist logic as the "formula" of the 1928 *Meriam Report* that led to the 1934 IRA. "Perhaps the most valuable contribution of the Meriam investigation [into the negative effects of decades of federal Indian policy] was the formulation of a basic concept of the task of administration which would advance the economic position of the Indians and foster social adjustment" (McNickle 1973, 92). He quotes the *Meriam Report*'s recommendation that the Indian Service devote "its main energies to the social and economic advancement of the Indians, so that they may be absorbed into the prevailing civilization or be fitted *to live in the presence of that civilization* at least in accordance with a minimum standard of health and decency" (italics supplied by McNickle). The radically energizing force of this statement was not lost on McNickle, as he comments, "The idea that the Indian people might 'be fitted to live' within the dominant society without being obliterated by it was, indeed, unprecedented as a statement of possible national policy." He carries the logic further to the heart of American ideals, as well as hypocrisies:

> The Meriam formula was also notable as a repudiation of the philosophy of administration which had prevailed since 1871, when the government adopted the thesis that it could legislate Indians into white Americans. It was a recognition [in the 1920s] that freedom of choice is an essential ingredient of a democratic society, a freedom that cannot be exercised unless true alternatives are available. (93)

True alternatives would constitute the prerequisites of a pluralist society. "To live in the presence of that civilization" as an alternative civilization—with autonomy and, again, "with their own aims and ideals, as an integral part of American life"—this would be a radical democratic pluralism as a future for a changed Native America and a changed America.

A few other salient comments in McNickle's account of this alternative presence of pluralism will reinforce our sense of his consciousness of, if not confidence in, this principle moving in history, of "a future for Indians as Indians" (104). By different terms, he traces an alternative pluralist perspective all the way back to the beginnings of the colonial era. This is a radically revisionist history, not changing the past, but rereading it for a more positive future without the inevitability of tragedy. McNickle identifies a humanistic trend, even "a core of positive accomplishment in the colonial policies and practices of the Spanish regime," and he follows such practice through the Dutch and English colonists to the early American republic's policies toward Indians. Grounded in the fifteenth-century papal Doctrine of Discovery, this reversed history, another negative space, actually codified recognition of aboriginal land rights into colonial law, whereby, under many different iterations, the colonists were required by the church or the crown "to give," as McNickle explains, "formal recognition to the occupancy rights of the Indians and to defer to tribal self-government." McNickle is not, of course, blind to the inhumane travesties of history, but he points out this remarkable understory.

> While Spanish policy changed from period to period and lax administration often defeated sound purpose, the effect of the Laws of the Indies was to bring the Indians under the protection of the crown and to anticipate the practice of trusteeship incorporated into law by the United Stands and Canada and provided for by the United Nations with respect to dependent peoples. (28–29)

Here McNickle not only identifies legal obligations of nation-states to their Indigenous populations, but he also anticipates the current global Indigenous movements codified another generation later in the UNDRIP in 2007. That UN document, again driven forward across decades by Indigenous peoples themselves, begins to map cultural and political pluralism on a global scale, precisely by the logic of ongoing Indigenous presence through the colonial and postcolonial eras.

Toward the end of *Native American Tribalism*, McNickle accounts for recent major events of Indian activism in the 1969 occupation of Alcatraz, the 1971 Trail of Broken Treaties, and the 1973 occupation of Wounded Knee. He places these dramatic events in the larger context of "Indian nationalism, pan-Indianism, and Red Power—terms used with some degree of common meaning—[that] indicate a growing sense of shared problems, shared goals, and a shared heritage" (170). Thus, the politics of American pluralism enters a new phase as the voices of difference find ways to consolidate their power. In his concluding chapter entitled "A Closing View," McNickle reflects the ongoing harsh realities, never sugarcoating the pluralist impulses in American or Native American political cultures. Always in context of the larger history, after tracing social protests, such as the long-fought success, "after sixty-five years of unremitting effort" by Taos Pueblo to regain ownership of its sacred Blue Lake, and after tracing new artistic expression highlighted by the 1969 Pulitzer Prize awarded to Kiowa Pueblo novelist, N. Scott Momaday, McNickle concludes, "if the Indian race is to be destroyed, the new voices avow, the destroying agent will have to contend with an integrating tribal people, not with isolated individuals lost in anonymity" (170). McNickle here proclaims that the divide-and-conquer practices of colonial history will no longer work against a "certainty" of "shared goals." His form and tone thus retain the tragic mode, as we can see most directly in the fiction, while his content gestures steadily toward the brighter future of pluralism, toward an America that welcomes rather than excludes Indians.

McNickle's nonfiction thus offers an early articulation of Indigenous pluralism in a modern nation-state. Redirecting the founding assumptions of colonial relations, he presages the goals and strategies of the turn-of-the-century global Indigenous movement, as we referenced Ravna's essay at the start. Again, Ravna observes a shift of recognition; in states where there are minorities and in particular Indigenous peoples, the state has a responsibility to let these nations participate in decision-making processes that concern them. Such participation is the stuff of pluralism, and it remained the purpose of McNickle's prose.

Let's look then at the fiction for similar gestures in which he dramatizes the stakes of pluralism.

"Bull's Voice Reminded Them of Old Days": The Fiction

If McNickle's critique of history was direct in his nonfiction, and if that nonfiction gestures toward pluralism more directly, his fiction mounts an even more dramatic critique of American history as tragic. Thus, his fictional gestures toward pluralism are more indirect. This juxtaposition by genre offers different challenges in parsing out McNickle's pluralistic tendencies and advocacies. His varying aesthetic choices as a historian and as a novelist resonate back and forth. An explicit but tentative pluralism in the nonfiction dares not to hope too much and contrasts with an implicit but commanding pluralism in the fiction and weeping for too little. Together they work to energize and to dramatize pluralism as an even deeper absent presence in American narratives.

McNickle's two major fictional treatments, *The Surrounded* and *Wind from an Enemy Sky* push pluralism beyond revisionist history to the limits of the untranslatable, while they take the next, though not inevitable, step into the tragic. As I hope to have shown above, his nonfiction adopts a somewhat more encouraging and positive outlook. He adopts tragedy in fiction for the same reasons that he strives to rewrite hope in history; he strives to transform his audience through these dramatizations, as well as to inform and re-educate them through history and commentary. Tragedy shapes imaginative narrative structure toward inevitability based on miscommunication or the irreconcilability of opposites. Inevitability is the sine qua non of tragedy. If the tragic ending were escapable, we would have comedy, but here all doors are closed. The author's choice of tragedy is all about McNickle's audience "with its own set of conventions and traditions" (Purdy 1990, 76), even as it evolves with the author's guidance.

Let's look now at how McNickle insists on authentic difference, with implications for re-envisioning America, especially through his central characterization of Bull in *Wind from an Enemy Sky*.[8] Eventually we shall see how the author's choice of a tragic mode in fiction serves the same political purpose as his choice to make visible the hope of pluralism in his nonfiction. McNickle chooses the most radical "hothead" (121) to make his point of difference and pluralism most dramatically. Yet this is not merely a dramatic strategy. To choose a radical, violent characterization in Bull is to probe precisely the dominant politics that would reduce pluralism to extremism. By branding difference as extreme—by criminalizing "the Indian"—the dominant system of power only deflects its ethical obligation to recognize difference and to "allow" pluralism into the fabric of society.

More specifically, I suggest that Bull reflects the historical figure of the Salish chief Charlo, who held out the longest—for four decades—against the Hellgate Treaty of 1855 and against relocating his people from their Bitterroot homeland 100 miles north to the Flathead Reservation where they were to be "confederated" with the Pend d'Oreille and Kootenai nations. In the novel the decades-long conflict between Bull and his brother Henry Jim reads like a metaphor of the historical divisions between one Salish faction, led by Charlo, who held on to their ancestral lands until the bitter end, and another faction, led by Arlee, who migrated to the reservation early on. Although the history was more complex—and thus less "inevitably" or tragically polarized—the Bull versus Henry Jim split picks up that internal divide by simplifying it into recognizable tragic oppositions. In reality, Charlo, who resisted relocation to the reservation, actually adopted strict Catholicism, while Arlee, who relocated early on, retained his Salish traditions less syncretically. Instead of the historical north-south divide between the Flathead and the Bitterroot watersheds, the novel splits these factions of the people between the mountainous foothills and the farming valley, between a resistant hunter camp and an assimilated farming economy.

In Bull's first response to his estranged brother's unexpected overture for reconciliation after decades of distrust, the narration maps the opposition.

> Bull stared, his lips parted for speech, but he could not yet bring himself to it. A hard center in his mind resisted. How could he push aside thirty years as if they had never troubled him or the people who stayed with him in their foothill camps and went hungry with him because he would not lead them down to the flats where they could have had government wagons and teams, flour and coffee, [and] fence posts? (20)

Bull's wariness in relation to his brother amounts to a suspicion of white culture, since Henry Jim has so aligned himself with assimilation of the white agricultural economy and rejection of things Indian, a denial of difference that pluralism would recognize.

Because of that wariness, Bull's character, and his Indian pluralist authenticity, throughout the novel are essentially criminalized in the eyes of white society—as Bull himself confirms in the shootout at the end. This outlaw dynamic further dramatizes the tragic, untranslatable nature of Bull's authenticity, even as it dramatizes the need for a pluralist alternative. Where pluralism is confused with extremism, as difference is confused with denial, tragedies ensue. An American federal policy founded on the erasure of Indians must reduce difference to a threat.

Thus, McNickle's agonized story line cries for a different view of colonial relations and of Indian manhood that does not drive a leader to violence. He summons not a view that rejects authentic difference but one, as we see in McNickle's other writing, that makes room for difference in a pluralist society. As the cross-culturally savvy Doc Edwards explains of the criminality projected onto Bull, "it would be an eagle feather in [the U.S. Marshal's] Stetson if he could pin it on Bull or one of his men. Every lawman who's ever been in here has been after him" (70). Edwards even recognizes that the issue is not the unsolved murder, not specific legalities, or not any specific crime against any particular law but Bull's more general colonial crime of resisting the dominant power and of insisting on his own people's difference.

Edwards even points away from the specific lawmen to "the country" itself who targets the "cantankerous" (121) Indian insurgent: "I hope you realize that Bull is one Indian this country would like to put behind bars, guilty or not. All these years he stood out against fellows like this Henry Jim, his own brother. If it hadn't been for him, more of this Indian land would be in white ownership." Doc Edwards names the dynamic: Indian bodies stand in the way of whites' seizing Indian land. The "legal" infrastructure for this seizure was set in place by the 1887 Dawes Allotment Act and the series of homestead acts since 1862. If Bull and his clan are declared criminals and thus thrown in jail, the human obstacles will be removed, and the land will be thrown open even farther to dispossession.

With this legislated, predatory economic base explicitly driving the plot, the characterization of Bull insists on his traditional warrior persona, only aggravating the absorptive-resistive oppositionality of capitalism, versus pluralism, and carrying it toward the final logic of violence. Following directly on a narrative comment about the impossibility of translation across the violent frontiers of colonialism, "the words men speak never pass from one language to another without some loss of flavor and ultimate meaning." The reader has been introduced to Bull, through his name, as someone, even something, radically different. "Bull, it was, the animal, but really something that was man and animal, and neither. Everyone knew him thus, knew his massive, eroded face, his strongly jointed frame, and his ponderous gaze when he considered a man and his words. He talked, though, in a lively, even lilting, voice, and that was an odd thing." (2)

McNickle's literary skill paints this potent character with a uniqueness and eccentricity, an almost feminine "lilting voice," that gives him more individuality, difference, and thus authenticity in the authority of his gaze and his odd tone. Rounding out Bull's "strongly jointed" character, the lilt of his voice, referred to at a number of points in the novel, eventually links the reader to Bull's protective feelings, feelings that in some societies would be identified with maternal qualities, but that McNickle portrays at the heart of the warrior.

This gentleness does not undercut the warrior persona, but underlines the protective, communal dimensions of traditional warrior roles in Native cultures. Across many Indian cultures, from Athabascan, to Pueblo, and to High Plains Lakota, and from Salish to Seminole, the nurturing qualities of fatherhood are paramount, even within the warrior.[9] We see such qualities in Bull's grief for his lost daughter, Celeste, in his grandfatherly care for Antoine, in his self-sacrificial efforts over the decades, and ultimately in the final, tragically violent moments of the plot. He lives and dies for his family, his clan, and his people. Inwardly, the authenticity of his personal difference upholds their sovereignty. Outwardly toward the whites, his warrior self is communal in the name of pluralism.

One of the initial scenes of confrontation with the U.S. marshal, Sid Grant, demonstrates this point of social responsibility in the warrior's role. After the marshal shouts from horseback at Bull's camp, the chief turns to

Two Sleeps, the old seer, and asks bitingly, "old man, what do you see now? Is this the way we are going to get help from the white man?" Charged by the dramatic pressure of the marshal, the scene continues with a description of this underground quality of a warrior's strength summoning the collective tribal spirit. "Bull's voice reminded them of old days. He had hardly lifted his voice, but the lilt they heard cut the air like a whiplash. The older ones felt a stirring in their veins, and a song came up in their throats. But they held back" (75). Bull's rallying vigor always, as here, speaks from and for the strength of the entire camp.

Yet as a leader he is also conscious, like the author, of the issues of translation, as he speaks to Son Child, the tribal police officer, known as The Boy. "You know our language, and you know this man's [the Agent's] language. I want you to be the man who talks between us. Anybody else would mix everything up. You are now like my son, and it will be that way between us" (180). Bull does not want to "mix everything up." He wants the pluralist recognition—and respect—of authentic translation. He wants a communication across cultures that retains authenticity in listener and speaker and that speaks the truth of and to each other. In this passage he recognizes the equilibrium of power he seeks as leader of his people, the reciprocity of translating authentic selfhood across linguistic and cultural barriers. Thus, at the heart of his cantankerous resistance, of his insistence on authentic translation, lies this hope of pluralism. The final tragic irony prevails against pluralist translation of authenticity when The Boy has to use his revolver to shoot Bull because the chief speaks with a rifle instead of with words. Or we may say, sadly, that The Boy's revolver directly translates Bull's rifle.

The warrior authenticity in Bull's final gesture is the ultimate assertion of pluralist difference in the novel. The violence of that gesture tends to reinforce difference as danger, a threat to life and community, because it primarily plays out the logic of colonial capital intruding and exploiting Bull's world. Here it is sufficient to link Bull's action to his own resignation, his failure—as the whites' failure—to achieve pluralist recognition. "'I told all of you my gun would speak for me, and I think the time has come. It is no good talking to these men. This is all they understand.' He patted the butt of the rifle" (255). According to Bull's experience, words don't translate into meaning across the bureaucratic frontier. Violence "is all they understand," and it is the only language that translates to white listeners who would assimilate, if not annihilate, difference. As Bull seizes the rifle and levers a cartridge into the chamber, his grandson Antoine (who stands in for Archilde revisited from *The Surrounded*) sees the claim of authenticity against denial of such difference in a desperate moment. "Antoine saw his grandfather's face in the same instant, and recognized the look of wild despair. He knew that the thing he had imagined would finally happen. Black blood would spill on the ground. His grandfather would feel strong again, and the boy was proud for him." Within the tragic, limiting terms of frontier confrontation, the grandfather's warrior choices again serve the strength of the ongoing generations. For that reason, for the linkages in this climactic moment between Bull's identity, his community, and the sovereignty of his people through his grandson, Bull's authentic life is not afraid of death, as he shouts his view of the wealthy exploiter, Adam Pell. "He can die like the rest of us! Now let them walk over our heads! We won't have to care anymore!" Difference denied is a dream of pluralism deferred.

Even as Bull starts shooting, McNickle returns us yet again to the theme of authentic translation and the failure of recognition. "Bull's words were never translated. With the rifle held hip high, he shot Adam Pell through the chest and saw him fall backward. The startled look in Adam's eyes dulled quickly." While the ultimate failure of translation here is the killing of life, we see in the seconds leading to the next death yet more thematic focus on miscommunication. Agent Rafferty, who precipitated this moment, this entire confrontation, has just seen "the fatal error of encouraging Adam to speak" about the death of the stolen Feather Boy bundle. The entire tangle of failed recognition of difference across cultures, in this misfired meeting and in the longer history of dispossession of land and culture, becomes "the fatal error" that kills Rafferty as well. Even in this crucial instant, Rafferty fails to read the situation. In his patronizing position as Agent he fails to translate the authentic depths of human anger in Bull. Lethally, Bull reads Rafferty's belated attempt to interact as only another intrusion:

> Rafferty could not believe it was happening. Even as Bull turned the gun on Adam, he had thought it to be no more than a quick flare of anger.
>
> After the shot, Rafferty leaped forward and at the same time called to The Boy, "Stop him! Grab the gun!"
>
> Bull saw the movement. He swung the gun as Rafferty lunged forward, and fired, hitting him high in the forehead, just below the receding hairline. (256)

Then as The Boy finally shoots and kills Bull, who "turned, knowing it would come" and who "had not tried to lift the rifle," the desperately murderous chief abruptly becomes the martyr. His resistance is not to protect himself but his people. His authentic difference serves tribal sovereignty. The scene is further complicated by the fact that the tribal police chief, The Boy, like the historical killers of Crazy Horse and Sitting Bull, is himself Indian, effectively locating the problem not in race but in internalized colonialism and the ultimate violence that drives colonialism against pluralism and hierarchy against democracy. Race logically becomes only a decoy, a shell game, for the real secret, the issue of domination and dispossession, and the land. Power. Land. Erasure. As we see this scene in the larger context of McNickle's work, neither race nor authentic ethnic difference can be erased, but power might be shared. He dramatizes the tragic opposite, where difference is no longer, or never was, the robust energy of community, but becomes the excuse for domination rather than pluralism.

Reflecting the pattern of his own life, McNickle set Native expression, political and artistic, as a prerequisite for an authentic America that lives up to its ideals. As the motto "from many, one" continues across the centuries to percolate through the evolving nation, engaging all classes, races, and genders, the logic of an authentic e pluribus unum requires that the pluribus, the Indigenous citizens of many dominated nations, step forth and tell their story to the unum.

Where the ethical structures of tribal sovereignty have existed "since time immemorial" in what Vine Deloria, Jr., describes as "inherent rights,"[10] the legal structures codifying those aboriginal land rights have varying histories in varying regions of the world. Treaty making in the United States until 1871, when the Congress declared an end to treaties by arrogating its own "plenary power," lead eventually to twentieth-century recognition of that "government-to-government" relationship between U.S. Indigenous nations and Washington. These codifications preceded much of the other arrangements across the globe, such as Sámi rights, which were codified, as Ravna explains, in the Finnmark Act in 2005 after years of efforts to recognize the land rights of the Indigenous Sámi.

As we have seen, McNickle called for such recognition in various voices, by the objective narrative of a historian and by the subjective dramas of a novelist. He raised the call in print throughout the twentieth century as a solid echo of the more ephemeral voices of millions of Indigenous peoples across those years who made the same claim to their rights on the land.

Notes

1. See, for instance, chapter 1 on sovereignty in my text *That Dream Shall Have a Name: Native Americans Rewriting America*. See also Deloria and Lytle (1984) *The*

Nations Within: The Past and Future of American Indian Sovereignty; Wilkins (1997) *American Indian Sovereignty and the U.S. Supreme Court: The Masking of Justice*; Anaya (1996) *Indigenous Peoples in International Law*; Williams (1990) *The American Indian in Western Legal Thought: The Discourses of Conquest*; and Bruyneel (2007) *The Third Space of Sovereignty: The Postcolonial Politics of U.S.-Indigenous Relations.*

2. See David L. Moore (2014) "'Through the Monster's Mouth': Contemporary Poetry of the Flathead Reservation."

3. For the clarity of this working definition, I'm grateful for conversations with Haudenosaunee philosopher Vera Palmer, who is now at Dartmouth College.

4. See the classic essay by Mary Louise Pratt (1991) "Arts of the Contact Zone" for a map of representational dynamics in the colonial encounter.

5. e pluribus unum (Latin for "out of many, one"), although not the official motto, has been on the Great Seal of the United States since it was adopted by an Act of Congress in 1782.

6. See the introduction to my 2013 text, *That Dream Shall Have a Name: Native Americans Rewriting America.*

7. See, for instance, Jose Barreiro's (1992) *Indian Roots of American Democracy*; Oren Lyons and John Mohawk's (1992) *Exiled in the Land of the Free: Democracy, Indian Nations, and the U.S. Constitution*, and for a more populist treatment, Jack Weatherford's (1991) *Indian Roots: How the Indians Enriched America.*

8. For the sake of space, I will concentrate on the latter novel, which functions as a dramatic summary of McNickle's life of thinking. A longer study might not only analyze *The Surrounded* as well but also explore reader response among McNickle's largely white readership and how the author strategically employs the Aristotelian catharsis of tragedy, as in *Wind from an Enemy Sky*, to shock bigots among his white readership out of the inhumanity of Marshal Sid Grant, or to nudge others to shift from the patronizing sympathy of Adam Pell to the more equitable humanity of Doc Edwards.

9. See, for instance, Joyzelle Godfrey, Bill Iron Moccasin, and Joseph M. White (2006) "American Indian Fathering in the Dakota Nation: Use of Akicita as a Fatherhood Standard."

10. See Deloria and Lytle (1984), *The Nations Within: The Past and Future of American Indian Sovereignty.*

References

Anaya, S. James. 1996. *Indigenous Peoples in International Law.* New York: Oxford University Press.

Barreiro, Jose, ed. 1992. *Indian Roots of American Democracy.* Ithaca, NY: Akwekon Press, Cornell University.

Berkhofer, Robert F., Jr. 1978. *The White Man's Indian: Images of the American Indian from Columbus to the Present.* New York: Knopf.

Bruyneel, Kevin. 2007. *The Third Space of Sovereignty: The Postcolonial Politics of U.S.-Indigenous Relations.* Minneapolis: University of Minnesota Press.

Deloria, Vine, Jr., and Clifford M. Lytle. 1984. *The Nations Within: The Past and Future of American Indian Sovereignty.* Austin: University of Texas Press.

Eck, Diana L. "What is Pluralism?" *The Pluralism Project*. Harvard University. http://pluralism.org/pages/pluralism/what_is_pluralism. Accessed May 2, 2012.

Godfrey, Joyzelle, Bill Iron Moccasin, and Joseph M. White. 2006. "American Indian Fathering in the Dakota Nation: Use of Akicita as a Fatherhood Standard." *Fathering: A Journal of Theory, Research, and Practice about Men as Fathers* 4(1):49–69.

Lyons, Oren, and John Mohawk, eds. 1992. *Exiled in the Land of the Free: Democracy, Indian Nations, and the U.S. Constitution*. Santa Fe: Clear Light.

McNickle, D'Arcy. (1936) 1980. *The Surrounded*. Albuquerque: University of New Mexico Press.

———. (1949) 1975. *They Came Here First: The Epic of the American Indian*. New York: Octagon.

———. 1973. *Native American Tribalism: Indian Survivals and Renewals* (Revised and expanded version of *The Indian Tribes of the United States*). Published for The Institute of Race Relations, London. New York: Oxford University Press.

———. (1978) 1988. *Wind from an Enemy Sky*. Albuquerque: University of New Mexico Press.

Meeker, Joseph W. (1972) 1996. "The Comic Mode." In *The Ecocriticism Reader: Landmarks in Literary Ecology*, edited by Cheryll Glotfelty and Harold Fromm, 155–69. Athens: University of Georgia Press.

Moore, David L. 2013. *That Dream Shall Have a Name: Native Americans Rewriting America*. Lincoln: University of Nebraska Press.

———. 2014. "'Through the Monster's Mouth': Contemporary Poetry of the Flathead Reservation." In *These Living Songs: Reading Montana Poetry*, edited by Brady Harrison and Lisa Simon, 132–49. Missoula: University of Montana Press.

Parker, Dorothy R. 1992. *Singing an Indian Song: A Biography of D'Arcy McNickle*. Lincoln: University of Nebraska Press.

Pratt, Mary Louise. 1991. "Arts of the Contact Zone." *Profession 91*. (Annual) Modern Language Association, 33–40.

Purdy, John Lloyd. 1990. *Word Ways: The Novels of D'Arcy McNickle*. Tucson: University of Arizona Press.

Reed, Ishmael. 1991. "What's American About America?" In *Ourselves Among Others: Cross-Cultural Readings for Writers*, 2nd ed., edited by Carol J. Verburg, 4–7. Boston: St. Martin's Press.

Smith, Anna Marie. 1998. *Laclau and Mouffe: The Radical Democratic Imaginary*. New York: Routledge.

Weatherford, Jack. 1991. *Indian Roots: How the Indians Enriched America*. New York: Ballantine.

Wilkins, David E. 1997. *American Indian Sovereignty and the U.S. Supreme Court: The Masking of Justice*. Austin: University of Texas Press.

Williams, Robert A., Jr. 1990. *The American Indian in Western Legal Thought: The Discourses of Conquest*. New York: Oxford University Press.

CHAPTER FIVE

Federal-Tribal Comanagement of the National Bison Range

The Challenge of Advancing Indigenous Rights Through Collaborative Natural Resource Management in Montana

Robin Saha and Jennifer Hill-Hart

The National Bison Range is . . . the heart of the Tribes' traditional home-lands, lands that have been occupied from time immemorial. Buffalo, then and now, form an inextricable bond between our people and our earth.

—MICHEL PABLO, TRIBAL COUNCIL CHAIRMAN,
CONFEDERATED SALISH AND KOOTENAI TRIBES[1]

Introduction

After over two decades of negotiations, the United Nations (UN) adopted the UN Declaration on the Rights of Indigenous Peoples (UNDRIP) in 2007. Key goals of UNDRIP are to confront discrimination and marginalization, protect human rights and treaty rights, maintain and strengthen Indigenous cultures and institutions, and support the self-determination of the world's 370 million Indigenous peoples. In particular UNDRIP recognizes that rights to lands, territories, and resources are essential to Indigenous cultures, subsistence, and development. Although UNDRIP is not legally binding and does not provide a specific blueprint for advancing Indigenous rights, it expresses aspirations and principles necessary to protect the rights of Indigenous people. The preamble of UNDRIP states that the recognition of Indigenous rights is essential to "harmonious and cooperative relations" between national governments and Indigenous peoples, "based on principles of justice, democracy, respect for human rights, non-discrimination, and good faith" (UN 2007). The preamble also states that "treaties, agreements and other constructive arrangements, and the relationship they represent, are the basis for a strengthened partnership." This proposition stems from the recognition that hundreds of years of historical injustices (e.g., conquest, genocide, colonization, dispossession, relocation, exploitation, and oppression) have necessitated a shift in favor of greater power and influence for Indigenous people, which requires constructive engagement and a complementary legal foundation. Thus, it is important to understand and appreciate how specific treaties, laws, and policies of the United States can facilitate partnerships between the federal government and Native American tribes in ways that can simultaneously advance Indigenous rights and help correct legacies of injustice.[2] It is also important to understand how such partnerships may be impeded and what can be done to overcome such challenges.

Although there are many federal laws, regulations, executive orders, and judicial rulings that either reserve or confer rights to the tribes in matters generally affecting tribal interests, the Tribal Self-Governance Act of 1994 (TSGA) provides the legal underpinning for the federal-tribal natural resource management partnerships between the U.S. government and Native American tribes. Specifically, it is the basis for the comanagement arrangement of the National Bison Range (NBR), the topic of examination in this chapter. The NBR, a unit of the National Wildlife Refuge System, is overseen by the United States Fish and Wildlife Service (US-FWS). It is located in the State of Montana (see map, p.145), entirely within the Flathead Indian Reservation, home to the Confederated Salish and Kootenai Tribes (hereafter referred to as CSKT or "the Tribes").

Comanagement under the TSGA is not an easy or straightforward path. We argue that such partnerships, if they meet certain conditions necessary for what we call "true comanagement," can strengthen tribal sovereignty and thereby advance Indigenous rights. True comanagement also helps advance Indigenous rights to the extent that it upholds key principles of justice and fairness embodied in UNDRIP and is consistent with several articles of UNDRIP. The case of NBR illuminates how contentious federal-tribal comanagement can be even when conditions of true comanagement are mostly met. Agency resistance initially frustrated comanagement efforts and persistent opposition from numerous quarters continues to impair progress. Still, there are signs that tribal sovereignty has been enhanced and Indigenous rights advanced, albeit incrementally and not

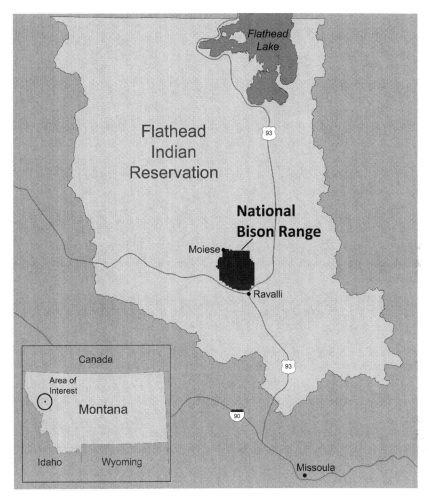

National Bison Range. Map by Matthew Nordhagen.

without numerous delays and setbacks. While the case of the NBR can be viewed through the lens of paternalism that characterizes much federal Indian law in the United States, we recognize that "undoing" hundreds of years of historical injustice is going to be a long-term project.[3] Thus, we seek to highlight what we see as an important step in the path to justice. It is apt to recall Martin Luther King, Jr.'s statement that the "arc of the moral universe is long but curves toward justice."

Our chapter proceeds in the following manner. First, we discuss specific articles of UNDRIP that pertain to Indigenous peoples' interests in natural resource management. Second, we discuss conceptual and practical aspects of comanagement and articulate how comanagement of natural resources can advance Indigenous rights by supporting tribal sovereignty if the conditions for true comanagement are met. Third, we discuss the TSGA as the crucial legal foundation for federal-tribal comanagement and explicate ways the TSGA is consistent with principles of UNDRIP; it thereby has potential to advance Indigenous rights. Fourth, we describe the historical and cultural context for the NBR that is useful for understanding the current controversial situation. The bulk of our case study analysis follows; it includes a detailed account of repeated rounds of comanagement negotiations between the USFWS and the Tribes, which was followed by implementation and cancellation of those agreements. In doing so, we consider some of the ways that comanagement of the NBR under the TSGA adheres to some of the principles embodied in UNDRIP, including the articles of the UNDRIP presented below. For our analysis we rely largely on secondary sources including news coverage and government documents, such as official correspondence, administrative records, congressional testimony, and judicial proceedings. These sources are supplemented with observations and personal communications from site visits in 2003 and 2009.

Our analysis reveals that, despite the difficulties and delays encountered, comanagement of the NBR exhibits the features of true comanagement. We argue that these characteristics of comanagement enhance tribal sovereignty in this case, although modestly. Finally, we conclude that comanagement of the NBR helps to advance Indigenous rights as articulated in UNDRIP. We temper this conclusion with the qualification that the comanagement regime at the NBR is precarious. Moreover, racially charged, anti-Indian community opposition and federal agency and employee resistance have posed tremendous obstacles that provide cautionary lessons for other attempts to advance Indigenous rights through federal-tribal comanagement partnerships.

United Nations Declaration on the Rights of Indigenous Peoples

Identifying specific rights related to land and natural resources, UNDRIP establishes the importance of effective federal-tribal relations and associated legal mechanisms that can guide the management of culturally significant resources. For example, article 26 recognizes Indigenous rights to traditional lands and resources, traditional ownership, and the protection of traditional lands and resources.[4] Article 27 refers specifically to relations between national governments and Indigenous peoples and requirements for inclusion and participation, including a "fair, independent, impartial, open, and transparent process," with "due recognition to Indigenous peoples' laws, traditions, customs, and land tenure systems." Article 29 similarly asserts the "right to the conservation and protection of the environment and the productive capacity of . . . [Indigenous] lands or territories and resources." Article 31 proclaims the right to "maintain, control, protect, and develop" Indigenous peoples' cultural heritage, traditional knowledge, traditional cultural expressions, and related intellectual property rights. The article also calls for national governments (states) to "take effective measures to recognize and protect the exercise of these rights." Article 32 concerns the "right to determine and develop priorities and strategies for the development or use of their lands or territories and other resources." The article also calls for states to "consult and cooperate in good faith with the Indigenous peoples concerned through their own representative institutions . . . [for] any project affecting their lands or territories and other resources, particularly in connection with the development, utilization, or exploitation of mineral, water, or other resources." Article 32 prompts states to "provide effective mechanisms for just and fair redress . . . and appropriate measures shall be taken to mitigate adverse environmental, economic, social, cultural, or spiritual impact."

Comanagement as a Type of Shared Jurisdiction and a Means for Advancing Tribal Sovereignty

Although multiple definitions of comanagement have been offered, no single definition has found wide acceptance. Comanagement can be thought of as a type of shared jurisdiction and a way to strengthen tribal sovereignty—a step toward reversing the historic legacy of injustice to Native Americans.[5] As such, comanagement is replete with the ambiguities and imperfections that surround the notion of tribal sovereignty and the practical challenges of sharing of power. Marcus Lane and Michael Hibbard (2005, 174), who also quote James Tully's chapter, "The Struggles of Indigenous Peoples for and of Freedom," in *Political Theory and the Rights of Indigenous Peoples* (2000), and interpret the struggles for tribal sovereignty this way.

> Indigenous claims to sovereignty are part of a systematic program of resistance to "internal colonization." . . . They are an effort to reconfigure

the terms of Indigenous-state relations. They do this by . . . creating the means for *sharing* jurisdiction. Shared jurisdiction is, in turn, enabled by providing for relations between "equal, self-governing and coexisting entities, and set up [*sic*] negotiation procedures to work out consensual and mutually binding relations of autonomy and interdependence." (Tully 2000, 53)

Ohlson and colleagues underscore the importance of examining power sharing to distinguish comanagement from other types of cooperative management, such as those involving consultation, public participation (so-called comment and review periods), advisory roles, consent, or informal collaboration. They state that though the federal and tribal governments may work together to protect, conserve, and restore natural resources, "comanagement only occurs where each management entity has legally established management responsibility; ideally, the two governments function as equal partners. In cooperative management arrangements, one agency or government has authority over the other" (Ohlson et al. 2008, 435).

In her paper in *Human Ecology* titled "Ecological Restoration and Local Communities" (quoted in Castro and Nielsen, 2001, 230), Fredrica Bowcutt also views comanagement as a partnership and similarly defines it as "a situation in which two or more social actors negotiate, define, and guarantee amongst themselves an equitable sharing of the management functions, entitlements, and responsibilities for a given territory or set of natural resources." We concur with Martin Nie's view that tribal comanagement "on federal land should be built upon basic principles of American Indian law," and "tribal comanagement should not be confused with other types of stakeholder cooperation or other public-private partnerships" (Nie 2008, 586). According to Nie, federal-tribal comanagement is the "sharing of resource management goals and responsibilities between tribes and federal agencies" (Nie 2008, 602). In his article in *Environmental Law* titled "Protecting Habitat for Off-Reservation Tribal Hunting and Fishing Rights," Ed Goodman offers two definitions of comanagement.

Comanagement embodies the concept and practice of two (or more) sovereigns working together to address and solve matters of critical concern to each. Comanagement is not a demand for a tribal veto power over federal projects, but rather a call for an end to federal unilateralism in decision making affecting tribal rights and resources. It is a call for a process that would incorporate, in a constructive manner, the policy and technical expertise of each sovereign in a mutual, participatory framework. (quoted in Nie 2008, 602)

In *Conservation Through Cultural Survival*, the Canadian Royal Commission on Aboriginal Peoples states that comanagement arrangements involving aboriginal communities in Australia and Canada have provided "significant vehicles for participatory power sharing" by providing "institutional arrangements enlarging the scope for local participation in decision making over resources, while also respecting Indigenous land claims" (quoted in Castro and Nielsen 2001, 236). Marren Sanders (2007) suggests that comanagement offers not just a seat at the table, but rather a means to nation-building achieved by strengthening tribal capacity for self-governance, improving government-to-government relationships, and reducing cultural barriers between tribes and federal agencies.

Comanagement has unsurprisingly attracted criticism. Since it is not synonymous with the restoration or repatriation of tribal land to autonomous tribal management, tribes themselves have been critical of comanagement for various reasons. For example, Western management approaches too often dominate and leave little room for relevant, unique tribal conceptions, which have often focused on "respect and duty" in contrast to the "[property] rights and claims" that characterize the Euro-American approach (Tsoise 1996, 281). In "Land, Landscape, Culturescape," included in the Report for the Royal Commission on Aboriginal Peoples, Land, Resource and Environment Regimes Project, Andrew Chapeskie states that Western models of comanagement are often "culturally foreign and not infrequently repugnant to most of those who continue to work on the land in accordance with their customs"; this is a view that has led to calls for "negotiations based on the holistic concept of coexistence rather than on the comanagement of a particular resource" (quoted in Castro and Nielsen 2001, 236). Speaking more generally, Sanders (2007, 129) asserts and laments that "federal Indian policy has created dependency among Indian nations such that tribes have to rely on 'someone else's institutions, someone else's rules, [and] someone else's models, to get things done.'" Sanders also points out that comanagement has sometimes been equated with state regulation of tribal lands and resources, thereby undermining tribal sovereignty. The potential shortcomings of comanagement serve as a reminder of the importance of bilateralism, that is, the government-to-government, that is, the tribal-to-federal relationship of comanagement.

Comanagement arrangements may not end up serving tribal interests if they are not afforded due consideration, if, for example, parity or near parity does not exist in negotiations, or if tribal participation in governance and representative bodies are overwhelmed by other stakeholder groups. Representation of tribal interests can be similarly affected by the way members of such groups are selected and appointed. The adequacy of tribal representation can be further complicated by a diversity of perspectives internal to a tribe (Castro and Nielsen 2001). Comanagement can be undermined by lack of support by governmental agencies or elements within them, whereby "agencies may seek to co-opt such initiatives, trying to guide activities so that the government remains the controlling partner" (Castro and Nielsen 2001, 232). Furthermore, political and personal interests can also fuel the desire to retain state control over natural resources. As Castro and Nielsen note, "resource managers may perceive more risks than benefits from formally incorporating the views of multiple stakeholders into their plans and activities" and state that in the end, "co-management can mean reduced authority, a decline in influence, and smaller budgets" (Castro and Nielsen 2001, 232). When comanagement is not perceived to be in the interests of or benefitting either party, lack of cooperation can prevent goals from being achieved to the detriment of natural resources and the exercise of Indigenous rights. Astonishingly, nearly all of these dynamics characterize the case of comanagement of the NBR.

Additional significant obstacles to effective tribal-federal comanagement more generally include the lack of supporting laws and policies and existing laws and policies that create uncertainty or that limit the scope of formal agreements, the role for tribal governments, or the extent to which power is shared. Consider, for example, the 1994 presidential memorandum on "Government-to-Government Relations with Native American Tribes" and Exec. Orders No. 13084 (63 Federal Register 27,655–57 (May 14, 1998)) and No. 13275, "Consultation and Coordination with Indian Tribal Governments" (65 Federal Register 67,249–52 (Nov. 6, 2000)), which require that executive agencies consult with tribal governments to the greatest extent practical and to the extent permitted by law prior to taking actions that affect tribes. These orders have the stated purpose to improve internal management but do not create any right to enforceable action. Even when seemingly promising, judicially enforceable laws exist, judicial interpretations may circumvent their use for advancing Indigenous rights (Zelmer 2002; Wiles 2010).

It is our contention that comanagement offers the potential to enhance tribal sovereignty in a number of ways, most importantly by enabling "*de facto* sovereignty" or sovereignty in practice, as articulated by Stephen Cornell and Joseph P. Kalt in "Myths and Realities of Tribal Sovereignty" (from the *2004–2003 Joint Occasional Papers on Native Affairs*). They distinguish *de facto* sovereignty from *de recto* sovereignty, that originating from a moral claim (or an expression of principles and aspirations), and *de jure* sovereignty, that afforded by having a legal framework in place. According to Cornell and Kalt, to exercise tribal sovereignty effectively, tribes must do more than make a de recto claim or exist under a de jure legal condition; de facto sovereignty "means Indian Nations have genuine decision-making control of their own futures, including use of tribal resources" (Sanders 2007, 128). As explained by Sanders (2007, 171–72), "De facto sovereignty . . . is not just making the federal government live up to its trust and treaty obligations. It is recognizing that regardless of the stated polices of self-determination and government-to-government relations, tribal sovereignty operationally falls to tribes who must assert sovereignty by performing the functions of effective government."

The above theoretical discussion leads us to our definition of true comanagement, which has the potential to enhance tribal sovereignty. True comanagement requires (1) power sharing, (2) responsibility sharing, (3) tribal control, and (4) supporting federal legislation.

We next provide specific background for the examination of our case. First, we discuss the TSGA, the legal foundation for federal-tribal comanagement of the NBR. That is followed by a very brief history of federal Indian policy on the Flathead Indian Reservation and the NBR itself, which will provide additional helpful background for our case study analysis.

Tribal Self-Governance Act as a Legal Foundation for Federal-Tribal Comanagement Agreements

In 1994 Congress passed the TSGA as an amendment to the Indian Self-Determination and Education Assistance Act (ISDEAA) of 1975 (U.S.C. § 450a(a), Pub. L. No. 93–638, 88 Stat. 2203 (1975)). The ISDEAA was enacted to establish a meaningful role for federally recognized Indian tribes in the planning, design, and implementation of health, education, and other programs and services to meet the needs of Indian people and communities. The ISDEAA sought to reduce the influence of the federal government in the daily lives of Indian people, while strengthening tribal institutional capacity and expanding opportunities for tribal leadership and self-determination (Lyons 2005). The ISDEAA enabled tribes to contract with and obtain grants from the federal government so they could manage programs and parts of programs that previously had been run solely by the federal government, specifically by the Bureau of Indian Affairs (BIA) and the Department of Health, Education, and Welfare (25 U.S.C. § 450a(a)).[6] Amendments to the ISDEEA in 1988 established the "Self-Governance Demonstration Project," which allowed ten tribes to conduct self-governance pilot projects (Public Law 100–472, 100th Cong., 1st sess., (October 5, 1988)). The ISDEEA granted tribes greater authority to administer, manage, and fund programs, activities, functions, and services such that the Tribes could redesign federal programs and services to meet the needs of their communities.

The TSGA made the Tribal Self-Governance Program permanent. For the first time, eligible tribes could enter into negotiated agreements with non-BIA agencies within the Department of Interior (DOI), particularly the resources management agencies, "to plan, conduct, consolidate, and administer programs, services, functions, and activities, or portions thereof" of those agencies (25 U.S.C. § 458cc(b)(2)). Tribes that meet the criteria for the DOI Tribal Self-Governance Program can petition to administer a non-BIA program or parts thereof when a program is "available to Indian tribes or Indians because of their status as Indians," or a program has "special geographic, historical, or cultural significance" to the tribe (25 U.S.C. § 458cc(b) (2) and 25 U.S.C. § 458cc(c)(b)).[7] Inclusion in the Tribal Self-Governance Program requires that tribes participate in planning activities and demonstrate financial stability and management capacity to the DOI (King 2007). As of 2012, 251 of the 565 federally recognized tribes participate in the program (Roberts 2012).

According to Mary Ann King (2007, 475), "the TSGA links tribal self-determination policy and federal land management, and has the potential to alter federal-tribal relationships and transform institutions for natural resource and public land management." King (2007, 476) states that "the TSGA acknowledges the effect that land management by federal agencies has had on tribal sovereignty," and adds that "the creation of public land has had devastating implications for tribes, their members, and tribal sovereignty." Federal land management has often led to the loss or direct expropriation of tribal land and resources, jurisdiction, and control. Thus, by creating new opportunities for tribes to participate in federal land management and administer programmatic funds, the TSGA offers significant potential to enhance de facto tribal sovereignty with respect to off-reservation resources and federally managed lands on reservations (Suagee 1998).

Under the TSGA, Annual Funding Agreements (AFAs) are the primary mechanism by which self-governance tribes can obtain authorization from the secretary of the interior to assume programs and parts thereof from DOI agencies. Tribes can apply to administer a federal program or carry out a part of one that the secretary of the interior determines is eligible for inclusion in an AFA. Eligibility is up to the discretion of the secretary of the interior and the agencies that ultimately "determine the degree to which tribes may participate in managing federal programs" (King 2007, 501). Annually, the secretary of the interior must publish lists of agency programs and parts of programs that are eligible for AFAs in the *Federal Register.* The notice for Fiscal Year 2013 included: twenty-three programs and sixty-two units of the National Park Service (NPS) in nineteen states; eight programs and nineteen units of the USFWS in nine states; nine Bureau of Land Management (BLM) programs but not specific BLM units; four Bureau of Reclamation (BOR) projects; and all BOR-managed Indian Water Rights Settlement projects (USDOI 2013).

Section 403(k) of the TSGA forbids the secretary of the interior from negotiating AFAs for federal programs, services, functions, or activities that are "inherently federal" or not specifically authorized by the statute (25 U.S.C. § 458cc(k)). Determining what is an "inherently federal function" was specifically at issue with negotiations of an AFA between the Tribes and the USFWS regarding the delegation of program authority at the NBR (Lyons 2005, 728–29). In 1996 the DOI solicitor issued an opinion that provided general guidance on what constitutes "inherently federal."[8] It referred to a doctrine that prohibits the delegation of federal functions "that have been determined by the courts not to be constitutionally delegable" and are "discretionary functions vested in Federal officials" (quoted in King 2007, 503). Drawing on a U.S. Supreme Court ruling (*United States v. Mazurie* 419 U.S. 544 (1975)), the Solicitor nevertheless concluded that the U.S. Congress and the executive branch may delegate power to tribal governments that is not delegable to private, non-governmental entities; they note the limits the doctrine may place on delegation are "relaxed where the delegation is to a tribe in an area where the tribe exercises sovereign authority" (quoted in King 2007, 503). According to a DOI solicitor's opinion, "the more a delegated function relates to tribal sovereignty over members or territory, the more likely it is that the inherently [f]ederal exception of section 403(k) does not apply" (quoted in King 2007, 503). The greater a tribe's cultural or territorial connection to the land or resource, the greater the likelihood of success of a comanagement agreement.

Regarding the delegation of discretionary functions vested in federal officials, the solicitor referred to the Office of Management and Budget Policy letter on "Inherently Governmental Functions," which defines an inherently governmental function as "a function that is so intimately related to the public interest as to mandate performance by Government employees" (quoted in King 2007, 504). The solicitor held that those functions include "the act of governing, i.e., the discretionary exercise of Government authority, and . . . monetary transactions and entitlements" (quoted in King 2007, 504). The solicitor's opinion leaves much open to interpretation and debate. It appears to express the view that TSGA constitutes a congressional delegation of federal authority rather than a congressional recognition of inherent tribal power.

Although the TSGA offers a means for tribes to participate in public land management, the final decision-making power regarding whether to enter into a non-BIA AFA lies with the affected federal agency and the secretary of the interior; however, under section 403(b)(2), agencies are obligated to negotiate, but not necessarily reach an agreement. Despite the retention of federal control, the TSGA requires a government-to-government negotiation process between the federal government and tribes and a corresponding degree of transparency. Congress must be notified ninety days in advance of an AFA going into effect.

The TSGA procedural measures clearly go a step farther than the weak mandates or entirely discretionary consultations of the past. Moreover, AFAs are legally binding and mutually enforcing, though agencies reserve the right to cancel them unilaterally if there is an imminent threat to resources (25 U.S.C. § 458aaa-6(a)(2)(A)). The TSGA requires the DOI to negotiate and enter into AFAs in "a manner consistent with the [f]ederal [g]overnment's laws and trust relationship to and responsibility for the Indian people" (25 U.S.C. § 458cc(a)). Tribes may nevertheless face various legal and financial impediments, as well as the risk of an unfavorable judicial precedent in attempting to enforce this provision.

A snapshot of AFA use under the TSGA suggests that it has received at best only lukewarm acceptance by DOI land management agencies; evidence of systematic resistance to TSGA implementation also exists. In FY 2012 there were only twelve non-BIA AFAs in place within the DOI, five AFAs involve tribes and the BOR, three with NPS, two with the USFWS, and one each with the BLM and Office of the Special Trustee for American Indians (USDOI 2013). The extent to which the AFAs as a whole are achieving true comanagement is not known, and such evaluation is beyond the scope of this chapter.

In her study of AFAs between tribes and the NPS, King concludes that the NPS has "narrowly construed the TSGA, and framed it within the NPS's conventional tools for sharing money and authority with non-tribal entities" (King 2007, 481). She observes that there were only four ongoing AFAs between tribes/consortia and NPS in 2007, adding that the AFAs generally involved "discrete projects—for example, river and watershed restoration, ethnographic and archaeological studies, and planning and construction efforts for NPS facilities—rather than programmatic control and

decision-making" (King 2007, 503). She concludes that "tribes may negotiate on a government-to-government basis with the NPS." She adds that
"it is not clear that the TSGA provides a sovereign nation with any more
programmatic control and decision-making authority than a contractor"
(King 2007, 481).

This outcome, according to King, is the result of resource and capacity
limitations of tribes (i.e., their opportunity, costs, and ability to qualify for
and enter into lengthy negotiations; opposition from external stakeholders,
often conservation groups; issues related to the potential loss of federal jobs;
and biases and resistance from within NPS). She further suggests that
agency responses may stem from NPS's perception that TSGA is in conflict with its legislative mandate and a threat to its control and ownership
of resources, and it views TSGA as a special contracting provision. More
fundamentally, she suggests NPS opposition may relate to seeing "TSGA
as a change in public land law and policy, rather than viewing it as a logical extension of Indian self-determination policy" (ibid., 524). She further
concludes that implementation of the TSGA to date by the NPS prevents
the achievement of TSGA legislative goals to move from tribal self-
determination to self-governance.

Even less is known about the use of AFAs by the USFWS, few in number though they are. Lyons provides several examples of the USFWS's rejection of tribes' petitions (Lyons 2005, 726). The case of the NBR, wherein
the Tribes initially sought substantial management rather than a narrow
set of discrete functions exemplifies many of the same characteristics as
those reported by King with respect to the NPS. Narrow interpretations of
the TSGA do not fulfill congressional intent or go far in advancing Indigenous rights under UNDRIP, in particular article 32, which calls for
good faith negotiations.

Insofar as the TSGA affords tribes legal recognition, it also upholds at
least some measure of Indigenous rights-related land and resource conservation of traditional Indigenous territories, as expressed in the introductory
pronouncements of UNDRIP and in articles 26 and 29. The TSGA's requirement that the federal government negotiate and enter into AFAs in a
manner consistent with federal law and the federal trust relationship to
tribes is consistent with article 27 of the UNDRIP which calls for a "fair,
independent, impartial, open and transparent process." The TSGA is also
in line with article 31, which calls for states to adopt "effective measures"
to protect rights related to "cultural heritage, traditional knowledge, and
traditional cultural expressions," insofar as such rights may be affected
by the management of lands and resources that are also eligible for

comanagement agreements. This suggests that the TSGA has potential for advancing Indigenous rights and correcting historical injustices. Whether comanagement under TSGA in fact constitutes an "effective measure" is an empirical question.

A Brief History of Federal Indian Policy on the Flathead Reservation

On July 6, 1855, the tribes of the Bitterroot Salish, Kootenai, and Upper Pend d'Oreilles signed the Treaty of Hellgate with the U.S. government. Under the provisions of this treaty, the Tribes ceded to the U.S. government over 20 million acres of traditional territory. In exchange for relinquishing ownership and occupancy rights for the ceded lands, the Tribes were promised 1.2 million acres of land to be reserved for their exclusive use. This area would become the Flathead Reservation, located in portions of four counties in western Montana (see map, p. 3). The three tribes were promised privacy and freedom from interference from the U.S. government and were also granted off-reservation hunting and fishing rights.

The General Allotment Act of 1887 (Ch. 119, § 5, 24 Stat. 388, 389 (1887)) reconfigured land ownership on Indian reservations and vastly reduced communal land ownership by dividing much of tribal lands into fee simple plots (typically of 160 acres). Allotment was an attempt to force individual Indians to live sedentarily much like American homesteaders, and after twenty-five years, the General Allotment Act allowed the unallotted land on reservations to be declared as "surplus" and open for sale to non-Indians without compensation to tribes. A separate act of Congress, the Flathead Allotment Act of 1904, thereby opened the way for non-Indian land ownership on the Flathead Reservation, a process that was accelerated by the Burke Act of 1906 (Whitehorn 2003). These policies resulted in the transfer of over a half-million acres from tribal ownership on the Flathead Reservation and resulted in a "checkerboard" pattern of land ownership (Williams 2007). The Office of Indian Affairs (renamed the BIA in 1947) governed nearly all aspects of tribal life on reservations until the Indian Reorganization Act of 1934 (IRA) whereby the federal government "restored" tribal self-governance and some degree of land management back into tribal hands. The IRA returned governing authority to federally recognized tribes but required the establishment of elected tribal councils and encouraged tribes to "adopt a model constitution and charter of incorporation that would give them the power to acquire and manage property"

(Act of June 18, 1934, Ch. 576, 48 Stat. 984 (1934)). This also meant the disempowerment of traditional tribal leaders as governing authorities or official representatives in negotiations with the federal government.

In 1935, having "reorganized," the tribes on the Flathead Reservation adopted the Constitution and Bylaws of the Tribes and officially established their tribal name, as well as becoming the first tribes to adopt a tribal constitution that would be recognized by the federal government.[9] In 1936, by vote, a majority of adult Indians on the Flathead Reservation ratified the Corporate Charter of the Tribes, which was issued by the U.S. secretary of the interior. The Tribes were thereafter able to receive revolving loan funds from the U.S. Treasury that were only made available to Indian chartered corporations for the purpose of promoting the economic development of the Tribes and their members (CSKT 1996a, 1996b). The Tribes were able to return to self-governance and reestablish government-to-government relations with the U.S. government, albeit under the rules established by the U.S. government.

In 1953, in an attempt to force Indians to assimilate into the larger society, the federal government adopted a policy of discontinuing federal trust responsibility to Indian tribes and tribes' abilities to self-govern. The 83rd U.S. Congress ushered in this termination policy by passing a resolution declaring that "Indian tribes and individual members thereof should be freed from [f]ederal supervision and control and from all disabilities and limitations especially applicable to Indians" (H. Con. Res. 108, 83rd Congress, Aug. 1, 1953, 67 Stat. B132). In the ensuing years various Indian tribes, including the Tribes, were targeted for termination whereby federal recognition was to be revoked along with the U.S. government's treaty obligations through the exercise of congressional plenary powers. These measures were also to be accompanied by the dissolution of tribal government and Indian reservations as political entities. With the support of the National Congress of American Indians and the Montana congressional delegation, the Tribes successfully fought to evade termination, citing their history of strong tribal government (Wilkinson 2005). The termination policy failed to dissolve the Flathead Reservation, therefore the CSKT Tribal Council maintained governing authority over lands on the reservation, and the Tribes worked to regain ownership of and expand management authority for their lands. Tribal regulatory authority on the Flathead Reservation is a source of tension because a majority of residents are non-Indians who cannot vote in elections of the Tribes' government officials, in spite of the fact that the Tribes allow and encourage non-member representatives to serve on their resource management boards (CSKT n.d.b). Some residents actively oppose greater tribal authority on the Flathead Reservation (Montana Human Rights Network [MHRN] 2000).

In the most recent era of tribal self-determination, ushered in by the ISDEAA, the Tribes obtained contracts to manage a wide range of programs and thereby established a track record of success in management of their own affairs. The Tribes also developed their own programs, including vibrant, widely recognized natural resources programs that employ numerous well-trained natural resource management professionals, and built a track record of conservation leadership (Lyons 2005; Krahe 2001). The Tribes also embarked on a number of economic development projects, attracted business to the reservation, and continue to use their managerial skills, business acumen, and financial success to repurchase former tribal lands lost during the allotment period.[10] The Tribes' successes enabled them to enter the Self-Governance Program, thereby making them eligible to negotiate an AFA with the USFWS. Moreover, the Tribes established strong government-to-government relations with the federal government, the state of Montana, and various local governments over the last several decades.

A Brief History of the National Bison Range and Its Herd

By the early 1880s, the vast bison herds in the United States had been decimated by the sustained slaughter designed to undermine the resource base and economy of the Plains Indians, facilitate the establishment of railroads, and make way for Euro-American settlers and their livestock in the American West (Smits 1994; LaDuke 1999). In the early 1900s the American Bison Society estimated that only 325 wild bison remained out of the tens of millions that had once roamed the West (Lyons 2005). Other estimates were even lower, and bison could only be found in isolated pockets, such as Yellowstone National Park. As a result, American conservationists and the public grew concerned about protecting the species from extinction. The American Bison Society lobbied President Theodore Roosevelt, and together they urged Congress to establish a protected area for bison on the Flathead Indian Reservation.

Although the bison were not naturally occurring on the reservation, members of the Tribes, Charles Allard and Michel Pablo, had previously maintained a small herd of free-ranging bison on the reservation. Allard and Pablo started their herd with four wild bison calves they obtained from another member of the Tribes; however, by 1906, the Allard-Pablo herd had been sold to various parties in Kalispell, Montana, and Canada (Lyons 2005).

In 1908 Congress authorized the creation of the NBR through the purchase of 18,524 acres on the Flathead Indian Reservation (Lyons 2005). Although Congress allocated funds to pay the Tribes $1.56 an acre for the land, it was land that the Tribes never intended to sell, and the Tribes received much less than the actual value of the land, even if one considers an additional settlement made in the 1970s (Lyons 2005). In 1909 to stock the NBR with bison, many of the animals from the original Allard-Pablo herd and from other locations were purchased with funds raised by the American Bison Society (Germaine White, Information and Education Specialist, CSKT, Fish, Wildlife, Recreation and Conservation Division, personal communication, January 13, 2009). Thus, the NBR herd directly descended from the free-ranging Allard-Pablo herd. It is currently maintained to consist of 350 to 500 animals (USFWS 1990).

The direct expropriation of the Tribes' land to create the NBR represented a loss of tribal jurisdiction and control (King 2007). The creation of the NBR was one of many changes to the landscape that adversely impacted the ability of the Tribes to steward the bison themselves. Most prominently was the previous loss of the Tribes' ability to hunt wild bison along with the subsequent land allotment policies that encouraged private land ownership and a farming lifestyle. In fact, Michel Pablo was forced to sell his herd because a free-ranging herd could not be maintained or otherwise remain economically viable under land allotment and attendant fence building (Germaine White, personal communication, January 13, 2009). The special cultural significance of the bison to the Tribes has nevertheless endured and is a deeply honored relationship held by many other American Indian tribes and First Nations Peoples in Canada. This strong cultural relationship stems from the central role of the bison in cultural traditions, spiritual practices, religious beliefs, and essential lifeways (Fahey 1974). It is this long-standing and close relationship that forms the basis of the Tribes' claims regarding participation in the management of the NBR. Based on various media accounts from 2003, Lyons (2005, 710) conveys the Tribes' perspective regarding their interest in the NBR in this way: "[they] argue, that this is, in the historical, cultural, and geographic sense, their land and their bison herd . . . a resource that would not exist but for the efforts of the ancestors of tribal members."

To the wider American society and many conservationists, the NBR would become an iconic unit of the National Wildlife Refuge System, in part because of the "story" of the powerful majestic bison, a symbol of lost wildness, rugged resourcefulness, and much more recovered from the brink of extinction. The direct involvement of President Roosevelt in the creation of the NBR adds to the mystique, which is considered by some to be one of the "crown jewels" of wildlife refuges in the United States. The powerful, emotive symbolism of the bison coupled with a reverential historic figure in U.S. history creates a natural constituency for preserving the status quo and may contribute to making tribal participation in the management of the NBR so strongly contested (Capriccioso 2003). However, as discussed below, threats to federal jobs and control, as well as strong anti-Indian sentiments, also prominently factor into the controversy that surrounds the attempts to exercise tribal sovereignty.

Early Attempts to Negotiate a Comanagement Agreement

In late 1994, shortly after the provisions of the TSGA were in place, the Tribes began planning to negotiate for comanagement of some of the various programs and operations of the NBR (*Char-Koosta News* 1994).[11] At the same time, the USFWS's Native American Policy with Native American Tribes appeared to signal the agency's readiness to recognize that tribal governments have the authority to "manage, co-manage, or cooperatively manage" fish and wildlife resources (USFWS 1994, 4). Although the Tribes formally requested to commence AFA negotiations and regularly communicated with the Interior Department's Office of Self-Governance, no agreement was reached. By September 1995, attempts at negotiating an AFA had failed, which prompted the Tribes and Montana congressman Pat Williams to contact high-level officials in the Interior Department urging the establishment of good faith negotiations. The Tribes efforts continued throughout 1996 and 1997 and resulted in several high-level meetings but little else. The Interior Department's appropriation bill for fiscal year 1998 included a terse mandate to the USFWS to enter into comanagement negotiations, and it indicated congressional oversight was needed in order jump-start negotiations (USDOI 1997).[12]

However, AFA negotiations did not occur for several more years. Most observers attributed the failure to begin earnest negotiations to the vigorous opposition of then-U.S. senator Conrad Burns and several individual activists. In a 1996 press release the senator accused the two parties (the USFWS and the Tribes) of engaging in secret closed-door negotiations on the future management of the NBR (Azure 1996). State and county elected officials also voiced early opposition to negotiations with the Tribes, and later on to federal-tribal shared management. Montana governor at the time, George Racicot, supported Senator Burns's call for public airing of opposing viewpoints in a clear effort to energize opponents of comanagement and support non-tribal constituents (Azure 1996). Joining the chorus was State Representative Rick Jore, who attended the various public meetings where he expressed his disapproval of the joint management of the NBR. Lake County officials also convened a public meeting that was covered by the local media and served to give voice to local opponents (Azure 1995b).

High-profile involvement of elected officials and local residents' organized efforts brought this issue national attention. Conservation groups were concerned about setting a precedent for federal-tribal comanagement and argued it had the effect of privatizing public lands. Conservation and sportsmen groups claimed that "management of the refuge could be altered, and public use could be changed or made more expensive" (Azure 1995a). For more than a decade, some community members and local and national groups continued to raise concerns about a comanagement agreement by citing fears over federal job loss based on misconceptions about tribal hiring practices, lack of public participation opportunities, and fragmentation of the NBR (Lyons 2005). Responding to these fears, Minette Johnson of Defenders of Wildlife said that people's fears about the potential change in management structure were unfounded because most of the Tribes' fisheries' employees and biologists were non-Indians. She believed that the Tribes would continue to hire employees based upon their qualifications (Azure 1995a).

During initial discussions about comanagement in the mid-1990s, some members of the public expressed opposition to the possibility of the Tribes' management of the NBR through racist commentary and discriminatory stereotyping (Azure 1995a). The Montana Human Rights Network (MHRN), which monitors anti-Indian and white supremacist activity in Montana, documented the anti-Indian opposition to a management role for the Tribes at the NBR. The MHRN report, *Drumming Up Resentment: The Anti-Indian Movement in Montana*, stated that the comanagement discussions "gave the anti-Indian movement its best opportunity for community organizing in years" (MHRN 2000, 30). The MHRN noted that it was common for the anti-Indian movement "to portray the issue as one of whites being oppressed by Indians." Lisa Morris, an ardent advocate against the Tribes having a management role on the NBR, wrote "it might even be fair to point out that when non-white people are up in arms about their lack of voice in the community and proclaim frustration with people in power, they are called oppressed. But when the situation is reversed, the hindered are called racists" (MHRN 2000, 37). The racially charged opposition embroiled the issue.

The AFA negotiation process was impeded by reluctance and resistance from USFWS as well, although local and national opposition groups no doubt prevented the agency from needing to put up its own overt resistance. Endorsements of comanagement by USFWS officials do not appear to be part of the public record or media coverage in the mid-1990s. Dan Ashe, deputy director of the USFWS, attempted to diffuse the local tension and allay some of the extreme fears by pointing out the Tribes' "ability to manage resources," and adding that "by working with the Tribes as a partner we can help each other and do a better job of managing the lands." Ashe said the federal government wasn't abandoning the NBR. It would "continue to be a part of the federal wildlife system and continue to belong to all Americans" (Azure 1995a).

Nevertheless, USFWS personnel, especially those at the NBR, were not eager to negotiate an AFA for comanagement of the NBR.[13] Purportedly needing to gain confidence in the Tribes' management abilities, the agency instead sought to have "discussions" about contracting functions and services but without use of an AFA, preferring to use Memorandum of Understandings (MOUs) that included only a scaled-back set of activities and retained greater responsibility and control for the agency (Azure 1996; David Wiseman, National Bison Range Complex Manager, personal communication 2003).

Underlying a cooperative public image maintained by the USFWS may have been a deep institutional interest in maintaining full control of the NBR. The Tribes' initial request for full or nearly full management of the NBR was perceived as a threat to agency authority, even though its statutory authority under the National Wildlife Refuge System Administration Act of 1966 (and subsequent amendments) was under no threat, particularly in light of the TSGA prohibition against delegating "inherently federal functions" (16 U.S.C. § 668dd(a)(2)). Still, the prestige and privilege of having full management control of one of the "crown jewels" of the National Wildlife Refuge System was at stake, and the principles of organizational behavior, to protect one's jurisdiction, appeared to predominate.[14] Such agency interests work against the non-discrimination principles of UNDRIP, and its call for negotiations free from bias.

Entrenched distrust of the Tribes' abilities to serve as effective comanagers was a common bias evident in the public discourse and input into the agency decision-making process. Agency silence, that is the absence of public pronouncements to the contrary from the NRB managers or regional officials, was a form of complicity that eventually necessitated intervention from the deputy director in Washington, DC. Public discourse that unfairly questioned tribal competency provided a socially acceptable smoke screen for underlying racism and beliefs in racial superiority evident in the public record (Azure 1995a). Not surprisingly, the fears and distrust enlivened by the political responses to the first attempts to negotiate an AFA foreshadowed and scripted a drama that undermined implementation of the agreement that would eventually be reached.

Impasse Overcome and Renewal of Controversy: The 2005–2006 Annual Funding Agreement

After the collapse of their initial attempts to negotiate, the Tribes sought ways to continue to be involved with the USFWS in the NBR. The Tribes developed relationships and built trust with the USFWS personnel who managed the NBR. In fact, the Tribes already had a long-standing record of cooperation with the USFWS on various programs and projects, including wildlife population surveys, grizzly bear management, and reintroduction of the endangered trumpeter swan and peregrine falcon. The Tribes and USFWS also signed MOUs that included financial contracts, whereby the Tribes provided vegetation monitoring, weed control, and fire management services (David Wiseman, National Bison Range Complex Manager, personal communication 2003). The USFWS also involved the Tribes in cultural resource inventories in the National Bison Range Complex ([NBRC] USFWS 2001).[15] Other units within the NBRC, Ninepipe and Pablo National Wildlife Refuges, are managed by the USFWS on federal trust land with the Tribes as the beneficial owners who granted USFWS conservation easements while retaining tribally reserved rights to these properties (Matt 2004b). These informal and formal agreements occurred outside of the Self-Governance Program, but nevertheless provided an opportunity for tribal resource management and USFWS personnel to gain familiarity working together and understanding of their capabilities.

When the Tribes formally requested resumption of AFA comanagement negotiations in 2003, the Tribes had strong justifications ready. In making its case for an AFA, the Tribes maintained that they could offer outstanding resource management skills as demonstrated by the successful management of over seventy tribally established programs (CSKT 1996a, 1996b).

The Tribes had experienced many successes managing programs formerly controlled by the federal government, as well as implementing their own unique programs to protect the physical, historical, cultural, and spiritual priorities of the Tribes in keeping with articles 25 and 26 of UNDRIP.[16]

In his 2003 testimony before the U.S. Senate Committee on Indian Affairs, Tribal Council chairman D. Fred Matt, described the Tribes' long-standing expertise and leadership in natural resource management, particularly in fisheries and wildlife management. He noted that the Tribes' Division of Fish, Wildlife Recreation, and Conservation had a professional staff of nearly fifty employees. He highlighted the *Flathead Lake and Upper River Fisheries Comanagement Plan* written and implemented with the Montana Department of Fish, Wildlife, and Parks. He stated, "the Plan represents the coming together of two governments and two cultures voluntarily, in a common direction for the shared fishery of the West's largest freshwater lake." Chairman Matt also mentioned the Tribes' mitigation and habitat improvement efforts to offset the impacts of Kerr Dam on fish and wildlife of the Flathead River. He referred to the tribally designated and managed Mission Mountains Tribal Wilderness Area, which was established in 1982 and covers some 92,000 acres of tribal lands in the Mission Mountains (including 10,000 acres of a Grizzly Bear Conservation Zone) and 97,000 acres of tribal lands protected as tribal primitive areas (Statement of D. Fred Matt 2003). He concluded by stating:

> The Confederated Salish and Kootenai Tribes have always been good stewards of the natural resources. . . . Our efforts include continuing our cultural traditions, interdisciplinary consultation, setting high standards and professional qualifications, providing due process and public involvement as part of the regulation development process, including non-Tribal members on regulatory boards, staying active in the political process and coordination with Federal agencies and State Government. These efforts have gained us recognition by Federal agencies and benefit Tribal Government, Tribal members, the reservation economy, and all Americans. (ibid.)

Chairman Matt further expressed the Tribes' aspirations to comanage the NBR by remarking that the Tribes "clearly have historic, geographic, and cultural connections to the National Bison Range lands" (ibid.).

To commence negotiations for an AFA with the USFWS, the Tribes had to establish firmly a strong connection in at least one of the above areas. They were able to do so for all three (Germaine White, personal communication 2009). Historically, the Tribes traveled to follow the bison every year along the Northern Rocky Mountain Front on the east side of the Continental Divide. Bison provided food, clothing, shelter, and tradition for the Tribes. Noting the central role the bison played in tribal culture, the Tribes explained that their interest in stewardship of the bison extended beyond the conservation/preservation ethic that prompted the creation of the NBR. The Tribes have a historical relationship with bison, and tribal members have personal and familial ties to the NBR land and its particular bison herd. Before the negotiation began in 2003, the Tribes provided the USFWS with documentation of their cultural connections and direct historical relationships with this particular herd of bison, as well as their geographic connection, as the NBR is entirely within the Flathead Reservation on lands reserved for the Tribes under the Hellgate Treaty.[17] In Chairman Matt's words:

> The National Bison Range sits at the heart of our reserved homelands. Historically, we are connected by the foresight of our direct ancestors who preserved the forebears of the bison that roam the range today. And most importantly, the life-sustaining, cultural connection to the bison, and the land of the range, is also an honored part of our tradition and value system as Indian People today. (Matt 2004a)[18]

Recognizing that negotiations would occur in a politically charged environment and be subject to public scrutiny and oversight by lawmakers, the Tribes and USFWS presented a unified front to the public and proceeded in a very deliberate and open manner. In February 2003, the two parties developed and publicly released a *Draft Principles and Plan of Action*, which included mutually agreed-upon principles and a timeline to guide the negotiations (CSKT and USFWS 2003b). One of the principles was an acknowledgment of the special historical, cultural, and geographic connections possessed by the Tribes to the NBR land and the bison. Other principles pertained to the retention of federal authority and ownership, no doubt in response to mischaracterizations and fear-mongering from the first AFA negotiations (Azure 2004). These latter principles were restated in a joint press release, as follows:

> Interior also has clear legal guidance that requires a Fish & Wildlife Service manager to remain and Fish & Wildlife Service concurrence on inherently federal responsibilities. "The refuges will remain federal assets, and they will continue to be managed for the wildlife for which they

were established and public access will continue as long as that is consistent with the refuge purposes." (CSKT and USFWS 2003c)[19]

The *Draft Principles and Plan of Action* also included joint goals to conduct media outreach, keep interested parties informed (especially elected
officials), and obtain public input at key decision points.

Although the public could comment on the *Draft Principles and Plan
of Action*, it could not be invited to comment on the most crucial matter,
the draft management agreement, until it was developed and made public.
The scope and specific details of the agreement still needed to be ham-
mered out, and this required intense negotiations between USFWS and
the Tribes, during which time various stakeholders grew impatient and demanded information. Still, the two parties were adamant in publicly avow-
ing the need to conduct the negotiations in private until a draft agreement
was reached, though lawmakers or their designees were invited to attend
(CSKT and USFWS 2003d). The early public notification and transparency about the process seemed to refuel concerns about the public being
left out and rekindle suspicions.

In April 2003, the two parties publicly agreed to work collaboratively on
a number of issues that pertained to the management of other units in the
NBRC that required coordination between the USFWS and the Tribes
(CSKT and USFWS 2003a). In a letter from the Region 6 director, the
USFWS claimed and continued to insist as it had for over a year that "uses
of the refuges that are incompatible with refuge purposes" were matters
that had to be resolved before AFA negotiations could proceed (Morgenweck
2004). However, the Tribes argued that the matters either had already been
resolved, were in the process of being resolved, or were being held up by
USFWS inaction. If they were valid concerns, they would require a formal
process to be resolved properly, and USFWS had not begun to undertake
that process (Matt 2004b). The Tribes also contested the necessity and
legality of addressing these ancillary issues as a condition for negotiating
an AFA in good faith (Matt 2004b). Before a congressional hearing in May
2004, the Tribes voiced concern about roadblocks and repeated delays with
the negotiation process, presumably referring to the "incompatibility" issues that delayed agreement negotiations (Statement and Prepared Testimony of D. Fred Matt 2004). Stall tactics and equivocation on the part of
the USFEW are inconsistent with the principles of bargaining in good faith
expressed in article 32 of UNDRIP.

Local opponents again organized, this time by hosting websites, forming
advocacy groups, holding and attending public meetings, gathering petition

signatures, writing letters to newspaper editors, and gaining support from national organizations and retired USFWS managers. Three particular local groups voiced their opposition to the Tribes' management of the NBR and rallied others living on the Flathead Reservation and in the nearby Bitterroot Valley to do so: The Citizens Equal Rights Alliance; its sister organization, Citizens Equal Rights Foundation; and the Flathead Reservation-based All Citizens Equal. From these groups an ad hoc group called The Concerned Signatories of the Bison Range Petition formed (MHRN 2000, 36). These groups were led by the same individuals who generated the most vigorous opposition to the early comanagement discussions in the mid-1990s. All three groups were known to fight against Indian projects and jurisdiction and have been closely watched by the MHRN for "anti-Indian" activity. The groups and their supporters questioned the fairness of tribal hiring preferences under the Tribes' management and repeated the claim that comanagement would unfairly disadvantage non-Indian workers at the NBR, and set up "racial discrimination on federal lands with federal dollars" (Selden 2003). Some even objected to the possibility that American Indian spiritual beliefs would be publicly shared at the NBR (MHRN 2000, 35).[20] Believing that national parks, forests, and refuges should be managed exclusively by the federal government, these groups expressed concern over the precedent an AFA could set for tribal comanagement or management of other public lands, which they contended was illegal and unconstitutional.[21]

At least forty conservation organizations, including the National Wildlife Refuge Association, Ducks Unlimited, Wilderness Society, American Bird Conservancy, and Chicago Zoological Society, eventually expressed opposition to the AFA (Fitzgerald 2004). These organizations provided public input on the negotiations and draft agreement (Branigan 2003). Leading the charge was the Public Employees for Environmental Responsibility (PEER), a national organization representing federal employees of land management and environmental agencies. The organization, PEER, questioned the legality of the negotiations and expressed their belief that it is inappropriate to have tribes manage a national resource (Branigan 2003). Terry Z. Riley, director of conservation at the Wildlife Management Institute, said the AFA would "only lead to more problems and lots of hard feelings over time" (Montgomery 2003). Expressing concerns about "reverse discrimination" and echoing the talking points of the anti-Indian activists, Riley stated that under tribal management, tribal members will be given hiring preference, "a prospect that has many envisioning the harassment and firing of non-Indian employees" (Montgomery 2003). "[Tribal members] may isolate the few Fish and Wildlife employees already working on the refuges," Riley predicted. "They can make life miserable for federal employees and their families" (Montgomery 2003).

The well-publicized, closed-doors negotiations led Senator Burns to request a public meeting to allow opposing views to be aired and to gauge public sentiment, once again lending even more public attention to the negotiations (Devlin 2003). Over 500 people attended the public input meeting in May 2003. The majority of those who testified supported CSKT-USFWS comanagement of the NBR. Negotiations proceeded throughout 2003 and the first part of 2004, culminating with the release of a draft AFA on July 14, 2004, with a 90-day public comment period before the AFA was to be finalized (Devlin 2003). Under the draft AFA, the Tribes would take responsibility for activities in five categories: Management, Biological Program, Fire Program, Maintenance Program, and Visitor Services (with the USFWS retaining ownership of and ultimate management authority for the Bison Range). Public information and "open house" meetings took place in September 2004 (Stromnes 2004a). Nearly two dozen conservation groups, including the American Bird Conservancy and several regional Audubon groups, registered their opposition to the AFA and argued that the AFA was virtually turning over inherently federal functions and would put protected natural resources in jeopardy (Stromnes 2004b). In addition, 121 USFWS retirees contacted by PEER asked Interior Secretary Gale Norton to scuttle the comanagement arrangement (Stromnes 2004c).

Nevertheless, in December 2004, the Tribes and USFWS signed the *Fiscal Years 2005–2006 Annual Funding Agreement* (2005–2006 AFA) with the Interior Department concurrence for the operation and management of the parts of the NBRC, effective March 15, 2005, through September 30, 2006.[22] The 2005–2006 AFA was referred to the appropriate congressional committees for the required ninety-day notification period, though no objections were raised in Congress. The 2005–2006 AFA closely resembled the draft. The Tribes were wholly or partially responsible for the following: annual bison roundup and health monitoring; migratory non-game bird surveys; waterfowl pair counts; bird banding; vegetation monitoring; digital mapping; invasive plant control; wildfire suppression and prescribed burning; collection of federal public use fees; and custodial/maintenance services (Stromnes 2005). A detailed work plan that exceeded 1,000 pages was created to guide the Tribes' personnel (USFWS 2006).

The USFWS would contract a majority of the fieldworker jobs to the Tribes, and these amounted to about half of the budget for the NBRC (Stromnes 2005). The AFA allowed for about ten positions to be overseen by the Tribes' coordinator, including a wildlife biologist, fire management personnel, and maintenance staff. Positions retained by the federal government included the USFWS refuge manager, senior biologist, outdoor recreation planner, law enforcement officers, and a maintenance foreman, which USFWS asserted were "inherently federal."[23] Although USFWS employees of the NBR could opt for reassignment to another USFWS unit, the Tribes agreed to employ directly any federal NBR worker whose job it contracted, and the USFWS agreed to offer its employees the option to receive a special assignment by USFWS under the Intergovernmental Personnel Act to work for the CKST but retain federal employee status (Stromnes 2005). Existing USFWS personnel were given adequate notice to make employment decisions.

After the 2005–2006 AFA went into effect, most USFWS workers chose reassignment rather than positions working with the Tribes, though two chose to be assigned to the Tribes.[24] Although the Tribes felt well-poised to manage the NBR fully, they accepted the AFA as a comanagement project and as another step in a long journey to regain control over land and wildlife on the Flathead Reservation.

Trouble on the Range

The 2005–2006 AFA allowed for AFA renewal and for a temporary extension of the contract once it expired if a new contract was under negotiation. Beginning in the spring of 2006, the parties began negotiating for the next AFA, but by the summer of 2006 difficulties that arose during implementation of the 2005–2006 AFA reached a boiling point. Although the USFWS issued a temporary extension of the 2005–2006 AFA in September 2006, pending negotiation of a new AFA,[25] the USFWS refused to renew the AFA and entirely severed the working relationship with the Tribes in December 2006 (CSKT, n.d.a).

Not surprisingly, there are different accounts of how the 2005–2006 AFA was executed, what went wrong, and why. The Tribes' workers reported that they experienced a lot of tension, as well as lack of communication and cooperation from much of the USFWS staff (CSKT, n.d.c). This poor working relationship posed significant challenges for the Tribes' personnel in the performance of AFA work, though the Tribes nevertheless reported significant accomplishments (CSKT, n.d.a). However, the USFWS alleged that the Tribes' work suffered from significant deficiencies, which were detailed in the agency's 2005 *Report on Implementation of the Annual*

Funding Agreement at the National Bison Range Complex (Backus 2006). The report was issued on February 17, revised, and reissued on March 1, and revised again and reissued on July 10, 2006, presumably in response to the Tribe's thirty-eight page rebuttal to one or both earlier versions (US-FWS 2006). The report covered AFA work conducted during the 2005 calendar year (CY) and was critical of much the Tribes' comanagement work, except for the annual bison roundup (Backus 2006). Of the 116 activities performed, nearly half were deemed as "needing improvement" or "unsuccessful." Numerous deficiencies were also noted in the CY 2006 *Preliminary Performance Evaluation Summary.* The Tribes issued a 114-page response contesting the evaluations were inaccurate, biased, and unfair (CSKT n.d.c). The Tribes' response contended that the Tribes' personnel encountered more resistance, lack of communication, and other impediments in 2006 than in the previous year. The Tribes' response stated:

> The FWS evaluation of the Tribes' performance relates to a work plan that prioritized nearly every work activity as of "High Importance" to the FWS, without comparing the allocated resources, including man-hours, to the achievability of the activity. FWS failed, for example, to compare Tribal CY 2006 accomplishments to a baseline of total FWS accomplishments completed in the same time period with the same amount of resources. We repeatedly raised this issue of resource allocation and prioritization of work to the FWS; but in each instance, the FWS refused to address the issue (CSKT n.d.c, 1).

Supporting the claim that the USFWS used a different standard to evaluate the Tribes than it did for its employees, the report included data showing USFWS personnel only completed 25 percent of their scheduled waterfowl nest counts during the ten years leading up to tribal involvement, then used 100 percent completion as the performance standard for tribal employees assigned the duty (Devlin 2007a).

The Tribes' response also indicated that the Tribes had not been notified of the alleged deficiencies, and therefore, inadequate opportunity was provided to correct any problems that existed.[26] The Tribes accepted some of the findings in the evaluation report, but disputed many others as incorrect (Devlin 2007a).[27] The USFWS finalized its report without changing any of the allegations against the Tribes, despite the correct information provided by the Tribes.[28]

Although the USFWS evaluation reports provided tremendous ammunition to opponents, a USFWS official in the Mountain-Prairie Regional

Office who had recommended the termination of the AFA to the USFWS director in Washington, DC, publicly downplayed concerns about the performance evaluation by stating:

> I have worked directly with the CSKT's Wildlife Program and I rank them among the best in tribal programs and as good as many state fish and wildlife agencies. . . . I have no doubt that the CSKT Wildlife Program can do a good job in managing the National Bison Range. The 2005 Accomplishment Report should not be construed as a negative report. That report was developed as a tool for use in identifying strengths and weaknesses during the first year of a very complicated agreement. Many have misused this report by focusing solely on the weaknesses in the report and ignored the successes. I am confident that the CSKT management activities at the Bison Range will continue to improve and that this partnership will be a success. (quoted in Devlin 2007c)

The 2005 and 2006 evaluations were "developed by some of the same USFWS employees who had previously submitted the October 8, 2004, letter opposing the AFA prior to its approval"[29]—a circumstance that gave credence to the Tribes' claim that the 2006 evaluation, like the 2005 evaluation, was "not an objective assessment of AFA implementation" (CSKT n.d.c, 2).[30] Events and facts make it hard not to conclude that key USFWS personnel at the NBR sought to make the AFA unsuccessful by using whatever means available to sideline the agreement and the prospects of its renewal.

The USFWS's refusal to address the grievances raised about the fairness of its evaluation and its insistence on using a different standard, which was a seemingly impossible standard to meet, appear to have been a clear violation of the call in the UNDRIP for "harmonious and cooperative relations" between national governments and Indigenous peoples "based on principles of justice." The USFWS actions are also contrary to article 27, asserting the right to "fair, independent, impartial, open, and transparent process." The federal agency's actions in the last few months of 2006 continued to violate this right.

During discussions for a new AFA, seven USFWS employees at the NBR filed an informal grievance with the USFWS in September 2006, alleging that the agency, by signing and implementing the AFA, created a hostile work environment characterized "by harassing, offensive, intimidating, and oppressive behavior" by the Tribes' employees, and asked that the existing AFA be terminated.[31] In October 2006, the Tribes repeatedly requested information from the USFWS about the allegations, specifically what they entailed and who was involved, but its requests were denied. As a result, the Tribes conducted their own investigation and issued a 153-page report, which documented claims by the Tribes that USFWS employees actively undermined the ability of the Tribes' employees to perform their duties at the NBR (Steele 2006). A USFWS investigator from the Mountain-Prairie Regional Office conducted a separate investigation of the USFWS employees' allegations that relied largely on summaries of interviews of USFWS personnel. The USFWS investigator's report found that USFWS employees felt their jobs were threatened and that the tribal hiring preference was discriminatory (Devlin 2007e). The DOI referred this matter to the Equal Employment Opportunity Office (EEO), which conducted a preliminary investigation; however, no formal EEO complaints were filed by USFWS employees (McDonald 2007).

The Tribes' requests for information about the USFWS employees' grievances were effectively rendered moot on December 11, 2006, when the USFWS director Dale Hall terminated the 2005–2006 AFA (Devlin 2008a). A last-minute notice from the USFWS Regional Office made several days before about the Tribes' alleged failure to feed bison properly and a "withdrawal of authorization" to do so was used to help justify the termination decision. In January 2007, the Tribes appealed the termination notice to the Interior Board of Indian Appeals (IBIA). They contended that, among other things, the USFWS terminated the AFA based on incorrect information.[32] The Tribes noted that termination was done without any notice of performance deficiencies or notice of allegations, nor opportunity to respond or correct any actual deficiencies, as required under § 10.A.3.b(2) of the 2005–2006 AFA.[33] The situation clearly had deteriorated to the point that a resumption of comanagement with the same personnel must have seemed untenable to all involved.

The 2005–2006 AFA failed (Devlin 2008a). A subsequent investigation by the Interior Department's Office of Inspector General (OIG) found that Interior Department officials "did exert considerable and unusual influence directing the USFWS to enter into the annual funding agreement with the tribe(s)" and the OIG added, "but such influence was neither improper nor illegal" (Devlin 2007d). It was also reported later that the DOI was in discussions with the Tribes about a complete management transfer of the NBR to the Tribes when the USFWS abruptly cancelled the 2005–2006 AFA (Devlin 2007b). Intra-departmental discord and agency resistance were important factors in the failure of the 2005–2006 AFA. It is also clear that high-level support in the Interior Department was crucial to negotiating the first AFA and subsequent resumption of negotiations (Devlin 2007e).

Comanagement Revived: The FY 2009–2011
Annual Funding Agreement

On December 29, 2006, deputy secretary of the interior, Lynn Scarlett, expressed her disappointment with the termination of the 2005–2006 AFA in a letter to USFWS and the BIA.[34] She stated the termination order would remain in place, but the working relationship between USFWS and the Tribes would be reestablished with the direct involvement of high-ranking DOI officials and with a goal of working toward a new AFA for fiscal year 2007. The Tribes submitted a proposal to work toward that goal, but USFWS Director Hall preferred to have some type of other cooperative agreement for the NBR. As a result of continued intervention of high-level DOI officials, much of 2007 was devoted to arranging mediated dispute resolution.[35] The new AFA negotiations finally began in January 2008, after the DOI assistant secretary for Fish and Wildlife and Parks, Lyle Laverty, issued an action plan to restart negotiations with a neutral third-party facilitator.[36] The resulting AFA, covering fiscal years 2009–2011 (FY 2009–2011), was signed on June 19, 2008, more than one and one-half years after the termination of the first AFA.[37] Although the circumstances leading to the cancellation of the first AFA clearly violated article 32 of the UNDRIP, which also calls for "effective mechanisms for just and fair redress," in a longer-term view, the intervention of the DOI to resume negotiations and effect a new AFA could be seen as such a mechanism.

The FY 2009–2011 AFA called for nearly all of the same program activities, functions, and services to be carried out by the Tribes as the 2005–2006 AFA, but it gave the Tribes an explicit management role. The FY 2009–2011 AFA called for the Tribes to designate a deputy refuge manager, a lead biologist, and an administrative support assistant. The Tribes' deputy refuge manager was to serve as a "senior staff advisor to the refuge manager" and "provide substantive input to management decision making at NBRC."[38] The AFA recognized and formalized "the partnership between the Service and the Tribes in operating and maintaining all programs of the NBRC."[39] In an effort to address previous difficulties and encourage collaboration and regular communication, the AFA also called for creation of a refuge leadership team that included the USFWS refuge manager, USFWS deputy manager, the Tribes' deputy manager, and the Tribes' lead biologist.[40] Final authority, however, was to remain vested in the USFWS refuge manager, which was consistent with all TSGA AFAs, and the USFWS would reassume responsibility for activities managed by the Tribes if the USFWS director found the Tribes were "causing imminent jeopardy to natural resources or public health and safety."[41] The USFWS and the Tribes brought in new faces to fill the management positions, and various sources indicated that the FY 2009–2011 AFA was implemented smoothly in 2009 (Devlin 2009; USFWS 2012).[42] Associate deputy secretary of the interior, Laura Davis stated, "a true partnership and spirit of cooperation has developed from the history of controversy between the FWS and the Confederated Salish and Kootenai Tribes of the Flathead Nation over the National Bison Range Complex in Montana. . . . [The] FWS sponsored trainings and the bison round-up event in October 2009, was highly successful."[43] Although a detailed work plan for the Tribes was never developed for the new AFA, the previous year's work plan guided the Tribes' operations, which had not substantially changed (USDOI 2011). However, a performance evaluation of the Tribes' work was not conducted before litigation brought the agreement to a halt.

Comanagement Rescinded—Federal Lawsuits

In December 2008, a few months after the FY 2009–2011 AFA took effect, several former USFWS employees and PEER filed suit in Federal District Court for the District of Columbia against the DOI and USFWS. They claimed that the AFA violated a number of federal laws, including the National Wildlife Refuge System Administration Act (Refuge Act), the National Environmental Policy Act (NEPA), and TSGA by constituting an alleged illegal delegation of inherently federal functions (Devlin 2008b). In April 2009, another set of former wildlife refuge employees and the Blue Goose Alliance[44] filed a separate suit making similar claims but also contended that the defendants violated the Endangered Species Act.[45] These cases, *Reed v. Salazar* and *Blue Goose Alliance v. Salazar*, were combined (744 F. Supp. 2d 98 [D.C. Dist. 2010]), and the Tribes joined the DOI and USFWS as a defendant.

On September 28, 2010, the district court held that the USFWS had violated the Administrative Procedures Act by entering into the FY 2009–2011 AFA without properly invoking a "categorical exclusion" under NEPA. A categorical exclusion can be applied to an action or activity that, due to its routine nature (such as ordinary day-to-day operations, maintenance, management, and the like), can reasonably be asserted not to result in adverse environmental impacts that would need to be evaluated under NEPA prior to deciding on an action. Such a predecision evaluation could take the form of an Environmental Assessment (EA) or Environmental Impact Statement. However, questions existed about whether a categorical exclusion appropriately applied and whether or not "extraordinary circumstances" existed so as to prohibit the application of a categorical exclusion and require a predecision environmental review.[46] The court found that the administrative record did not show that the USFWS made such considerations, nor did USFWS or DOI repudiate the plaintiff's claims in this regard that the "highly controversial" AFA was a qualifying condition. The court held that "in light of substantial evidence in the record of past performance problems by the CSKT," the USFWS decision to execute the AFA was an "arbitrary and capricious" agency action under NEPA and ordered that the FY 2009–2011 AFA be set aside and rescinded.[47]

The court did not make a finding on the validity of the alleged performance deficiencies. The court also did not rule on the plaintiffs' other claims, for example, that the AFA violated the Refuge Act, TSGA, Freedom of Information Act, or the Intergovernmental Personnel Act. It is a virtual certainty that such claims will be revived with respect to a future AFA, considering the entrenched interests, past behavior, and capabilities of the opponents of federal-tribal comanagement of the NBR.

The Recent Status

On November 10, 2011, the Tribes submitted a request to USFWS to negotiate a new AFA. Since then, the DOI/USFWS and the Tribes have drawn up a draft AFA for the fiscal years 2013 to 2016, which substantially resembles the rescinded AFA (USFWS 2012). The USFWS also posted on its website a Notice of Intent (NOI) to conduct an EA for the draft AFA— indicating that it will not attempt to invoke a categorical exclusion for the new AFA, but will comply with NEPA in a more rigorous manner (USFWS 2012). The NOI is part of the scoping process under NEPA whereby interested parties can submit input to USFWS regarding the scope of the EA. The closing date to submit such input was June 15, 2012. As of 2013, it was not yet clear what the public input process would be for the EA itself.

A Case of True Comanagement and Enhanced Sovereignty?

We began with the proposition that true comanagement must effect power sharing and sharing of significant responsibilities. True comanagement must do more than merely afford tribes an influence in the management of federal lands; it must allow for a good degree of tribal control. We further posited that true comanagement strengthens tribal sovereignty and can thereby advance Indigenous rights. We also argued that successful comanagement requires a supporting legal foundation. By considering the manner and degree to which comanagement of the NBR achieved these conditions, we can address whether de facto tribal sovereignty was enhanced in this case, and then consider whether Indigenous rights were advanced.

During the period when comanagement agreements were in effect on the NBR, the CSKT were responsible for nearly all of the programs, services, functions, and activities on the NBR, with law enforcement being one exception. It employed the majority of the NBR staff, but during the 2005–2006 AFA, the ability of the Tribes' personnel to carry out their duties was hampered by lack of communication and cooperation with USFWS staff. However, when the FY 2009–2011 AFA was in place, those difficulties were surmounted. Moreover, by creating a CSKT deputy refuge manager position and a leadership team composed of an equal number of CSKT and USFWS senior personnel, the AFA provided a significant level of influence for the Tribes in decision-making. Although a revised work plan and associated performance standards were not developed before the judicial rescission of the AFA, it was clear that a high level of CSKT involvement and influence in planning and operations was provided for. These elements are consistent with those necessary for true comanagement agreements, in particular, the inclusion of provisions that detail each party's obligations and responsibilities, legitimate structures for tribal involvement, specification of working groups with balanced representation and operational procedures, and flexibility and modifiability (Sanders 2007; Goodman 2000). In addition, significant measures were put in place for "zero tolerance" of harassment and discrimination and for dispute resolution. These aspects of the FY 2009–2011 AFA are consistent with article 27 of UNDRIP.

The conditions under which negotiations occur, such as the degree of parity between the parties, is an important factor in the degree to which the resulting agreement affords tribes the ability to protect tribal interests and in assessing fairness of the process. The issuance of joint press releases and the involvement of high-level Interior Department officials indicate that a functional government-to-government relationship existed leading up to and during the negotiations. Although our study did not look closely into many of the specific details of the negotiations, we are aware that the Tribes successfully advocated for a larger role in the management of the bison herd than USFWS initially desired. The TSGA and associated regulations allow tribes to propose which programs, services, and activities it would like to take on and thereby set the agenda and determine the content of negotiations. The TSGA does not limit tribes to petitioning only for programs, service, and activities identified by the federal agency.

More importantly, the TSGA compels the DOI agency to negotiate with tribes, though not necessarily to reach an agreement, thereby giving tribes a seat at the table, and thus, an opportunity to exercise tribal sovereignty within their aboriginal territories. In the case of the NBR, racially motivated community opposition, politically well-connected intervention, and agency resistance combined to delay good faith negotiation for nearly a decade. Eventually, Senator Burns stood aside, negotiations proceeded, and an agreement was reached. This accomplishment resulted from the Tribes cultivating powerful interveners, such as Congressman Pat Williams, who successfully lobbied DOI officials to commence negotiations in earnest (Williams 2007). Supported by its legal office, the Tribes established constructive relationships with DOI officials who they directly lobbied along with members of congressional oversight committees to send the message to USFWS that its resistance would not be allowed to persist indefinitely.[48] As a result of this pressure following the cancellation of the 2005–2006 AFA, USFWS renewed comanagement negotiations, signed the FY 2009–2011, and subsequently made personnel changes that significantly improved cooperation between USFWS and the Tribes, and afforded the Tribes an expanded role in management of the NBR.

The short amount of time that the FY 2009–2011 AFA was in effect before the PEER-Blue Goose Alliance lawsuit resulted in its rescission is suggestive of limited tribal influence and control. While this may be true in the short-term, the procedural shortcoming that undermined the agreement can be remedied by executing a new AFA that adheres to NEPA, which the two parties are in the process of doing. The Tribes see the lawsuit as a temporary setback and will continue to persist in their comanagement efforts. Because of the previous agency resistance, judicial intervention, and congressional oversight, the success of implementation of controversial legislation, such as the TSGA, must be evaluated over decades not years.

The TSGA itself, which provides the essential legal foundation for AFAs, recognizes that tribes are sovereign governments and incorporates the United States' trust responsibility. These recognitions by high-level officials in the Interior Department over multiple presidential administrations and congressional oversight committees under bipartisan leadership[49] have helped to keep negotiations and comanagement efforts progressing, albeit in a punctuated manner. This insight underscores the importance of a strong legal foundation for comanagement.

The Tribes' reputation as outstanding resource managers and their ability to utilize significant political connections, public relations, lobby prowess, legal expertise, and financial resources have enabled the Tribes to establish themselves firmly as legitimate comanagers and to confront effectively the oppositional forces and entrenched interests in this case. This is no small feat, and it serves as strong evidence that the Tribes are exercising a good degree of de facto sovereignty.

We can see this by taking an extended view, even though de jure sovereignty is limited in the manner that TSGA authorizes the federal agency unilaterally to cancel an AFA, as was done for the 2005–2006 AFA. Nevertheless, the Tribes vigorously contested this decision and its fairness and thereby legitimized negotiations for a new AFA. The Tribes also overcame entrenched agency resistance at all administrative levels and seemingly irreparable working relationships with USFWS personnel at the NBR. The Tribes also contested PEER's allegations of the Tribes' operational deficiencies in implementing the FY 2009–2011 AFA. As a result, the Tribes were vindicated by a March 2011, OIG investigation that dismissed the allegations (USDOI 2011). However, the OIG report came out after the *Reed v. Salazar* ruling, in which the U.S. District Court cited the USFWS's performance review of the 2005–2006 AFA. The court side-stepped the Tribes' challenge of the review's factual basis, bias, and lack of associated due process and nullified the FY 2009–2011 AFA due to a USFWS procedural misstep in its NEPA categorical exclusion for the AFA. Nevertheless, the Tribes are still in the process of negotiating a new AFA with a new NEPA review process.

The USFWS avoided earnest comanagement negotiations requested by the Tribes for nearly a decade. After ten more years, the USFWS cultivated a more constructive government-to-government relationship with the Tribes and exhibited itself as a more cooperative and trusting partner in the Tribal Self-Governance Program. Likewise, the Tribes no doubt gained a better understanding and appreciation of the challenges of federal-tribal comanagement of non-BIA programs under the TSGA. The Tribes' persistence and decades-long interactions with its federal partner, staffing of the NBR Visitor Center, and media outreach have created greater awareness of tribal cultural perspectives on the history of the NBR and significance of bison within the USFWS and the general public. The ability of the Tribes to tell their story can be seen as a work in progress.

Conclusion

The case of comanagement of the NBR illustrates the importance of procedural justice and the right to meaningful participation, as embodied in article 27 of the UNDRIP. Article 27 calls for establishing and implementing "a fair, independent, impartial, open, and transparent process . . . to recognize and adjudicate the rights of Indigenous peoples pertaining to their lands, territories, and resources" and a "right to participate in this process." The TSGA supported by the federal trust relationship clearly establishes such a right. The CSKT have worked extraordinarily hard to exercise this right and attempt to ensure a fair process.

Yet the process in many respects has not been fair, and as noted above, many aspects of comanagement of the NBR did not adhere well to the UNDRIP and appeared to be clear violations of Indigenous rights. A few examples warrant highlighting. First, the refusal of the federal government, the USFWS in particular, to negotiate an AFA for nearly ten years as required by § 403(b)(2) and 458cc(a) of the TSGA is inconsistent with article 32, the call for good faith negotiations. This recalcitrance followed a pattern that King found with regard to NPS AFA negotiations (King 2007). Reinforcing this conclusion is the fact that the CSKT were among the first self-governance tribes who were part of the demonstration project authorized by ISDEAA of 1988, which preceded the TSGA. Second, the circumstances involved with the cancellation of the 2005–2006 AFA were also contrary to article 27, asserting the right to "fair, independent, impartial, open, and transparent process."

Nevertheless, TSGA, especially the provision affording tribes the ability to negotiate agreements for programs with "special geographic, historical, or cultural significance," insofar as it establishes a right to comanagement, in essence codifies articles 26, which states that "Indigenous peoples have the right to the lands, territories, and resources which they have traditionally owned, occupied, or otherwise used or acquired."

Still, our account suggests only a modest advancement of Indigenous rights in the case of the NBR despite our claim that the Tribes have exercised significant de facto sovereignty bounded within the federal system. The Tribes will still likely have to face challenges involving litigation and will need to continue actively to attract and cultivate support from powerful entities, as well as maintain political support in the Interior Department, Congress, and elsewhere. Under the TSGA, the USFWS will continue to retain ultimate authority when it comes to entering into, continuing, and renewing comanagement agreements.

Even if agency resistance fades away for good, DOI support stays strong, and congressional oversight continues, it remains to be seen if comanagement under TSGA can be an effective legal foundation given that the courts may determine that it conflicts with other federal laws. Future judicial rulings related to section 403(k) may constrain the types of activities that can be conducted by tribes without being considered inherently federal, thereby restricting the types of programs, activities, and functions eligible for AFAs. The case also raises the question about how well TSGA provides opportunities for comanagement for tribes that may not have the track record of resource management and legal and financial resources on par with those of the CSKT. The case further suggests the need to apply article 29 of UNDRIP, which calls for "assistance programs for Indigenous peoples for such conservation and protection, without discrimination." Even for recognized self-governance tribes, it is still unclear whether the U.S. government will "take effective measures to recognize and protect the exercise" of Indigenous rights "to maintain, control, protect, and develop" cultural heritage, traditional knowledge, traditional cultural expressions, and related intellectual property rights as called for in article 31. Twenty years after the passage of the TSGA, the verdict is still out.

These uncertainties leave open the possibility that comanagement under the TSGA may not achieve its stated purpose to promote tribal self-governance to a significant degree. Because land repatriation appears to be a rare, unlikely, often politically impossible option, for now, comanagement appears to afford one of the best opportunities to advance Indigenous rights and serve as an important step in the path to tribal management and the greater exercise of tribal sovereignty. If true comanagement under the TSGA cannot be achieved, if the CSKT are not ultimately successful for themselves and in paving the way for other tribes, we may see calls for federal legislation to create tribal parks that would give tribes more control, albeit within the confines of the federal trust relationship.[50] We may also see a push to further amend the Indian Self-Determination and Educational Assistance Act and other related laws. Regardless, the "arc of history," insofar as it curves toward justice as suggested by Martin Luther King, Jr., appears to have a gentle curve.

Notes

1. This was stated in request to the U.S. Department of the Interior to negotiate a comanagement agreement; it is quoted from *News from Indian Country Today* (Capriccioso 2003).

2. The term "Tribes" used in this chapter refers to American Indians, Alaskan Natives, and Native Hawaiians in the United States.

3. See Kathryn Shanley's introduction chapter for a discussion of the Marshall Court rulings from the nineteenth century through which the federal trust relationship became etched into law.

4. Similarly, article 25 of the UN Declaration states: "Indigenous peoples have the right to maintain and strengthen their distinctive spiritual relationship with their traditionally owned or otherwise occupied and used lands, territories, waters and coastal seas, and other resources and to uphold their responsibilities to future generations in this regard."

5. There are many types of partnerships between governments and local communities variously referred to collaborative natural resource management, cooperative management, participatory management, stakeholder cooperation, community-based management, community forestry, social forestry, and watershed management. We heed Castro and Nielsen's (2001) call for a narrow definition of comanagement.

6. The U.S. Department of Health, Education, and Welfare has since been reorganized into two departments: the Department of Health and Human Services and the Department of Education.

7. The Self-Governance Program began as a demonstration project authorized by the 1988 amendments to the ISDEAA. The CSKT were among the ten tribes included in the original demonstration project.

8. Memorandum from the Office of the Solicitor, U.S. Department of the Interior, on Inherently Federal Functions under the Tribal Self-Governance Act.

9. Statement of D. Fred Matt, executive director, Tribal Council, CSKT of the Flathead Nation. 2003. In Hearing Before the Committee on Indian Affairs, United States Senate, 108th Congress, 1st Session, on Status of Tribal Fish and Wildlife Management Programs Across Indian Country (S. Hrg. 108–21). Washington, DC: U.S. Government Printing Office, June 3.

10. Statement and Prepared Testimony of D. Fred Matt, chairman, CSKT. 2004. In *Hearing Before United States Senate Committee on Indian Affairs on S. 1715*, 62–65; 95–102. Washington, DC: U.S. Government Printing Office, May 12.

11. However, the NBR was not specifically listed among the FWS units eligible for an AFA in the statutorily-required annual *Federal Register* announcement until October 21, 1997, for the 1999 Fiscal Year (USDOI 1997).

12. Presidential Executive Order 12996, "Management and General Public." Use of the National Wildlife Refuge System," issued on March 25, 1996, also encouraged federal-tribal partnerships on National Wildlife Refuges (*Federal Register* 61 no. 61 [1996]: 13647–48).

13. The negotiations concerned other units of the National Bison Range Complex, which is referred to here and below as the NBR for convenience.

14. Notably, it would be nearly ten years after the TSGA was signed into law that FWS would enter into its first Self-Governance AFA in 2004, with the Council of

Athabascan Tribal Governments contracting for various projects at the Yukon Flats National Wildlife Refuge in Alaska. The Tribes' were not alone in having requests for comanagement rejected by the FWS (Lyons 2005, 726).

15. The NBR is part of the National Bison Range Complex, which includes additional wildlife conservation areas that also are part of the National Wildlife Refuge System but are located entirely within the boundaries of the Flathead Indian Reservation.

16. The CSKT have two culture committees that provide advice and support for integrating traditional cultural perspectives and knowledge into tribal government policy making and decision-making.

17. There was no formal process or requirement to document these geographic, historical, and cultural ties for the Department of the Interior or the USFWS.

18. See also "Testimony of James Steele Jr., Tribal Council Chairman, CSKT of the Flathead Indian Reservation." 2008. Submitted to the Senate Committee on Indian Affairs' Hearing on Proposed Legislation to Amend the Department of the Interior Provisions of the Tribal Self-Governance Act, May 13. Accessed Feb. 7, 2013. http://www.indian.senate.gov/public/_files/Steeletestimony.pdf.

19. Quoting Interior Deputy Assistant Secretary Paul Hoffman, lead negotiator for the Interior Department.

20. Citing a *Missoulian* newspaper story that quoted Lisa Morris.

21. See, for example, comments from Susan Campbell Reneau in Stromnes (2003).

22. Fiscal Years 2005–2006 Annual Funding Agreement Between the United States Fish and Wildlife Service and the Confederated Salish and Kootenai Tribes of the Flathead Reservation (Dec. 1, 2004). Accessed on Nov. 12, 2012. http://cskt.org/documents/nbr/nbrc.afa.joint.pdf.

23. Fiscal Years 2005–2006 Annual Funding Agreement, § 11.E(3) (USFWS 2006).

24. Amended Memorandum of Points and Authorities in Support of the Confederated Salish and Kootenai Tribes' Motion for Summary Judgment ([April 27, 2010] *Reed v. Salazar* [744 F. Supp. 2d 98]) (hereinafter "Amended memo"), citing *Confederated Salish and Kootenai Tribes v. United States*, 437 F.2d 458 (Ct. Cl. 1971).

25. United States District Court for the District of Columbia, Memorandum Opinion, *Reed v. Salazar* (744 F. Supp. 2d at 107), (hereafter "Memorandum Opinion"), citing Dec. 29, 2006 DOI Memorandum, September 28, 2010, at 11.

26. Amended memo, 41–45.

27. See also Amended memo, at 41–45.

28. Amended memo.

29. Amended memo, 41–42.

30. Quoting CSKT, "Response to CY-2006 Preliminary Performance Evaluation Summary," at 2. As noted in a U.S. District Court brief (Intervenor-Defendant Confederated Salish Kootenai Tribes' Memorandum of Points and Authorities in Reply to Plaintiffs' Opposition to Defendants' and Intervenor-Defendants' Motions for Summary Judgment, *Reed v. Salazar* [Civil Action No. 08–2117, April 8, 2010, 11]) an employee adamantly opposed to the 2005–2006 AFA, one of the authors of the USFWS performance evaluation of the AFA, and a plaintiff in *Reed v. Salazar*, Delbert ("Skip") Palmer, who had also been, in the 1990s, a board member of All Citizens Equal (ACE),

an anti-Indian organization with racist roots based on the Flathead Reservation that opposed the AFA (see previous discussion of early attempts at negotiating and AFA and MHRN (2000, 20, 37, 38)).

31. Memorandum Opinion (*Reed v. Salazar* [2010, 11]). U.S. Fish and Wildlife Service employees also filed a formal grievance on Jan. 18, 2007.

32. *Confederated Salish and Kootenai Tribes of the Flathead Nation v. Mountain-Prairie Regional Director*, Docket # IBIA 07–60-A). Later that month the IBIA put CSKT's appeal on hold, pending efforts to resolve the issues through negotiations for a new AFA.

33. Amended Memo.

34. Memoradum Opinion, 14 citing Dec. 29, 2006 Memorandum.

35. Exhibit A of Memorandum of Points and Authorities in Support of CSKT's Motion to Intervene in *Blue Goose et al. v. Salazar* (Civil Action No. 09–0640 [CKK]), p. 21.

36. Memorandum Opinion (744 F. Supp. 2d at 107), referencing Nov. 26, 2007 FWS Memorandum.

37. Fiscal Years 2009–2011 Annual Funding Agreement between the United States Department of the Interior Fish and Wildlife Service and the CSKT of the Flathead Reservation (FY 2009–11 AFA). The FY 2009–11 AFA went into effect Oct. 1, 2008, and was to extend until Sept. 30, 2011 (FY 2009–11 AFA § 24).

38. FY 2009–11 AFA § 7(C).1.

39. FY 2009–11 AFA § 2(A).

40. FY 2009–11 AFA § 7(D).

41. Memorandum Opinion (744 F. Supp. 2d at 107), at 15 citing FY 2009–11 AFA § 17(C).

42. The first author visited the NBR with a group of college students on October 15, 2009, and met with the USFWS Refuge Manager and Project Lead, Jeff King, and the CSKT Deputy Project Leader, Mike Carter. Both reported excellent communications, coordination, and cooperation between USFWS and the CSKT personnel.

43. Testimony of Laura Davis, Associate Deputy Secretary, U.S. Department of the Interior. 2010. House Natural Resources Committee on H.R. 4347, The Department of the Interior Tribal Self-Governance Act. June 9. Accessed Feb. 5, 2013. http://naturalresources.house.gov/uploadedfiles/davistestimony06.09.10.pdf.

44. The Blue Goose Alliance, co-founded by former FWS mangers, is dedicated to promoting national wildlife refuges and supports the creation of a separate National Wildlife Refuge Service within the DOI.

45. Rob Chaney, "Group Files Suit over Bison Range Plan," *Missoulian* (Apr. 9, 2009).

46. The "extraordinary circumstances" trigger is covered under NEPA regulations (43 C.F.R §46.215).

47. *Reed v. Salazar*, 744 F. Supp. 2d 98, 120 (D.D.C. 2010).

48. Letter to Secretary of the Interior Dirk Kempthorne from House Natural Resource Committee Chairman Nick Rahall (D-LA) and Ranking Minority Member Don Young (R-AK); Exhibit C of Memorandum of Points and Authorities in Support of CSKT's Motion to Intervene in *Blue Goose et al. v. Salazar* (Civil Action No. 09–0640 [CKK]), p. 33–35.

49. In a May 2007, joint letter to Secretary of the Interior Dirk Kempthorne, House Natural Resource Committee Chairman Nick Rahall (D-LA), and Ranking Minority Member Don Young (R-AK) attempted to counteract agency resistance by stating that "we are concerned that the lack of support for this agreement by some individuals within FWS may have resulted in a distorted record concerning NBR activities under the AFA," cited from Exhibit C of Memorandum of Points and Authorities in Support of CSKT's Motion to Intervene in *Blue Goose et al. v. Salazar* (Civil Action No. 09–0640 [CKK]), at 33.

50. Examples include the Cape Flattery Wild Areas on the Makah Indian Reservation in Washington State, several parks managed by the Navaho Nation, the Sinkyone Intertribal Park in California, and a tribal park on the Ute Mountain Reservation in Colorado.

References

Azure, B. L. 1995a. "Bison Range-Management Opponents Try to Buffalo Officials." *Char-Koosta News*, Sept. 1.

———. 1995b. "Bison Range Rally Airs Opposition to Tribal Management: Tribal Speaker Shunned by Crowd." *Char-Koosta News*, May 19.

———. 1996. "Burns Accuses Tribes, USFWS of Secret Bison Range Negotiations." *Char-Koosta News*, Nov. 29.

———. 2004. "Tribes' Aspirations Moving Forward." *Char-Koosta News*, Sept. 16.

Backus, Perry. 2006. "Report Critical of Bison Range Management." *Missoulian*, July 30.

Branigan, Tania. 2003. "Groups Lock Horns over Bison Range, Conservationists Criticize Administration Plan That Would Let Tribes Run Montana Refuge." *Washington Post*, A19, Sept. 2.

Capriccioso, Robert. 2003. "Salish-Kootenai Management of Bison Range more than a Beef over Buffalo." *Indian Country Today*, Nov. 17.

Castro, Alfonso Peter, and Erik Nielsen. 2001. "Indigenous People and Co-management: Implications for Conflict Management." *Environmental Science & Policy* 4(4):229–39.

Chaney, Rob. 2009. "Group Files Suit over Bison Range Plan." *Missoulian*, April 9.

Char-Koosta News. 1994. "Tribes Prepare Proposal to Manage National Bison Range." Dec. 9.

CSKT (Confederated Salish and Kootenai Tribes). 1996a. *Comprehensive Resources Plan, Volume I*. Pablo, MT: Author.

———1996b. Comprehensive Resources Plan, Volume II. Pablo, MT: Author.

———. n.d.a. "Final Report National Bison Range Complex: Fiscal Years 2005 and 2006 Annual Funding Agreement Between the CSKT and USFWS." Accessed Nov. 8, 2012. http://www.cskt.org/documents/press/finalreport_annualfundingagreement.pdf.

———. n.d.b. "Fish, Wildlife, Recreation, and Conservation." Accessed February 5, 2013. http://www.cskt.org/tr/fwrc.htm.

———. n.d.c. "Response to CY-2006 Preliminary Performance Evaluation Summary: Annual Funding Agreement between CSKT and FWS, January 1 to November 30,

2006," Accessed Nov. 12, 2012. http://www.cskt.org/documents/press/response2cy
2006report.pdf.

CSKT (Confederated Salish and Kootenai Tribes) and USFWS (U.S. Fish and Wildlife Service). 2003a. "Draft Compatibility Issues Plan of Action," April 1.

———. 2003b. "Draft Principles and Plan of Action." National Bison Range an Affiliated Refuges Annual Funding Agreement, Preliminary Discussions and Draft Plan
of Action, Feb. 20.

———. 2003c. "Tribes and Fish & Wildlife Service Announce Plans to Negotiate Joint
Management of Bison Range." Joint Press Release, April 2.

———. 2003d. "U.S. Fish & Wildlife Service and Confederated Salish & Kootenai
Tribes Hold Negotiations Meeting June 9–10 in Washington," Joint Release,
June 10.

Devlin, Sherry. 2003. "Emotions High over Bison Range Management: Tribes' Bid for
Control Sparks Heated Debate." *Missoulian*, May 15.

Devlin, Vince. 2007a. "CSKT Report Defends Tribes' Work on Bison Range." *Missoulian*, Aug. 23.

———. 2007b. "Feds Find Progress in Bison Range Dispute." *Missoulian*, Jan. 24.

———. 2007c. "Feds Say They Want Relationship with Tribes at National Bison
Range." *Missoulian*, Dec. 30.

———. 2007d. "Official Seeks End to Bison Range Conflict." *Missoulian*, Dec. 7.

———. 2007e. "Report Details Bison Range Charges." *Missoulian*, Jan. 10.

Devlin, Vince. 2008a. "CSKT, Feds Say Talks Restoring Bit of Trust." *Missoulian*,
Jan. 19.

———. 2008b. "Group Files Suit against Tribes' Deal on Bison Range." *Missoulian*,
Dec. 9.

———. 2009. "Second Group Seeks To Halt CSKT Involvement in Bison Range."
Missoulian, Jan. 15.

Fahey, John. 1974. *The Flathead Indians*. Norman: University of Oklahoma Press.

Fitzgerald, Mary. 2004. "Wildlife Staff Protest Pact with Tribes Indians Would Share
Management of Montana Bison Range." *Washington Post*, Oct. 19.

Goodman, Ed. 2000. "Protecting Habitat for Off-Reservation Tribal Hunting and Fishing Rights: Tribal Comanagement as a Reserved Right." *Environmental Law*
30:284–85.

King, Mary Ann. 2007. "Co-management or Contracting-Agreements Between Native American Tribes and the US National Park Service Pursuant to the 1994 Tribal
Self-Governance Act." *Harvard Environmental Law Review* 31:475–50.

Krahe, Diane L. 2001. "A Sovereign Prescription for Preservation: The Mission Moun-
tains Tribal Wilderness." In *Trusteeship in Change: Toward Tribal Autonomy in
Resource Management*, edited by Richmond L. Clow and Imre Sutton, 195–221.
Boulder: University Press of Colorado.

LaDuke, Winona. 1999. "Buffalo Nations, Buffalo People." In *All Our Relations: Native Struggles for Land and Life*, edited by Winona LaDuke, 137–62. Cambridge,
MA: South End Press.

Lane, Marcus B., and Michael Hibbard. 2005. "Doing it for Themselves Transformative
Planning by Indigenous peoples." *Journal of Planning Education and Research*
25(2):172–84.

Lyons, Erin Patrick. 2005. "'Give Me a Home Where the Buffalo Roam': The Case in
Favor of the Management-Function Transfer of the National Bison Range to the

Confederated Salish and Kootenai Tribes of the Flathead Nation." *The Journal of Gender, Race, and Justice* 8:711–33.

Matt, D. Fred (Tribal Council Chairman, CSKT). 2004a. Letter to the Editor, *Char-Koosta News*, Aug. 26.

———. 2004b. Letter to U.S. Fish & Wildlife Service Regional Director, Ralph Morgenweck, May 4 (on file with first author).

McDonald, R. 2007. "PEER Gets It Wrong Again." Guest Editorial, *Char-Koosta News*, May 31.

MHRN (Montana Human Rights Network). 2000. Drumming Up Resentment: The Anti-Indian Movement in Montana. Helena: Montana Human Rights Network. http://www.mhrn.org/publications/specialresearchreports/DrummingUp.pdf.

Montgomery, Erin. 2003. "This Land is Your Land? Two Indian Tribes Try to Take Over a National Wildlife Refuge. Conservationists Concerned." *The Weekly Standard*, July 17.

Morgenweck, Ralph. 2004. Letter to D. Fred Matt, Chairman, Tribal Council, CSKT, March 5 (on file with first author).

Nie, Martin. 2008. "Use of Co-management and Protected Land-Use Designations to Protect Tribal Cultural Resources and Reserved Treaty Rights on Federal Lands." *Natural Resources Journal* 48:585–647.

Ohlson, Davinna, Katherine Cushing, Lynne Trulio, and Alan Leventhal. 2008. "Advancing Indigenous Self-Determination Through Endangered Species Protection: Idaho Gray Wolf Recovery." Environmental Science and Policy 11(5): 430–40.

Roberts, Lawrence. 2012. "Testimony Before the Committee on Indian Affairs, United States Senate on Advancing the Federal-Tribal Relationship through Self-Governance and Self-Determination," September 20, Accessed Oct. 26, 2012. http://www.doi.gov/ocl/hearings/112/FederalTribalRelationship_092012.cfm.

Sanders, Marren. 2007. "Ecosystem Co-management Agreements: A Study of Nation Building or a Lesson on Erosion of Tribal Sovereignty." Buffalo. *Environmental Law Journal* 15:97–176.

Selden, Ron. 2003. "Montana Bison Range and Refuge Management in Question." Indian Country Today, June 25.

Smits, David D. 1994. "The Frontier Army and the Destruction of the Buffalo: 1865–1883." *Western Historical Quarterly* 25(2):313–38.

Steele, James L., Jr. 2006. "National Bison Range: The Rest of the Story." *Char-Koosta News*, Aug. 24.

Stromnes, John. 2003. "Be Patient, Burns Tells Opponents of Tribal Bison Range Takeover." *Missoulian*, Aug. 29.

———. 2004a. "Burns: Go Slow on Bison Range Process." *Missoulian*, Oct. 30.

———. 2004b. "Public Comment on Bison Range to Close Nov. 4." *Missoulian*, Oct. 21.

———. 2004c. "Tribes Amend Bison Range Management Proposal." *Missoulian*, Dec. 5.

———. 2005. "Sen. Conrad Burns Promises Hearing on Bison Range." *Missoulian*, Mar. 16.

Suagee, Dean B. 1998. "Tribal Self-Determination and Environmental Federalism: Cultural Values as a Force for Sustainability." *Widener Law Symposium Journal* 3:229.

Tsosie, Rebecca. 1996. "Tribal Environmental Policy in an Era of Self-Determination: The Role of Ethics, Economics, and Traditional Ecological Knowledge." *Vermont Law Review* 21:225–333.

Tully, James. 2000. "The Struggles of Indigenous Peoples for and of Freedom." In *Political Theory and the Rights of Indigenous Peoples*, edited by Duncan Ivison, Paul Patton, and Will Sanders, 36–59. Cambridge, UK: Cambridge University Press.

UN (United Nations). 2007. United Nations Declaration on the Rights of Indigenous Peoples. http://www.un.org/esa/socdev/unpfii/documents/DRIPS_en.pdf.

USDOI (U.S. Department of the Interior), Office of Inspector General. 2011. "The National Bison Range" [Evaluation Memorandum/Report with attachments]. Report No. NM-EV-FWS-0001–2010. March.

USDOI (U.S. Department of the Interior), Office of the Secretary. 1997. "List of Eligible Programs for Inclusion in Fiscal Year 1999 Funding Agreements to be Negotiated with Self-Governance Tribes by Interior Bureaus other than the Bureau of Indian Affairs." *Federal Register* 62:54644–01.

——. 2013. "List of Programs Eligible for Inclusion in Fiscal Year 2013 Funding Agreements to be Negotiated with Self-Governance Tribes by Interior Bureaus Other Than the Bureau of Indian Affairs." *Federal Register* 78(15):4861–65.

USFWS (U.S. Fish and Wildlife Service). 1990. "National Bison Range Fenced Animal Management Plan." Lakewood, CO: USFWS, Region 6.

——. 1994. *The Native American Policy of the U.S. Fish and Wildlife Service.* Washington, DC: U.S. Fish and Wildlife Service.

——. 2001. "Wildland Fire Management Plan for the National Bison Range Complex." Moiese, MT: U.S. Fish and Wildlife Service.

——. 2006. "Calendar Year 2005 Report on Implementation of Annual Funding Agreement at National Bison Range Complex," May 23. Accessed Oct. 28, 2014. http://www.peer.org/assets/docs/fws/06_20_7_nbrc_report.pdf..

——. 2012. "Notice of Intent to Prepare an Environmental Assessment Regarding the Interest of the Confederated Salish and Kootenai Tribes to enter into an Annual Funding Agreement with the Department of the Interior, U. S. Fish and Wildlife Service, for the Operation and Management of Programs at the National Bison Range Complex." Accessed on Oct. 21, 2012. http://www.fws.gov/bisonrange/AFA/Final_Public_Notice_AFA.pdf.

Williams, Pat. 2007. "Intent of Act was to Encourage Tribes to be More Self-sufficient." Guest Editorial, *Char-Koosta News*, Apr. 12.

Whitehorn, W. Clark. 2003. "The National Bison Range," *Montana—The Magazine of Western History* 53(3):63–65. Accessed Oct. 30, 2012. http://www.visitmt.com/history/Montana_the_Magazine_of_Western_History/fall2003/bisonrange.htm.

Wiles, Jessica M. 2010. "Have American Indians Been Written out of the Religious Freedom Restoration Act." *Montana Law Review* 71:471–502.

Wilkinson, Charles. 2005. *Blood Struggle: The Rise of Modern Indian Nations.* New York: W.W. Norton & Co.

Williams, Jason. 2004. "Beyond Mere Ownership: How the Confederated Salish Kootenai Tribes Used Regulatory Control of Natural Resources to Build a Viable Homeland." *Public Land & Resources Law Review* 24:121–37.

Zellmer, Sandra B. 2002. "Sustaining Geographies of Hope: Cultural Resources on Public Lands." *University of Colorado Law Review* 73:413–520.

CHAPTER SIX

The Sámi Influence in Legislative Processes

Adoption of the Finnmark Land Act of 2005

Øyvind Ravna

The right to govern an ancestral homeland is the iconic struggle of Indigenous peoples that echoes around the globe. At the heart of the contest is the vital relationship of people to their homelands, whether they now share their homeland with other cultures or whether they live as nations-within-nations. Control of resources means control of culture and continuance. The disputed ownership and management of Salish tribal lands that has been ongoing for more than a century typifies the dilemma of Native Americans seeking control of their homelands (Robin Saha and Jennifer Hill-Hart in chapter 5 and David L. Moore in chapter 4). Like the Salish in Montana, the Sámi in Finnmark have sought recognition of their land and natural resource rights for decades and have had varying influence on political, legal, and legislative processes concerning those rights.[1] On June 17, 2005, the Finnmark Act (Fm Act), a land code relating to legal relations and management of land and natural resources in the county of Finnmark in Norway, was adopted as a result of this process. Section 1 of the Fm Act outlines that "the purpose of the [Fm] Act is to facilitate the management of land and natural resources in the County of Finnmark in a balanced and ecologically sustainable manner for the benefit of the residents of the county and particularly as a basis for Sámi culture, reindeer husbandry, use of non-cultivated areas, commercial activity, and social life." More than a land code, the Fm Act is also a law borne through Indigenous participation and consolations.

Generally we must assume that in states where there are minorities, and in particular Indigenous peoples, the state has a responsibility to let these nations participate in decision-making processes that concern them. For states that have ratified the United Nations' *International Labor Organization* (ILO) *Convention No. 169 Concerning Indigenous and Tribal Peoples in Independent Countries* (ILO 1989), as Norway did in 1990, the commitment to give Indigenous people substantial influence in decision-making, including participation in legislative processes, is binding (see article 6 of the Convention). Norway is also bound by a consultation agreement between the government and the Sámi Parliament, which was completed in May 2005. It can be seen as a side effect of the Fm Act process.

The commitment is further strengthened not only by the fact that Norway signed the United Nations' Declaration on the Rights of Indigenous Peoples of 2007 (UNDRIP), but also by the fact that Norway actively promoted it. Although this is a declaration and not a binding treaty, Norway's vote to adopt it incurs obligations to comply with its contents, especially since the cabinet minister responsible has stated, "the UN's Declaration on the Rights of Indigenous Peoples is in line with government policy towards the Sámi people." Its articles 18 and 19 ensure Indigenous peoples the rights to consultations and to participate in decision-making in matters that would affect their rights.[2] In the case of adoption of the draft, Nordisk samekonvensjon (2005), the Nordic states will be bound to negotiate on matters of significant importance to the Sámi people for decisions taken. According to the draft ILO Convention, negotiations must be conducted in such a way "that the same things [in the Nordic countries] can influence the procedure and results" (Nordisk samekonvensjon 2005, 15). Furthermore, the same things veto against the states to adopt or allow actions that "can significantly damage the essential conditions for the Sámi culture, Sámi industries, or Sámi community."

The problems addressed in this chapter are discussed in two parts: first, I examine the Indigenous peoples' influence on the legislative process leading to the adoption of the Fm Act; and, second, I describe and discuss the extent of the clarification process authorized by the Fm Act, including the procedural law requirements. Of particular interest in this context is chapter five of the Fm Act, which initiates a process of legal clarification of land rights for areas that previously were considered to be state-owned land (Ravna 2011b, 425–29). The process is to be performed by a body called the Finnmark Commission (cf. Fm Act § 29, para. 1), while a special court, the Land Tribunal (Tribunal) for Finnmark, is to settle disputes arising once the Finnmark Commission has investigated a field or specified area (cf. Fm Act §36, para. 1).[3]

The sources examined will mainly be preparatory works supported by case law and legal literature. The current legal clarification process in Finnmark is discussed in the literature only to a small extent for the last two sources. The theme is actualized since it proposes similar schemes for clarification in the Sámi areas south of Finnmark (Norges Offentlige Utredninger (NOU) 2007, 31–68).

Sámi Participation in Legislative Processes Before the Fm Act Process

Sámi participation in public surveys and preparatory works has relatively long traditions in Norway, even if the extent of the Sámi influence on the process and result is arguable. Already in 1875, when the government initiated a work to elaborate a Reindeer Husbandry Act of Finnmark, two reindeer herders, John Persen Jox the elder and Ole Isaksen Hætta, were included in the Law Commission (Bull 2001, 112).[4] When the first general reindeer husbandry act covering the whole country should have been developed, the Sámi party was not invited to the law committee, which among others can be explained from the prevailing Norwegianization policy at that time. Instead the Sámi proposed a law of their own, which partially contributed to the first Sámi Congress held in Trondheim on February 6, 1917 (Berg 2009). Today February 6 is celebrated as Sámi National Day, but the attempt to write a bill didn't win significant influence. The Norwegian politicians preferred to adopt the bill written by public prosecutor P. Kjerschow (Kjerschow 1922).[5]

In the 1950s, the political winds had turned, and establishing a reindeer committee without herding Sámi was virtually impossible.[6] When the Reindeer Husbandry Act Committee of 1960 was founded, two reindeer herding Sámi were included as members. The law committee set forth a proposal that was forward looking in terms of intervention in the herding areas and in relation to expropriation compensation for such intervention. This radical proposal, however, met huge opposition among the Ministry of Agriculture and the parliamentarians. Although the act that passed in 1978 was better in many ways than the former act, the legal protection of Sámi reindeer herders was barely better than the Kjerschow Act of 1933.

Of greater interest in our case is the work process preparatory to the previous Fm Act, adopted in 1965 and in effect until 2006. In contrast to the preparation of the Reindeer Husbandry Acts, there was historically no tradition to appoint representatives of the Sámi in the law commissions. The

Sámi were not appointed when the law committee was given the mandate in 1962 to prepare a new "land sales act," or Fm Act. The law committee's bill provided neither significant change nor advantage for the Sámi, despite the fact that the committee's mandate was to draft an act to serve as a tool for managing and governing outlying fields and mountainous areas in a core Sámi area. For example, the law committee refused to follow suggestions from the Sámi committee, which had proposed that Sámi should have priority for purchase of land from the state (Innstilling 1959, 35), but the law committee concluded instead that "there is no reason to provide legislation that gives the Sámi a special right to purchase or lease state property" (Innstilling 1962, 15). The view was supported by the Ministry in charge who stated that, "the rights of the Sámi must be respected in any context. But the Ministry supposes, as the committee, that there is no need to institute advantages for the Sámi in purchasing or leasing of land" (Ot.prp. nr. 59, 1984–1985).

Another example of a preparatory work that did not take into consideration Sámi representation is the work in relation to an outfield (uncultivated) commission act in the 1980s, which included the counties of Nordland and Troms, but which also included Finnmark County (ibid.). All these counties have Sámi populations. In the preparatory work there was no Sámi representation; furthermore, the bill was put forward despite an almost unanimous protest from a number of Sámi organizations (ibid., 14). This shows that the state authorities have set up a much higher threshold for Sámi representatives to achieve influence on the preparatory works and the determination and management of ownership rights and titles to land in the Sámi areas. It also brings into question the reindeer husbandry rights. The situation may be explained by the old doctrine stating the nomadic use of land could not form a basis of ownership, which in practice meant that the ownership belonged to the state or the king (Stang 1911, 3).[7]

When the Sámi Rights Committee, which in reality was a law committee, was established due to pressure from Sámi organizations and activists, the state could not avoid including Sámi representatives. The original committee, appointed in 1980 and a modified committee that wrote the first draft of the Fm Act (Naturgrunnlaget for Sámisk kultur [The Natural Resource Base for Sámi Culture]) published in NOU (1997, 4), consisted of a relatively large proportion of Sámi. It must in any case be pointed out that in perhaps the most important subgroup under the Sámi Rights Commission, the so-called law group, there were no Sámi representatives.

The Preparatory Work of the Fm Act
and the Sámi Influence

The Sámi Rights Committee Draft
and the Governmental Response

As already mentioned, the Norwegian state in the 1980s prepared and established a judiciary commission to determine the boundaries of state property in the mountainous areas of the counties of Nordland and Troms:
Utmarkskommisjonen for Nordland og Troms (the Uncultivated Land
Commission for Nordland and Troms [1985–2004]). The county of
Finnmark was not included in the jurisdiction of this committee even if
it was discussed, which can be explained partly by the previously mentioned opinion about the state ownership of the unsold land (Ot.prp. nr.
53, 2002–03, 13–14) and partly by opposition from the Sámi parties to
such establishment.

The investigation of Sámi rights to "land and water" in Finnmark was
therefore left to the Sámi Rights Committee.[8] But the committee did not
assess actual ownership and rights of use acquired in the area by the Sámi
and others at the time it was considered state property. Instead the already-
mentioned subgroup, the Law Group, consisting of reputable property lawyers (but no Sámi) assessed the ownership to the land of Finnmark. The
subgroup concluded that "the State must be regarded as the owner of the
former unregistered land in Finnmark. This applies not only to the outer
part, but also to the inner part" (NOU 1993, 266). This was the case even if
the ownership acquisition is "not based on contract, clear expropriation decision, or legislation but is rooted in misunderstandings" (ibid., 263). Implications of the lack of Sámi representatives in this expert group are not
discussed here.

The Sámi Rights Committee itself, in any case, found that the Sámi and
other locals had certain rights of use and proposed an act for the management of the land in Finnmark whereby the title should be transferred from
the State Forest Company (Statskog SF) to an independent ownership body
called the *Finnmark grunnforvaltning* (Finnmark Estate Management).
This body should be controlled by a board appointed in part by the Finnmark County Council and in part by the Sámi Parliament.

The Sámi Rights Committee also proposed a governance model in
which local people would be assured influence over resource management
through locally appointed "outfields boards." It further proposed that
community common land should be clarified and determined based on

local tradition, which could be considered as a kind of "modern *siida* system"[9] (NOU 1997, 241).

In addition the Committee also made a proposal for a procedure to clarify such common land. Although at the time the Commission for Nordland and Troms was at the peak of its productivity, the Sámi Right Committee proposed no corresponding mechanism to clarify the properties and land rights in Finnmark. Instead it suggested that the community common land be determined by a committee appointed for each municipality. This was justified by the fact that such clarification demanded local knowledge.[10]

Even though the Sámi Rights Committee also undertook a general discussion of the legal basis for natural resources in Finnmark, it did not conclude upon the rights of ownership and use for specific groups in designated areas. The legal standing of land rights and ownership of state-held land in Finnmark at that time remained unresolved.

The question of Sámi rights to natural resources in Finnmark was controversial. Six years after the Sámi Rights Committee submitted its proposals, the Bondevik government finally presented a bill. During that period, an acknowledgment appeared from state authorities that the state ownership of the "unregistered land" in Finnmark was based on a legal opinion of the Norwegian state that was no longer valid. So when the Bondevik government presented their draft of the Fm Act in 2003, they concluded this ownership could not be upheld in full (Ot.prp. nr. 53, 2002–2003, 43).[11] This resulted in a governmental proposal to transfer the ownership to a body controlled by the Sámi Parliament and the Finnmark County Council.

But at the same time the government omitted the Sámi Rights Committee proposal for local community management of outlying fields. This was justified in that outfield resources should be managed uniformly, not to "harm a desired and appropriate allocation of resources in their entirety" (ibid., 98–99). The Sámi Rights Committee proposal to clarify community common areas was an attempt to survey and recognize their rights over "land and water."[12] The government acknowledged in section 5 of the draft that "Sámi and others have acquired rights by prescription and immemorial usage" (Ot.prp. nr. 53, 2002–2003, 106) and that there may be "private or collective rights based on prescription or immemorial usage" (ibid., 8, 122, cf. draft § 5) of the former state land. The proposal for clarification was omitted from the bill too. No other suggestions were made to identify such rights. The government's aim, instead, was "to make good arrangements for the rights and the management of land and water in Finnmark by law, rather than by dispute resolution in the courts" (ibid., 97), and by transferring the land to an ownership body called the Finnmark Estate.[13] Accordingly it did not put forward any proposals or procedures to conduct such clarification.

The draft act was met with considerable criticism from the Sámi Parliament, who argued that the bill was not in accordance with obligations under international law, especially the ILO Convention (Innst. O. nr. 80, 2004–2005, 14). As a result, the Parliamentary Standing Committee of Justice asked for an independent assessment of the proposed act, which Professors Geir Ulfstein and Hans Petter Graver were engaged to undertake. They concluded that the government's proposals on key points were insufficient to meet the ILO Convention. In relation to article 14, it was stated:

> If the Finnmark Act shall meet ILO Convention requirements for recognition of land rights, the decision rules must be changed in such way that the Sámi secure the control according to an ownership position. Is this not relevant for the entire county? The special Sámi areas need to be identified with a view to ensuring the Sámi the control and rights to these areas. (Ulfstein and Graver 2003)

The criticism, in particular the requirement for the bill to comply with international minority and Indigenous people law, initiated a new era for constitutional practice in Norway.

The Sámi Influence Through the Consultations with the Parliamentary Standing Committee of Justice

On the initiative of the Parliamentary Standing Committee of Justice (Standing Committee), four consultations with the Sámi Parliament and Finnmark County Council took place in 2004 and 2005. The majority of the Standing Committee of Justice pointed out that "Norway's international obligations to consult the Sámi are thus included in Parliament's work. This is a constitutional innovation. Consultations have pushed the case forward and have been very useful" (Innst. O. nr. 80, 2004–2005, 15). The consultations led to rather extensive changes in the bill, which included a new first paragraph of section 5 stating "the Sámi have collectively and individually through prolonged use of land and water acquired rights to land in Finnmark." This statement represents an important principle and final political recognition that such rights exist (ibid., 15, 37).

Due to these consultations, the majority of the Standing Committee, with the exception of the members from the Progress Party and the Socialist Party, acknowledged that identification of existing rights must be included as a key element in the Fm Act (ibid., 15, 37). The majority thereafter proposed establishing "a surveying commission and a judging tribunal to identify existing rights to land and water in Finnmark" (ibid., 17).

The majority points out that the surveying commission had to report on the legal situation on the land the Finnmark Estate would take over from the State Forest Company. The statements of the Commission would, according to the majority of the Standing Committee, provide a good basis for people in Finnmark to make up their mind about whether conflicts over land rights actually exist (ibid., 15). The intention is that the ambiguities and disagreements can be resolved through negotiations and consensus, which was reasoned in Sámi traditions (ibid., 21).

Remaining legal disputes may be brought before the Special Land Tribunal during a period of one and one-half years. Based on that, the majority proposes a new chapter five of the Fm Act entitled "Surveying and Recognition of Existing Rights" (ibid., 17). Other significant changes in the draft Fm Act as a result of the four consultations with the Sámi Parliament included that the preamble (section 1) was somewhat strengthened in relation to Finnmark's interests pertaining to Indigenous interests, since the reference in the preamble to the general public outside Finnmark was taken out of the text. Also of importance was a new provision (section 3), which lifted up the commitments to international law and stated that the Fm Act shall apply to the limitations imposed by the ILO Convention and a section 10 that stated authorities have a duty to take Sámi concerns into consideration by changing the use of outlaying fields and uncultivated land. Further, the Finnmark Estate is given more independent possession because (1) the language that states the government shall appoint a board member is taken out of the act and (2) by the fact that the Finnmark Estate is given general expropriation protection. The possibilities for locals to get special rights to the utilization of natural resources are also a part of this picture (ibid., 15). The review shows that the Sámi interests have had a huge overall influence on the final result of the Fm Act. In the following section I look at the most central part of this scenario, the surveying and recognition unit and the definition of asset in practice.

A Survey of the Clarification Process in the Fm Act

Reflection of the Sámi Influence in the Finnmark Commission's Procedural Law Requirements

As we have seen, the Finnmark Commission was not included in the government bill, but it was introduced under consultations with the Sámi Parliament. The Finnmark Commission was formally established by a Royal Decree March 14, 2008, pursuant to the Fm Act, § 29, para. 1. Its mandate was to investigate the rights of use and ownership the Finnmark Estate took over from the state according to current national legislation.

Establishing the Finnmark Commission follows up on obligations to which Norway is bound by the ILO Convention to consult Indigenous peoples under article 6, para. 1(a) and to a larger extent establish adequate procedures within the national legal system to settle land claims of Indigenous peoples under article 14(3). The latter aims to facilitate the clarification process in relation to the Sámi, who, for the most part, are locals living in villages or reindeer herders. This holds not only for the formal process but also for the application of substantive law, including the use of legal sources as Sámi customary law.

Of importance to note is that the majority of the Standing Committee, after consultations with the Sámi Party, expressed great skepticism to the ordinary court of law system. It stated that according to the ILO Convention, the scheme selected in the Fm Act was preferable to the ordinary courts where "it is clearly not acceptable under international law to hand over to the ordinary courts the question of which and the extent of rights acquired in Finnmark" (ibid., 28).[14]

As an additional argument for the proposed arrangement, the majority mentioned that there had been similar arrangements, regardless of Indigenous peoples' rights and obligations under international law elsewhere in the country. The reason the Standing Committee of Justice proposed the identification process was partly due to Norway's international legal obligations to the Sámi. It was also in part because the people of Finnmark—Sámi and non-Sámi—should not be put in a worse position than people elsewhere in the country when it came to legal clarification of the status of outlaying fields and mountainous areas.

The establishment of the Standing Commission can also be seen as a direct result of the Fm Act, § 5 that recognizes the Sámi and others have acquired rights on the Finnmark Estate through prescription and immemorial usage. The Finnmark Commission consists of five members, a majority of whom are lawyers with qualifications as judges (cf. Fm Act § 29, para. 2); however, the act does not set any requirement for Sámi or other representation except the fact that "at least two members shall be resident in or otherwise have a strong affiliation to the County of Finnmark." It is assumed that the Sámi Parliament is permitted to comment on the composition before the member is appointed by the government.[15] The actual composition can be said to reflect a political balancing act with great emphasis placed upon correct ethnopolitical distribution and a rather large representation of the Sámi.[16]

In relation to the application of law we noted that the majority of the Standing Committee emphasized that the surveying of rights should be based upon current *national law*. The term national instead of "Norwegian" was chosen to "better point out that consideration must be given to Sámi customs and sense of justice" (ibid.). This means that Sámi customs and customary law must be taken under consideration as substantive law within the framework of article 8 of the ILO Convention.

Although the objective of this chapter is not to analyze the weight of Sámi customs in contradiction to Norwegian statutory law, it does merit comment.[17] Where Indigenous people's customary law stands in contrast to other sources of law, the Sámi Rights Committee II has found that the weight of such law must be determined by the quality of the customs. The Sámi Rights Committee does not preclude Indigenous customary law be given greater weight than customary law among the majority population. Rather, it concludes that "customary law will not take unconditional precedence when in conflict with internal laws, nor in questions of laws that do not apply fundamental legal principles" (NOU 2007, 222).

Two prejudicing cases, *Selbu* and *Svartskog*, published in the Supreme Court journal, *Norske Retstidende* (2001: 759 and 1229, respectively) are important sources when Sámi land rights are to be clarified. The majority of the Standing Committee stated that "assessment of evidence in the recent case law has been satisfactory." Modern Norwegian case law, particularly the *Selbu* and *Svartskog* cases, has given instruction on how traditional Sámi use shall be considered as a basis for acquisition. These will be important sources of law for the Commission and Court (Report to the Parliament 80 2004–2005, 36).[18]

The Committee actually went so far as to discuss whether this recent case law should be codified in the Fm Act, but it did not make this proposal since it would mean that statutory provisions and not case law would be the sources in the identification process. This shows, in any event, that these cases represent important foundations of law in answering substantive questions about when rights are to be acquired. The majority also pointed out that in the assessment of whether rights exist, and, if so, to what extent, reasonable results have to play a certain role (ibid., 36). This may indicate that policy considerations could also be a relevant source of law.

Finally, the commitment has been strengthened through Norway's signing of UNDRIP, which in article 40 states that the settlement of disputes relating to Indigenous peoples shall take into account "the customs, traditions, rules, and legal systems of the Indigenous peoples concerned and international human rights." This provision can be compared with the ILO Convention's article 8.

Other Procedural Law Requirements of Importance

As mentioned, the mandate of the Finnmark Commission is to investigate the rights of use and ownership of areas taken over from the state by the Finnmark Estate, according to current national legislation. But the Commission is not a court of law, so it is not going to file any binding judgments. Its report can in any case be charged by bringing the matter to the Tribunal. Although the Finnmark Commission is not a court, the provisions against bias of the courts exert an influence (cf. Fm Act §46, para.).

It is particularly noteworthy that examination of reindeer husbandry rights, without any good reasoning, is performed only upon demand by a person with a legal interest. We can also note the rights to salmon fishing in the large rivers of Tana and Neiden are not included (Forskrift March 26, 2007, Nr. 277, § 5–6). In contrast to the Uncultivated Land Commission of Nordland and Troms, the process for the Finnmark Commission does not begin with a claim, suit, or other party subpoena. The Finnmark Commission is neither assigned investigation fields by central authorities, as was the Mountain Commission, but shall *itself* determine which fields it will investigate and the sequence of treatment (cf. Fm Act §, 30 para. 1). This may be in conflict with the principle of party disposal.

Section 30 also states that consideration shall be placed on "natural and appropriate delimitation of the field as regards extent and legal and historical context and the need to clarify the legal relations." Based on experience from the first three fields, which have been taken for investigation,[19] it can be said that the Commission has placed greater emphasis on natural and appropriate delimitation rather than the need for clarification. The selection of field 4, Karasjok/Kárášjohka signals, however, a change because the Commission will investigate one of the most demanding Sámi areas where there is a great need for internal legal clarification of the reindeer husbandry rights and areas.

The Commission can omit consideration of cases "that are clearly inappropriate for investigation by the Commission" (cf. Fm Act §30, para. 3). For such a decision, emphasis should be put in the category of the right and its legal basis. The majority of the Standing Committee has pointed out that this assessment must be based on the background and purpose of the clarification process where "a right based on immemorial usage will normally fit better than a right based on contract. Uncultivated areas will normally be better suited for investigation than a right to rent or lease ground" (Innst. O. nr. 80, 2004–2005, 19). It was further stated that the Commission primarily shall investigate rights of use and ownership that are based on long-term and traditional use. But the mandate cannot be limited to this. "According to the majority's opinion, it is therefore difficult in a precise way to specify in more detail the legal relations the Commission shall examine" (ibid.).

The Finnmark Commission has responsibility for case illumination (cf. Fm Act §32, para. 1). The Fm Act further states that "the Commission may in the manner it finds appropriate obtain statements, documents, and other material and conduct surveys and investigations, and so on concerning actual and legal circumstances that may be significant for the Commission's conclusions." However, this does not prevent the parties themselves from explaining the facts or the evidence to the Finnmark Commission. Representatives for interest groups may also be appointed to follow the working of the Finnmark Commission. The cost shall be covered by the state (cf. Fm Act §32, para. 3).

The final result of the investigation of the Finnmark Commission shall be submitted in a report on the legal situation of the field. The report has to contain information about (a) who, in the view of the Commission, are owners of the land; (b) what rights of use exist in the Commission's view; and (c) the circumstances on which the Commission bases its conclusions (cf. Fm Act §33). The Commission cannot refuse to consider an ownership dispute, for example, by concluding that it is other than the Finnmark Estate who is the owner of a particular piece of land. The majority of the Standing Committee here points out that the Commission in such cases "must decide what result has the best basis in law." It is not acceptable to conclude that the Finnmark Estate is not the owner of the area in question without also indicating who is assumed to be the owner (ibid., 21).

The Finnmark Estate shall, without undue delay, assess the conclusions of the Finnmark Commission (cf. Fm Act §34, para. 1). This is natural and necessary since the Finnmark Estate holds the title to the lands examined by the Commission and is otherwise regarded as the landowner and thus party to the investigation. The Standing Committee has held that the Finnmark Estate is more than an ordinary landowner and party, but has commitments in the identification process beyond what can be termed as ordinary party commitments (ibid., 21). The Finnmark Estate thus has an obligation to actively consider the Commission's report. To the extent the Finnmark Estate agrees that others have rights on "their" land, it is obliged to confirm and without undue delay attend to the rights to be registered. Through agreement, negotiated consensus, or unilateral declaration the process will terminate at this stage (cf. Fm Act §34, para. 2).

Private parties have no obligation to act on the report of the Finnmark Commission. The majority of the Standing Committee in practice assumed the opposite when it stated "if the parties do not want to put the question to rest by bringing it to the Tribunal, they can allow the Finnmark Estate to continue to manage the grounds without cutting off the possibility of raising the issue at some future point in time" (ibid., 21). That statement virtually proposes leaving the legal issues unresolved without any legal effect, and it sustains speculation in waiting to put forward a claim of strategic reasons. Such reasons assume that the prescription period is not yet reached; future change in the interpretations of the law gives better possibilities or other circumstances that may later work to one's benefit. Likewise, parties can wait if they would prefer the matter be dealt with by the ordinary courts instead of the Tribunal.

According to the Fm Act, section 35, parties that do not agree with the Finnmark Commission's conclusions or who need assistance to have the conclusions set out in binding agreements can ask the Finnmark Commission for mediation. We also note that disputes are assumed to be resolved according to Sámi tradition. The majority of the Standing Committee here refers to the Sámi Parliament, which has emphasized that "conflicts as far as possible and in line with Sámi traditions shall be resolved through negotiations and not through court proceedings. The majority completely support such a procedural approach" (ibid., 21). The Commission's report will not produce any legal effect by itself. Forcible decisions depend on agreements between the parties, unilateral declarations, or cases brought further to the Tribunal.[20]

The Land Tribunal for Finnmark

Matters not resolved through negotiations and agreements can be brought before the Land Tribunal for Finnmark. It has a mandate to settle rights disputes that arise after the Finnmark Commission has investigated a field (cf. Act §36, para. 1).[21] The Tribunal recognizes no demand for Sámi representatives, locals, or other special knowledge by the members, not even a connection to the county of Finnmark. General civil procedural rules apply in the same way for the Tribunal as they did for the Uncultivated Land Commission for Nordland and Troms so far as they are applicable, and nothing else is specified in the act (cf. §46, para. 2). But like the Commission for Nordland and Troms, there are a number of special procedural rules. As we have already seen there are particular rules on arbitration in which the Finnmark Commission is given a role in mediation. However, the mediation is not compulsory (Innst. O. nr. 80, 2004–2005, 22), which means that legal proceedings can take place once the Commission has submitted its report. The Tribunal is not assumed to carry out court mediation or other forms of mediation.

According to the Fm Act, section 36, the Tribunal can hear disputes about the rights that arise after the Finnmark Commission has investigated a field. A period of one year and six months is set to bring the dispute before the Tribunal. This period runs from the time the Commission has submitted its report (cf. §38, para. 1); the deadline is assumed to be long enough to allow the Finnmark Estate time to consider the report and to give the parties time to negotiate. The extended period of time can also clearly be explained as an answer to the interests of the Sámi nomadic use of land and nature, assuming that their way of life means that they need longer time to respond (ibid., 23). The preparatory work does not discuss the effect of a long deadline in relation to the requirement for trial within a reasonable time, according to the European Convention on Human Rights ([ECHR] 1950; Ravna 2011a, 184–205). The deadline is not exhaustive either. The Tribunal may deal with matters that come in at a later stage if not all cases in a field have been brought to conclusion and if it finds the case appropriate for such consideration (cf. §38, para. 2).

The Tribunal has exclusive jurisdiction (cf. §36, para. 3), which means that cases that fall under the Tribunal cannot be brought before the ordinary courts or the land consolidation courts except in specified circumstances. Such circumstances occur when the Tribunal has dismissed a case pursuant to section 39 or the deadline for bringing proceedings before the Tribunal has expired (see below). The exclusive competence means that *lis pendens* (pending legal action or notice) if a certain case occurs when the deadline for bringing the matter before the Tribunal has ended and the Commission has submitted its report (ibid., 23). In fact, exclusive competence will block lawsuits of the ordinary courts until the last item in an investigation field is processed.

Matters that are "found inappropriate for consideration" by the Tribunal may be dismissed in whole or in part (cf. §39, para.). Such rejection can be done ex officio, and it cannot be appealed (cf. §39, para. 2). The plaintiff, however, shall be allowed to respond before dismissal occurs. When it comes to matters that are not suitable for treatment, it is comparable to those questions the Finnmark Commission can refuse to investigate, pursuant to Fm Act section 30, para. 3. The threshold for rejecting a claim is somewhat lower, since it is not required "that the case is obviously not suitable for treatment" (ibid., 23). Although an appeal cannot be posed against rejection of the Court rulings, the majority of the Standing Committee of Justice means that the interests of the plaintiff are met since he is allowed to respond before the Tribunal settles the question. The majority also states that the Tribunal should "be able to concentrate on the major and fundamental issues, so that minor matters, such as adjusting the boundaries between two properties, or interpretation of contracts for the sale of property, could be left to the ordinary courts or land consolidation courts."

The judgments of the Tribunal can only be appealed directly to the Supreme Court (cf. Fm Act §42). The majority of the Standing Committee points out that a "similar solution was selected for the Commission for Nordland and Troms" (ibid., 25). But it didn't mention that the rules of appeal were amended by Act 22, May 1981, No. 24, Amendment to the Civil Procedure Act, which proposed to limit the appeal right. This meant that the right of appeal was severely limited in terms of the rules that applied to the Mountain Commission.[22]

This appeal procedure means that presumably only a minority of the appeals will be heard since the Supreme Court is not an ordinary court of appeal but rather a court for settling principle questions of broad significance outside the concerned parties. Another objection against this appeal scheme is that the Norwegian Supreme Court can neither make on-site inspections nor examine witnesses.

Conclusion

The review shows that the Sámi parties and the Sámi Parliament in particular have had a major influence on the legislative process, at least after the consultations were initiated between the Sámi Parliament, the Finnmark County Council, and the Standing Committee of Justice in 2004. In my view it is not incorrect to call this a constitutional innovation. Such

consultations give Indigenous peoples significant influence on the legislation process in matters that concern them, and countries that have ratified
ILO Convention No. 169 are obliged to provide this to Indigenous peoples.
In this area it must be said that Norway has fulfilled its international obligations and is close to creating a law based on the principle of free, prior,
and informed consent.

Looking at the recently adopted land code, one can say that the surveying and recognition process for Finnmark is innovative and unique, not only
because of the influence of the Indigenous people in the legislative process but also because it aims to take into account Sámi customary law and
other customs and traditions including a particular way of life. The construction itself, with two independent bodies put together in a unified system, may also be called an innovation.

But at the same time, the process is challenging. The provisions chosen
to clarify and recognize land rights and titles in Finnmark deviates significantly from ordinary civil procedure and former commission procedures
in Norway. Of procedural law requirements we can point out the principle
of party disposition, which is not implied, specifies that the appeals go directly to the Supreme Court and that the force of law of the Commission
is not well deliberated. That two separate bodies have been created, which
together constitute a unified system but at the same time must remain
strictly independent of each another, is a kind of innovation. But such a
procedural model may also imply that trial within a reasonable time be difficult to access.[23]

Also in relation to the substantive side of the law, the process might be
challenging, not only because the Finnmark Commission and Land Tribunal have a far wider mandate than comparable commissions, but also
because they have less guidance from preparatory works and case law than
the comparable commissions had. That the process occurs in a part of the
country, or in a culture, where property law traditions have lower standing
than elsewhere, also adds to the difficulty.[24] Even if it is a lack of case law
and property law traditions, those who apply the law must be aware of the
prejudicing guidelines in the landmark *Selbu* and *Svartskog* cases, which
set up norms for how the rules on immemorial usage are to be applied to
Sámi land claims. But other case law indicates it will take time to establish
norms for clarifying and ensuring the quality of customary law (Norsk
Retstidende [Nrt.] 2001, 1116 and 2008, 1789).

Sámi customary law is also an important source of law not only because
of the ILO Convention and the emphasis placed on such sources in the
preparatory work of the Fm Act, but also because of the allowances to Sámi

legal culture we must expect from Norwegian legal culture. Since the Fm Act overall has few constraints and few sources and precedents to depend upon, one problem might be the predictability of a case or a legal question. Consequently, it can be difficult for the claimant or parties to predict the result of a particular case. While the previous Uncultivated Land Commissions for Nordland and Troms only had to investigate whether the state owned the land, the boundaries between state and private land, and what rights of use existed on the land belonging to the state, the legal issues to be investigated in Finnmark have no such limitations. Here the Finnmark Commission and Land Tribunal have to examine the whole bundle of rights and resources that might be found on what today is the Finnmark Estate, which might include community commons, joint ownership, and Sámi siida.

Even if the current Commission is well situated with Sámi members, it might be problematic that there is no requirement for Sámi representation or knowledge, neither among the members of the Finnmark Commission nor among the members of the Tribunal. Local knowledge is generally important for reaching a right and reasonable result de facto acceptable to all parties. It is also important for parties to know their peers have contributed to the decision. Sámi customs, customary law, and legal traditions are infrequently taught in law schools today, so Sámi local knowledge is, therefore, of paramount importance.

The problems pointed out above mandate relevant questions about the Sámi influence on the legislative process. For example, it has contributed to adopting the most appropriate scheme for the legal clarification process. As a rule of thumb, there is always room for improvement, and this is obviously the case here. At the same time we must recognize that the Sámi Parliament, in consultation with the Norwegian Parliament, accomplished what was possible in 2005. The results might have been more extensive if the negotiations were done today. We can also note that the Sámi Rights Commission II, in investigating similar legislation for the Sámi areas south of Finnmark, has stated that "it can be concluded that the Fm Act system as a whole clearly must be considered to meet the requirements of ILO Convention articles 14(2) and 14(3)" (NOU 2007:13, 453).[25] Despite the shortcomings of the Fm Act, there is no reason to renounce such statements. Space does not permit a *de lege ferenda*, that is, "law as it ought to be," discussion. However, this review shows that people in Finnmark, Sámi and non-Sámi alike, would probably gain from amendments to the law. To ensure trial within a reasonable time, the legislation could be changed to set a shorter period of time to bring cases before the Tribunal, whereas the Finnmark Commission itself is advised to be aware of time-consuming delays.

Transferring the Finnmark Commission to a court of law could also be given consideration, as this would benefit the appeals system, use of time, and provide the opportunity to obtain enforceable decisions. The Tribunal could then be a purely appellate body. With such amendments, cases should naturally start with a writ or a lawsuit with the Finnmark Estate and those who appoint its board, the Sámi Parliament, and Finnmark County Council playing an active role. The Finnmark Commission and Land Tribunal should then be ensured in law a larger proportion of qualified lay persons, especially with knowledge of local Sámi customs.[26]

Finally, and in spite of the criticism raised above, the author emphasizes that this review illustrates that Norway *is recognizing* Sámi rights to land and natural resources, giving the Sámi representatives a rather substantial influence in the legislative process of the Fm Act, and the management and self-determination of the natural resources in the core Sámi area. This was pointed out in the United Nation's Special Rapporteur on Indigenous Peoples' Rights. James Anaya, in 2011, stated that the Fm Act "offers important protections for the advancement of Sámi rights to self-determination and control over natural resources at the local level, setting an important example for the other Nordic countries" (Anaya 2011).

At the same time he expresses certain reservations when he points out that since "the process for identifying rights to land under the Fm Act is currently underway, the adequacy of the established procedure is not yet known" (ibid., para. 49). While such a reservation is relevant, it cannot be ascribed to failure to uphold the aim of ILO Convention, absence of recognition of Sámi self-determination, or lack of Sámi influence of the legislative process. It is more correct to look at the Fm Act as a result of what was possible to accomplish in 2005 and consider that some failures might be explained as a result of uncoordinated and inadequate preparatory work when the constitutional innovation was created.

This means that even if people in Finnmark—Sámi and non-Sámi—can live with the current Fm Act, there is considerable room for improvement. It is clearly possible to establish a process that *better* meets the requirements of the ILO Convention than the current Fm Act as it stands. That improvement is a job for legislators to ensure that the Sámi representatives are participating according to the principle of free, prior, and informed consent based on the international legal commitments and moral obligation Norway committed to give the Sámi as one of the two nations on which the country is founded.

Notes

All translations of quotations are done by the author.

1. Finnmark is the northernmost county of Norway and is the central part of the traditional area of the Indigenous Sámi people. The Sámi territories—*Sápmi* or *Sámiid eanan in the Sámi language*—span the northern and middle parts of Finland, Sweden, and Norway as well as the Kola Peninsula in Russia. The Sámi consists totally of 50,000–80,000 persons, with approximately 40,000 living in Norway (Gaski 2013). Of these, 13,890 are registered voters in the Sámi Parliament in Norway. See http://www.sametinget.no/artikkel.aspx?MId1=269&AId=2962&back=1&sok=true. Accessed September 12, 2011.

2. The articles state:

> (18) Indigenous peoples have the right to participate in decision making in matters which would affect their rights, through representatives chosen by themselves in accordance with their own procedures, as well as to maintain and develop their own Indigenous decision-making institutions.

> (19) States shall consult and cooperate in good faith with the Indigenous peoples concerned through their own representative institutions in order to obtain their free, prior and informed consent before adopting and implementing legislative or administrative measures that may affect them.

3. The term "Uncultivated Land Tribunal for Finnmark" is often used in English translation. It does not reflect the Sámi point of view, since livelihood and cultural activities historically have not depended on actual land cultivation. The outlying land and mountainous areas are consequently Sámi cultural land. Therefore, the more neutral form, the Land Tribunal for Finnmark, is used.

4. The preparatory work resulted in Lov (Act) June 23, 1888, nr. 2 om forskjellige Forhold vedkommende Fjeldfinnerne i Finmarkens Amt.

5. *Utkast til Lov om rendriften*, utarbeidet av riksadvokat P. Kjerschow (1922).

6. We can here point out the work of the Sámi Council for Finnmark, headed by the Sámi politician and educator Per Fokstad, see Innstilling fra komiteen til å utrede samespørsmål (The Sámi Committee, Oslo, 1959) 1. The Sámi Council for Finnmark was established in 1953 by Finnmark County Council. In 1964 the Sámi Council for Finnmark was replaced by the Norwegian Sámi Council.

7. "As long as people live as nomads, so long as the earth is wide enough to give all the space they need, the land is, however, not subject to ownership. Only when a tribe settles down and starts agriculture does ownership to land arise." See also N. Gjelsvik (1919), Kristiania (1919, 114 [repeated in the editions of 1926 and 1936]). Such prevailing legal opinion made it difficult for locals, and especially Sámi, to achieve recognition of their rights to hunting, fishing, and grazing based on right by prescriptions and immemorial usage. For more reading, see Ravna (2011a).

8. The Sámi Rights Committee, appointed in October 1980, worked up to 1997. A renewed Committee, the Sámi Rights Committee II, was appointed in June 2001.

9. In former times siida was a Sámi community that managed a physically determined territory; see Solem (1933) *Lappiske rettsstudier*, 81–84. Today the concept

is used for a family-related working unit in reindeer husbandry (cf. Reindeer Husbandry Act, § 51–56).

10. The Sámi Rights Committee also proposed the land consolidation court would be the appeal body, since the procedure to determine boundaries under Sections 88 and 89 of the Land Consolidation Act seemed the most natural "process form" when it came to delineation questions.

11. An important reason for the governmental acknowledgement was the Norwegian ratification of the United Nations' ILO Convention No. 169 concerning Indigenous and Tribal Peoples in Independent Countries in 1990.

12. See also Gauslaa (2012).

13. The Finnmark Estate [Finnmarkseiendommen] is defined in Fm Act Section 6 as "a separate legal entity with its seat in Finnmark, which shall manage the land and natural resources . . . as the owner in accordance with the purpose and provisions of the Act in general." The Sámi Parliament proposed to appoint three board members, Finnmark County Council three, and the state one nonvoting member, cf. Fm. Act Section 7.

14. This was later opposed by the Sámi Rights Commission II, see NOU 2007: 13, p. 453.

15. Report to the Parliament, No. 80 2004–2005, 19.

16. Ole Henrik Magga is a respected Sámi politician, who among others has been leader of the Norwegian Sámi Association (1980–1985) and president of the Sámi Parliament (1989–1997). Anne Marit Pedersen also has Sámi background and has among others contributed to the work of the draft Nordic Sámi Convention appointed on the recommendation of the Sámi Parliament. See http://www.domstol.no /Enkelt-domstol/Finnmarkskommisjonen/Om-kommisjonen/Medlemmer-og-ansatte/. Accessed September 27, 2011, and Nordisk samekonvensjon. Utkast fra finsk-norsk-svensk-Sámisk ekspertgruppe, October 26, 2005, 86.

17. For further reading, see Ravna (2010).

18. For more about the cases, see Ravna (2011a, 2011b, and 2011c).

19. The three first fields of the commission are Stierdna-Sievju/Stjernøya-Seiland (field 1), Unjarga/Nesseby (field 2), and Sállan /South Island (field 3). Fields 1 and 3 consist of islands in the Alta Fjord in West-Finnmark, while field 2 is a municipality in eastern Finnmark.

20. For more reading (in Norwegian), see Ravna (2011b).

21. The tribunal must also be seen as part of Norway's obligation under article 14 of the ILO Convention No. 169. The Tribunal is not yet established (October 31, 2011). However, as the Commission has still to submit its first report, the current status of the Tribunal is not problematic.

22. The amendment had its origin in that the Supreme Court in 1979 proposed to limit the appeal right so that the Appeal Committee of the Supreme Court could refuse to promote the case under the Civil Procedure Act, section 373, para. 3(4), if it found "that neither the decision importance beyond this case or other circumstances give reason that the appeal will be tried by the Supreme Court."

23. Effective remedy of appeal and trial within a reasonable time can be seen as conflicting interests, but both these requirements must be met according to article 6 of the ECHR, ILO Convention No 169, article 12 and 14(3), and the UN Declaration on the Rights of Indigenous Peoples, article 40.

24. Comparable arrangements in other countries could be discussed, but there is probably not much to be mentioned. For an overview, see NOU 2007: 13, pp. 247–71.

25. The Committee has also pointed out that the process "is assumed to be 'in line with Norwegian objectives of loyalty for achieving the purpose of the Convention.'"

26. Transferring the Commission to a court of law also raises other issues, for example, a question of independence, cf. ECHR article 6, and the Norwegian Constitution, article 22 and 88. However, this is not to be analyzed in this paper.

References

Anaya, S. James. 2011. Report of the Special Rapporteur on the situation of human rights and fundamental freedoms of Indigenous people. The situation of the Sámi people in the Sápmi region of Norway, Sweden and Finland, see: http://unsr.jame sanaya.org/docs/countries/2011_report_Sámi_advance_version_en.pdf. Accessed September 20, 2011.

Berg, Bård A. 2009. Daniel Mortenson, Norsk biografisk leksikon, February 13. https:// nbl.snl.no/Daniel_Mortenson. Accessed November 3, 2014.

Bull, Kirsti Strøm. 2001. Reindriften i Finnmark, Rettshistorie 1852–1960. Oslo: Cappelen.

ECHR (European Convention on Human Rights). 1950. Article 6. November 4. Rome.

Forskrift March 26, 2007, nr. 277 (regulation 16 March 2007 no. 277) om Finnmarkskommisjonen og Utmarksdomstolen for Finnmark.

Gaski, Harald. 2013. Samer. Store norske leksikon. fra https://snl.no/samer. November 26. http://snl.no/samer. Accessed November 4, 2014.

Gauslaa, Jon. 2012. "Lov om rettsforhold og forvaltning av grunn og naturressurser i Finnmark fylke (finnmarksloven)" (Gyldendal rettsdata), note 3.

Gjelsvik, N. (1926, 1936) 1919. Norsk tingsrett. Kristiania.

Innstilling fra komiteen til å utrede samespørsmål. 1959. Oslo. [A White Paper].

Innstilling om lov og forskrift om Statens umatrikulerte grunn i Finnmark fylke. 1962. (A law bill/White Paper).

Innst. O. nr. 80 (2004–2005) Innstilling fra justiskomiteen om lov om rettsforhold og forvaltning av grunn og naturressurser i Finnmark fylke (finnmarksloven) [A law bill / White Paper].

ILO (International Labor Organization). 1989. Convention No. 169 concerning Indigenous and Tribal Peoples in Independent Countries.

Kjerschow, P. 1922. Utkast til Lov om rendriften, utarbeidet av riksadvokat Kjerschow, Oslo [A law bill / White paper].

Nordisk samekonvensjon. 2005. Utkast fra finsk-norsk-svensk-Sámisk ekspertgruppe, Oslo 26. Oktober.

Norsk Retstidende (1836–) Christiania/Kristiania/Oslo (NRT) [A Supreme Court journal / archive].

NOU (Norges Offentlige Utredninger). 1993. 34 Rett og forvaltning av land og vann i Finnmark. [Norwegian Public Report - A White Paper].

———. 1997. 4 Naturgrunnlaget for Sámisk kultur [Norwegian Public Report - A white Paper].

———. 2007. 13 Den nye sameretten, [Norwegian Public Report - A white Paper], 31–68.

Ot.prp. nr. 59 (1984–1985) Om lov om utmarkskommisjon for Nordland og Troms. [This is a law bill/white paper/Proposition to the Parliament no. 59 (1984–1985)].

Ot.prp. nr. 53 (2002–2003) Om lov om rettsforhold og forvaltning av grunn og natur- ressurser i Finnmark fylke (Finnmarksloven—The Finnmark Act).

Ravna, Øyvind. 2010. 'Sámi Legal Culture—and its Place in Norwegian Law in Rendezvous of European legal cultures, eds. Jørn Øyrehagen Sunde and Knut Einar Skodvin, Fagbokforlaget, Bergen.

———. 2011a. "The Finnmark Act 2005 Clarification Process and Trial 'Within a Rea- sonable Time.'" Nordic Journal of Human Rights 29(2–3):184–205.

———. 2011b. "The Process of Identifying Land Rights in parts of Northern Norway: Does the Fm Act Prescribe an Adequate Procedure within the National Law?" Year- book of Polar Law (3):423–53.

———. 2011c. 'Rettsvirkningen av rettskartleggings og anerkjennelsesprosessen i Finn- mark,' Lov og Rett, 50(4):220–40.

Solem, Erik. 1933. Lappiske rettsstudier, Aschehoug, Oslo.

Stang, Fr. 1911. Norsk formueret. Indledning til formuesretten, Aschehoug, Kristiania.

Ulfstein, Geir, and Hans Petter Graver. 2003. Folkerettslig vurdering av forslaget til ny finnmarkslov, Oslo. See http://www.regjeringen.no/nb/dep/jd/dok/rapporter_planer /rapporter/2004/folkerettslig-vurdering-av-forslaget-til.html?id=278377. Accessed 28 September 2011.

CHAPTER SEVEN

Authenticity and the Construction of "Indianness" in Visual Media, or Trickster Goes to the Movies

Bob Boyer

I recall a very formative moment in my youth. My father and I attended a special screening of *Little Big Man* (1970) at the Saskatchewan Indian Federated College in Canada sometime in the early 1980s. The film, set around the time of the Battle of the Little Big Horn, was what we now call a revisionist western.[1] I was about eleven years old, and imagine, if you will, an entire theater filled predominantly with American Indians, some of whom were actively involved in the American Indian Movement of the period—imagine them absolutely going nuts over this film. We knew the people in this film, as many of the extras were friends and family members from within our own communities. Chief Dan George was an active presence in our communities and represented common ties with the many Native American actors in the film.[2]

The historic presence of the events portrayed in the film was fresh and relevant in the minds of the audience. It was as though we were watching ourselves as we participated in viewing the film. It was a raucous, animated event. Laughing, crying, yelling, and the throwing of popcorn. I recall little of the film itself in this initial viewing, as I was overcome by something in the audience. Here I felt like I was a part of something. For the first time in my young life I became aware of the power of the media. Somehow this film was charging the room with a political and cultural vigor I sensed was

We thank Susan Margaret Gray Boyer sincerely for her permission to edit and publish the chapter submitted by Bob Boyer, who died unexpectedly on January 19, 2013. Every effort has been made to honor Bob's voice and ideas in editing.

always present but was at the time not publicly displayed in such an outward manner.

Beyond this, I sensed somehow, I was Little Big Man. This film was talking about me. I personalized the character of Little Big Man and took the tragic longing for harmony and understanding to heart. This has stayed with me my entire life.

The thing is, this was not an Indigenous production. In fact, the people in this theater were not the savage cartoon "Indians" of the big screen that we were watching on the big screen in front of us. In this room were future doctors, lawyers, educators, activists, and politicians; participants in the modern cultural diaspora of a people scattered and removed from their ancestral lands.[3]

Now, some years later, I am faced with somehow defining this cultural split in the world. A voice in the back of my mind is constantly questioning the weaving of these images. The truth is often disguised. Who were those "Indians" in Little Big Man? Was this really our heritage? Where did this film come from? If there is another truth, where is it being portrayed?

In the mid-to-late twentieth century, media was a fairly centralized entity. Hollywood was at its zenith. The industry consisted of a tight group of people because the technology allowed it to be so. Today this is no longer true. For the greater part of the last century, Hollywood has created a Tribe of Indians wholly constructed upon the ideals and images of a white society's view of how the West was transformed. "This regression could be taken all the way back through John Smith to Columbus, each representation building the myth a piece at a time, construction reality as it best suited the purpose at hand. The resulting invention is an imaginary Indian—not a group of widely diverse peoples—that could be easily digested by the consumer" (Kilpatrick 1999, 35). By not taking the time to invest the truth in the images it created, an entire industry was able virtually to construct the image of the Plains Indian as defeated loser of life, liberty, and sovereignty. In its own particular way, Hollywood has aided in the misconceptions that prevail today in a postcolonial North American culture.

The history of this constructed image is well documented and persists through to the present. The once-popular band No Doubt's lead singer, Gwen Stefani, received criticism for and therefore was forced to remove images of the band in a music video playing cowboys and Indians with Gwen dressed as the prototype Plains Indian princess. The look she achieved was similar to that of Cher in the 1990s video for her song "Half-Breed." No Doubt, however, takes the image a step farther with "Stefani being bound and tied by her bandmates, which they construed as a message of violence and dominance over women; particularly disturbing when combined with the racial aspect" (Geller 2012).

Recently, accurately portraying more viable images of Indigenous peoples from within our own Indigenous communities has been possible. The accessibility of digital filmmaking technologies has not only revolutionized independent filmmaking, but also Indigenous film projects. In the same way that early Native American painters in the Western style and writers of literature with Indigenous backgrounds faced challenges within the time and place of their own artistic struggles, today's young Indigenous filmmakers face tough artistic choices. With this new accessibility come further questions, questions regarding authenticity, even though authenticity questions have always plagued Native artists. Perhaps the propensity of non-Natives to want to "play Indian" perpetuates the need for Native artists to search in turn for authentic artistic expression.[4]

Julie Cajune, an educator on the Flathead Indian Reservation, observed that "American Indians get the unique experience of being asked to validate our ethnic identity, our 'Indian-ness,'" because the identification of "Indianness" is defined by the colonial system. And individual Indigenous people frequently find themselves in the awkward position of having to clarify their tribal identities in opposition to the colonial identity. While her identity is derived from the historical belief that her people belong to the land, Cajune grew up in her mother's community, among the Salish Tribe, who refer to themselves as the "flesh of the land" (Sakariassen 2011).

As a filmmaker, and educator, I can only proceed with the knowledge that as I write this, mine is but a single opinion in a vast ocean of varied attitudes toward American Indian "authenticity," specifically authenticity in the world of Indigenous filmmaking. My views come more from my experiences than from books.

A shift is occurring from the dark days of the past to the present state of tribal self-determination. Resistance to the loosely disguised corporate culture of postcolonial America is partly inherent in this "post-Indian" reality in which we can participate in a progressive and authentic representation of the truth. Gerald Vizenor captures the challenge Native writers and visual artists face when he writes, "my thought is that memory, that visual sense of presence, and the scenes we create in stories, must outwit something. How about manners? Maybe tricky stories undo the comfy creases of tradition. The trickster is never a narrator, so in stories the trickster must tease the tragic out of piety and victimry" (Vizenor 1999, 20).

From an Indigenous point of view, there are no real *Indians* in the Americas. We are tribal peoples each with a rich and distinct history and cultural makeup. As it is, we will often begin any formal presentation identifying our tribal affiliation. My own background is a complicated and shady series of events leading to a present sense of pride and indignation. I am Red River Métis—*Métis* being a French term for "mixed blood." We are a unique nation of peoples who have risen through the colonial processes of manifest destiny as cultural refugees striving to maintain a contemporary presence within the tribal dialogue. We are only one of the many tribal identities that exist today who are hanging on to important *sacred* knowledge, as it is present in the contemporary world. We are actively resisting the mainstream pull toward the creation of a hybrid homogenized pan-Indian culture by continuing to practice local cultural ceremonies and actively preserving our unique *Michif* language.[5]

Postmodernism is a tough academic beast to wrangle. As an "educated" postmodernist, I sometimes have to ask myself, does culture really matter? Does it have relevance in the modern world? Clearly, the answer is yes. It is crucial for all people to preserve and pass on to their children an honest sense of identity in opposition to the postcolonial corporate elements that seek to destroy all remnants of the Earth we have been taught is our Mother. It is something my traditional grandfather would always repeat to me when I was a child and as I struggled with the teachings of our ancestors in the face of a fast-moving modern world that still has relevance: "we are all the human beings."

Media as Power—Whose Image Is This Anyway?

"The commercialization and commodification of a race emerges after there has been a power struggle and one culture has been clearly marked as dominant" (Goodyear 1996). The great struggle for European dominance over the vast empty lands of the Americas in the nineteenth century has been popularly portrayed through images of cowboys and Indians from before filmmaking technologies existed. In popular books and magazines, early settlers wrote of their great domination of the dark savage woods. "The tradition of stereotyping the Native American through visual imagery has a long history dating back to the painted ethnographic portraits of the 1600's, which typically show fanciful images of so-called primitives with seemingly realistic or authentic details and props" (Mason 1998).

Some of the first films ever produced in the Americas were of the American West. Even before Hollywood's domination of the popular media, in the early development of film technology, filmmakers had established a formative fascination with portraying Manifest Destiny in all its glory. By 1890, when the massacre of Lakota occurred at Wounded Knee, American Plains Indians in particular had been subjugated to white control. The great fight against savagery and the other primitives were popular topics culminating in portrayals of the *tragic* events of General George Armstrong Custer's great massacre at the Battle of the Little Bighorn. In 1912 Thomas Ince, one of America's early producers of feature-length films turned his cameras to this mythology in his film *Custer's Last Fight* (1912). Filmed at a cost of $30,000, it was then the most expensive motion picture ever made, which reproduced "in faithful accordance with government records and recognized historical authorities" the events of the Little Bighorn Battle, billed as a record of how Custer, unconscious of his loss of support, led his command "into the very jaws of death." Some of the very same images that would be replayed over and over again in the popular mythology of the event were set in the graphic images of "thrilling charges" and "sensational hand-to-hand conflicts" culminating in the Indian "Circle of Death" (*Custer's Last Fight*). These images predominantly displayed by the motion picture industry evolved from negative stereotypes created by chronicles of the earliest white settlers.

Contradictory views of Indians, from gentle and good to terrifying and evil, stem from an ethnocentric ambivalence toward an entire "race" of people that Euro-Americans attempted to destroy (Deloria 1995). The stereotypical image of American Indians as childlike, superstitious cultures, a subhuman species that really has no feelings, values, or inherent worth, remains intact in the popular American mind to some extent. Whether these images are inaccurate, fabricated, or overly simplistic matters little. They have become the established truth as the postcolonial American culture has constructed the historical myth of the American Indian.

For over a century, Hollywood has shaped the public's view of Indigenous people. The wise elder (Old Lodge Skins in *Little Big Man*); the drunk Injun Joe (in *Tom Sawyer*); the Indian princess (*Pocahontas*); and the loyal sidekick (Tonto) are images that have become engrained in the consciousness of North Americans. Hollywood's invention of "how the West was won" relies completely on the presence of Native tribes, who were to be wiped out or reined in. The predominant device used by Hollywood to reinforce colonial attitudes toward Indigenous peoples has been to enlist a white character to narrate the storyline. *Cheyenne Autumn* (1964), *A Man Called Horse* (1970), *Soldier Blue* (1970), and *Little Big Man* (1970) are all good examples of this popular practice, and the master narrator dominates the subject and subjects of the film. In attempts to be sympathetic to the

Indian, these films completely overlook the state of Indigenous peoples in the present and continued to portray through non-Indigenous eyes a state of the mythological past, even through comic reversals, such as *Little Big Man*.

Hollywood's role in the perpetuation of this myth is well documented and continues to play out this paradox of the "noble savage," while the dominant image of Indians in the early movies was that of "savages," with John Wayne leading the U.S. Calvary against the Indians. Today, a shift to the "noble savage" with American Indians viewed as a once great but now dying culture is prevalent: a culture that could talk to trees and animals or a culture that had no human relevance beyond the magical connection to nature that Europeans have lost somewhere in their own historical past (Mander 1991). On another front they were often depicted as nothing more than the sad residue of a colonial past with a whole range of social problems arising out of their maladjustment to society and seeming inability to be absorbed into mainstream culture. Hollywood's portrayal of American Indians figures into the continued political subordination and material exploitation of tribal nations. Dehumanization and the appropriation of identity are powerful tools in the symbolic destruction of the cultural identity of a people. In this way the historic achievements of a people are erased from the public record and replaced with the colonial version of events.

As the portrayals of Indigenous characters—as primitive, violent, and deceptive or as passive and full of childlike innocence—evolved in the media, they became familiar, comfortable signposts for much of Western civilization whenever it needed to acknowledge the Indigenous presence. Since few people, especially in larger urban centers, actually came into contact with Indigenous populations, these portrayals, however inaccurate, had all the more impact. Needless to say, Indigenous peoples were never hired as actors to depict themselves. Instead mainstream actors, such as Salvatore Mineo, Jr. (*Rebel Without a Cause*, 1955) and Natalie Wood (*The Searchers*, 1956), were put in heavy brown makeup to represent Indians. These images do not become diminished after one season. They play over and over. Non-Indigenous actors continue to be sought out to play Indigenous characters, such as Johnny Depp as Tonto (*The Lone Ranger*, 2013). Hollywood has a long way to go before it becomes culturally responsive to the images of Indigenous peoples. In the presence of this political pressure Hollywood seems to go out of its way sometimes to write American Indians out of the picture altogether.

In recent years, it has been more common than not to portray a new myth of the American West—one where either American Indians are nonexistent as in the 2007 remake of the film *3:10 to Yuma*, or, if they are present, they were a friendly bunch who went out of their way to be friendly with the white man. *Cowboys and Aliens* is the most outrageous representative of this new Hollywood mythology where not only is the conflict of the West rewritten with "savage aliens" replacing the historic reality of entire Nations resisting the onslaught of Manifest Destiny, it portrays conflicting tribal groups as allies under the leadership of the dominant white settlers a la *A Man Called Horse* (1970). It is clear in this latest incarnation of the history of the West that either there were no peoples in the Americas worth representing or, if there were, they were simpletons in need of a great white leader to command their otherwise hopeless causes.

Beyond the historical image of the American Indian in which we are portrayed as existing primarily within a roughly fifty-year period set somewhere at the middle to the end of the nineteenth century, it is apparent that American Indians did not survive into the contemporary world. In "Media Foster Stereotypes About Indians," the blog *Stereotyping Indians by Omission* notes that:

> With over 40,000 Indians living in and around New York City, one might wonder why there is never a Native attorney or police officer on *Law and Order* or *NYPD*. They haven't even had an Indian perpetrator. With the size of Chicago's Native population, it is surprising that not one Indian ever received emergency care in *ER* or was ever treated at *St. Elsewhere*. Not one medical show has ever had an American Indian doctor. And where are the Indian nurses; a primary career choice for many native women? Countless Indian teachers are working in schools across the country but they, too, are invisible in the media. Native programmers, firefighters, auto mechanics, pilots, ranchers, shopkeepers, and secretaries never seem to make it into the plots of our routine TV or big screen fare.[6]

The omission of these images sends a message that suggests American Indians do not exist within contemporary society. If aboriginal peoples are portrayed, they are often done so in supporting roles or relegated to the background. Rarely speaking, their character is often only revealed through their interactions with white people.

If left to Hollywood's inclinations, we are in danger of perpetuating a society that suffers from historical amnesia. "A society that finds it difficult to pressure the memory of those who have resisted and struggled over time for the ideas of freedom, democracy, and equality" (West 1993).

Consultation of Indigenous peoples in the production of these images has been nonexistent and tenuous at best. These recycled cultural myths, almost all of which were mostly established by white inventors of Indian images, continue to find their way into the portrayal of Indigenous peoples in contemporary media. Hollywood has undoubtedly played a role in blurring, merging, and marginalizing the cultural specificities of Indigenous peoples.

Accommodating Stereotypes

When northern explorers first interacted with the nations of the Arctic region in the late nineteenth century, they established and commonly practiced commodification of the Indigenous peoples of the Americas. They continued these practices into the twentieth century. In order to profit from the exotic nature of these newfound Arctic peoples, they taught them to use traditional carving techniques to sculpt soapstone and ivory images of their day-to-day lives. In doing this the peoples of the Arctic regions quickly turned away from their traditional images to those that sold well in a modern non-Native market.

The exotic translated to profit for the traders of the North. Like the early photographs of Edward S. Curtis, who carried wigs for his subjects to wear in order that they would appear "authentic," these "traditional" items were sold to the public as true artifacts of the primitive peoples of the North. As Thomas King writes in *The Truth About Stories*, "Curtis was fascinated by the idea of the North American Indian, obsessed with it. And he was determined to capture that idea, that image, before it vanished" (King 2003, 32). He amassed over forty thousand negatives, and with those images an idea of a pristine past, a dying or vanishing Noble Savage became immortalized.

It was not only traders and explorers who participated in the practice of "collecting" the idea of vanishing Indigenous cultures. R. Steward Culin, the first curator of the Brooklyn Museum, frequently commissioned works from the different Native American tribes. Culin would often provide the "correct authentic" materials to aid the Indians. It was understood that the Indians themselves had forgotten their history and had to have it recreated for them. Through nineteenth-century eyes, he was helping the Native Americans to learn about their past and educating the white population about their history at the same time (Moyer 2004). Indigenous peoples of the Americas have in the past been silenced. Their stories have been appropriated by the mainstream and, as such, have represented the fears and desires of the oppressor rather than any "real" Indigenous worldview. The concept of Indigenous did not even exist before the coming of the European. Rather, Indigenous peoples identified themselves and others according to tribal groups, bands, or on the basis of their relationship to specific traditional societies. The process of colonialism for Indigenous peoples has manifested such catastrophic effects on their lives that there has been little time to theorize these changes or ask questions relating to identity and what Indigenous peoples want now that their entire way of life has been altered. Instead it has been the oppressor who has sought to define the *Indigene.*

In the modern era, Hollywood has profited from the distorted and misplaced imagery of the American Indian. In the process Indigenous peoples have marginally participated in the recreation of these false images of "native-ness." The American Indian acting community is a small group of individuals. What limited roles that are available to Indigenous performers are far and few between. Commissioned to do voice-overs for cartoon characters or often to lend an "authentic" Indian voice or perhaps to play a limited role in live movies, a few well-known Indian actors find themselves in the unenviable position of committing cultural suicide professionally in order to maintain consistent employment in the media industry. They have to find ways in their private lives to counteract the personal costs of acting out their stage roles.

Initially, Hollywood did not bother to use Indigenous peoples in the portrayal of the American West. Today, however, in the attempt to create "authentic" Indigenous images, the employment of Indigenous actors serves to justify the supposed valid nature of these stereotypes. Indigenous actors having limited access to significant or relevant roles leads to their being at times a somewhat complacent group of individuals who cannot be blamed for their contribution to the continued myth. Because one sees "Indian faces" does not make it an Indigenous story.

Although these predominantly non-Indigenous productions generally present a patronizing view toward the subject of *Indians* in their films, some have come close through the skilled use of Indigenous consultants on their sets. Bruce McDonald's 1994 film *Dance Me Outside* is a highly respected film for not only the filmic skill of the director, but the authentic representation of the community in which it takes place on a reservation in Ontario, Canada.

In Jim Jarmusch's 1995 film *Dead Man*, Gary Farmer plays "Nobody" in an outstanding performance of an Indigenous man moving through the turn of the nineteenth century. This film in its odd independent form somehow portrays the truth of the West from an Indigenous point of view. Jim Jarmusch provides a rare example of how film can transcend "race." It is not the case that one must be of the "race" or culture of the film they are producing. In some real way we are all descendants of Indigenous cultures. Not so long ago, we all lived as tribal entities in some form or another. Through careful research and empathetic understanding of the content of the story, non-Indigenous producers and directors can effectively portray Indigenous life. Often when directors understand the human stories that lie underneath the exterior trappings of the culture, their portrayals ring more true.

Searching for an "Authentic" Image

If the popular media is not portraying an authentic version of the culture, what is an authentic American Indian image? Somewhere in here the Trickster exists. As the inheritors of these misplaced images, we must take some of the responsibility for the recreation of the myth. "In American politics real ethnic issues that should be addressed take over the platform. And the real, meaningful things, the ethnic questions, aren't really addressed. They are shoved aside" (Hope 1989). As a creator of images, the contemporary filmmaker is faced with a dual problem. Popular films must meet the desires of the hegemonic culture to present *authentic* tales of the *Other*.

Audiences seek to view these stories within the well-established images already possessed in relation to "Otherness." The pressure from within our own Indigenous communities is the desire to have Indigenous communities "authentically" represented to the hegemonic culture. Without replaying the previously established imagery of the dominant culture over the worldview of the American Indian communities, what serves as an authentic Indigenous image? Often the argument itself serves to constrain the Indigenous filmmaker. The truth has been historically silenced in the retelling of the Western mythology. Indigenous stories have been appropriated by the postcolonial media machine and as a result have represented the fears and desires of the oppressor rather than any authentic Indigenous worldview (Foucault 1980).

The concept of race did not exist before the coming of the Europeans in the Americas. Ethnicity differs from tribalism, since traditional tribal structures are not based on race. Communities were defined by membership and participation in common ceremonial procedures and language groups. American Indian cultures have endured such tremendous change in their communities that it is difficult to identify what contemporary Indigenous communities want now that their entire way of life has been forever altered.

The contemporary state of reservation cultures does not represent the true identity of Indigenous peoples in the Americas. Rather, it is the postcolonial image and situation that continues to define "us" versus "them." The oppressor has too often defined the terms we use to define the image of the American Indian. These terms, a product of European preoccupation with racial classification, eventually became part of the cultural vocabulary of North Americans. Such names were then "fleshed out" with visual and verbal images and prompted by governmental policy. Early American writers wrote romances filled with images of "the Indian" as an inhuman savage with a taste for the blood of white women and children (Larson 2000). Westerns, such as John Ford's *The Searchers*, defined the image of the American Indian as the fearsome aggressor and the cowboy as the hero who kills and tames the wild tribes, who not only threatened the settlers, but worse, threatened to take their women.

Authenticity within the context of a postcolonial America becomes somewhat elusive. The problem of understanding what authentic Indigenous images are comes from the process by which it was first destroyed by colonial forces, then reconstructed in ways that served the colonial purpose. Indigenous filmmakers find themselves in the odd position of re-creating that which was previously invisible, that which was systematically destroyed by the dominant Western culture.

In the face of a prevailing image created by others, the task can become so overwhelming that it is impossible to portray the truth without taking into account the dominant images. When Indigenous filmmakers contribute to the dialogue regarding authenticity, the dominant Western culture constrains these images to those that conform to the already established views. Oddly, it has been the federal government and the American legal system that has largely assumed the authority to speak for Indigenous identity/authenticity through a system based on blood quantum, which makes the search for authenticity on other terms nearly impossible. In order to get through to the sadness of the oppression, to the authentic identity the dialogue within Indigenous communities, the effort hinges somewhat on the identification of "the human beings." In a precontact state, Indigenous communities all identified the basic human values associated with common participation in the world as we experience it; basic human values such as raising our children in a good way and letting them know we are all equal are a central ideology that remains present in traditional Native American communities. This concept flies in the face of the colonial power structures and is even reflected somewhat in the subjected communities of Indigenous peoples.

The colonial images of the "Other" are based on a belief system foreign to the Indigenous communities of the Americas. They are justification for the controlling of the "Other." Policies of extermination, genocide, segregation, assimilation, and the systematic removal of children from their families or entire tribes from their ancestral lands are the result of this worldview that is still present today. The result is often a watered down version, or a default "humor," that serves to diffuse the threat a non-Indian audience might experience in the face of such hard postcolonial realities. Films, like *Pow Wow Highway* (1989), offer a humorous portrayal of a stark "Indian" reality that garners moderate box office success in their appeal to the dominant Western culture. Issues that would threaten a mainstream audience are not the focus of films like *Pow Wow Highway*, which represent a somewhat limited view of the state of Indigenous peoples in the Americas.

In telling their own individual stories, Native American filmmakers are placed in the unique position of representing more than their own personal experience but somehow contributing to a great body of discourse that contributes to the Native American discourse as a whole. In the process a complex negotiation between the filmmaker and the audience is expressed. When creating images, the Indigenous artist is limited to images that the audience recognizes as "authentic" and must create a story that will not threaten the non-Indian audience. This process creates an environment where a nonthreatening film then raises the question of "authenticity" for the Indigenous community itself.

How does one portray an "authentic" Indigenous image in the face of having been removed from your family or having grown up in an urban community removed from the reservation? Or even those who continue to live in reservation communities? How do they portray an "authentic" Indigenous worldview in the face of overwhelming postcolonial pressures? Addressing these questions in a postmodern, contemporary world that can overstep the divisive effects of colonialism is essential in the identification of an authentic voice. When Native Americans contribute to the dialogue on authenticity we do not do so from a place of origination. We are constrained by prior discourse and are placed in a position of having to identify in terms of what postcolonial audiences recognize as valid on issues seen as "authentic" and in terms that do not threaten. "Placing this discussion in a postmodern context is a way to acknowledge the fear and terror generated by the process of colonization upon the Indigenous peoples of the Americas, while ultimately pointing to ways of imagining a better future" (Larson 2000).

We are in a state of continued flux as the North American Indigenous community seeks to reclaim its voice from the oppressor. Ideas surrounding the establishment of "authenticity" are being redefined. The Western notions of duality are being redefined, and a more inclusive image of the human experience is being explored. Traditional Indigenous views of inclusivity and shared human experience are beginning to emerge.

If the historical hierarchies of race, class, and gender manipulate those dualisms, strategies for political action, for identity construction, and thus for narration, are not limited to absorption or resistance. Instead the actual triangulations of each oppositional moment offer relations and exchanges that redefine the possibilities for survival (Moore 2010). Breaking through the barriers of the postcolonial mythology, Indigenous peoples are reinstating traditional values into the dialogue. The duality of the "us" and "them" is being replaced with the more traditional exploration of the human experience as a whole. Not to be confused with a pan-American homogeny but as recognition of the unique individual experiences of all human beings present in the continuity of the world within a present context.

Revitalization of Indigenous Peoples and Perspectives

Indigenous peoples are often fond of pointing out how we continue to "live in two worlds," but in some ways a parallel world does exist. While the dominant culture perpetuates its own myths, the Indigenous peoples of the Americas have managed to maintain and evolve their unique perspectives. In the face of hardship and government-sponsored destruction of our original cultures, the sacred ways of our ancestors were forced underground, and the accommodation of the Western myth became a method of preserving the truth behind these false images. A split was created in the world for Indigenous peoples. While the dominant postcolonial culture shaped its mythology, Indigenous cultures preserved theirs, hidden away in small enclaves throughout the Americas. Not all people went to the reservations; the government authorities weren't able to put everyone in boarding schools. A culture of resistance preserved the histories and ancient teachings of the first nations of the Americas.

In the past, with a lack of access to media-making tools, Indigenous peoples have maintained a vital oral traditional culture. Access to contemporary tools through advances in digital media technologies extends that oral tradition into wider spheres and that way creates a platform for Indigenous voices that did not exist in the recent past. A whole new generation of Indigenous artists and storytellers are beginning to emerge. Indigenous peoples all over the globe are gaining control of their own narratives instead of passively waiting for Hollywood to abandon its inaccurate and racist stereotypes. Indigenous peoples are challenging perceptions of traditional peoples today, as they are tasked by the need to tell their own stories. Their work connects us to belief systems and philosophies; it captures the daily life and the spirit of Indigenous communities.

No longer held back by the limitations of access to technology, Indigenous contemporary artists are beginning to tackle the tough job of counteracting the damaging images of the dormant postcolonial Western cultures. A new generation of Indigenous artists is aggressively striving to reclaim their stories and to promote their cultural heritage and dignity. James Sterngold, in reviewing Spokane Indian novelist, poet, and filmmaker Sherman Alexie's film *Smoke Signals*, summarizes Alexie's perspective this way: "One of his primary goals was to take away from so called white experts the responsibility for describing contemporary Indian culture." His aim is "not to avoid criticism of Indian society but to make sure it is Indians doing the criticizing and interpreting" (quoted in Sterngold 1998, 14).

Indigenous communities throughout the Americas are encouraging their community members to take on the mantle of storytelling through the medium of digital filmmaking. The evidence is visible in the growing number of film festivals that showcase these emerging artists. The Red Earth Film Festival, First Nation's Film and Video Festival, and the American Indian Film Institute's American Indian Film Festival are only a few of the long-standing organizers of these events. All across the Americas you can find emerging festivals and showcases for the works being produced by young artists today.

The rise of independent filmmaking has also found a Native American voice with numerous rising Indigenous production companies, such as Two Shields Production Company out of Utah and Chris Eyre's production company, Seven Arrows Signature. Recently, a number of Indigenous producers and scriptwriters have begun to emerge. They have produced works that challenge audiences to see a different perspective on Native American culture. Chris Eyre's 1998 film *Smoke Signals* was an early film in this contemporary movement. "No single film or even dozens of films by Native

Americans could reverse this topsy-turvy history, yet *Smoke Signals* was celebrated as an important start" (Wood 2008). His film achieved widespread recognition while utilizing a predominantly Native American production team. It remains one of the few Hollywood films that found wide distribution in which the narrative is formed almost entirely by Native Americans.

The Inuit film *Atanarjuat: The Fast Runner*, produced in 2001 and directed by Zacharias Kunuk, exemplifies the approach to storytelling indicative of traditional cultures. With its plot unfolding in a precontact past, *Atanarjuat* is unique among contemporary Indigenous films in North America. It received tremendous critical acclaim. "These accolades came to a film situated as far toward the Indigenous end of the Indigenous to non-Indigenous continuum of films as is possible" (Wood 2008). This film is important in that it used the traditional language, Inuktitut, in the feature and was created by a predominantly Indigenous production crew. Unique among contemporary North American Indigenous filmmaking, in terms of its subject matter and its formal solutions, the film raises important questions about the possibilities of Indigenous self-representation in contemporary postcolonial societies.

This use of Indigenous languages is a bold but important movement within the world of Indigenous filmmaking. The Sámi film director Nils Gaup from Norway is an early innovator in this concept. His 1987 film *Pathfinder* is the first full-length movie with all of the dialogue in Northern Sámi. Again, critically acclaimed, the film garnered an Academy Award nomination for Best Foreign Language film.

As a global movement, Indigenous feature films are gaining some recognition and are not limited to the Indigenous peoples of the Americas. The 2002 Maori film *Whale Rider* exemplifies the wide appeal of these Indigenous stories and the powerful effect they can have on the larger dominant cultures. "Films that tell Indigenous stories can change local traditions on a scale inconceivable within dominant cultures" (Wood 2008). Non-Indigenous audiences can come away from these films with a greater knowledge of the lives of traditional Indigenous peoples.

A rising talent in the world of feature films is Sterlin Harjo, whose recent films represent the rationale behind the call for more Indigenous films by Indigenous peoples. His recent feature, *Barking Water* (2009), is a low budget independent film shot entirely on location as he traveled with his small crew and cast to create a rich story about an aging Native American couple on a journey that has them confront contemporary issues of home, the past, love, and self-discovery. Void of any cliché, the film does a beautiful job of representing Indigenous peoples honestly in the world today. Gone are the stereotypes of the past, and we are confronted with a rich and touching human story to which all peoples can relate.

These films represent an insistence that Indigenous peoples are here still. In their uncompromising portrayals of reservation or urban realities—of communities and individuals suffering from unemployment, poverty, alcoholism, and alienation—alongside stories of physical survival and cultural resistance, Indigenous film has aimed to reinsert Indigenous people into the material realities and historical timeline of North America. After almost a century of silence as a creative voice in screen culture, Indigenous filmmakers are, within a generation, becoming a vibrant presence in the world of filmmaking. As we continue to move forward into the twenty-first century, Indigenous filmmakers stand on solid ground within the contemporary film industry, as they continue to write, direct, and produce television series, shorts, documentaries, and feature films.

Thanks to the trailblazers who continue to advocate for the creation of training and education opportunities in the film industry, many individuals will continue to be nurtured, and we will continue to see the development of emerging Indigenous talent. As a new generation of filmmakers gains an increased understanding and awareness of Indigenous peoples and their cultures, the identity of the Indigenous cinema will continue to undergo further transformation. Moving forward in an age of increased awareness and access to information, there is a great positive force behind the re-imaging of the Indigenous experience we all participate in as human beings.

Notes

1. *Little Big Man*, directed by Arthur Penn, written by Calder Willingham, and based on a satirical novel by Thomas Berger is a film that recounts "how the West was won through the eyes of a white man raised as a Native American." Berger's novel is

> a comic yet stinging allegory about the bloody results of American imperialism. As a misguided twentieth-century historian listens, 121-year-old Jack Crabb (Dustin Hoffman) narrates the story of being the only White survivor of Custer's Last Stand. White orphan Crabb was adopted by the Cheyenne, renamed "Little Big Man," and raised in the ways of the "Human Beings" by paternal mentor Old Lodge Skins (Chief Dan George), accepting nonconformity and living peacefully with nature. Violently thrust into the White world, Jack meets a righteous preacher (Thayer David), and his wife (Faye Dunaway) tries to be a gunfighter under the tutelage of Wild Bill Hickock (Jeff Corey) and gets married. Returned to the Cheyenne by chance, Jack prefers life as a Human Being. The carnage wreaked by the White man in the

Washita massacre and the lethal fallout from the egomania of General George A. Custer (Richard Mulligan) at Little Big Horn, however, show Crabb the horrific implications of Old Lodge Skins' sage observation: "There is an endless supply of White Men, but there has always been a limited number of Human Beings." (Rovi Lucia Bozzola, www.rottentomatoes.com/m/little_big_man/)

2. Chief Dan George's real name was Geswanouth Slahoot; he was born in 1899 on the Burrand Indian Reserve Number Three (today known as Tsleil-Waututh First Nation) in North Vancouver. Upon entering boarding school, his last name was changed to George as part of the assimilation process designed to eliminate Native languages (www.imdb.com/name/nm0313381).

3. Bob Boyer's father, Robert Boyer, Sr. (1948–2004), taught on and off at the Saskatchewan Indian Federated College in Regina, Saskatchewan, from 1978 to 2004. He was a highly acclaimed Canadian Metís artist.

4. For a thorough discussion of the American ideological habit of "playing Indian," see Philip J. Deloria, Jr.'s (1999) book *Playing Indian*.

5. The Michif language, described often as a creole, is a mixture of French and Cree, with some borrowings from other Native languages. See http://www.native languages.org/michif.htm.

6. *Stereotyping Indians by Omission*, http://www.bluecorncomics.com/omis sion.htm.

References

Deloria, P. 1999. *Playing Indian*. New Haven, CT: Yale University Press.

Deloria, V., Jr. 1995. *Red Earth, White Lies: Native Americans and the Myth of Scientific Fact*. New York: Scriber Press.

Foucault, M. 1980. "Truth and Power." In *Power/Knowledge: Selected Interviews and Other Writings, 1972–1977*, edited by Colin Gordon, 109–33. UK: Harvester Press Ltd.

Geller, W. "No Doubt Pulls Controversial Cowboys and Indians' Themed Video After Complaints." *Stop the Presses! Yahoo Music Blog*. https://ca.music.yahoo.com /blogs/stop-the-presses/no-doubt-pulls-controversial-cowboys-indians-themed video-161819208.html, Sunday, November 4, 2012.

Goodyear, F. 1996. "The Narratives of Sitting Bull's Surrender: Bailey, Dix & Meads' Photographic Western." In *Dressing in Feathers*, edited by Elizabeth S. Bird, 29–44. Boulder: Western Press.

Hope, A. 1989. "Is Ethnicity Obsolete?" In *The Invention of Ethnicity*, edited by Werner Sollors, 226–36. New York: Oxford University Press.

Kilpatrick, J. 1999. *Celluloid Indians*. Lincoln: University of Nebraska Press.

King, Thomas. 2003. *The Truth About Stories*. Minneapolis: University of Minnesota Press.

Larson, S. 2000. *Captured in the Middle*. Seattle: University of Washington Press.

Mander, J. 1991. *In the Absence of the Sacred: The Failure of Technology and the Survival of the Indian Nations*. San Francisco: Sierra Club Books.

Mason, P. 1998. *In Felicities: Representations of the Exotic.* Baltimore: John Hopkins University Press.

Moore, D. 2010. "Cycles of Selfhood, Cycles of Nationhood: Authenticity, Identify, Community, Sovereignty." In *Native Authenticity*, edited by Deborah L. Madsen, 39–58. Albany: State University of New York Press.

Moyer, K. 2004. "Going Back to the Blanket: New Outlooks on Art Instruction at the Carlisle Indian Industrial School." In *Visualizing a Mission—Artifacts and Imagery of the Carlisle Indian School, 1879–1918.* Curated by Latini Fraust. Carlisle, Pennsylvania: The Trout Gallery, Dickinson Gallery.

Sakariassen, A. 2011. "Growing Pains—The University of Montana and Its Native American Students Are Getting Closer Even as They Remain Worlds Apart." *Missoula Independent* 22(45):14–17.

Sterngold, J. 1998. "Film: Able to Laugh at their People, Not Just Cry for Them." *New York Times*, June 21, 14.

Vizenor, Gerald, and A. Robert Lee. 1999. *Postindian Conversations.* Lincoln: University of Nebraska Press.

West, C. 1993. *Beyond Eurocentrism and Multiculturalism: Prophetic Thought in Post Modern Times.* Monroe, ME: Common Courage Press, 1993.

Wood, H. 2008. *Native Features: Indigenous Films from Around the World.* New York: Continuum Press.

CHAPTER EIGHT

Crossroads on the Path to Mental Decolonization

Research, Traditional Knowledge, and Joy Harjo's Music

Laura Castor

And in such a world of conflict, a world of victims and executioners, it is the job of thinking people, as Albert Camus suggested, not to be on the side of the executioners.

—HOWARD ZINN, *A PEOPLE'S HISTORY OF THE UNITED STATES*

In the opening lines of Joy Harjo's song "Equinox," the narrator evokes an image of the ongoing trauma kept in motion by the legacy of conquest of Native North America. "I must keep from breaking into the story by force," she begins, "for if I do I will find myself with a war club in my hand / and the smoke of grief staggering toward the sun / your nation dead beside you" (Harjo 2002, 184). The "story" to which Harjo alludes is part of a popular mythology of the American West, in which the stakes are high for potential winners and losers and for those called friends or enemies of progress. These dualistic categories of analysis have assumed an ever-greater force in a twenty-first-century popular imagination haunted by fears of the perceived "Other" who may take the shape of a wide range of people from a victimized refugee to a terrorist. As historian Howard Zinn suggests, such perceptions easily slide into unspoken beliefs in a world of executioners and victims. Writing in the early 1980s, Zinn is among the post–World War II generation of historians who have rethought nineteenth-century notions of American and Western history as a progressive unfolding of "civilization" in the face of "savagery." Zinn argues that documenting history is a function not only of accurately interpreting events in chronological time, but also of constructing narratives with cultural and ideological power.[1] It is also a matter of selective memories developed in all areas of culture, not least of all music.

In its many functions, music participates in the making of history. It may serve as a call to war, or entertainment to provide relief from combat. It may function as ceremonial healing from personal and collective trauma, as communication, and as education. In the twenty-first century, because many of its expressions are available on the Internet, music also has the potential to function as a cultural crossroads for those with diverse views of the past. As such, music complicates ideological oppositions between potential "executioners" and "victims." Yet global access also means that it is part of a pervasive consumer culture that often confuses rather than clarifies the difference between choices made by "thinking people," and tastes constructed by the forces of global capital.[2] Listeners and musicians alike are complicit, regardless of our race, gender, or ethnic ancestry.

The title of the anthology Joy Harjo edited with Gloria Bird, *Reinventing the Enemy's Language* (1997), suggests a way of working with this challenge. At a superficial level, the "enemy's language" for Harjo is English. But in her multimedia art, it also suggests epistemological challenges for her readers and listeners. In a world of limited material resources, the consumer culture in which we all participate is rooted in Enlightenment worldviews that privilege competition for material acquisition over cooperation for the benefit of mutual survival. The Western epistemologies that form the basis for these views have also privileged the material authority of written texts over the relationality of the oral, and they have separated poetry from its Indigenous beginnings in song. Harjo participates with other Indigenous peoples to reconnect the two (Harjo 2009).[3]

Since the year she and Bird published this anthology, Harjo has transformed many of her earlier poems into spoken word pieces and songs. She has released them on five albums, performed internationally, received popular acclaim, and made several of the entire CDs available on her website. Harjo and Bird's phrase "reinventing the enemy's language" therefore poses two related questions. In what ways does Harjo intend to "reinvent" the language of Euro-American westward "progress" through her integrated music and poetry? Equally important, how does Harjo's music do the culturally revitalizing work of reconnecting poetry with its Indigenous roots in song? This work has two parts: the first deals with the issue of historical memory, while the second participates in the politicized (as opposed to polemical) process of cultural revitalization through art.

In our time, the work of cultural revitalization often depends on outside participation and support. Harjo certainly relies on exposure to audiences beyond Indian Country, and her music and poetry open her to the wider audience she needs to thrive—and survive—as an artist. Like many other Indigenous artists, Harjo quite naturally wants to be part of a globalized music market. And that's a good thing. As respected Sámi scholar Harald Gaski observes, "the cultural area that globalization has had the greatest impact on within Indigenous culture is without doubt popular music" (Gaski 2008, 347). Among the successful Sámi musicians, Norwegian Sámi yoikers Mari Boine, the duo Lawra Somby and Sara Marielle Gaup who perform as Adjagas,[4] and the Finnish yoiker Wimme Saari thrive internationally.[5] The choir, Sámi Jienat (Sámi Voices) also continues to bring attention to Sámi culture for international audiences throughout Scandinavia and in the United States (Sámi Jienat). Like Harjo, these artists combine traditional forms with contemporary instruments and styles. The rewards of widespread acclaim aside, Gaski notes that contemporary yoik nonetheless should be understood with a "contextualized interpretation of a cultural expression, which, first and foremost, is not *merely* text, nor just music, but both of them and even more than just the sum of lyrics and melody" (Gaski 1999). A similar approach is relevant for interpreting Harjo's work.

For researchers, activists, teachers, students, and others who advocate for Indigenous people's issues, the practice of reading Indigenous texts, such as Harjo's, in the context in which they were produced has been a long-term project. In the 1980s Patricia Limerick was one of the first scholars to convince a mainstream audience of historians of the American West that "many complicated environments [were] occupied by natives who considered their homelands to be the center, not the edge" (Limerick 1988, 26). A growing discussion in a variety of fields about the process of healing the intergenerational historical trauma of colonization necessarily includes a discussion of the personal, emotional dimensions of this process. These can be characterized broadly as a process of mental decolonization.[6] Mental decolonization goes hand-in-hand with the larger political processes on every continent, and it takes place through psychological therapy, education, and the arts in a variety of media.[7] Harjo's art provides especially good examples of this work in progress.

A number of scholars have engaged with Harjo's poetic texts in ways that have created openings for an analysis of the decolonizing power in her combined words and music. For example, Azfar Hussain, drawing on Foucault's use of the "episteme," notes that Harjo's work "tends to resist the production of an organically and ontologically coherent episteme" (Hussain 2000, 27).

He writes that scholars should not try to characterize her "work as a whole" because while her discourse in many cases is characterized by postmodern playfulness, it also remains historically grounded (Hussain 2000, 28–29). Nor can Harjo's art be interpreted as neoliberal multiculturalism (Hussain 2000, 28). For Hussain, Harjo's commitment as an artist stays anchored in careful attention to the institutional sites of power that produce colonizing knowledge. This commitment, I suggest, includes attention to the virtual and actual spaces for listening to music throughout the globe.

Mary Leen takes Hussein's notion of "attention" to the sites of power where cultural knowledge is produced in a different direction. She cites the poet Leslie Ullman's observation that "as a storyteller, Harjo steps into herself as a passionate individual living on the edge" (quoted in Harjo and Leen 1995, 1). Leen argues that Harjo's artistic risks have allowed her to remember and recreate memories through storytelling in a way that is "vital and generative" (Harjo and Leen 1995, 1) and that music is central to this process. "Rather than being another form of time, the Muscogee world is music and motion in calisthenics. In Muscogee epistemology, the past and the future are the same struggle" (Harjo and Leen 1995, 2). I would add that Harjo's capacity to convey this sense of time to a broad audience has to do with her willingness over the past thirty years to work at the edge of various genres and modes: poetry and music, music and dramatic performance, film and music, storytelling and poetry, and criticism and art. Not all memories can be addressed adequately using a single artistic expression, and Harjo's skill at playing with multiple forms allows her to explore the nuances of historical truth and visions for the future as she sees them.

Like Thomas King in *The Truth About Stories*, Harjo engages in a process of transforming mythical and personal stories while preserving some of their core elements through historical time (King 2003, 91). In King's retelling of the mythical creation story of the *Woman Who Fell from the Sky*, for example, the ground in one world becomes the sky in another. What remains the same is a spirit of aliveness in the story expressed through the resourcefulness of various creatures that cooperate to help the woman King calls "Charm" to anchor herself on what becomes solid Earth. In an interview Harjo notes a similar intention for her music. In whatever form and on whatever stage she performs, she says that what matters most is "to preserve the spirit of the song" (Harjo interview with Kauanui, 2009). The "spirit" at the core of her work might be described as energy that infuses a relationship with the material world. Artists and listeners share a sense of belonging to it, and they trust the energy of the performance to enact a shift in their consciousness, however slight.

This approach is likewise at the core of ceremonial healing rituals in traditional cultures from Aboriginal Australia to the Innu First Nations people of Eastern Canada, from the Lakota in the Midwestern Plains of the United States to South Africa, and from Sápmi to Turkic Siberia. The Lakota singer and writer Howard Bad Hand, for example, describes an experience of listening to the recorded words of sacred Lakota songs given to him by his uncle. "Whether the words were from the past, or just created for the ceremony about to take place, a pattern was beginning to emerge in my mind showing the real value of the word usage. I was being directed in how to see the world, spirit, and material, and I was also being directed in how to think of the reality of the present moment" (Bad Hand 2002, 32). Considering that any analysis of this "spirit of the song" is at best a translation that misses the dynamism at its core, it is not surprising that most scholarly discussions of Harjo's work have focused more on her written poems than on her music. Nonetheless, studies such as Hussain and Lien's open spaces for a consideration of how her words and music express the sort of "reality of the present moment" described by Bad Hand.

In a Sámi context, the multimedia art of Nils Aslak Valkeapää provides a good illustration of this reintegration process. Valkeapää in 1991 was awarded the Nordic Council's Literature Prize for *Beaivi Ahcazn* (*The Sun, My Father* [English translation 1997]). In part, his acclaim can be attributed to his innovative approaches that, beginning in the 1970s, combined the spirit of traditional yoik with forms such as pop, jazz, and classical music, as well as visual art (Gaski 1994). Like Harjo in her work to reconnect poetry to song, Valkeapää worked to renew interest in yoik for contemporary Sámi listeners who had not learned their native language, as well as for non-Sámi audiences.

One of the earliest examples of his work internationally is a story told about Valkeapää from the first meeting of the World Council of Indigenous Peoples in Port Alberni, Canada, in 1975. At the gathering, it was through Valkeapää's yoiking that the other participants, initially skeptical of his white skin color, were able to recognize him and the Sámi as Indigenous (Gaski 2008, 358). Historian Jukka Nyyssönen, in his discussion of Sámi politics in Finland from the 1970s to the 1990s, notes how Valkeapää, together with author Kirsti Paltto, actively promoted a radical identity, political strategy that questioned the global rights discourse strategy used by the Sámi Delegation established in 1973 (Nyyssönen 2008, 92). In 1979 in Finland, the first of two *Daavi Suvva* (Breeze from the North) festivals arranged by the Finnish branch of the Sámi Council, brought together musicians and other artists from a diversity of circumpolar Indigenous cultures (Nyyssönen 2008, 93).[8] In recent years, the annual *Riddu Riddu* international festival has continued this work of cultural and political renewal in Kåfjord, a small town in Northern Norway. The festival, made possible through the organizers' ability to gain outside funding, has been a venue and inspiration for the internationally recognized, as well as local performers whose music fuses yoik with contemporary instruments and styles.[9]

These developments in Sápmi suggest some of the ways in which the work of cultural revitalization for many Indigenous people has increasingly depended on outside participation and support.

"Equinox" as Historical Memory

By exploring various layers of meaning in "Equinox" beginning with historical contextualization, we can identify ways in which Harjo uses poetry as song to address, and begin to heal, the historical trauma to which she alludes in line three with her image of "the smoke of grief, staggering toward the sun." At first glance, the collective memories Harjo evokes in "Equinox" paradoxically seem to keep historical polemics alive. At least it can be said that Hussain's observation is accurate in that it is difficult to pin down exactly what Harjo's central message is—her title "Equinox" suggests that at some level she may question an overly polemical approach. At the time of the spring and fall equinox, everyone in the world experiences twelve hours each of light and dark. Harjo hints that perhaps a similar balance between opposites might characterize the events she narrates.

On the other hand, the first verse of the poem can be read as a retelling of a clearly defined military opposition between Harjo's ancestor, Chief Menawa, who with one thousand Red Stick warriors, fought the then-future president Andrew Jackson's 2,600 Euro-American forces (supported by 500 Cherokee and 100 "Lower Creek" Muscogee) at the Battle of Horseshoe Bend in Alabama on March 27, 1814 (Horak 1999, 20). Although Menawa survived the battle, Harjo's last line of the first verse could well describe his awareness that "his nation [lay] dead beside [him]": 557 Red Stick warriors were killed; 250–300 drowned as they tried to escape across the river. On Jackson's side, only 49 soldiers died. The following August, Jackson negotiated the Treaty of Fort Jackson. This treaty prepared for a wave of Euro-Americans to settle in Alabama and Georgia, whereas the Muscogee were forced to cede twenty million acres, about half of their land (Horak 1999, 21).

Jackson's treaty also introduced the precedent of granting individual ownership to Indian lands, thus separating Indians from each other as communal land holdings broke up, and Natives were increasingly encouraged to adopt the competitive spirit of capitalism (Zinn 2005, 128). As Zinn observes wryly, this approach "fitted well the old Jeffersonian idea of how to handle the Indians by bringing them into 'civilization'" (Zinn 2005, 128). In the following decades, White expansion into their lands grew exponentially, while Menawa led the contingent of Muscogee that continued to struggle against their territorial invasion, "war club in hand" (Harjo 2002, 184).[10] An illustration of the intensity of his opposition is that when the Mestizo Chief William McIntosh attempted to cede remaining Muscogee territory, the Muscogee party led by Menawa sentenced him to death (Horak 1999, 22).[11]

Recounted from the perspective of the Euro-American victors, the 1814 Battle of Horseshoe Bend and its aftermath have become part of the grand "story" that Harjo's narrator says she "must keep from breaking into by force." This story is a frontier narrative that combines a series of contradictory assumptions about Native peoples from history and popular culture. Its ideological sense of entitlement was expressed well by journalist John O'Sullivan. In his 1839 "The Great Nation of Futurity," he states

the expansive future is our arena, and for our history. We are entering on its untrodden space, with the truths of God in our minds, beneficent objects in our hearts, and with a clear conscience unsullied by the past. We are the nation of human progress, and who will, what can, set limits to our onward march? Providence is with us, and no earthly power can. (O'Sullivan 1839)

At the end of the nineteenth century, Frederick Jackson Turner's lecture on "The Significance of the Frontier in American History" given at the 1893 Chicago Exposition, and the Wild West Shows of Buffalo Bill Cody, became especially influential in reinforcing the rhetoric Sullivan had expressed in the late 1830s. Turner argued that American identity was shaped by the existence of an area of "free" land that gradually disappeared as waves of pioneers, traders, and farmers made their way west to cultivate and civilize it. In this view of the American landscape as an empty space of abundant land awaiting development, Native peoples were rendered virtually invisible. Bill Cody, starting in 1883, represented a very different idea of a

"Wild West" in his outdoor shows that enacted the West as a dangerous territory populated by savage Indians who were heroically defeated by whites in battles where they earned their right to the land (Szaloky 2001, 49). As Thomas King notes in his discussion of Edward Curtis's sympathetic photographs of Indians, popular sentiment shifted in favor of Natives only when it seemed to many whites that Indigenous peoples no longer stood in the way of American "progress" (King 2003, 32).[12]

Yet the conceptual oppositions between Indians and whites, between savagery and civilization, would remain intact, and these oppositions are part of the "story" that Harjo's narrator seeks a way to resist in the opening lines of "Equinox." Since the 1970s, part of the cultural work of revisionist historians and imaginative writers, including Harjo, has been to expose the blindnesses in earlier mainstream narratives of American history, such as those represented by Turner and Cody (Drinnon 1997 [1980], 462, 285). "One of the ways history is not merely professional or a matter of research," historian Dominick LaCapra asserts, "is that it undertakes to create a critically tested, accurate memory as its contribution to a cognitively and ethically responsible public sphere. Memory of this sort is important for an attempt to acknowledge and relate to the past in a manner that helps to make possible a legitimate democratic polity in the present and future" (LaCapra 2001, 91). Harjo would share LaCapra's conviction that historical narratives have ethical consequences. Whereas the first stanza of "Equinox" expresses the overwhelming grief of loss that was personally and politically colonizing, the poem as a whole can be read as a process of mental decolonization that opens spaces for thinking critically about the psychological and ethical consequences of the frontier narrative of American history. In her final line, as her final saxophone riff fades out, we are left to ponder what it means to "[break one's] addiction to war and desire" in a world as politically polarized as ours (Harjo 2002, 184).

In the first two lines ("I must keep from breaking into the story by force / for if I do I will find myself with a war club in my hand"), the history to which Harjo alludes is a function of selective remembering, and the choice about how to remember is part of the equation (Harjo 2002, 184). Although Harjo speaks on behalf of her ancestors and relatives, she also provides spaces for empathic listening that includes a broad audience. In line three, the listener enters such a space where we confront a personified image of grief "staggering" drunkenly as if struggling to numb the pain of loss after attempting, without success, to retaliate. Harjo's reference here alludes to the historical roots of alcohol abuse at the same time that it reminds the reader that alcohol abuse is a continuing issue in many

Native communities. Whereas the need to react "war club in hand" has historically led to overwhelm, despair, and internalized victimization that drinking cannot numb. Yet in the "smoke of grief," the capacity lingers, however diminished, to survive intact. This hope suggests the possibility for developing a different historical narrative that might promote collective well-being rather than continued victimization.

"Equinox" as Cultural Revitalization

One approach to reading line five, "I keep walking away / though it has been an eternity," is through the lens of unconscious trauma. For Cathy Caruth (1996, 91), post-traumatic stress can be understood as a figurative inability to walk away from the site of trauma. "The response to an unexpected or overwhelming violent event or events cannot be fully grasped as they occur, but return later in repeated flashbacks, nightmares, or other repetitive phenomena." Caruth identifies a paradox below the mental suffering triggered by trauma in which "the most direct seeing of a violent event may occur as an absolute inability to know it; that immediacy, paradoxically, may take the form of belatedness" (ibid., 91). Long after the original trauma, chronological time may seem to collapse in a flash, overwhelming the present with an involuntary, crippling immersion in relived experience. Painful memories dissolve into an unbearable, confusing present, and the victim may do anything to avoid feeling them. Yet, for a traumatized person to begin functioning again, perhaps in a way that may benefit other survivors, what she or he needs is neither a numbing indifference nor an immediate retaliation against the perpetuator (Zinn 2005, 10). Rather, she or he must allow time to gain psychological distance from the event.[13] As Dominick LaCapra writes, emotional and critical thinking distance is needed for a person to work through trauma rather than simply to act it out in the kind of self-sabotage that Harjo's image of a "staggering" drunk suggests.

Caruth observes that at the heart of traumatic experience is also an ethical question about perceived responsibility. Irrational as it may be, victims easily slide into survivor's guilt, asking themselves if they had something to do with triggering the event. In Harjo's image of her ancestor's witness to the death of hundreds of his tribe, many whom may have been relatives, the reader has the chance to speculate on the survivor's guilt with which Menawa could have lived. Harjo's subsequent verses open spaces for imagining intergenerational healing.

At the beginning of line six, "and from each drop of blood," Harjo reminds her readers of the blood quantum laws developed by U.S. government authorities to determine Indian status beginning a century before the Battle of Horseshoe Bend. Considering that the federal government most widely applied these laws after the Indian Reorganization Act of 1934 to determine qualification for financial benefits (Spruhan 2006, 47), Harjo's reference is less transparent than it may appear at first glance. It includes the shifting historical relationships in that blood holds symbolic, as well as literal meaning; the idea of blood has been used as a means of exclusion from benefits, as a metaphor for the cost of resistance, and as a symbolic link between the generations of "sons and daughters" whose ancestors' lands, languages, and cultures were invaded. In lines six through eight, it also includes the non-human living world of trees and mountains. The image of sons and daughters "springing up" with "mountains of sorrows, of songs" in lines seven and eight also suggests ways of gaining conceptual and emotional distance, not necessarily through the conscious will to heal historical trauma but through the slower, rhythmic support of seasonal cycles in the living, non-human world.[14] Harjo reinforces this process figuratively; her reference to "walking away" may be interpreted not only as about a post-traumatic attempt to avoid remembering as discussed above, but also as part of this healing process.

This process is reinforced through repetition of the melody and through the saxophone breaks at the end of each verse. The saxophone opens the listener to another dimension of decolonization directly through music. More specifically, Harjo's commitment to returning poetry to its Indigenous roots in song affirms Indigenous epistemologies, which value the processes of coming to know the world over the goals of recording knowledge about it through written documents.[15] Even more to the point, hearing Harjo's poetry through music opens an imaginative space for listeners to begin to enter a Muscogee reality. In such a world, says Harjo, "past and future are part of the same struggle," and they are both present in the moments of listening (Harjo and Leen 1995, 2).

Whereas line five of the written text marks a verbal shift from trauma to resilience, in the song version, the enactment of healing begins with the instrumental introduction. In the first four beats of the song, the saxophone in the foreground is accompanied by a slowly beating drum, rattle, and keyboard in the background. Musically, the poem expresses proximity, through the saxophone riff and distance with the percussion. In effect, before the listener begins to respond to the words, we hear the piece as if from afar through sound vibrations and rhythm. Harjo thus transports us into a sonic environment that hints of temporal distance and of the possibility for psychological distance from the site of the historical traumas of invasion, land losses, and exile. Such emotional distance, notes LaCapra, is needed for a trauma victim to begin working consciously with repressed memories that otherwise return in flashbacks and nightmares (Caruth 1996; LaCapra 2001, 90). At the same time, the opening beats of the song symbolically enact a Muscogee world where past loss and future hope continue their "tug of war" (Harjo and Leen 1995, 2).

Harjo's drumming throughout the song can be understood through insights from cognitive psychology and music therapy research, as well as in the context of traditional ceremonial drumming. Swallow notes that recent studies in cognitive neuroscience suggest that the rhythm of drumming may stimulate certain kinds of vibrations in the body that "jog" cell membranes where some neuronal patterns may be strengthened and others inhibited (Swallow 2002, 51).[16] Likewise in many traditional practices, ceremonial drumming has long been acknowledged as a core element in supporting the well-being and emotional health of individuals, as well as the health of local economies. In South Africa, for example, Robert Thornton notes that the work of the sangoma healers is most widely experienced as publicly performed dances with *ngoma* (intense singing and drumming). Each dance repeats specific patterns of drum beats which, continued for long periods of time, are performed to entertain audiences, but also to "wake up the spirit" or "lift up" the consciousness of *thwasana* (apprentice healers) undergoing advanced training (Thornton 2009, 28). Among the Sámi, seventeenth- and eighteenth-century Christian missionaries recognized and feared this sort of communal power when they chose the shaman drum as one of their main targets for eradicating signs of the "devil" from Sámi culture (Rydving 1991, 29). Peter Armitage discusses a similar pattern among the Jesuit missionaries to the Innu of Eastern Labrador and Quebec (Armitage 1992, 68–89). This persistent presence of drumming across historical time and geographical place is a vital force in Harjo's "spirit of the song" that survives in her contemporary expression of its power in a global music context.

In "Equinox," "spirit" is evoked not only in her way of reclaiming poetry as song and in her instrumentals, but also through the use of breath as vocal percussion in the second half of the poem. In recent years Harjo has lived in Hawaii, and the album in which "Equinox" appears as a song, *Winding Through the Milky Way*,[17] also includes the piece, "No Huli" inspired by a Native Hawaiian story.[18] In "Equinox" she includes the Indigenous Hawaiian word *ha* which translates into the English "breath." Harjo repeats the sound ha from the last line of the third verse beyond the end of the last line of the poem, through to the fading out of its last saxophone riff.[19]

Harjo's use of breath in this song also links her performance to a traditional Muscogee story about the Master of the Breath who is the Creator whose spirit comes from the four cardinal directions (Bierhorst 1985, 188). She may be alluding to this story in several ways. The first and second verses, in the historical context of Indian Removal signal a geographical movement from East to West.[20] In line five, "I keep walking away" might be contextualized historically as a figurative continuation of the Trail of Tears. Layered between her lines are historical memories that, for particular listeners, might include periods defined in mainstream nineteenth- and twentieth-century histories as assimilation, self-determination, termination, and renewed self-determination and literary renaissance (Limerick 1988, 195). But whatever histories are evoked, in line nine, Harjo has expanded the listener's spatial orientation, as well as our sense of time. Here she speaks "from the dusk of a small city in the north / not far from the birthplace of cars and industry" of Dearborn, Michigan (Harjo 2002, 184; Klepper 2001). If we had expected a continuation of the clear opposition between Indians and Whites suggested in the poem's opening lines, by line nine she has complicated it. Here, the narrator's capacity to survive and thrive in an industrialized "new world" replaces the memory of Indian Removal. The geographical and temporal distances, as much as they dislocate members of the tribe, threaten their continued loss of tradition, nonetheless lead to a revitalized, poetic expression of the old Master of the Breath story. As such, Harjo enacts a new, imaginative space for her dynamic poetry. This space is one in which the rhythm of breath connects the drumming and vocal percussion in the song with it verbal images of geese, crocuses, trees, and humans all sharing the same larger pulse of the earth's aliveness. This process may seem to last "an eternity," but it also heals as it supports the politicized transformation of "mountains of sorrows" into cultural spaces for Indigenous revitalization.

Possibilities for contemporary creative expression aside, as LaCapra reminds us, the process of transforming traumatic memory into art does not endow that memory with redemptive value (LaCapra 2001, 156). What Harjo does is to offer a more modest invitation to experience a few elements of Muscogee cosmology during the moments of our listening. At the same time, her words speak to the need for continued concerted effort toward decolonization in many areas of culture. This process is expressed musically and verbally throughout the poem where the virtual absence of "breaks" in the song's regular beat and tempo contrast a series of repeated images about breaks with a victimized past. First, the drunken "staggering" of the first verse becomes "walking" in the second. Second, the narrator carries her listeners from a warning against a violent break-in in lines one through four, to an image of crocuses breaking through frozen earth at the time of the spring equinox in lines eleven and twelve, to an assertion of the narrator's emotional strength in "breaking my addiction to war and desire" in lines thirteen through seventeen. This hope of achieving a sense of equanimity in the midst the struggle between past and future conflicts is reinforced in the "Equinox" of the poem's title. Although the phenomenon of light and dark held in balance is a fleeting one, Harjo's image might nevertheless be seen as an opening for nondualistic ways of relating historical memories to imagined futures.

In lines thirteen through seventeen, Harjo's words have a decisiveness that resist the chaotic figurative noise of American commodity culture that Harjo calls the global "overculture" (Harjo interview with Kauanui, 2009). "Soon they will come for me and I will make my stand / before the jury of destiny. Yes, I will answer in the clatter / of the new world, I have broken my addiction to war / and desire. Yes, I will reply, I have buried the dead / and made songs of the blood, the marrow" (Harjo 2002, 184). By this line, the earlier focus on an external enemy has moved into the space of "internal processes." This shift, Marie Smyth observes, is central to the clinical work that music therapists do with trauma victims (Smyth 2002, 76). For Harjo, "making songs of the marrow" does not imply surrender to the forces of colonization represented in the "clatter of the new world," nor does it condone passivity in the face of continued oppression. Rather, the creative process reinforces the link between Muscogee mythologies and revitalized Indigenous song in Harjo's performance of "Equinox."

Challenges for Harjo's "Spirit of the Song" in an Era of Globalization

Harjo recalls in an interview some of the ways in which her soft jazz style connects her with her ancestors. She notes that since the arrival of the first African slaves, Indigenous and Black communities exchanged musical inspiration; in listening to traditional Muscogee music, one hears rock, jazz, and the blues. New Orleans' Congo Square, she adds, was a Muscogee ceremonial ground before it served as the grounds where African slaves gathered on Sundays to sing, dance, and perform the music that developed into what we now know as jazz. Harjo's early inspiration for playing jazz saxophone grew when she discovered that her grandmother had played the instrument, as well as by listening to artists such as Miles Davis, the Argentinian Gato Barbieri, and through studying with the Kaw/Muscogee saxophonist Jim Pepper. Pepper, in particular, mentored Harjo in her early development as a musician (Harjo 2009).[21] Both of these references are electronic and so have no pagination.[22]

Connections to tradition aside, Harjo, like many other contemporary Indigenous musicians, including Sámi artists whose music is distributed internationally, reaches far more listeners through private spaces on Internet screens and through earphones than she does in face-to-face community venues. These venues risk separating her listeners from each other rather than gathering them for collective action as part of the sort of "democratic polity" of which LaCapra speaks.[23] The question remains, then, as to whether listening to Harjo's music most often provides only momentary relief from the daily stresses of twenty-first century urban life.[24]

Harjo is well aware of this apparent contradiction. As she has noted in interviews, she does not simply aim to promote herself as a multimedia artist who appeals to the broadest possible audience. In the global commodity "overculture," music has no spirit, and hence no space for holding art that does the work of revitalizing traditional knowledge. To the contrary, she sees her music and poetry as part of a larger process of resisting the forces of commodity culture (Harjo 2005). The ways in which this resistance becomes possible through Harjo's art depend not only on how one reads her poetry, but also on how one listens, unconsciously through the power of the music to activate physiological healing and consciously through reflection on the historically contextualized, living presence of her words. Developing the ability to listen in more integrative ways can serve as a force for mental decolonization that heals historical trauma, as well as act as a catalyst for advocacy. Perhaps for scholars, teachers, and students, this process begins in academic settings, but it also extends beyond them to wherever the work of cultural revitalization is practiced.

Notes

1. Patricia Limerick notes that the idea of culture as a "whole system of ideas and beliefs" emerged only in the late nineteenth and early twentieth century, and that it moved only gradually from professional academic contexts to mainstream thought. In the mid-twentieth century, when historians began to apply the concept of culture to

their analysis of white-Indian relations, a whole new way of thinking about each other became possible (Limerick 1988, 190).

2. For a discussion of the psychological relationships between the Western advertising market and the consumer, see John Berger (1972). For a more recent discussion of the ambivalent relationship between Sámi music in a global era, see Gaski (2008).

3. Harjo has evolved through a variety of forms that speak to her commitment to healing the effects of historical trauma. Born in Tulsa, Oklahoma, in 1951, she is a member of the Muscogee Creek Tribe. Encouraged first to become a visual artist, she studied painting and theater at the Institute of American Indian Arts and graduated in 1968. She earned a degree in Creative Writing at the University of New Mexico in 1976, followed by a Master's of Fine Arts at one of the leading creative writing programs in the United States, the University of Iowa, in 1978. While at Iowa she also studied at the Anthropology Film Center, completing a nondegree program in filmmaking. Harjo has taught at a number of institutions, including the Institute of American Indian Arts, Santa Fe Community College, and the Universities of Colorado, Arizona, New Mexico, and the University of California Los Angeles. In addition to her coedited 1997 anthology *Reinventing the Enemy's Language*, she has published seven collections of poetry and two children's books. Harjo also created the screenplay for the film of the National Museum of the American Indian in Washington, DC, and wrote and performed two one-woman plays, *Wings of Night Sky, Wings of Morning Light* (2014 on joyharjo.com) and *I Think I Love You: An All Night Round Dance* (2013 on joyharjo.com) She has received widespread acclaim for her work, including the Josephine Miles Poetry Award, the William Carlos Williams Award (Harjo, Poetry Foundation interview on joyharjo.com), and the Eagle Spirit Achievement Award for overall contributions in the arts (Press Kit on Joyharjo.com).

4. "Adjagas is a Sámi word describing the state between sleeping and waking. For Mari Boine, see www.mariboine.no/biography-php. See also Ragazzi (2007), *Firekeeper*.

5. In her first CD, released in 1997, Harjo performed many of her earlier poems as music through spoken word, saxophone, and other instrumentals. Since then she has produced four additional CDs and has won an award as Best Female Artist of the Year for *Winding Through the Milky Way* (2008), and a New Mexico Native American Music (NAMY) award for "Equinox," one of the pieces on that album (Harjo 2008).

6. This process has a wide range of expressions, not only for members of Indigenous communities and for others who identify as Indigenous. It is also relevant for individuals from a wide variety of backgrounds whose education and lived experiences have made them aware of the ways in which the histories of Indigenous losses have profoundly influenced larger national and transnational histories. Ato Quayson's writing on postcolonial discourses provides useful perspectives on this need. He prefers the active sense of the term "postcolonizing" work to the objectified theoretical idea of "postcolonialism" (Quayson 2000). I share Quayson's view that in the early twenty-first century, "postcolonizing discourses" are major discourses, wherever one's geographical location is and whatever one's cultural background may be. I use the term "decolonizing" processes that music poetry promotes rather "postcolonizing" in order to emphasize the mental processes that are a precondition for long-term "postcolonizing" work.

7. Franz Fanon (1952) is probably the most acclaimed early writer about the need for this process, but a cursory Internet search reveals current studies in history, political science, gender studies, psychology, visual arts, and music, education, and religious

studies. These have come from Africa, Haiti, Iran, India, Canada, the United States, and Sápmi. See, for example, Lynne Davis (2010) *Alliances*, Smith College's homepage describing a recent conference"Beyond Freire," and Hilde Methi and Kristin Tårnesvik's (2011), *Hotel Polar Capital: The Sámi Art Festival, 2008–2011.* See especially the chapter "The Road to Mental Decolonization," 91–96.

8. A second Daavi Suvva festival was held in Karesuando, Sweden, in 1993. See Angell (2009).

9. An excellent example is Hilder's doctoral dissertation, *Sami Soundscapes* (2010), in which the author argues that the Sámi festival functions as a living "museum" for performing, negotiating, and transmitting Sámi traditions. For cultural histories of the *Riddu Riddu* festival, see Hansen (2009) and Leonenko (2008). Gaski (Sami Culture in the Nordic Countries) discusses the internal as well as external challenges to developing a serious body of critical scholarship around these expressions.

10. In Alabama, for example, the white population grew from 9,000 in 1810 to 310,000 in 1830 (Horak 1999, 22).

11. It is not in the scope of this chapter to discuss the multilayered negotiations between Southeastern tribes and the federal government that led from the Treaty of Fort Jackson to the Jackson administration's policy of Indian Removal in the 1830s. It is, nevertheless, important to note that the events leading to Indian Removal cannot be reduced to a simple Hollywood-style prolonged battle between Indians and whites. The southeastern tribes targeted for removal—the Cherokee, Choctaw, Seminole, Creek (Muscogee), and Chickasaw—had become known to Euro-Americans as the "Five Civilized Tribes" for good reasons. Limerick notes that by the 1820s the Cherokees, for example, were in many respects on their way to fulfilling the Jeffersonian hope of transforming from "savages" to "citizens." They had a constitution, had developed an alphabet, published a newspaper, had friendly relations with missionaries, and in some cases, even ran plantations and owned slaves (Limerick 1988, 192). The U.S. Supreme Court upheld the Cherokee tribe's treaty rights in *Cherokee Nation v. Georgia* (30 U.S. 1 1831). Despite this ruling, many Jeffersonians still were impatient with the overall pace of Indian "progress" toward civilization. Together with the more virulent Indian-haters, land-hungry settlers, and Georgians who resented the slow pace at which they felt the federal government rescinded Indian titles in their state, they joined ranks in support of Indian Removal. Later in the decade, Harjo's ancestor Memawa was among the 25,000 Muscogee forced to walk many thousands of miles to Oklahoma Territory in what historians now call the notorious "Trail of Tears" (Horak 1999, 22).

12. For examples of a wide range of Curtis's extensive project starting around 1900 that documented Natives from a wide variety of cultures and geographical locations, see the Library of Congress's American Memory project on *Edward S. Curtis's North American Indian.* http://memory.loc.gov/ammem/award98/ienhtml/curthome.html. May 3, 2012.

13. Seligman (2007, 135–44) discusses the difficulty in treating post-traumatic stress through talk therapy.

14. For an extended essay discussion of the Indigenous meaning of a "living world" as distinct from a Eurocentric view, see Hogan (1995).

15. Aikenhead and Ogawa (2007, 553) discuss a number of differences between Eurocentric knowledge in a Cartesian tradition and what the authors call "Indigenous ways of living in nature." The authors note that in many Indigenous languages no

equivalent to the Western concept of "knowledge" as an object exists. Drawing on examples from the Nehiyawak (Plains Cree) tradition, they consider ways in which, for a Cree person "coming to know" is "a quest to become wiser in living properly in their community and in nature. This approach to knowing engages imaginative thinking. It has parallels with Toni Morrison's observation that the role of the artist in shaping historical memory is to make certain traumatic events bearable (Morrison 1987).

16. A number of ongoing research developments in a variety of fields are important to mention because they suggest that people from many backgrounds have experienced music not only as entertaining but also as part of a larger effort on the path to mental decolonization. Sutton's (2002) anthology *Music, Music Therapy, and Trauma: International Perspectives*, for example, includes the reflections of a number of music therapists on their clinical work with trauma victims in a variety of geographical locations. Often, these studies have been done in regions of ongoing military conflict where the danger of developing post-traumatic stress is real for many people (Sutton 2002). Smyth (2002, 76), for example, notes that for her clients in Northern Ireland, music provides "a third way in the face of polarization and deep division." Her studies show that music facilitates the "removal" of attention and focus from an external "enemy" and places it instead on the "subjective and internal processes of those who have been hurt" (ibid.). Swallow observes that an important aspect of the internal processes is physiological; what might be happening through listening to and playing music is that cell membranes are "jogged" by the vibrations of the rhythm, and neurons are then encouraged to fire, or to keep from firing (Swallow 2002, 51). Melody and tone can activate long-term memories stored in the brain's limbic structures, such as the hippocampus, registering conscious emotional memories, and in the amygdala, a small almond-shaped structure near the hippocampus that registers unconscious fear, as well as strong positive emotions. Whereas the amygdala and the hippocampus may be damaged through exposure to repeated trauma or less extreme stress, recent research in cognitive neuroscience suggests that listening to music exercises these structures (Levitin 2006, 91). Listening to and playing music might also activate the release of the pleasure-seeking hormone dopamine (Levitin 2006, 191) and show short-term effects similar to medication. Music therapy cannot replace other forms of psychotherapy or activism but for many people, it is part of the larger mental decolonization effort.

17. Fast Horse. R1434293. MP3Download.

18. "No Huli" is about a canoe that tips and the ability of the person paddling it to get it back up, and by extension, to recover balance in the choppy waters of everyday life.

19. In *How We Became Human*, the title of the poem that follows "Equinox" is "Ah, Ah." In this piece, Harjo may again be playing with various expressions of this sound as breath directly connected to spirit, merely changing ha to ah for a similar effect. In the poem's seventeen lines, ah, ah functions much like the rhythm of breath as it becomes the voice of a crow, the ocean, human beings, the reader's lungs, a plane, the sun, and the "soul" of the poet (Harjo 2002, 185).

20. In Harjo's introduction to *How We Became Human* (2002, xxiii), she discusses the historical importance of the Trail of Tears on her poetry.

21. See also "Joy Harjo: Interview About Her New CD" http://www.youtube.com /watch?v=_tXCtqNdFaU. 5 November 2011.

22. According to music critic Bill Siegel (2008), "Pepper underscores the role that jazz plays in the formation and expression of cultural identity—through his music, he says that 'Indian' isn't a very meaningful label, that there are many 'Indians' of many nations, many heritages, many cultures—and they are still here, still alive, still vibrant, still growing." Pepper's music, he says, opened up the awareness of a broad listening audience to the wide range of Indigenous musical vibrancy. Harjo extends this musical vibrancy to her poetry.

23. For a discussion of a similar development in a Sámi context, see Kvifte (2001). Kvifte places contemporary expressions of Sámi yoik within the larger framework of the Progressive Music Movement. This movement, he believes, may be winning the battle in terms of the expression of creative forms of yoik and song, but it is losing the larger political battle.

24. Campbell (2011) considers a variety of ways individuals listening to music through headphones respond to it. http://thedianerehmshow.org/shows/2011-10-13/healing-speed-sound.

References

Aikenhead, Glen S., and Masakata Ogawa. 2007. "Indigenous Knowledge and Science Revisited." *Cultural Studies of Science Education* 2(3):539–620.

Angell, Synnøve. 2009. "Daavi Suvva 1979: Being Sámi, Becoming Indigenous: Vocal and Musical Manifestation of Sámi and Indigenous Movement." MA thesis. Tromsø: University of Tromsø.

Armitage, Peter. 1992. "Religious Ideology Among the Innu of Eastern Quebec and Labrador." *Religiologiques* 6:64–114.

Bad Hand, Howard. 2002. *Native American Healing.* Chicago: Keats Publishing.

Berger, John. 1972. *Ways of Seeing.* London: Penguin.

Bierhorst, John. 1985. *The Mythology of North America.* New York: Quill.

Campbell, Don. 2011. Interview with Susan Page, The Diane Rehm Show. National Public Radio. http://thedianerehmshow.org/shows/2011–10–13/healing-speed sound. Aired November 6, 2011.

Caruth, Cathy. 1996. *Unclaimed Experience: Trauma, Narrative, and History.* Baltimore: Johns Hopkins University Press.

Curtis, Edward S. 2012. Edward S. Curtis's The North American Indian. American Memory, Library of Congress. http://memory.loc.gov/ammem/award98/ienhtml/curthome.html. May 3, 2012.

Davis, Lynne. 2010. *Alliances: Re/Envisioning Indigenous-Non-Indigenous Relationships.* Toronto: University of Toronto Press.

Drinnon, Richard. (1980) 1997. *The Metaphysics of Indian-Hating and Empire-Building.* Norman: University of Oklahoma Press.

Fanon, Franz. (1952) 2008. *Black Skin, White Masks,* translated by Richard Philcox. Paris: Editions du Seuil.

Fjellheim, Frode. http://vuelie.no/?page_id=80 14 March 2014.

Gaski, Harald. 1999. The Secretive Text: Yoik Lyrics as Literature and Tradition. Nordlit 5 spring, 3–27. http://www.hum.uit.no/nordlit/5/gaski.html. November 6, 2011.

———. 1994. "Preface: A Hunting Shaman in the Media Age." In *Trekways of the Wind*. Guovdageaidnu: DAT and Nils-Aslak Valkeapeää, translated by Ralph Salisbury, Lars Nordström, and Harald Gaski. No pagination.

———. 2008. "Yoik-Sámi Music in a Global World." In *Indigenous Peoples: Self-Determination, Knowledge, and Indigeneity*, edited by Henry Minde, Harald Gaski, Svein Jentoft, and Georg Midré, 347–60. Delft: Eburon.

Gaski, Harald, and Tr. John Weinstock. Sámi Culture in the Nordic Countries-Administration, Support, Evaluation. http://www.utexas.edu/courses/sami/dieda /hist/nordic.htm. October 28, 2014.

Hansen, Lene. 2009. "Riddu Riddu-Fra Verken Eller til Både Og." In *Mangfold eller Enfold*, edited by Trond Giske, 24–40. Oslo: Aschehoug.

Harjo, Joy. 2002. *How We Became Human: New and Selected Poems, 1975–2001*. New York: W. W. Norton & Co.

Harjo, Joy. 2005. "If There's Mother Nature There's Also a Father Nature." *Joy Harjo's Poetic Adventures in the Last World Blog*. http://joyharjo.blogspot.com/2005/02/if theres-mother-nature-theres-also.html, February 27.

———. 2009. Interview with Kauanui, Kehaulani (24.4.09). Indigenous Politics, Wesleyan U. Podcast.

———. 2010. Interview by Poetry Foundation. http://www.poetryfoundation.org /bio /joy-harjo. November 5, 2011.

Harjo, Joy. 2012. Oklahoma Historical Society's Encyclopedia of Oklahoma History and Culture. http://digital.library.okstate.edu/encyclopedia/entries/H/HA021.html. May 4, 2012.

Harjo, Joy, and Gloria Bird. 1997. *Reinventing the Enemy's Language: Contemporary Native Women's Writings of North America*. New York: W. W. Norton & Co.

Harjo, Joy, and Mary Leen. 1995. "An Art of Saying: Joy Harjo's Poetry and the Survival of Storytelling." *American Indian Quarterly* 19(1):1–16. Literature Resource Center. http://www.jstor.org/stable/1185349. November 6, 2011.

Hilder, Thomas Richard. 2010. *Sámi Soundscapes: Music and Politics of Indigeneity in Arctic Europe*. London: Music Department, Royal Holloway, University of London.

———. 2012. "Repatriation, Revival, and Transmission: The Politics of a Sámi Musical Heritage." *Ethnomusicology Forum* 21(21):61–179. DOI: 10.1080/17411912.2012 .689473.

Hogan, Linda. 1995. *Dwellings: A Spiritual History of the Living World*. New York: W. W. Norton & Co.

Horak, Virginia. 1999. *The Battle of Horseshoe Bend: Collision of Cultures*. National Register of Historic Places. Washington, DC: National Park Service.

Hughes, Richard T. 2004. *Myths America Lives By*. Urbana: University of Illinois Press.

Hussain, Azfar. 2000 (Fall). "Joy Harjo and Her Poetics as Praxis: A 'Postcolonial' Political Economy of the Body, Land, Labor, and Language." *Wicazo Sa Review* 15(2):27–61. DOI:10.1353/wic.2000.0008.

King, Thomas. 2003. *The Truth About Stories*. Minneapolis: University of Minnesota Press.

Klepper, Steven. 2001. The Evolution of the U.S. Automobile Industry and Detroit as its Capital. http://www.druid.dk/uploads/tx_picturedb/dw2002-440.pdf. November 2011.

Kvifte, Tellef. 2001. "Hunting for the Gold at the End of the Rainbow: Identity and Global Romanticism, on the Roots of Ethnic Music." *Popular Musicology Online*.

Salford: Popular Music Research Unit at Salford U, England. http://www.popular
musicology-online.com/issues/04/kvifte.html. March 11, 2014.

LaCapra, Dominick. 2001. *Writing History, Writing Trauma.* Baltimore: Johns Hopkins
University Press.

Leonenko, Anastassia Valerievna. 2008. "Riddu Riddu, Joik or Rock–n-Roll? A Study
of the Riddu Riddu Festivala and Its Role as a Cultural Tool for Ethnic Revitalization." Tromsø: University of Tromsø.

Levitin, Daniel J. 2006. *This Is Your Brain on Music: The Science of a Human Obses-
sion.* New York: Plume.

Limerick, Patricia. 1988. *The Legacy of Conquest: The Unbroken Past of the American
West.* New York: W. W. Norton & Co.

Methi, Hilde, and Kristin Tårnesvik. 2011. *Hotel Polar Capital: Accounts from the Sámi
Art Festival, 2008–2011.* Kirkenes: Sámi Art Festival.

Morrison, Toni. 1987. *Profile of a Writer* (VHS). RM Arts. Home Vision.

Nyyssönen, Jukka. 2008. "Between the Global Movement and National Politics: Sámi
Identity Politics in Finland from the 1970s to the early 1990s." In *Indigenous Peoples:
Self-Determination, Knowledge, Indigeneity,* edited by Henry Minde, Harald Gaski,
Svein Jentoft, and Georges Midré, 87–107. Delft: Eburon.

O'Sullivan, John. 1839. "The Great Nation of Futurity." *The U.S. Democratic Review*
6:426–30. http://web.utk.edu/~mfitzge1/docs/374/GNF1839.pdf. November 5, 2011.

Quayson, Ato. 2000. *Postcolonialism: Theory, Practice, or Process?* Cambridge: Blackwell Publishers.

Ragazzi, Rossella. 2007. *Firekeepers.* Digital Beta, 57 minutes. Norway: Sonar Film.

———. 2010. *The Road to Mental Decolonization.* Kuratorisk Aktion and The Sámi
Art Festival. 978–82-998333-2-5.

Rydving, Håkon. 1991. "The Saami Drums and the Religious Encounter in the Seventeenth and Eighteenth Centuries." In *The Saami Shaman Drum,* edited by Tore
Ahlbäck and Jan Bergman, 28–51. Åbo, Finland: The Donner Institite for Research
in Religious and Cultural History.

Saari, Wimme. *Wimme.* www.rockadillo.fi/wimme/.

Sámi Jienat. 2014. Back from Tour in U.S.A. http://www.samijienat.com/bloggaacute
/back-from-tour-in-usa. November 30, 2014.

Seligman, Martin. 2007. *What You Can Change and What You Can't: The Complete
Guide to Successful Self-Improvement Learning to Accept Who You Are.* New York:
Vintage Books.

Siegel, Bill. 2008. The Jazz Legacy of Jim Pepper: An American Original. http://jim
pepperlives.wordpress.com/. November 4, 2011.

Smyth, Marie. 2002. "The Role of Creativity in Healing and Recovering One's Power
after Victimisation." In *Music, Music Therapy, and Trauma: International Perspectives,* edited by Julie Sutton, 57–82. London: Jessica Kingsley Publishers, Ltd.

Spruhan, Paul. 2006. "A Legal History of Blood Quantum in Federal Indian Law to
1935." *South Dakota Law Review.* 51(1):1–50.

Sutton, Julie, ed. 2002. *Music, Music Therapy, and Trauma: International Perspectives.*
London: Jessica Kingsley Publishers, Ltd.

Swallow, Michael. 2002. "The Brain—Its Music and its Emotion: the Neurology of
Trauma." In *Music, Music Therapy, and Trauma: International Perspectives,* edited
by Julie Sutton, 41–53. London: Jessica Kingsley Publishers, Ltd.

Szaloky, Melinda. 2001. "A Tale N/nobody Can Tell: The Return of a Repressed Western History in Jim Jarmusch's Dead Man." In *Westerns: Films Through History*, edited by Janet Walker, 47–69. New York: Routledge.

Thornton, Robert. 2009. "The Transmission of Knowledge in South African Traditional Healing." *Africa* 79(1):17–34. DOI: http://dx.doi.org/10.3366/E0001972008000582.

Valkeapää, Nils Aslak. 1994. *Trekways of the Wind*, translated by Ralph Salisbury, Lars Nordström, and Harald Gaski. Kautokeino: DAT.

———. 1997. *The Sun, My Father*, translated by Ralph Salisbury, Lars Nordström, and Harald Gaski. Kautokeino: DAT.

Zinn, Howard. (1980) 2005. *A People's History of the United States, 1492–Present*. New York: Harper Perennial.

CHAPTER NINE

Looking Both Ways

Future and Tradition in Nils-Aslak Valkeapää's Poetry

Harald Gaski

The aim of this chapter is to analyze one of the key poems by the Sámi poet Nils-Aslak Valkeapää from his award-winning book, *Beaivi, áhčážan* (*The Sun, My Father*). The book is a lyrical composition consisting of old documentary photographs of Sámi everyday life over the last 120 years from the entire Sámi area, that is from Kola peninsula in Russia, in the east, to the mid-regions of Norway and Sweden in the west and south, extending to more than half of Finland as well. The Sámi are the Indigenous people of this northern region, and thus enjoy specific rights to land and waters. Sámi language and culture are thriving, and a unique oral tradition lives side-by-side with new arts and literature created on the basis of tradition and innovative new perspectives on life and existence in the high north. Nils-Aslak Valkeapää, a multimedia artist who excelled in poetry, as well as music and painting, was for several decades the leading voice of the Sámi revival. He contributed to the new interest in traditional Sámi music, the *yoik*—a vocal genre—at a time when it was almost extinct, and he was the organizer of the first Indigenous peoples' cultural festival in 1979, when he gathered singers and poets from all over the Indigenous world to Karesuando on the borderland between Sweden and Finland.

In this chapter I propose an interpretation of Valkeapää's 1989 Poem 558, *The Sun, My Father*, based on a Sámi approach, that is, using my own Sámi language and cultural background in my analysis. Sámi aesthetics, cultural values, and wordplay are the foundation of my investigation. This does not imply any assumption of this being the only or the correct understanding of the poem. But, in keeping with the new approach represented by Indigenous methodology,[1] my reading is intended to offer an interpretation that treats Sámi views and values seriously and advances an analysis that tries to unite Sámi traditional aesthetics with general literary norms, thus presenting an Indigenous reading of the poem. The methodology and the theoretical approach are implied in my analysis, as befits Indigenous practice; there's no need to extract a specific theory, because the theory should be integrated into the analysis as part of a holistic understanding, not only of the singular poem, but of the poem as an expression that has a message to Indigenous peoples today.

In the analysis of this poem I refer primarily to the English translation of the book *The Sun, My Father*, published in 1997. The Sámi original, *Beaivi, áhčážan*, came out in 1989, and the Scandinavian rendition, *Solen min far*, was awarded the Nordic Council's literature prize in 1991. However, where it is important for the interpretation I will go back to the Sámi original. From a perspective grounded in theoretical concerns about the difference in the actual interpretive situation when one uses the original and the translation at the same time, my reading of Nils-Aslak Valkeapää's Poem 558 can be considered to be a cross-cultural, cosmopolitan analysis that draws heavily on Sámi language fluency and cultural competence. My interpretation takes its point of departure in the cultural meeting between two languages, where communication and understanding (mediation, for my part) is the main intention behind the analytical endeavor.

The poem concentrates several central themes in the book *The Sun, My Father*. This is not least the case with the creative process in several aspects, for example, as commentary on the artist's role in creating his own product as a parallel to earlier eras' religious practices by making figures in stone and on drums as powerful signs with influence on people's well-being. The temporal dimension is another central theme in the poem—time in extent and as the medium within which change happens. The poem is simultaneously backward-looking and future-oriented; it is in the "timeless" condition when the poem's first-person speaker has crossed "over to the other side," that he "sees" both ways.

Love of the tundra land and the mountain landscape are also central elements in the book as in Poem 558. This love even seems to surpass the occupation with the Sámi people's future, where nature as a whole is more important than that which humans happen to live in at any given time. The meta-perspective is double-layered. Beyond commenting on the creation of the world, the poem's first person has also withdrawn to another position from which he can observe and evaluate his sisters' and brothers' acts, more in a futuristic perspective than a contemporary. The poem ends with a wish by the first-person speaker to return to the Sun. As is known, the Sámi are descendants of the sun, which, for Poem 558, means that one is almost required to read the poem in this mythological context.[2] In returning to the sun the poem's first person wants to contribute to closing the circle for the Sámi people through a return to the origin. Whether this also entails the end of the Sámi people, neither the poem nor the book says, but there is little doubt that the question of the further existence of the Sámi on the earth is an underlying theme in *The Sun, My Father.*

In many ways Poem 558 is also entirely concrete and, with regard to figurative language, a summary of *The Sun, My Father.* Many of the same images used earlier (and later) in the book are repeated in this poem, though not necessarily identically, yet with such clear parallels to the other poems or poetic passages that the references are obvious. This is also the case for the themes in the shorter individual poems elsewhere in the book and the various themes that are treated more "conclusively" in Poem 558. One already sees this in the first meaning-bearing component "as if / I myself / inscribe." This is a variant of the images used in the cycle of poems beginning with Poem 31, where the first-person speaker begins his work by inscribing the images, the figures, the creatures on the drum and on stone. While in the book's early poems it is clearly a first person who inscribes and beats, the underlying power is more prominent at the beginning of 558 than, for example, in number 32 and beyond. In 558 it is phrased "as if I myself inscribe," in other words a toning down of the subject's free performance of his mission, directing more attention to the following passage where the first person "[flies] to the other side." It seems as if the report of what the first person sees and experiences "on the other side" is more important than the repetition of the theme from Poem 32 and beyond, where, through his inscribing, he is involved in the actual creation of all the individual elements that are mentioned in the following poems. This is a sort of parallel to the ontological-hermeneutic discussion about a medial or pragmatic view of language, about whether the thing comes into existence by acquiring a name, or at least stands out for our consciousness as something comprehensible through the naming of the thing. In 558 the poem's first person becomes more a medium for announcing what "life" and the other powers want with us.[3]

It is life that gets us to act, even if for the individual it can appear "as if I myself was doing it," as it reads later in the poem, which thus provides a variant of the discussion about free will versus predestination. The poem continues with "and I draw /sometimes I believe / that this is me / these images / and / however I change / the images, images of me, / or I myself /

so many shapes of me, aspects, I could have been / so many, or almost anything / in another condition." Here another of the poem's main themes is
introduced, namely the metalevel, with commentaries on the actual creation of the text, and, at the same time, a concern about the poet's place in
society. This theme becomes clearer farther along in the text, but it is appropriate to introduce it at this point because the way of expressing this
theme definitely has something to do with—to put it discreetly—the Sámi
way of broaching a topic; namely, carefully hinting in an almost indirect
and evasive way to "get it said"—*geažideapmi.*

Geažideapmi is, for one thing, often used in traditional yoik poetry and
Sámi narrative art. These constitute an important sounding board for
Valkeapää's poetry, and he gives the practice an extra refinement in his texts.
Geažideapmi can be used in everyday communication, in artistic contexts,
and also in pedagogical contexts where it is up to the child himself or herself to discover the content in what the grownups have intimated.
Geažideapmi can be characterized as "an art of intimation," a way to hint
at the path along which the speaker wants the listener's associations to move.
So, even if the thematic concern is the artist's position in society, it is, from
the perspective of an ethos that takes the Sámi communicative situation as
primary, very important to pay attention to, and label, the distinctive aesthetics in connection with building up the thematics and as drama in the
text. Here the inspiration from and the allusion to yoik poetry's circular
structure emerge in the same way that the thematic building up of the text's
"message" is packed into a traditional Sámi communicative context. For
this reason it is important to emphasize the steady return to themes that
have already been taken up earlier, in the same way that themes that have
been alluded to earlier in the text can turn up again at a later point in a
somewhat more explicit form. Often this is somewhat more precise than at
the first hint, perhaps also turned in a somewhat different direction than at
the first mention, just as a yoik melody, a *luohti,* too, can select a "loop" or
an ornamention of that sort. This is an example of the way Valkeapää uses
yoik performance patterns in his poetry. It is one of the reasons that his poems ought to be read and interpreted as more than just writing; they are
music and poetry at the same time—*lyrics* in the original meaning of
musical words.

If one compares the individual sections of the poem to each other, it becomes evident that the third section, the one that begins with "life," appears as a main section on the first page of this long poem. At the same
time the passages from "was doing it" in the middle of the page all the
way to "in another condition" stand for the more concrete images of the

first-person speaker as a representative of himself and of us all because we resemble each other. The poem's first person is a part of life, just as an author is part of the total artwork's depiction, reflection, and processing of life. This aspect, too, has its reference earlier on in the book, in Poem 21, where "I" and "those like me" grow out of this earth, to the earth.[4] This could, for that matter, represent still another dimension of the speaker's relationship to himself and surrounding society, namely the *one* artist in relation to other artists, and, on the other hand, the artist in relation to the rest of society. In Poem 21, however, the focus is more on "growing up," becoming—possibly being *initiated as*—an artist. Typographically, too, this way of thinking or problematizing emerges best of all in the Sámi original, in that a number of central words farthest to the right in the poem can be read together as a unit, as a sequence; namely the words:

[I] myself	ieš
these images	dáid govaid
or I myself	vuoi mungo
[I] find	gávnnan

Actually, the literal translation of this passage is "I myself / these images / or I / find," but from the context in English the translators have changed the emphasis on "myself" somewhat. This little example shows that the first-person speaker remains a separate individual, with a separate individuality, and as a parallel to the subject in a yoik. Yet the speaker is neither isolated nor alone, nor segregated from the rest, but rather remains a part of a whole, of a collective where the part makes up a whole in itself, and becomes part of a larger unit. Seen this way, Poem 558 becomes a concrete image, even typographical, of what the text expresses, which, in turn, is a representation of yoik's traditional ideology that affirms the individual's position and place within the collective.

The last line at the bottom of the page should be read as a provisional conclusion to the page, but at the same time re-read, or repeated, as a beginning of what follows on the next page. Or, to put it differently, it represents neither a conclusion nor a beginning, but on the contrary shows continuity, an eternal continuation of the poem's themes. This can be considered as recognition of yoik tradition's contention that a yoik has neither beginning nor end. Therefore, one often hears the yoik form described as cyclical. One can read Poem 558 in the same way but more as a repetition of certain parts—both to emphasize these and as a little circle in the great cycle. Our reading of the poem will be more wavy than circular, though, since we tie the pages together by reading the last line twice, as belonging to the preceding and the following blocks of text. This is reminiscent of the tradition in yoik with *geasašit*, as well as *guorastit*, and, to a certain degree, *deattastit*. Geasašit refers to accenting certain parts of the yoik by stretching them out in length, preferably in repetitive form, while guorastit means taking up a yoik sound and exploring it further. *Deattasteapmi* has to do with the way the individual yoiker chooses to stress selected themes through accents and emphases on especially important parts. All these yoik concepts fit perfectly into an analysis of Nils-Aslak Valkeapää's poetry and underscore the importance of understanding his poetry in its Sámi origin (*al*), where the tradition's interpretive possibilities are included.

The poetic first person thus finds many forms of himself, and sees that he could have been so much, in another condition or situation (*eará dilis* in Sámi), at the same time as he discovers a readiness within himself to be like all others, "to do everything that people do, and even more," as the poem says. To "unfold an open human" as it is stated in the continuation, read together with the following line "and when I draw myself, I suppose I draw others too," must indicate a need to mention that which seems to be familiar can still be more closely examined. One can learn something about oneself, and others can discover new meanings by having to relate to the familiar through having to explain what one presumes to know inside out. In number 558 this passage, moreover, obviously goes into the first person's need to affirm to him that he is like everyone else, even if he is equipped with a number of characteristics that distinguish him from the rest. He is a "seer."

In the following section he leaves himself again to "fly away / to see / how I am." Here, moreover, we encounter italic writing for the first time in this poem. The italicized sections can be read together independently from the normal script as a separate poem within the poem, where many of the same themes are taken up as in the nonitalicized sections. The italicized parts are still clearer poetic bits than the long, prose-like lyrical passages in normal script. In that way there is an extra intensity in the italicized sections; they are, in a way, "the yoik ornaments" in the poem, those places where important themes are given a new dimension or emphasis through italicization. This is a deattasteapmi. Thus, we once more have to deal with another parallel, or, possibly, an allusion to the yoik's rhythm, formulation, and ideology.

My primary aim is to interpret the poem from an approach grounded in Sámi language and culture, in addition to using general literary critical

methods of reading to draw out the richness in Valkeapää's texts. Therefore, I have included references and comparisons to the text in its Sámi original throughout. This is what a cross-cultural cosmopolitan reading promises, but, of course, I know well that my strong focus on the Sámi cultural
context entails an over-representation of the specifically Sámi in Valkeapää's
poetry. I do not see any problem with this per se, for it ought to be legitimate for a Sámi scholar to read Sámi texts with Sámi glasses—that is, for
example, what most Norwegian literary scholars have done with Norwegian literature throughout time, without anyone having criticized them
for being narrow minded or ethnopolitical in their reading. In any event,
I would still claim that my interpretation in no way excludes other possible
readings of Valkeapää. I would rather make his own words mine and quote:
"with many meanings / the symbols too / more to choose from." However, I
guard against claiming that the author plays exclusively on the parallelism
to the Sámi yoik in his aesthetic-rhetorical formulation of Poem 558, because I do not want to force any straitjacket of opinion onto the reader.
Nevertheless, I must be allowed, as a (well-) informed reader with a given
set of analytical tools, to view the text in a cultural and historical context
and to frame it within an interpretive tradition that has already existed for
a long time among the Sámi: namely, the way yoik lyrics have been used—
and understood—in Sámi communities.[5]

In the poem, the first person appears as a *noaidi*, a shaman.[6] He "flies
away," just as the noaidis could fly. Or is it perhaps only in the actual drawing, the inscribing, that he leaves himself in order to better be able to see
how he is? In any case, it is clear that the speaker is looking at himself, wondering what he looks like.[7] This can be intense and moving as becomes
evident in the two following lines: "I feel fire / billowing." These two lines
can equally well be read as an introduction to the longer section that follows; but, as earlier argued, this poem demands a circular reading that occasionally results in some lines, and smaller sections, having to be read
twice, in repetition, belonging both to the preceding text block and to the
following.

In a wider interpretive perspective it is also possible to read this self-
searching process as an activity that has brought to light some impurities
in the collective mind of the people, that the artist sees and mentions, but
does not go into any further. He just socializes himself into the collective,
"and nothing is strange / everything appears as if it was mine."

From page two to page three in the poem we find the same type of transition we had from page one to two, namely, the last line on page two
forms the end of the page, but at the same time also constitutes the

transition and introduction to the next page. Accordingly the speaker's thoughts that he is "the animal keeping away from the others" (*eaidánas ealli*) form a commentary about the artist's role in society, belonging to it and, at the same time, staying on the fringes of society as its observer, who, from his more or less self-chosen "outsider" role, can evaluate what goes on in the crowd. Eaidánis ealli also has its clear parallel in the book's Poem 272, on the poem's fifth page. Here it is placed at the top of the page, a good way from the other reindeer, with an adjective in addition to eaidánis to further emphasize that it is a very obstinate individual, namely *menodahkes*, which means a reindeer that tries to avoid being taken hold of. On the whole it is typical of Poem 558 in which sequences, images, and themes from other poems in the book are brought in and in that way take on a summing-up effect as discussed earlier in this article. Also the references to parallelisms within the author's writing—what I have elsewhere called intra-textuality—expand the dimension of the identification with "the Other" that the poem's first person undertakes.[8] It is not just a matter of other people as comparable personages or individuals, since the other references are, to a large extent, also anthropomorphized or equipped with a separate will and capacity to act. The wind, the fire, and the stones can speak; or, as a reader, one has the impression that they are active listeners to the speaker's conversation with them. Allusion is used in the same way—and *here* we can speak of an allusion—to eaidánis ealli in Poem 558 when the two lines "and even I / the animal keeping away from the others" is read in context.

Gradually the first person's space expands, for in the following line it says "a world within me too, boundless, a universe." The "part/whole" idea is relevant because the small reflects the large and the individual reflects aspects of the collective; but both are subordinate to nature and natural forces represented in the poem by "the wind" in the next line. This is also an allusion to previous poems in the book, for example Poems 12, 22, and 58. The wind takes the poem's first person with it, or the speaker goes with the wind, "and I disappear / with the gusts of wind / to the sea of time." There is motion in the poem, almost a transformation that occurs; the wind has earlier blown, causing the clouds to travel and has made the fire talk (number twenty-two); but here it is the poem's first-person speaker himself who goes along.[9] The motion simultaneously foreshadows a change in form, a transformation, almost alluding to a religious dimension of disappearing with the gusts of wind to the sea of time. The transport and the trans-*form*-ation also bring "tomorrow is a new day" into the image. Again, this is the first mention of a theme that is taken up more broadly a little later in the text. On the whole, again, one can find many similarities in this poem with the structure of epic poems, especially in the case of the use of parallelisms, adapted here to a Sámi communicative situation while also using Sámi aesthetic modes of expression. That the next day is a new day with new possibilities is, for that matter, almost a cliché, but in the poem the possibilities are not explicitly mentioned; the new day appears here as representative of "something else." Then the speaker will no longer have the views he now sees, so the new day represents a futuristic Otherness where the questions gradually come to be how large and extensive the change will be, who will still exist, what they will stand for, and who they will be.

In spite of the poem's first-person disappearance with the gusts of wind, there is, all the same, a question of continuation. Though perhaps it is in another form, yet a continuation nevertheless, possibly a continuation of the circle, the cycle. This follows in the italicized section immediately afterward where time is now the theme: "*I flow in time / with time / in time / in time's deep river.*" Between "nature / the powerful ruler," and "tomorrow," fire is thematized in the line "I converse with the fire." In a way, "tomorrow" becomes the mediator for the metamorphosis about which the hint is directed because the fire also has another language tomorrow; the fire can transform, as well as destroy. It is therefore also a force, an element, at the same time that it is part of nature; perhaps it is a servant of nature, as it is *nature* that is referred to as the powerful one who rules. In any case, the words *Time, Wind, Nature,* and *Fire* come one after another as important concepts of the theme in this part of the poem. The poem's first-person speaker has already, earlier in the same poem, felt the fire's billowing in the connection between his own image of himself, on the one hand, and "the mind's night / impure / the shame of deeds" on the other. In that context, one could almost get an image of the fire as something that makes clean, purifies, while on the next page it is not valorized in any way; it only represents something new for the new day.

"[N]ature," "tomorrow," and "alien" are to a degree emphasized in the text, standing alone as they do on one line each. It almost seems that there is a motion along the axis on which they stand toward the end (rounding off) of the page, and over to the next page where the first word is "ambiguous," as a continuation—again—of the last statement on the preceding page: namely, "strange voices speak in my thoughts." Where the poem's first-person speaker refrains from valorizing it differently in the language of the fire, it appears as if he is more positive about the ambiguous and the equivocal in the multitude of images, signs, and symbols, because he ends the passage with the commentary "more to choose from tomorrow." This, of course, can be read as an ironic expression of the day's variety in the media world; for instance, the poem moves within its own (rhetorical) definition of timelessness, and thereby gives itself freedom to comment on past and current events, as well as to peer "wonderingly" into the future without having to be precise in terms of time.

Let us, nevertheless, leave out the possible ironic voice in the poem with regard to this greater choice tomorrow and rather read the commentary in the serious connection that is evidently present in the first four lines at the top of the fourth page, when it is a matter of the abundance of signs. Here the translators clearly had to make choices when they took the text from Sámi to English, choices that could give, or do give, other associations in English than in Sámi.[10] This is, of course, completely normal with all translations; my errand is just to comment on this specific part of the text on the basis of both versions through a comparison of the Sámi original and the English translation.[11]

The end of the third page and the first part of the fourth page circle around "change," "the alien," "tomorrow," and the meaning of (the new) images and symbols that show themselves as "visions of wonders" for the poem's first-person speaker. In that way an alienation motif is brought into the text together with the change that leads to fire having another language, the new day's reindeer having new migration routes, and the stones other shapes "tomorrow." In Sámi the concept pair is *amasmuvvat* and *amasmahttit*, that can best be translated "to become alienated" and "to alienate," which will be relevant for discussing the context of the text.[12]

Amasmuvvat is the process that happens to someone who becomes alienated from something as the result of the more active verb *amasmahttit*. Another Sámi language parallel would be the concept pair *dáruiduvvan* and *dáruiduhttin*. The Sámi are becoming culturally assimilated as a result of Norwegianization. Norwegian authorities hoped, for example, that their active Norwegianizing policy, *dáruiduhttin*, would lead to Norwegianization, *dáruiduvvan*. In addition to these meanings, *amasmuvvan* and *dáruiduvvan* can describe the passive process of alienation or Norwegianization because one is not observant of the process one is exposed to and part of or does not care about it. Therefore, the poem actually carries on, without at all naming the concepts, an underlying discussion with its readers about identity and keeping identity alive, and almost promotes an ideological-critical consciousness. In any case, it is possible to read this perspective into the text without moving too far away from it, I would contend.

At the top of page four of Poem 558 *govadas*—in the Sámi text—is translated into English as *sign* or *figure* in the first line, and in the fourth line as *symbol*. The translators evidently chose familiar metaphors of images, signs, figures, and symbols to avoid introducing another of the meanings of gov-adas in Sámi, namely shaman drum, which in a more direct translation of the Sámi term would become the object one made figures on: *govva* (image) + *das* = govadas (something with images). For grammatical reasons there is just one "v" in the derived noun govadas. Some of the tension and richness lies, too, in the level of associations in the original text, in the play between the basic words *girji* (today, primarily in the meaning "book," but also "pattern") and *govva* "image." From these nouns one can make adjectives (*girjái* "patterned" in the sense of rich in patterns, *girjjat* as a synonym of *girjái*, and *govvái* "imaged," colorful) and also other nouns, such as govadas, that can mean something with images on it. Furthermore, govadas can mean something with *gohpi* in it, or that someone has *gohpan*, thus having made a hollow or depression in. Still it would be appropriate as a name of a magic drum, but it can also designate other hollowed out objects. To really make the image extra ambiguous girjái could also be an illative case form of the noun girji (book), in the meaning "to the book" or "into the book," both of which would be possible interpretations of the first word on the fourth page. Then the last line on page three and the first line on page four could be translated as "strange voices sound in the thoughts / to the book." If one, however, keeps to girjái and girjjat as adjectives, it would probably better correspond with the third line in the poem, *girját*, which is the comparative of *girjái*, thus even more patterned, more colorful.[13]

A tentatively more direct, and less poetic, translation of the first four lines on page four would accordingly be "multicolored / the drum rich in images, varied / richer in images / still more drums." The fifth line does not change, and still functions as a conclusion to the four previous lines. Thus, the content changes a little from *The Sun, My Father* translation to this tentative word-for-word translation, where the issue would be the number of shaman drums compared to the richness of colors. In order to make it still more precise, the content of the third and fourth lines can be rendered that it would have been even more colorful had there been, or had there existed, even more drums. This hardly changes the interpretation appreciably, but I feel that it is important to include the dimension of the shaman drum and the spirituality belonging to it in the interpretation of the text. The fifth line, though, is still unchanged, mediates the same commentary on the ambiguity and colorfulness as in the original translation, in that there are many possible choices that are emphasized in the case of "tomorrow."

Then the script returns again to italics, and the first line of this block ascertains that "*time does not exist.*" Time, and the concept of time, are steadily returning themes throughout the book and are decisive elements in this entire sequence, which has to do with the new day. We are all in time, so time both exists and does not exist, as it says in Poem 566, where even the typographical formulation of the poem looks like half of a circle; thus a cyclical understanding of time is proposed. But at the same time, regarded from the inside of the poem, seen from left to right, the typography rather suggests an arrow form for the poem, that is, a representation of the linear conception of time. As if this weren't enough, the arrow shape becomes even more clear in the Sámi original, *Beáivi, áhčážan*, where the images are included because the black and white photo that remains under Poem 565 can be seen through the paper and thereby forms the actual arrow; while Poem 566 is the arrow point!

The poem comments obliquely on the presumably contradictory conceptions of time—the linear and the cyclical—and it may be read as a mediator between these two understandings. Therefore, the typography, the visuality, in Nils-Aslak Valkeapää's poetry is important because the poems alongside their word content also have a musical, primarily yoik-based, dimension and, not least, a visual formulation that also carries meaning. This not only poses great ordeals for translators but also for book designers.[14]

There are no clear visions of what the first-person speaker has about the new day; in any case, they are termed "visions of wonders" together with fog in the thoughts. Another contributory cause could also be that the hearing impressions become disturbed or confused, for in this sequence it says *"and not the river either with the same words."* Because the rushing river "speaks" with different "voices" that the rushing varies quite a lot over a short time, everyone would know who has stayed by a river. This is caused by variations in the wind's way of bringing sound to our ears, but there are undoubtedly also other causes in the acoustic space that encloses the river and the listener. Therefore, the river's other words in the poem need not imply anything beyond the simple fact that the speaker hears other voices, other languages' words, brought on sound waves. But it is doubtful whether the poem's entire meaning should be just that. Therefore, this passage becomes part of all the other "strange voices" that appear gradually. But the figures the first person sees are foggy, and the symbols in this concrete poem sequence, in accordance with the foggy, give (and are presumably meant to give) associations of fuzziness and dimness. And, finally, the question as to whether they really are visions arises. Perhaps everything is reality— perhaps this is now, today, as it appears in the next line with italicized text. Nevertheless, the italicized part ends with a speculation about whether this, too, might just be a dream.

Before the italicized section there are three lines where "I" says he has filled the vessel or the drum. (In Sámi there is just "*gárri,*" but the translators obviously wished to include both dimensions of the word and therefore used "vessel" and "drum.") This statement returns farther on in the poem but in the form of a question—actually the opposite motion from what we would expect because we as readers probably at first anticipate a question that can be answered. Here the motion goes the other way, however, from the speaker who says he has filled the vessel and thereby has also been filled himself. In a way having fulfilled his intention, his calling, or command, he marvels later in the text "when will I [be] complete / when will I become whole."[15] One can surely argue that these two statements do not necessarily have anything to do with each other, or, that in the second sequence, there is not really a question of having completed his destiny here on earth before the poem's first-person speaker leaves it. This would imply that "the river of loneliness / a path" and the later lines "hitch up the draft reindeer / leave . . ." should be read with a wider implication than merely the completion of "the creative process" on the drum. But this can also hint at an "omen" or an approach to a problem, a point of view that will be discussed again later.[16] I base such an understanding, too, on the Sámi text's use of words, like "lean deavdán dán gári, lean devdon" (I have filled this vessel, I am filled) and, farther on in the poem, "*goas dievan čavddisin / goas šattan ollisin*" (when will I [be] complete / when will I become whole). Gárri and čavddis belong together because one says about a vessel when it holds water that *dat lea čavddis*, while becoming whole (become grownup) is *šaddat ollisin*.

The next line, "image on top of image," is still an assertion that the drum is full of figures, meaning *that* creative process is complete, that the speaker has done what he could.[17]

The following image, "a door out, the desire to open / increasingly often," however, brings a new element into the text. It is important not to close oneself in, not to hold the door to the outer world closed. But, before we let in all the impressions from the outside it is important to be ready, to have filled the vessel, and to be filled oneself, too, so one knows what, in fact, is one's own. When the vessel is filled and when we are sure of ourselves, it is important to open the door; "I open the door outward when I enter," as it goes in the next section with normal script after the intervening italicized sequence. Again, this is an entirely everyday phenomenon and a description—to open the door outward when one enters a room. But in the juxtaposition between the expressions, and in the movement in the symbolism from one image to another, it is also natural to read this as an invitation and admonition to be open to impulses from the outside and not to reject what we can learn from others. It is important to know one's own values, but it becomes even more exciting to see one's own world in relation to the outer world.

The text then turns and asks whether this, too, is just a dream. It is at this moment that things are happening—it is *now* we must think about what we are doing, because it will be decisive for what we want to be, what we will become tomorrow. There is an appeal, or at least a doubly, communicatively mediated admonition, to assess today what we are doing with the tradition. In spite of the rather direct highlighting of the importance of having presence of mind today, the poem's first person seems to think that the message might still not reach its destination. Perhaps it will remain in his dream of "an open door," where the movement can happen in both directions, and where the poets, the artists, can be important conveyors of new impulses inward into their own society just by "stepping in" through a door that opens outward. In such a situation the artists can become mediators and filters, "Sámifiers"—for the mediation of impulses from outside—for better or for worse.[18]

This is to stretch the text rather far. But in keeping with the epic yoik tradition of bringing an extra dimension to the understanding of the poem's oppositional content, especially for Sámi listeners, the mediation of the doubly communicative message was a central form of expression.[19] Poem 558 can be considered as a continuation of this tradition, and, as such, as having an aspect of a doubly mediated message and almost as having a dichotomized addressee. Against this background it is, in my opinion, possible to read the above "out of" the text, or out of the text's "other" content, even if I realize that many will say that here I am reading things "into" the text, rather than out of it. Nevertheless, I want to insist on a broad interpretation of the poem, especially considering the long second section on page five of Poem 558, the sequence with the many Sámi place names. But before we get to the place name section, I just want to finish the shorter text in italics right before it.

There is no apparent connection between the fourth and fifth pages of Poem 558, in any case, not as clearly as on the preceding pages. The poem's first-person speaker is, in a way, finished with the creative process that is his original work. He has filled the vessel, is filled himself, and is now moving into the next phase of the work; he is in the process of interpreting his visions, as presumably the noaidi, the shaman, interpreted his drum's figures and the way the pointer (*árpa*) moved between them when the noaidi hit the membrane or drum skin with the hammer. The speaker has also explained, or at any rate problematized, his relationship to the rest of society and the rest of the herd, as eaidánas ealli, as the animal who thrives best by himself and thus maintains a distance toward the rest of the herd. He is absorbed by the new day and by the process of change he feels is underway. This process is, in many ways, tied to nature's own processes—its rhythm, growth, and even change. Something dies and disappears, while something else remains, and something new springs forth. But how much of "what was" remains in the new that "grows up"? And how much of the tradition needs to live on for the new to be able to still call itself by the same name as that which has been? The poem's first person grapples with such questions, while time, the wind, and nature continue. Life above him continues, in spite of the individual's existence being limited, but the continuity constitutes the bigger cycle.

The strophe, or section, at the top of the fifth page is more wordplay and rhetoric than essentially new information within the poem's frames.[20] The three first lines represent a type of deattasteapmi, an earlier theme that is mentioned again as emphasis that these are important elements to have in mind and as a type of parallelism that introduces a series of rhetorically constructed oppositions: "would light exist / if there was no shadow," "must get lost to be / die to live," and "am I asleep when I dream / dream that I am awake."[21] Still, there is more than only contradiction and wordplay behind the first statement because the image with the light and the shadow contributes to turning a truth upside down to let the producer become dependent on the product. In a way, there is a parallel to taking the side of the weaker party by elevating the weaker and letting him control the premise. The phrase "must get lost to be" plays more on the fact that a person only really learns to know himself through his mistakes and fallacies, while "die to live" must be seen in the connection between the individual and the collective, the part and the whole. Life continues, but the only certain thing in a human's life is that she or he will die sometime, and from this fact we have to shape our lives, make our life projects. So the first-person speaker turns back to wondering whether what he experiences and sees is really true—or whether the real is real—before he comes out with his declaration of love for his beautiful, dear Sámiland.

The Sámi place names contribute to providing the Sámi-language reader the feeling of being on familiar ground, out on well-known terrain, something that is, of course, very essential for feeling secure and at home.[22] The landscape is recognizable; it consists of Sámi appellative names, and their first reference is to the region where Nils-Aslak Valkeapää grew up and where his family migrated with the reindeer. On the other hand, the poet has chosen names describing terrain formations that are very common all over the northern Sámi area, so actually the reader may be several places at the same time as she or he is in a specific region of Sámiland. This is a parallel to the first-person speaker's feeling, in his situation, that he cannot completely manage to decide what and where he is. The essential thing is that the rattling off of the Sámi place names clearly fits the poem within a Sámi context, which is also confirmed and corroborated in what follows on the next pages.[23]

At this stage, however, the speaker is in the process of searching for the track and interpreting the visions. He stuffs his shoes with grass sitting on a reindeer pelt, fur side down. If this has any specific mythological significance, I have not been able to discover it. Significantly, though, the speaker puts on the red Sámi *gákti* that has always been reserved for especially meaningful journeys and is ready to meet what is awaiting him.

Following this is a line particularly worth noticing because the first-person speaker, for the first time in the poem, expresses an activity that includes being occupied with keeping a herd together, or, at any rate, showing concern for the herd, namely the indented line "I herd." (NB, the English text in *The Sun, My Father* has "I *heard*.") That line in the next round is followed by the contrasting statements about having to get lost to be and to "die to live," making the preceding statement even more interesting. For who is it that gets lost? Is it the speaker, while he is herding the herd? Does this imply that he is leading the herd astray, or is the statement just a declaration of universal and unchangeable facts that apply to the individual just as much as to herd and people? Read in this way there is motion in the text. To begin with, in this thematic block the speaker searches for the track, and toward the end of the page he finds a path. However, it does not seem as if the speaker has—if he has ever really had—responsibility for the herd any longer, because "the river of loneliness" seems to end up as the path the first person wants to, or may even have to, follow. That being a shaman led to a rather lonely existence is quite clear, so in that respect it could just be this aspect of the spiritual leader's position that is mentioned farther up on the page with the two lines cited earlier: "happiness rejoicing an old demand boundless / grief." A shaman would in the course of his period of activity surely come to experience all these aspects of life—which in turn would lead to a rather isolated, or at least lonely, existence for him.

In spite of this, or perhaps because of it, the poem's first-person speaker is in a position to feel an enormous love for this land with the crooked birches, the stones, and the wind. "I kiss these stones / embrace the twisted birches / the wind, my dear beloved, elated." It is hardly an accident that this declaration of love to what must be Sápmi comes immediately after all the place names farther up the page, and the references to a reindeer hide on which to sit and from which to make footwear. The Sámi reference points continue with Silbajávri, probably a place name—but at the same time, of course, any lake that the moonlight happens to strike, (the reference has to be to evening or night, at any rate it has to be so dark that the stars can appear because it is precisely the star over Silbajávri that is mentioned).

Another important dimension of this little text sequence is the underlying stress on love for the land and nature that continues, even if people come and go. The stones, the birches, the wind, and Silbajávri represent the speaker's affinities. The wind's position in this case is a little unclear, or to say it with the text, it is "ambiguous" and "equivocal." In addition to being a deity, a messenger, and one who clears (the air) in the case of the wind, there could also be an allusion to the oldest written Sámi literary text, which mentions "the boy's will." The young man's temperament is to be akin to the wind, and it is a wish to be free and unfettered.[24] That the two wishes can also lead to loneliness ought to be well known, such as they seem to do in the traditional yoik text "Oarrejávri," written down by the Sámi minister in training, Olaus Sirma, for Professor Johannes Schefferus in Uppsala, and included in the book *Lapponia*, published in Latin in Frankfurt am Main.

I have already commented on the first two lines in italics on the sixth page of Poem 558 in interpreting the line on the fourth page that reads "I have filled this vessel, this drum, I am filled." So I will not delve more into the questions on the sixth page ("when will I [be] complete / when will I become whole") other than to point out that it can, again, be suggested as a possibility of reading page five and page six together, so that "loneliness," "a path," and "whole" have something to say to about each other. However, the tension and drama increase in the following strophe in normal script that begins with "hitch up the draft reindeer." This is a foreshadowing of the ultimate journey that the poem's first person makes—or promises, almost proclaims, to undertake—on the poem's last page in the shouted statement "I'm coming, / the Sun, my father." At the same time it is an allusion to the second of the two traditional yoik texts that the aforementioned Olaus Sirma wrote down, namely "Guldnasaš," which is the name of the draft reindeer of the first-person speaker on his journey to his beloved.

With the lines "hitch up the draft reindeer / leave to arrive," the final portion of Poem 558 begins. Two times earlier, right at the beginning of the poem, the poem's first-person speaker has departed: "but often / I fly to the other side" and further on "again I leave / fly away." The use of the verb "to fly" provides more associations to a shamanic journey than is the case on the sixth page where the speaker hitches the draft reindeer, something that is apparently more reminiscent of a journey on the ground. There is, to be sure, no trace left after this journey; at the same time as there is no track to follow, but, in any case, the lands, the stony cradle, and the tundra follow immediately after in the poem. I am not going to comment on the foreshadowing much here. I will deal with that when I analyze the last page of the poem where the speaker obviously returns to the Sun. What is important to note in this section is simply the fact that a new phase of the poem begins on the sixth page where the bell reindeer, the one the others are supposed to follow, trots "away." It is important to note that it is the bell reindeer that trots, and a certain connection or hint arises of an affinity between the bell reindeer and the speaker in the second strophe of normal script where it reads "I meander across the tundra / the belled reindeer / trots, the swan's yoik." In the "circular" or "cyclical" way of reading described earlier, the bell reindeer in this case will point to "I" in the line above (I, the bell reindeer) and to "trots" in the line below (the bell reindeer trots). Thereby, we again have a hint of a certain connection between "I" (self), "the herder" (the door opener, the mediator), and "the bell reindeer" (local guide), which corresponds to the two-fold position that "the self" has as "the animal keeping away from the others" but also as "the bell reindeer" to be followed. This corresponds to the shaman's (the artist's?) position as belonging to both sides, the everyday plane (on this side) with practical work like herding and hitching up the draft reindeer and the more elevated (the far side) with visions, dreams, and journeys of the type where no trail can be made out and no tracks remain.

I haven't commented on the line "leave to arrive," which at first glance seems to be one of those expressions of contradiction, but which is actually just an ascertaining of reality.[25] It is only by leaving that one is able to return, and it is not least important in relation to the artistic creative process to have been somewhere, "have left"—in order to experience new things, to learn. "Come" need not include returning at all—it does not say "come back," just "in order to be able to come." Again he uses this ambiguity, this double meaning that there are so many examples of in the book.

The expression "these lands, the stony cradle / I meander across the tundra" belongs among the text's ambiguities. This image is perhaps even better known from Nils-Aslak Valkeapää's LP record from 1979 *Sámi Eatnan duoddariid*, a record where the title tune—a combination of yoik and jazz where both music forms' distinctive qualities are attended to—almost got the status of a new Sámi national anthem.[26] In itself the image is genial as an expression of the love and warmth a Sámi feels for Sámiland's tundras, even if they are actually barren and cold (!). A stony cradle does not immediately sound attractive because stone has the association of something cold and hard, in any case not something for making a cradle. Nevertheless, the cold, negative image is interrupted by the second part of the word syntax; a cradle gives associations of warmth, security, and love. That is also the feeling the image desires to convey, namely, how beloved and close this barren, cold land is for the Sámi. It is our home; it has the hard and loving side about it: "I kiss these stones / embrace the twisted birches." In the Sámi language edition it is possible to keep this cradle association, as well in the following line because *"sugadan badjel duoddariid"* means not only "I meander across the tundra" as in the translation, but also "I am lulled across the tundra."

Otherwise, there is a tinge of pessimism on this page of the poem, which, for that matter, provides a counterpart to one possible way of reading the entire book *Beaivi, áhčažan.* "Rain / jaeger / so black / sea of demands" and the conclusion on the page "in the evening / the ice roars / breaks / and wrestles the air" bring both thoughts over to something melancholy and painful. The jaeger belongs in Sámiland like the Sámi themselves. In juxtaposition with rain and the sea of demands, it is nevertheless entirely natural to read a darker nuance into the jaeger too. It is clearly moving toward fall at this juncture in the poem's timeline, so the swans' yoik is a song of departure to the land and the people. "The long fall / the water / shines the ice" is a parallel to the black in the italicized strophe above because wet fall ice—before the snow comes—is about the darkest one can imagine. At the same time it is brittle and breaks easily—it thunders and the air clears. A pain is mediated, it is as if the one who reads is prepared for something sorrowful; perhaps another comparison between nature's preparation for the long fall, with the even longer—and even less lively—winter. The human mind prepares for the dark period and cold, for hearing house walls lament in the winter chill, and, on the other hand, for *not* hearing the sounds of the summer's bird life.

This loss continues on the next page, the seventh and second-to-last page of this long poem. And it gradually changes to becoming a lack of something, before it takes on a more futuristic perspective toward the end of the page where someone sometime in the future will contemplate these innocent images in stone and on drum, and ask why they were made. But, all the same, the words of the yoiks are powerful and the imagery metaphorical. As mentioned, the conclusion of the poem begins on the previous page, with the draft reindeer being hitched up. On the connotative level there are associations with the oldest written Sámi literary texts by Anders Fjellner and Jakob Fellman.[27] On this page there is first an allusion to the myth of the Sun's daughter, "the sun / your hair, rays, gold flowers" before the allusion at the bottom of the page to the long epic poem about "Sámiland's first inhabitants." None of the allusions are direct, but one dimly perceives some of the same atmosphere and thought process in Valkeapää's text as in the old Sámi epic-poetic texts.

The myth about the Sun's children includes the long epic poem "The Son of the Sun's Courting in the Land of the Giants" and the shorter poem "The Death of the Sun's daughter." The first one is in many ways the Sámi's heroic poem, about the proud Son of the Sun who leaves his land to find himself a wife and meets the Giant's daughter after having been at sea for an entire year. In the land of the Giants he must undergo a test, with which the Giant's daughter helps him. They are married in the Giants' way and return to the Sun side with the Son of the Sun's ship. The brothers of the Giant's daughter try to pursue the two, but the Giant's daughter has tied three magical knots in a kerchief, and by untying the knots increases the wind all the way to storm strength. In this way they escape, and at their destination on the Sun side, they are married in line with the traditions there. Eventually they get strong, sinewy sons who become the forefathers of the Sámi. This is the narrative that is supposed to give the Sámi faith in their own strength and pride on behalf of their tradition.

The much shorter poem about "The death of the Sun's daughter" ought to be read in connection with the longer epic poem because it balances the pride of this poem with an uncertainty about the Sámi people's continued existence here on earth. The Sun's daughter is about to die. She is the one who persuaded her father to give reindeer to the Sámi as a gift when they were suffering. Originally the reindeer were wild, but she taught the Sámi how to domesticate them.[28] They came wandering down to the earth along the rays of the sun. The Sun's daughter has always had a good eye for the Sámi, and has been their advocate vis-à-vis the Sun, her father, but now she is concerned about how it will go with the Sámi when she returns to him. She sees many dangers threatening, and in the dark night, the wolves are slinking around, ready to attack. Invariably the line is repeated: "Morning will come, will it not" (*Idit boahtá, iigo dáidde*), which gradually takes on the character of a prayer. This is in line with, and a continuation of, her earlier activity for the good of the Sámi people, but the poem as a whole presents a humble picture of the Sámi rational about the future. However, it is very interesting to notice that the identity question focuses quite clearly on *ethnic* identity, and that it is so prominent already in these old texts.[29]

Returning to the conclusion of Poem 558, again it is a matter of a pair of oppositions: a retrospective view versus a futuristic, the bright, and optimistic in the sun's rays versus the gloomier in "coastal avalanches / fog." The meta-perspective on the poem and its possibilities also returns in a somewhat different ornamental "loop," another expression like a *guorasteapmi*, with a somewhat different take on the role of the artist than earlier. This struggle between the optimistic and the pessimistic continues through the last page of the poem in the oppositional pair of "the white snow" and "the sea's ocean / blackens." It also continues in the apparent opposition between the pure, the delicate, and the untouched, with "the snow-whiteness" as something positive and beautiful, and the simultaneous characterization of the snow as representative of the cold that creeps in under the skin. This is a clear parallel to the mood, the senses' intuitive feeling of an underlying accord in the traditional Sámi texts mentioned, where the bustle about the Sámi people's continued existence on earth runs like a "*doalli*," an invisible but nevertheless perceptible trail through the text. Neither the epic-poetic yoiks nor Nils-Aslak Valkeapää's poem provide any answers to the questions, but they get the listeners and readers to think about what it is that threatens this existence, the future, and also about why some people have other customs, other languages, and other images than the Sámi.

The interaction between the individual and the collective aspect in the poem continues on its last two pages. Otherwise the use of symbols in the text is familiar: loss, reflection, and nature as projected on the forces of the human mind. I have already commented on the allusion in the final strophe on the seventh page of the poem, but it also contains a meta-level that again turns back to the discussion about for whom the artist creates his art. Here the allusion to the fictive observer / commentator / critic in the epic-poetic yoik "Sámiland's first inhabitants" emerges most clearly. The traditional text explains to those who came after about the first inhabitants and their primitive dwelling places and survival "tricks." The text insists that the first inhabitants were very resourceful and managed well in the severe climate and landscape, and that their descendants, rather than laugh at them, should honor and praise their forebearers. With Valkeapää the perspective has shifted to a future observer, who, in line with the traditional text, is presumed to want to make fun of the unsophisticated images that are "inscribed in stone on the drum in the air to itself."

Poem 558 argues against an undervaluation of earlier times' "word power / image, the symbolic / imagery." It is as if one hears the shaman's voice in the antiphony between "The Thief and the Shaman," where the shaman, after having admitted that the thief has become master in the land of the shamans, yet again resorts to the power of words to expel the invaders from the land.[30] In the case of Poem 558 there is no talk of driving anyone out from any place, but my point in bringing in the old antiphonal song is purely to note the corresponding sound in Valkeapää's poem, and to remind about its emphasis on the Sámi's faith in the power of words. This is an important dimension to keep in mind when one evaluates Sámi history in general because faith in words and in the language as a medium of argument, encouragement, and opposition have been a contributory reason for the Sámi never having gone to war against anyone; though they have tried to argue for, insist on, and even appeal to their rights. If that did not help, they did not see bloodshed as a solution to conflict but continued the linguistic argument for their own point of view. In the last few decades, of course, we have gotten laws and regulations that are supposed to look after Sámi rights and enjoin the country's authorities to organize the conditions for the Sámi to be able to maintain and develop their language, their culture, and their social existence.[31]

There is potential in "these dreams . . . / these images, the yoiks of the images, the images of the yoiks" that should be noticed "if they are left behind." It is possible that the artist has "inscribed in stone on the drum in the air to itself" these "yoiks, powerful words, word power," but, no matter what, they represent something valuable for more than just the artist, even if they may come to seem unsophisticated to future generations. It is a strong argument for the importance of knowing one's own background, one's traditions, of knowing who one is, in order to better know what one is in the process of becoming, of evolving into. It is this aspect of the poem, and the book, that has the appeal, the insistent inaudible voice about caring, not just flowing in "time's deepest channel," but making an effort for our common obligation to the Earth, our mother who gets her life-giving light from the Sun, our father. It is in the allusions to the mythical past that the future is invoked as an unfulfilled scenario, which only we ourselves can determine the content of if we do not wish our images to just be "inscribed in the air itself."

I have already commented on the first part or strophe in italics on the last page of the poem, but I also want to underscore the allusion to the traditional poem about "the death of the Sun's daughter" in the lines "the cold / sneaks under the skin." The Sun's daughter has an unpleasant feeling about an unsure future for the Sámi people as she is lying on her deathbed because the darkness threatens, and the wolves are out in nature. An insidious cold also creeps under the skin, even though the sky is glowing.

But the last image is more tied to the departure, to the trip back to the Sun. "The sea's ocean" farther up in the same strophe is a parallel to the sea's high and low tide on the preceding page, while "coastal avalanches" corresponds to "roars" from the sea's ocean. The whole time there is motion in nature's elements. The sea tightens and loosens its grip, climbs and falls, and the tundra billows; even the ice roars and clears the air. There is a lot of *sound* in the poem; nature has its own language that must be interpreted and understood on the same level as human language. Nature, however, is more predictable in its cyclical, periodic rhythm, and it is more eternal than peoples' behavior, represented by "life" that (no matter what) is above us, without asking.

The draft reindeer was hitched up on the sixth page, so we are already prepared for the journey. On the final page of Poem 558 the sky glows as a reminder, or perhaps an invitation, to the poem's first-person speaker to get to work on the journey to the Sun, something he expresses with the statement "the Sun, my father / I am coming, I come." In the Sámi original there is a particle—*han*—connected to the verb for coming: "*boadánhan mun, boadán.*" The particle gives an association that there have been a few disturbances en route that have delayed the speaker from coming earlier, but with "I am coming, I come," he can affirmatively answer an invitation that we as readers have not seen or heard, but that we can dimly perceive as a conclusion to something—life, perhaps?

The line "I remember" seems to be connected with the first "I'm coming" three lines above, so it can read as *I'm coming and I remember.* In that case the memories refer to what follows, namely roping the young white reindeer cow. Seen this way, "I remember" is probably an admonition to us readers to remember the tradition of the young white doe and a white thread in the right ear, what it has meant, and means, for the Sámi.[32] "The young white doe" may allude to Olaus Sirma's "Guldnasaš," who also was a young doe and draft animal, while the white thread in the right ear represents a symbol that the traveler is out on his last journey. In this reading the line "to the sun" fits in well, because it clearly represents a return to the Sun, not just for the singular speaker, but also as a completion of the circle, a rounding off, and a conclusion of the cyclical course of both the book as such, and of this one poem in particular. This is also a summation of the most important themes in the entire book. It may be regarded as a "return of the Sun gift," a way of showing gratitude for the gift the Sámi have received from the Sun by retelling the myth so that it can live on, and a statement that the Sámi can still be proud of their background. The speaker, however, returns to the Sun; it seems as if it is the Sun's daughter who is preparing to go "home," as in the epic poem "The Death of the Sun's Daughter." The route to the sunlight is, of course, the Sun's rays, upon which the wild reindeer—the Sun's gift—in its time came wandering along on their way down to the earth. The speaker will also follow the same rays back to the Sun, and, seen this way, complete the motion in both directions.

The poem's first-person speaker has given plenty of tracks to follow to find the way forward. He has also urged us to think ourselves, to mull over our way of living, and where it is leading. Perhaps the first person was meant to be nothing more than someone who poses the questions that get us to think further. The speaker seems to share the concerns for the future with the myths of the Sun's daughter, but neither of them is defeatist, only afraid of the dark. Obviously, there is a "night bird" over us, as is life, as well, right at the end of the poem. Neither asks for permission, they don't ask at all, they are just there, perhaps as an appeal to us to dare to be. "Without asking" is the conclusion of the three preceding lines, but at the same time it is the beginning of the next sentence that we must formulate ourselves. It is, you see, up to the Sámi, to decide what we want to be when the new day comes. As an answer to the Sun's daughter's wondering "morning will come, will it not?" Will we awaken as Sámi still, or will we awaken from a Sámi dream that belongs to yesterday? Or does the dream, and do we, belong to the utopian tomorrow?

Notes

1. There is neither space nor any specific need, I would say, to go at lengths in this chapter at a presentation of Indigenous methodology, since I gather I'm speaking to an audience who is already cognizant of the last decade's debates about Indigenous peoples' involvement in academia. This is an ongoing debate all over the Indigenous world. The deliberations are of a philosophical and methodological nature, as well as more particularly focused on specific subjects and fields of study. The literary discourse has probably been articulated most clearly in North America, also as part of a subjective discussion on the ownership to Native American and First Nation Studies, while Maori research in New Zealand has been more concentrated on transforming the current situation into programs that will strengthen Maori involvement in the whole of society. In the Sámi case, Indigenous methodology is just in its incipient stage but is getting stronger every day. To learn more about the field, see for example: Foster (2008); Huhndorf (2005); Justice (2004); Krupat (2002); Kuokkanen (2007); Smith, G. (2000); Smith, L. (1999); Weaver (2007, 1997); Wilson (2008); Womack (1999); and Gaski (2013).

2. See explanation of this later in the text and also a brief synopsis of the myth. More information can be found in my book *Bieijjien baernie—Sámi Son of the Sun* (Gaski 2003).

3. The first person speaker in Poem 32 can, on the other hand, be read as a divine "I"—as a creator—I, independent of the book's first person singular voice. Even though I have assumed that the voice is a male, mainly because of the gender of the author and the affinity to the practice of a shaman—who usually would be a male—it still is fully possible to regard the voice as female, although I acknowledge it as male in my text.

4. Compare the same type of thematics that are in the poem "I have jumped off life's circle" (Olsen 1991) and Valkeapää's own book *Nu guhkkin dat mii lahka* (*So Far the Near*), 1994.

5. See, for one, my essay, "When the Thieves Became Masters in the Land of the Shamans" (Gaski 2004, 25–35), about the way epic poetic yoik was used among the Sámi in earlier centuries to mediate the Sámi's own view of history and knowledge about past times and to express opposition to the increasing colonization of Sámiland. This essay is available on the Internet at http://www.utexas.edu/courses/sami/diehtu /giella/music/tyven.htm.

6. The noaidi was a key figure in the traditional Sámi belief system. Most often he was a man, but there are also accounts of female noaidis. The noaidi was the main tradition bearer, the medicine man, and the main interpreter of the messages given by the sacred drum, which was instrumental in reading the future, not least the outcome of hunting and the result of curing and healing.

7. This is a clear parallel to what we Sámi academics do the whole time, namely research ourselves, study our own culture to understand both ourselves and others better. From my perspective in the Sámi world I read this passage as a clear defense of a "researching" approach to one's own in all respects, in the discussion about "staying home or going out" with regard to research. In the Sámi literary tradition there is a strong appeal to do both, all the way from the epic mythical texts of Sámi authors like Fjellner and Fellman, via Paulus Utsi and Nils-Aslak Valkeapää to Inger-Mari Aikio-Arianaick, Rose-Marie Huuva, and Sigbjørn Skåden.

8. Intratextuality means that the author refers to or makes allusions to his or her own text. In Valkeapää's case, I have written more thoroughly about this in an essay called"Nils-Aslak Valkeapää: Indigenous Voice and Multimedia Artist" (Gaski 2008, 167).

9. The lines here are parallel to the oldest Sámi literary text (which Nils-Aslak Valkeapää, for that matter, knew well), namely Olaus Sirma's two yoik texts in Johannes Schefferus' book, *Lapponia*, from 1673. In the poem "Moarsi fávrrot" the protagonist desires to travel to his beloved. See more about this in Gaski (2011, 16–17).

10. I know this well because I was one of three members in a translation group for both the Scandinavian and the English renditions of the book. For the Scandinavian version I worked together with Kristina Utsi and Jon Todal, and for the English translation I collaborated with the Native American poet and novelist Ralph Salisbury and the Swedish emigrant and poet Lars Nordström. For this reason, I'm very cognizant of the choices made. However, under the circumstances of this chapter, I feel I'm writing from another position when analyzing the poem. Still, I find it meaningful and valuable to consider the different interpretive possibilities that open up by reading the existing text versions against each other because this contributes to developing several approaches to the text. Translation is, as is well known, the first interpretation, and as such, one angle from which to consider the content of the text.

11. However, what is special in my situation is that I am trying to put myself into an intermediate position between several authorities. I was, as mentioned, involved in translating the poem to Norwegian, and later to English in a team effort both times. I undertake here a literary analysis of the same poem on the basis of the Sámi and English texts. I do this in several respects, first and foremost the purely professional in an analytical context, but then also in a role as mediator between Sámi and English. It could, therefore, be worthwhile to point to the significance of being able to mediate between two (and in fact three, including the Scandinavian rendition of the book) not just linguistically different means of expression, but also very different cultural and culture-historical bases for the expressions. This is mainly what I am thinking of when I mention the distinctiveness of my situation; occupying the position between text analyst with a scholarly approach to the material, and on the other hand, a person who in his scholarly activity tries to consider, attend to, and to foster a Sámi text practice. In my interpretation I attempt to mediate the Sámi perspective and context that the text is built on. While, as a researcher, I'm also concerned about the relation between language and the translator, and I'm trying to give the translation a professionally defensible expression.

12. Parallel to Brecht's concept pair *Entfremdung* and *Verfremdung*, a non-intended and an intended alienation; *defamiliarization* for the Russian formalists, and *alienation* in today's literary discourse.

13. Kathleen O. Dana also comments on the different meanings of *govva* in her PhD dissertation (Dana 2003) and in an essay on Valkeapää and his image drum (shaman drum) (Dana 2004). In the essay she writes "the poet also speaks explicitly about the power of images to evoke images. For example, he writes epigrammatically and enigmatically about the nature of symbols and images in his very synthesized Poem 31 at the beginning of *Beaivi, áhčážan*, reinvoking similar imagic powers in his final creed-like and prophetic Poem 55" (ibid., 8). For Dana, it seems, however, to be a point to read Valkeapää as a shaman-poet and read his poetry accordingly as "books of poetry that are image drums of the postmodern era for his people. Nils-Aslak Valkeapää has not only made an image drum, but he is also a powerfully adroit shaman-poet who knows how to use natural and native symbols to see into the past and into the future" (ibid., 31).

14. The crowning example of Valkeapää's typographical game with the book format is, of course, Poem 272 in *The Sun, My Father*, where the poem (re)presents a reindeer herd on the move (see Gaski [2008, 165–73]).

15. Parallel to being "ready to jump off life's circle," as expressed in a poem that appears in an anthology ([Olsen 1991, 35–40] not yet translated into English). In this poem the "I" contends that he and his alike are ready to jump off life's circle.

16. This is very common in Nils-Aslak Valkeapää's manner of expression; perhaps it most clearly emerges in the poem cycle "My home is in my heart" in *Trekways of the Wind* where he has built up the poem almost as a thesis, with arguments and references—although only oral references—despite which the first-person speaker is not believed by the colonists, by the Other (see Gaski 2008, 160–64).

17. In line with what I have written farther on in the text about the yoik's form, one can say that the text's repetition, "verification of the affirmation," is a parallel to the yoik melody's deattasteapmi, underscoring a theme or a distinctive feature of the one yoiked. "Image on top of image" here emphasizes the completion of the creative

process: the creation of the actual figures, the images on the drum, and the poem itself.

18. "Sámáidahttit" as parallel to "dáruiduhttit" (see explanation earlier in the text), thus "Sámify" instead of "Norwegianize."

19. See more about this in Gaski (2004, 35–45).

20. This, too, is a special feature of Nils-Aslak Valkeapää's poetry. These change from the great vistas with important questions of principle to entirely normal everyday affairs and practical tasks. An example is the abrupt shift in a poem in *Eanni, Eannážan* (*The Earth, My Mother*), where the first part of the poem is almost a cultural-political statement, only to suddenly turn entirely around to really claim that the most important thing in life is the beauty in nature: "every culture / will promote its cultural / points of view / ITS OWN / duty / right / like the others / LIFE / and so beautiful / is the grass meadow / the high mountain glen / in the splendor of flowers."

21. This is also among the most prominent themes in Valkeapää's only text for theater, *Ridn'oaivi ja nieguid oaidni* (The Frost-Haired and the Dream-Seer). It was inspired by the Japanese Noh-theater tradition and actually performed for the first time in Sapporo in 1995. Later it was adapted in its Sámi original by the Sámi *Beaivváš* theater company, and it premiered in Guovdageaidnu, Norway, in 2007.

22. Kathleen O. Dana (2003, 122–24) discusses the meaning of the place names and shows that they are from the very region, the Arm of Finland, that Nils-Aslak Valkeapää made his home as a child. The place names are kept in their Sámi original in all the translations, but a glossary of the terms gives us an idea of the descriptive meaning of these place names.

23. This is a parallel to the place name usage in the central poem suite "My home is in my heart" in *Ruoktu váimmus* (*Trekways of the Wind*), where the Sámi place names tie the poem to a Sámi area, even if the thematics are relevant for all Indigenous people. The accompanying image material in the *Trekways* book consists of pencil sketches that are an important part of the suite. They are more reminiscent of Siberian Indigenous cultures and also motifs from the Southwest United States. In Poem 558, however, the entire context is Sámi, and besides, the poem consists only of words.

24. See among others, Gaski (2011, 17).

25. Cf. *Ruoktu váimmus, Trekways of the Wind*'s last poem: "I leave / to arrive/ go away / to be closer."

26. The LP was reissued in 1992 as a CD with the title *Sápmi lottážan*, DAT CD 12, I, II.

27. I'm thinking here of the mythical texts by Fjellner about the Sun's children, and the oral historical accounts written down, according to his informants, by the Finnish minister, Jakob Fellman in the northernmost region of Finland around 1830.

28. It is plausible to believe that the domestication happened by letting the wild reindeer listen to yoik. The myth does not confirm this idea, but there are plenty of traditional Sámi stories that hint at the fact that the reindeer become calm when they hear yoik.

29. The ethnic identity, as relational and different from the intruding neighboring people's identity, is perhaps even more clearly expressed in the historical-epic yoik texts that J. Fellman wrote down in Ohcejohka around 1830 (cf. footnote 27). The texts are even older than that, and they express a clear consciousness about themselves as Sámi, and thereby as something other than the Scandinavian.

30. See Gaski (2004, 35–45).

31. This was stated in an amendment to the Norwegian constitution, and also in a separate Sámi act, adopted by the Norwegian Parliament in 1989.

32. The white thread in the right ear is also mentioned in Poem 20 in *The Sun, My Father.* In that poem it is a token of celebrating spring as "a path / to the sun." This "path to the sun" is, of course, also essential for the way back to the sun as the final journey (see also Dana [2003, 196–97]).

References

Dana, Kathleen Osgood. 2004. "Áilloha¿ and His Image Drum: The Native Poet as Shaman." *Nordlit* 15: 35–45. Summer, University of Tromsø.

———. 2003. *Áilloha¿ the Shaman Poet and His Govadas-Image Drum. A Literary Ecology of Nils-Aslak Valkeapää.* Acta Universitatis Ouluensis, Department of Art Studies and Anthropology, University of Oulu. Also available at http://herkules.oulu.fi/isbn9514269446.

Foster, Tol. 2008. "Against Separatism: Jace Weaver and the Call for Community." *American Literary History* 20(3):566–78. Available at http://alh.oxfordjournals.org/content/20/3/566.full?sid=3d0c01d8–24ad-4553–844c-c73b4ba2eabc

Gaski, Harald. 2003. *Bieijjien baernie—Sámi Son of the Sun.* Karasjok: Davvi Girji.

———. 2004. "When the Thieves Became Masters in the Land of the Shamans." *Nordlit* 15, Summer, 35–45, University of Tromsø.

———. 2008. "Nils-Aslak Valkeapää: Indigenous Voice and Multimedia Artist." *AlterNative—An International Journal for Indigenous Peoples* 4(2):155–78.

———. 2011. "Song, Poetry, and Images in Writing. Sámi Literature." In *From Oral Tradition to Rap: Literatures of the Polar North,* edited by Langgård, Karen and Kirsten Thisted, 15–38. Ilisimatusarfik/Forlaget Atuagkat, Nuuk, Greenland.

———. 2013. "Indigenism and Cosmopolitanism: A Pan-Sami View of the Indigenous Perspective in Sami Culture and Research." *AlterNative—An International Journal of Indigenous Peoples* 9(2):113–24.

Huhndorf, Shari. 2005. "Literature and the Politics of Native American Studies." *PMLA* 120(5): 1618–27. (Oct. 2005). Modern Language Association. Available at http://www.jstor.org/stable/25486272.

Justice, Daniel Heath. 2004. "Seeing (and Reading) Red: Indian Outlaws in the Ivory Tower." In *Indigenizing the Academy: Transforming Scholarship and Empowering Communities,* edited by Devon Abbot Mihesuah and Angela Cavender Wilson, 100–23. University of Nebraska Press: Lincoln and London.

Krupat, Arnold. 2002. "Nationalism, Indigenism, Cosmopolitanism: Three Perspectives on Native American Literatures." In *Red Matters: Native American Studies,* edited by Arnold Krupat, 1–23. Philadelphia: University of Pennsylvania Press.

Kuokkanen, Rauna. 2007. *Reshaping the University: Responsibility, Indigenous Epistemes, and the Logic of the Gift.* Vancouver: UBC Press.

Olsen, Per Kristian. 1991. *Å, eg veit meg eit land.* 20 forfattere i Nord-Norge. Oslo: Tiden Norsk Forlag.

Smith, Graham Hingangaroa. 2000. "Maori Education: Revolution and Transformative Action." *Canadian Journal of Native Education* 24(1):57–72.

Smith, Linda Tuhiwai. 1999. *Decolonizing Methodologies: Research and Indigenous Peoples*. London: Zed Books.

Valkeapää, Nils-Aslak. 1983. *Greetings from Lapland*. London: Zed Press.

——. 1985. *Ruoktu váimmus* (*Trekways of the Wind* [1994]). Norway: DAT, Kautokeino.

——. 1989. *Beaivi, Áhčážan* (*The Sun, My Father* [1997]). Norway: DAT, Kautokeino.

——. 1994. *Nu guhkkin dat mii lahka/Så fjernt det nære*. (Not available in English.) Norway: DAT, Kautokeino.

Weaver, Jace. 1997. *That the People Might Live: Native American Literatures and Native American Community*. New York: Oxford University Press.

——. 2007. "More Light than Heat: The Current State of Native American Studies." *American Indian Quarterly* Spring, 233–55.

Wilson, Shawn. 2008. *Research Is Ceremony: Indigenous Research Methods*. Halifax: Fernwood Publishing.

Womack, Craig. 1999. *Red on Red: Native American Literary Separatism*. Minneapolis: University of Minnesota Press.

The Montana-Tromsø Project

A Scholarly Conversation on Indigenous Peoples and Multicultural Societies

Bjørg Evjen

The point of departure for this anthology arose, as Dr. Shanley says in the introduction, from the SIU-Funded project "Indigenous Peoples and Multicultural Societies," between 2008 and 2012. As scholars of Native American and Sámi studies, we aspired to strengthen our respective educational programs: Native American Studies (NAS) at the University of Montana, Missoula, and the Master's Program for Indigenous Studies at the Center for Sámi Studies, University of Tromsø. We intended that this happen by encouraging students of differing backgrounds to move between countries and programs of study and by bringing professors together in order to discuss and take part in different programs and jointly to develop future programs of study. Needless to say, these activities have been important for programs that focus on Indigenous peoples and for programs in studies at both universities; yet the time went by so quickly that many of us feel as if our exchange of ideas has only just begun.

The anthology illustrates the multidisciplinary approach and activity that the project covered—with chapters within the fields of history, health studies, pedagogy or education, environmental studies, law, literary history and literature, performance art, film, and linguistics. The multidisciplinary approach mirrors the way our project was planned and developed. Researchers from the two universities carrying different cultural backgrounds and to a certain degree also different academic-cultural backgrounds, met to discuss academic topics relevant to Indigenous peoples' contemporary situations, especially those Indigenous peoples who live within multicultural nations—"nations within nations," as the expression often goes in the United

States. What was the most time consuming was to overcome the academic-cultural differences and to make sure we understood one another's ways of approaching Indigenous research. This exists, of course, due to the different Indigenous contexts in the United States and in Norway.

Although during the beginning of our project, we had aimed to create an anthology consisting of jointly authored essays with thoroughly comparative perspectives. We soon recognized that the logistics involved, given our great distances, involvement of faculty in particular fields, and limited time, as well as limited knowledge about each other worked against that. Since we hoped to write about place-based knowledge, we needed, first, to know one another's place, and then to evolve our scholarly perspectives. Moreover, in our respective Indigenous Studies units, scholars from particular disciplines did not always match those from the other side. So ultimately we opted to speak together in some chapters and as individual voices in others. We have all, nevertheless, learned so much from one another, things that will no doubt show up in other projects, individually and collectively, going forward. Disciplines as conceived with the academy do not always reflect Indigenous ways of knowing.

Conferences and workshops at both universities served the important aim under this joint project of organizing annual workshops where researchers could meet to develop common research and to cooperate in publishing articles, as well as to allow us generally to become familiar with one another and with each country's Indigenous peoples, their histories, and cultures.

In the fall of 2008, we met at the University of Tromsø to start a fruitful long-term cooperation based upon Indigenous perspectives of past and present multicultural societies. We asked questions such as: How do we understand the terms "multicultural" and "Indigenous"? What have national governments done when trying to demographically and geographically define their nations' minorities? How do Indigenous nations within nation-states configure themselves against and despite outside societal expectations?

Participants from Norway and the United States met in 2009 to discuss Indigenous identities, rights, and research at the Indigenous Knowledge Traditions and Research Communities Conference at the University of Montana. The Indigenous self-definitions and intellectual property rights we discussed included: Who owns the stories, how does oral tradition maintain identity, and how do Indigenous cultures intersect with the mainstream?

The conference focused on the alliances that have grown up among Indigenous peoples from around the world, as those peoples have recognized their common political, historical, cultural, and social experiences under colonization and globalization. At the same time, conference participants explored ideas and issues related to Indigenous place-centered identities. The richness and depth of local histories and cultures fostered conversations around the protection of intellectual property rights from theft, appropriation, and distortion on the part of the government, as well as at the educational and entrepreneurial levels. The emphasis was on oral representation and histories. How do stories of place carried through oral traditions, arts, and literatures provide groundings for Indigenous identity? What do Indigenous peoples stand to lose when they share those stories with outsiders? How do commercial and educational efforts contribute toward and against sustaining traditions, while those peoples adapt to global change? How does language figure into the mix of cultural treasures needing to be preserved as part of a people's distinct heritage? How do local stories empower people to respect their homelands and fight for their ecological health?

We continued our discussions in a workshop at the University of Tromsø, in January of 2010, around ideas of representation and self-representation. In this workshop our researchers extended the topic of the second conference to discuss what happens with global collaborations and broad definitions, the double consciousness of Indigenous self-representation for political and economic reasons, and the role research communities play in sharpening the discussions around such issues. The emphasis was on visual aspects of cultural representation: How are Indigenous peoples represented in different visual media, such as films, photos, and museum exhibitions, by cultural outsiders, and by the Indigenous peoples themselves? An open seminar was given during the Tromsø International Film Festival that addressed the following question: While the representation of Indigenous peoples in general has changed over years, from a picture of "the noble savage" to a presentation of the modern, urbanized Sámi, Salish, or Cree, what knowledge is to be gained from seeing the change in terms of differences and similarities between Indigenous America and Indigenous Norway?

Our fourth workshop took place on Indigenous rights, politics, and self-determination in Tromsø, in 2010. The question of Indigenous rights has come to the forefront of the international human rights agenda, especially since the passage of the United Nations Declaration on the Rights of Indigenous Peoples (UNDRIP). Different groups throughout the world, albeit often in limited ways, have succeeded in their efforts to gain rights and establish institutions for self-determination. Internationally, developments within the UN system, most as noted with UNDRIP in September 2007, seem to have made major changes with respect to international law. Given that the different groups are rather small and separated from one another, they have suffered oppressions, abuses, and subjugations for a long time, and have lacked fundamental resources. The current situation represents an important shift ideologically and materially.

At the same time, however, discussions about minority rights are often rife with controversy in multicultural societies. Discussions vary among countries, but are often double-edged as concern is given to the justification of minority rights in general and to the justification of differences between different minorities, such as national immigrants, national minorities, and Indigenous peoples. Typically the discussions have unique internal, national elements, and external elements, as well as conflicts between demands from international law, on the one hand, and the role of national democratic institutions on the other.

The aim of the conference was to discuss Indigenous rights at various levels and in diverse contexts with a focus on minorities in international law and implications for processes in nation-states. To what extent is the development of Indigenous rights in different contexts an outcome of international law? How is international law transformed to rights and institutions for self-determination for a diverse group of Indigenous peoples? How are Indigenous rights legitimized, and to what extent are different rights challenged by the majority and other minority groups? How important are political processes compared to the role of courts and lawyers? Can Indigenous rights be more accurately seen as continuous struggles with setbacks, or is it processes characterized by progress where new milestones are achieved?

We met for the last time in 2011 to discuss "Intergenerational Indigenous Knowledge and the Global Village," at the University of Tromsø. The final conference brought together the themes of Indigenous self-representation, rights, and the ecology of place, and it addressed the role of research communities in producing knowledge that supports sustainability of Indigenous life and environmental integrity. The importance of preserving the communal values and traditional knowledge of the "village" was weighed with the influences and innovations of a broader community, a "global village." In matters of health and education, in particular, the conference focused upon indicators of well-being at the individual and collective levels. Environmental integrity in Indigenous worlds contrasted with what is often termed "environmental racism," and we focused on cooperative "development" of Indigenous peoples' lands. We sought to bring together interdisciplinary perspectives for analyzing the importance of intergenerational Indigenous knowledge and the challenges to its preservation. This conference consisted of a workshop on knowledge and generations, a visit to the Indigenous cultural festival Riddu Riddu, and a concluding meeting for the research collaborators. Questions guiding the discussions were intended, first and foremost, to include ways of assessing the benefits and limitations of our exchanges, what we will continue into the future, and the knowledge we will disseminate.

Place matters for Indigenous peoples. As part of the Western world, the United States and Norway share a Western worldview in terms of capitalist and democratic values. At both the Centre for Sami Studies and the Native American Studies Department, new ideas around Indigenous methodologies have been discussed and, at least to some extent, integrated into teaching and research. These developments reflect the fact that historically, many of the same processes have taken place during similar time periods. The international trends were also reflected in political history connections and contemporary realities among Indigenous peoples. Instruments used on national political levels during the span of time were surprisingly similar; for example, parallels include the role of missionaries in Christianizing the Indigenous people and educating them in reading Christian texts; the effort to bring up the children in the majority culture and the use of boarding schools; and the gathering of human remains and items of cultural patrimony by research museums. All occurred at similar times in both countries as did the increased educational level of Indigenous peoples—education, that is, into Western epistemologies.

Major differences were also found. Evjen and Beck discuss ways in which the United States vacillated between segregating American Indians on reservations and forcing or encouraging them to leave reservation communities to assimilate into American society (although on the basis of being equal citizens). In Norway the policy of assimilation focused entirely on forcing everyone living in the Norwegian society to be Norwegians. Reflecting this vacillation, land-use issues, on-reservation and off-reservation, dominated much of the relationship between Indian tribes and the United States. This was not as prevalent in Norway.

It is one thing to read about the dynamics of these relationships, but quite another to experience them in practice. We experienced each other's worlds through our cooperative work, not only within academia, but also outside our institutions. In Montana we met on two different reservations—the reservation of the Confederated Salish Kootenai Tribes and Rocky Boy's Reservation, which is home to Chippewa and Cree peoples. In Norway we worked together in social settings outside the University of Tromsø. These various levels of practice had the effect of mirroring the ways in which place matters. When our different geographies, cultures, and research met in that conversation, they made visible the different conditions that characterize the lives of Indigenous groups in our two national states.

The annual meetings were also a means of being physically present in place and practices, as well as the social, cultural, and physical context of our partners' lives. This led to a wider understanding while discussing experiences and to understand the nature of differences and similarities. It also made a fruitful contrast when doing comparative research. The local people's point of view became more accessible as we got to know each other's social contexts. Place can be a reflection of local conditions. It is also based on relationships that connect places to each other on much larger scales. Such a conceptualization is a highly dynamic definition of place as a specific conjunction of social practices and social relations, which have been constructed over time, consolidated, decayed, or renewed. From such a perspective, it is also possible to understand how global processes and changes are present in local processes.

Place might also constitute an important context for learning, sometimes in contrast to institutional teaching, other times as an extended kind of learning and experiencing. The students given grants from the project reflected the differences. This is brilliantly shown in the film produced with grants from our project, *Eagle Boy*, by Gry Elisabeth Mortensen; it tells how students and their children met the Norwegian culture and society. In total, ten graduate students participated in our program in one capacity or another, six of whom earned Master's degrees either in Tromsø or in Missoula.

The two main educational institutions involved have different histories. The Centre for Sámi Studies at the University of Tromsø is the most recently developed, since it was established in 1990. Through its strategic development and planning, the Centre is an important contributor in strengthening Sámi and Indigenous perspectives in research established within a wide range of fields at the University of Tromsø. The Master's Program in Indigenous Studies and the Forum for Development Cooperation with Indigenous Peoples provide examples of international cooperation. One part of the program involved providing scholarships for North American students to obtain their Master's degree in the program.

The Master's Degree Program in Indigenous Studies at the University of Tromsø is a part of the general focus on internationalization at the university. The program is an international graduate study program with its multidisciplinary approach to comparative Indigenous issues. During the program the student acquires broad knowledge of interdisciplinary perspectives and issues in the study of Indigenous peoples. The program covers a variety of mandatory courses that aim to give the students broad knowledge of varied perspectives and issues in the study of Indigenous peoples. In addition they are taught how to plan and carry out their own research. As one of the international programs at the University of Tromsø, we aim to develop this study to be a meeting place for research activities, communication, and knowledge exchange connected to Indigenous issues from a local and international perspective.

The Native American Studies Department at the University of Montana began as a student support program in the late 1960s. It became the American Indian Studies Program in 1970 with the addition of a director and academic course offerings. In 1997 it graduated its first three students of its major. And Native American Studies became an academic department in 1999. Today NAS offers a wide variety of courses served by six core faculty. The NAS faculty often serves on graduate committees for students working on their Master's and PhD's in Interdisciplinary Studies when at least one component of their work focuses on what would be regarded as a Native American Studies comparative topic.

By working together to understand each other's regional Indigenous experiences, social contexts, histories, and cultures, we hope to bring Sámi and Native American Studies perspectives into focus in new ways, "mapping" our presence as peoples of place. The field of Indigenous Studies benefits from such efforts, we believe, by showing our diversity as Indigenous peoples within broad categories and our cultural specificity at any given time in relatively narrow and dynamic definitions. The UNDRIP not only seeks to protect Indigenous cultures from forced assimilation efforts but also to allow for educational resources that will help to assure survival of Indigenous lifeways. Being within nation-states, such as Norway and the United States, the Indigenous peoples reflected in our project, Sámis and American Indians of Montana, participate in democracies that must honor their visions of self-determination and social development. The global challenges facing us all behoove us to develop cross-cultural understandings represented by our efforts. We look forward to future collaborations.

Contributors

S. James Anaya is a regents professor and the James J. Lenoir Professor of Human Rights Law and Policy at the University of Arizona, James E. Rogers College of Law, where he teaches and writes in the areas of international human rights, constitutional law, and issues concerning Indigenous peoples. Anaya is a graduate of the University of New Mexico (Economics 1980) and Harvard Law School (JD, 1983). Among his numerous publications is his acclaimed book, *Indigenous Peoples in International Law* (2004). Prior to becoming a full-time law professor, he practiced law in Albuquerque, New Mexico, and represented Native American peoples and other minority groups. For his work during that period, *Barrister* magazine, a national publication of the American Bar Association, named him as one of "twenty young lawyers who make a difference."

Unn-Doris Karlsen Bæck holds a PhD in sociology from the University of Tromsø, Norway. She currently works as a professor at the Department of Education, University of Tromsø, Arctic University of Norway, and as an adjunct professor in sociology at University of Oulu, Finland. Her research interests include studies of sociocultural perspectives on learning and education, education, and social inequality, with special emphasis on aspects related to social class, ethnicity, cultural diversity, urban/rural dimensions, and parental involvement, as well as sociology of education and sociology of youth in general. Bæck has managed a number of Norwegian and international research projects funded by, among others, the Norwegian Research Council. Recent publications include the anthology *Rural Futures? Finding One's Place Within Changing Labour Markets*.

David R. M. Beck is a professor in the Department of Native American Studies at the University of Montana in Missoula. He is the author of several books on tribal histories, including *Seeking Recognition: The Termination and Restoration of the Coos, Lower Umpqua, and Siuslaw Indians, 1855–1984* and a two-volume history of the Menominee Indians of Wisconsin: Vol. 1, *The Struggle for Self-Determination: History of the Menominee Indians since 1854*; and Vol. 2, *Siege and Survival: History of the Menominee Indians, 1634–1856*. Most recently he is coauthor with Rosalyn R. LaPier of *City Indian: Native American Activism in Chicago, 1893–1934*. His current work is on American Indians who worked at and for the 1893 World's Columbian Exposition in Chicago. He previously served as Dean and Senior Resident Faculty of the Native American Educational Services College, a private, American Indian–controlled college in Chicago.

Annjeanette E. Belcourt (*Otter Woman*) is an American Indian assistant professor in the College of Health Professions and Biomedical Sciences at the University of Montana's Pharmacy Practice and School of Public and Community Health Sciences Departments (enrolled member of the Three Affiliated Tribes [Ft. Berthold] and also affiliate to the Blackfeet and Chippewa). Raised on the Blackfeet Reservation, she is an alumnus of Browning High School and the University of Montana. Her doctorate is in clinical psychology. Research and clinical priorities include mental health disparities, trauma, post-traumatic stress reactions, risk, resiliency, and psychiatric disorder within the cultural context of American Indian communities. Dr. Belcourt has conducted grant-funded collaborative research projects with Native communities at the University of Montana and at the University of Colorado Denver's Centers for American Indian and Alaska Native Health. Publications have appeared in the *American Journal of Public Health, Psychological Bulletin, American Psychologist, Educational and Psychological Measurement*, and *Transcultural Psychiatry*.

Bob Boyer worked at the University of Montana in media arts and Native American studies until his untimely death in 2013. After graduating from university, he traveled with the Ringling Bros. and Barnum & Bailey Circus as a chaperone and English teacher. He moved to Montana in 1993 and taught high school in Ronan and Missoula before returning to further his education at the University of Montana for an MFA in Media Arts in 2009. Since 2009, Bob was an adjunct professor, teaching Media Arts and Native American Studies at the University of Montana. In the summer of 2012, Bob served as the head instructor for the Brazil Science Without

Borders Research Project. As a Canadian Cree who grew up in an educationally committed home—his father was a Native Studies professor at the University of Saskatchewan and a performing artist—Boyer understood the challenging issues in Indian Country well. A prolific poet, painter, photographer, and filmographer, Boyer was recognized for his short film "Apanii Ootukk" which won first place for short drama in two 2009 film festivals: the Big Island Indigenous Film Festival in Hawaii and the Cleveland Independent Film Festival. His film showed at the International Film Festival in Tromsø in 2011. He displayed his artwork in juried art shows and had several poem collections published. The chapter in this anthology is his first and only academic publication.

Laura Castor is professor in English literature and culture studies at the University of Tromsø where she teaches American literature and culture and Indigenous studies. Her research interests include collective memory, trauma studies, gender studies, Indigenous literatures, ecocriticism, and studies in short fiction. She has published articles on gendered power and Indigenous issues in contemporary American literature in journals, such as *MELUS*, *Nordlit*, and *American Studies in Scandinavia*, and book chapters in *Seeking the Self-Diasporic Narrative and the Ethics of Representation* (Cambridge Scholars 2008), *Less Is More: Short Fiction Theory and Analysis* (Novus 2008), and *The Art of Brevity: Excursions in Short Fiction Theory and Analysis* (University of South Carolina Press 2003). Currently she is working on a project where she explores the various ways in which memories of historical and personal trauma are transformed through fiction, poetry, and autobiographical writing.

Bjørg Evjen, Professor dr./Coordinator for the Master's Programme in Indigenous Studies, Centre for Sámi Studies, University of Tromsø, from 2007 to 2013, holds research interests in Sámi history, the history of research, women's history, Polar history, industrial and labor history, and local history. She has done research for the Sámi Rights Commission and for the Tysfjord region. Her recent publications include in English: "Custodial Reindeer and Custodial Goats, Part of Reindeer Herding and Animal Husbandry," in *Research, Management and Husbandry of Reindeer and Other Northern Ungulates* (2007); "One People—Many Names: On Different Designations for the Sámi Population in the Norwegian County of Nordland Through the Centuries" in *Continuity and Changes* (24[2] 2009); "Finn in Flux: 'Finn' as a Category in Norwegian Population Censuses of the Nineteenth and Twentieth Centuries" in *Axelsson and Skiold*, eds., *In-*

digenous Peoples and Demography, The Complex Relation Between Identity and Statistics (2014).

Harald Gaski is an associate professor of Sámi literature and culture at the University of Tromsø. Author and editor of various publications, he is published in Sámi, Norwegian, and English. Gaski's research includes Indigenous methodology, peoples' literatures with emphasis on Sámi literature, traditional and contemporary, and the late Sámi poet Nils-Aslak Valkeapää. Having played a key role in establishing Sámi literature as an academic field, Gaski was awarded *Gollegiella* (2006)—the Nordic Sámi Language Prize, as well as an award for best dissemination of research at the University of Tromsø (2006). He is currently a member of the international advisory panel for *Nga Pae te Maramatanga*, The National Institute for Research Excellence in Maori Development and Advancement, hosted by the University of Auckland, New Zealand, and is part of the editorial team for the associated journal on Indigenous peoples, *AlterNative*. Gaski is editor-in-chief for the academic series, *Sámi academica*, at the Sámi publishing house Cálliid Lágádus. He is a board member of the foundation for the rights and legacy after Nils-Aslak Valkeapää, Lásságámmi. He also served on the executive board of ARCUS, the US Arctic Research Consortium.

Jennifer Hill-Hart is a passionate advocate for social justice and finding policy solutions that create the systemic change to lift people out of poverty. She is a graduate of the University of Montana School of Law, with a certificate in Indian Law. Hill-Hart is completing her MS in Environmental Studies at the University of Montana, Missoula, with a portfolio emphasis on environmental justice in Indian Country. Her research interests include policies surrounding issues that create systemic change for people living in poverty, including: environmental justice, sustainability, healthy communities, food justice, public benefits, Indian Child Welfare Act (1978), tribal sovereignty, healthcare, education, and access to justice. Currently, Hill-Hart works for a legal aid law firm specializing in family law, domestic violence, and access to justice in Indian Country.

Allyson Kelley is a community health researcher and evaluator with interests in building community capacity to address the cultural, social, and environmental factors that contribute to poor health outcomes in American Indian communities in the Great Plains Region. Her work is driven by what communities identify as most important and is supported by advocacy and participatory worldviews. She uses community-based participatory research approaches and multiple conceptual frameworks, including socioecological and Indigenous theories. As a researcher with multiple community experiences, her primary interest is to help develop and sustain programs that will lead to social change through targeted community-health interventions informed by various cultural contexts. Kelley holds a doctorate in Public Health from the University of North Carolina, Greensboro, Department of Health and Human Sciences and a master's in Public Health from the University of Alaska, Anchorage. She currently serves as a consultant and evaluation research scientist for tribes in Montana and Wyoming.

David L. Moore is a professor of English at the University of Montana. His fields of research and teaching at graduate and undergraduate levels include cross-cultural American Studies, Native American literatures, Western American literatures, Peace Studies, Baha'i Studies, literature and the environment, and ecocritical and dialogical critical theory. He has taught previously at the University of South Dakota, Salish Kootenai College, University of Washington, and Cornell University. His book, entitled *That Dream Shall Have a Name: Native Americans Rewriting America*, is published by the University of Nebraska Press. He currently is editing a collection of essays on prominent author Leslie Marmon Silko, contracted with Bloomsbury Academic Publishers in the UK. Other publications include an edited volume of *American Indian Quarterly*, as well as numerous articles and chapters. He also cohosts *Reflections West*, a short weekly literary program on Montana Public Radio. He lives with his family in Missoula, Montana.

Phyllis Ngai holds a doctorate in education from the University of Montana, Missoula. She is the author of *Crossing Mountains: Native Language Education in Public Schools*, published by AltaMira Press. Her other recent publications include: "Multicultural Teaching Competence for Global Education: A Professional Development Model" in *International Journal of Education for Diversities*; "Indigenous Education for Critical Democracy: Teacher Approaches and Learning Outcomes in a K–5 Indian-Education-For-All Program" in *Equity & Excellence in Education*; "Implementing Montana's Indian-Education-For-All in a K–5 Public School: Implications for Classroom Teaching, Education Policy, and Native Communities" in *Journal of American Indian Education*; and "Indigenous Studies and Intercultural Education: The Impact of a Place-based Primary-school Program" in *Intercultural Education*. Dr. Ngai currently is teaching in the Department of Communication Studies in the University of Montana, Missoula.

Her research and teaching interests lie at the crossroads of language, culture, communication, and public education.

Øyvind Ravna is professor in law at University of Tromsø—The Arctic University of Norway. He holds a doctoral degree in law (University of Tromsø 2008) based on a thesis on legal clarification of reindeer husbandry rights and a master's in property and land law from the Norwegian University of Life Sciences (1987). His field of research is Indigenous law, especially land rights and protection of culture and livelihood, including the adaption and impact of the 2005 Finnmark Land Act, about which he has published many works including the anthology *Finnmarksloven—og retten til jorden i Finnmark* (2013). Ravna teaches Sámi law, property law, legal history, and human rights. Ravna is the head of the Indigenous law group under the Arctic Law Thematic Network under the University of Arctic. Ravna is editor-in-chief of the academic journal *Arctic Review on Law and Politics*. He was also the editor of four academic anthologies in the period from 2007 to 2012.

Gry Paulgaard holds a PhD in pedagogics from the University of Tromsø, Norway. She works as a professor in pedagogics at the Institute of Teacher Education and Educational Studies, UiT, The Arctic University of Norway. Her research includes studies of social learning and cultural identity, globalization and local belonging, marginalization, and social exclusion, with special emphasis on construction of center-periphery distinctions in sociocultural theory.

Robin Saha is an associate professor of environmental studies and an affiliate faculty with the School of Public and Community Health Sciences at the University of Montana. He is among the leading scholars in the area of environmental justice. He is coauthor of a 2007 update of the landmark report *Toxic Wastes and Race in the United States*. His articles in *Demography* and *Social Problems* have helped advance analytic techniques to assess racial and socioeconomic disparities in the location of environmental hazards. Professor Saha has expertise in conducting community-based participatory research with tribal communities on environmental health. He led the National Institute of Health-funded Blackfeet Healthy Homes Partnership Project, which developed community-based strategies to address mold and related health issues on the Blackfeet Indian Reservation. Professor Saha also has expertise in community engagement, collaboration, and partnership development in climate policy, planning, and broader sustainability initiatives.

Kathryn W. Shanley is a professor of Native American studies at the University of Montana, Missoula, and she works as the Special Assistant to the Provost for Native American and Indigenous Education. Her most recent publications include, "An Event of Distance: James Welch's Place in Space and Time," in *Native American Renaissance: Literary Imagination and Achievement* (2013) and "Intersubjectivity with 'Nature' in Plains Indian Vision-seeking," in *Re-imagining Nature* (2013). An enrolled Nakoda from the Fort Peck Reservation, Dr. Shanley has published widely on the work of Blackfeet/Gros Ventre writer, James Welch. Shanley coedits (with Ned Blackhawk) the Yale University Press Henry Roe Cloud, American Indians and Modernity series, and she served as president-elect, president, and past-president of the Native American and Indigenous Studies Association from 2011–2013. In addition to many other national service roles Dr. Shanley has filled, she has for the past ten years served as regional liaison for the Ford Foundation Fellowship Program and previously served for eight years on the American Indian Graduate Center board.

Gyda Swaney holds a doctorate in Clinical Psychology (University of Montana 1997); after working for her own tribe for thirteen years, she now serves as a University of Montana faculty member and Director of the Indians Into Psychology Program (a training grant to increase capacity and provide culturally competent care to Native Americans). She has served as consultant on research grants, trained providers, and delivered evidence-based practices to tribal communities. Her publications include cognitive behavioral treatment for trauma symptoms in Native American youth, health disparities and the boundaries of accessible care in Montana, and behavioral symptoms of eating disorders in Native Americans. Her current research focuses on community-based methods of inquiry into Native American grief, suicide, trauma, resilience, historical trauma, intimate partner violence, and health disparities. An enrolled member of the Confederated Salish and Kootenai Tribes of the Flathead Nation, Dr. Swaney also celebrates her roles as a proud daughter, niece, sister/cousin, mother, auntie, and grandmother.

Index